BUILDING BLOCKS FOR

Liberty

BUILDING BLOCKS FOR

Liberty

Critical Essays by Walter Block

Edited by
Iulian Tănase and Bogdan Glăvan

Foreword by
Llewellyn H. Rockwell, Jr.

First hardcover edition published in 2006 by Libertas Publishing, Bucharest, Romania (www.libertaspublishing.com).

First English edition © 2010 by the Ludwig von Mises Institute and published under the Creative Commons Attribution License 3.0. http://creativecommons.org/licenses/by/3.0/

Ludwig von Mises Institute
518 West Magnolia Avenue
Auburn, Alabama 36832
mises.org

Large Print Edition published 2012 by Skyler J. Collins.
Visit: www.skylerjcollins.com

Cover image by StockFreeImages.com.

ISBN-13: 978-1479133871
ISBN-10: 1479133876

Table of Contents

Acknowledgements

This book could not have been published without the advice and contribution of many libertarian colleagues and friends.

We are most grateful to Llewellyn H. Rockwell, Jr., President of the Ludwig von Mises Institute, for helping us pursue this project and writing a wonderful Foreword.

We should like to thank the editors of the *International Journal of Value-Based Management*, *Ethics, Place and Environment*, *Journal of Business Ethics*, *Journal of Social, Political and Economic Studies*, *Managerial Finance*, *International Journal of Social Economics*, *Journal of Libertarian Studies*, *American Journal of Economics and Sociology* for permission to reprint Professor Block's articles previously published by these prestigious journals.

It is a special pleasure to thank the outstanding scholars and Professors David Gordon, Jörg Guido Hülsmann, Thomas DiLorenzo and Peter Klein for reviewing the book.

Thanks to Tudor Smirna for designing the cover.

In the course of the preparation of this book we have received invaluable advice and assistance from Professor Walter Block. His very useful suggestions and comments helped us to improve the book further.

Iulian Tănase and Bogdan Glăvan

Foreword

Murray Rothbard, in his life, was known as Mr. Libertarian. We can make a solid case that the title now belongs to Walter Block, a student of Rothbard's whose own vita is as thick as a phone book, as diverse as Wikipedia. Whether he is writing on economic theory, ethics, political secession, drugs, roads, education, monetary policy, social theory, unions, political language, or anything else, his prose burns with a passion for this single idea: if human problems are to be solved, the solution is to be found by permitting greater liberty.

Yes, Walter Block is provocative. He is an admitted anarcho-capitalist, and his signature treatise is called *Defending the Undefendable*. But readers who spend time with his prose discover that there is far more to the Blockian method than simply breaking taboos. He is provocative not just because of his conclusions but also because he is relentlessly logical, unfailingly truthful, and unusually sincere. He wants answers to the most vexing human problems—whether they are small or large—and he is going to pursue that truth as far as human reasoning can take him.

I can recall looking through correspondence that Professor Block has had with colleagues in topics such as monetary policy, letters in which Block is sharply in disagreement with his correspondent. His argument on behalf of his position is so pointed and attractive that his opponent cannot resist attempting an answer, but of course that only elicits yet another response, and yet another rejoinder, and another response, and so on. The rounds of correspondence can go on for dozens of interchanges. Block persists not because he wants to beat anyone down, but because he is so sincere about finding truth and ferreting out error. If he is wrong about a point, he wants to know it. That's why his opponents always end up on the hot seat.

There is another aspect to his work that should be noted. His public persona is as a plumb-line libertarian but his method and mode of argument come from his core training in the science of economics. He deploys economic tools in the service of finding answers to social problems. This shows up not only in his exposition; he is also an inspired teacher, and never misses a chance to present his argument step by step so that the reader can come to understand economic logic along the way.

You might be surprised at how reasonable sounding Block can make what might otherwise be considered an outrageous idea. Not every reader will accept every one of Block's conclusions. But everyone will learn how a top-notch economic thinker in the Austrian tradition approaches a huge range of issues. If you disagree with him, you would do well to do so with the same method: that of thinking through problems with close attention to logical and analytical detail.

There is one final trait of Block that might be overlooked: his humility. In a world of academics with inflated egos and selfish ambitions, Block displays constant sincerity, even a kind of naïveté in believing that the truth demonstrated with patience and logic should be enough to carry the day. In our politicized world of charlatans and agenda-driven ideologues, this is rarely the case, of course. But Block charms us with his truth-seeking way, his desire to engage counterarguments of any sort, and his willingness to be shown where he is wrong.

A volume of all the "critical essays" by Walter Block would surely run into thousands of pages. But this is an excellent sampling, and a great tribute to one of the most inspired and hardworking intellectuals of our time.

Llewellyn H. Rockwell, Jr.
Ludwig von Mises Institute
Auburn, Alabama

Introduction

This book *Building Blocks for Liberty: Critical Essays* by Walter Block is dedicated to the notion that libertarianism is not only a political economic philosophy that is powerful and insightful, but it is also unique; it is neither of the right nor of the left (Walter Block, "Libertarianism is Unique; It Belongs Neither to the Right Nor the Left; A Critique of the Views of Long, Holcombe, and Baden on the left, Hoppe, Feser and Paul on the right," *Journal of Libertarian Studies*, 2010).

According to the view of most people, conservatism, or the right-wing philosophy champions economic liberty, but not personal freedom. And, similarly, socialism, or the left-wing perspective, favors personal liberty, but not that pertaining to buying and selling, trading, and other commercial endeavors.

Neither of these claims is exactly true. The adherence to the principles of free enterprise of Republicans on the right is easy to exaggerate. Many of them favor free trade, except when an industry they favor is facing foreign competition. At the time of this writing, President Bush is snarling at the oil industry for of all things price gouging; it is difficult to reconcile this with any adherence to a free economy. Similarly, Democrats on the left supposedly favor keeping the state out of the bedroom and the bathroom, but when they are in power, drugs, prostitution and pornography are virtually always illegal.

However, there is enough of a grain of truth in the standard view to make its inversion even more ludicrous. That is, it is just plain silly to assert that leftists favor economic freedom and rightists defend personal liberties. If anything is clear, it is that neither at all defends the freedom popularly ascribed to the opposite perspective. A socialist favoring free markets is as much of a contradiction in terms as a conservative who looks with favor upon liberties of the individual to ingest into his body what he pleases, or to do with his body anything other adults will permit him to do.

Nozick (1974, p. 163) put his finger squarely on the matter when he characterized libertarianism as favoring "capitalist acts between consenting adults." Here, in one fell swoop, this author exposes the weaknesses of both sides. The leftists, at least according to the received doctrine, are in favor of legalizing anything between consenting adults; similarly, the rightists are supposed to support capitalism. Neither really does. Certainly, no mainstream view is compatible with both kinds of freedom.

In order to find a political economic philosophy that espouses this vision, one must necessarily embrace libertarianism, the subject of the present book. It is only this perspective that travels to the furthest reaches of human endeavor, and consistently upholds the rights of people to do exactly as they please with their persons and property, so long as doing so respects the equal rights of everyone else to do the same.

The first section of *Building Blocks for Liberty: Critical Essays* by Walter Block is devoted to an exploration of economic liberty: what it is, how it helps promote the good life, why it is critically important if we are to keep whatever remnants of civilization we now enjoy, and put off our present descent into barbarism.

In the first essay, my co-author and I attempt to demonstrate that private property rights are the last, best, and only way to defend against exploitation, or rights violations. We make the point that one can only own the rights to *physical* property, not the value thereof. Chapter two is my and my second co-author's attempt to, among other things, answer the question of whether and under what conditions the possession of nuclear weapons, a *per se* invasive implement, may nevertheless legitimately be built and kept in a manner compatible with libertarian law. The burden of the third chapter is to show that, contrary to the views of many, "free market environmentalism" is not a contradiction in terms; that, indeed, our ecological systems can be best protected by a strict adherence to private property rights, not their denigration. In the fourth essay I and yet another co-author make the case that the last best hope for an educated public is the complete privatization of all schools. It is only under a regime of full private property in education that knowledge may properly be transmitted to the next generation. Chapters five and six address the complex issue of unionization in the free society. On the one hand, workers should have the right to quit their jobs; if they cannot do so, they are in a relation of slavery with regard to their employers. On the other hand, a strike encompasses far more than a quit, even a mass quit of all workers at the same time; it necessarily includes the initiation of violence against those ("scabs") potentially competing for the very jobs spurned by organized labor. The seventh article makes the claim that the most just and the most efficacious way to organize roads, tunnels, bridges, streets, and other thoroughfares is to, wait for it, privatize them. It is only under a regime of full private property in this sector of the economy that consumer welfare can be maximized. Chapter eight criticizes the public goods argument with application to the case of roads. The last contribution to this section evaluates the contributions of different distinguished economists to monetary theory and the gold standard. It makes and defends the claim that the gold standard is the only monetary system compatible with the free market philosophy.

Section two addresses issues of human rights and personal liberties. This is the opposite side of the coin from economic freedom for libertarians. In our view, liberty is all of a piece, inviolable, interconnected, inseparable. Left and right each have a very small bit of the answer to civilized living; both economic and personal liberties are required in the good society. What are the specifics?

In Chapter ten we examine the nonaggression axiom of libertarianism, the bedrock, along with private property rights based on homesteading, of the entire philosophy. Chapter eleven applies this insight to children's rights, while rejecting positive obligations. Read it and see the libertarian answer to the question of how youngsters can be protected without violating parental rights to ignore them if they wish. The twelfth essay in this compilation tackles head-on the issue of "social justice." Were this concept to depict "justice" in "social situations" whatever is meant by the former, it would, perhaps, be unobjectionable. Instead, however, it is a disguised attempt to smuggle into the conversation an unwarranted defense of compulsory egalitarianism, and must be rejected by libertarians out of hand.

Do people have a right to discriminate on the basis of race, or sex, or sexual preference, or beauty, or strength, or any other criteria they chose? The answer given in Chapter thirteen is an unqualified "Yes." Does this violate the rights of "victim" groups? Not a bit of it. Immigration is an issue that is widely debated within libertarian circles, and, of course, in the wider society as well. Chapter fourteen takes the side of open borders. In essay fifteen we tackle the issue of government. Is it a legitimate institution? Does it derive its just power from the consent of the governed? Do people have the right to withdraw that consent, on the (erroneous) assumption that they have first given it? Read this chapter and see. Chapter sixteen analyses the proper legal status of addictive drugs. For the libertarian, there can be no question: all adults have the right to place in their bodies whatever they wish. But will not legalization lead to crime, disarray, graft? No; these are the results of prohibition, just as in the case of alcohol. Decriminalization of addictive substances will eradicate these problems, placing them in a status similar to the one now occupied by beer, wine and liquor. Section two concludes with an essay addressing the confusion between libertarianism and libertinism.

Section three constitutes a short but very important contribution to libertarian theory. It is addressed to the very language in which we make our case for liberty. If we are constrained in this regard by considerations of political correctness, if we cannot use words fully, freely and correctly, then it will become difficult or even impossible to even articulate the libertarian message. The enemies of freedom have done yeoman work in eliminating crucial words from the "accepted" vocabulary. Even libertarians who ought to know better are in thrall to these linguistic conventions, and have thereby been weakened in their attempts to defend this philosophy. Words under dispute include: ms., developing countries, rent-seeking, social justice, tax subsidies, property rights, filthy rich, privileged, unearned income, freeman, ultra, profiteer, book burning, stakeholder, get something for nothing, free rider, fair trade, opportunistic, red states, blue states, liberal, and, last but certainly not least, libertarian.

Walter Block

Part One:
ECONOMICS

1 On Property and Exploitation

(with Hans-Hermann Hoppe)

1.

Whenever one says "I own a house," what one normally means is: I have the right to determine how that particular resource—described in objective, physical terms—is to be employed; I am free to employ it for any purpose whatsoever, provided that in so doing I do not impair the physical integrity of resources owned by others; I am likewise entitled to expect that the physical integrity of my resource, my house, remains unaffected by the actions others perform with the physical resources at their disposal. Property rights, then, are commonly conceived of as extending to specific, physical objects. These objects are economic goods and hence have value, otherwise no one would claim them. Yet it is not to the value attached to a specific resource that property rights extend, but rather exclusively to the physical integrity of such a good. I do not own the value of my house. I own a physically specified house, and I have the right to expect that others will not physically damage it.

Reprinted with kind permission of Springer Science and Business Media from *International Journal of Value-Based Management* 15, no. 3 (2002): 225–36. Hans-Hermann Hoppe, an Austrian school economist and libertarian/anarcho-capitalist philosopher, is Professor of Economics at University of Nevada, Las Vegas, Distinguished Fellow with the Ludwig von Mises Institute, Founder and President of The Property and Freedom Society, and Editor-at-Large of the *Journal of Libertarian Studies*.

2.

Plausible as this theory of property is,[1] in much of contemporary political economy and philosophy confusion abounds on the issue of whether property rights concern the value of physical things or, instead, it is the physical thing themselves which are of value.[2] It is thus necessary to clarify why the common notion of property rights as extending exclusively to physical things is indeed correct; and why the notion of property rights in values is flawed.

First, it should be noted that these theories are *incompatible* with each other. It is easily recognized that every action of a person may alter the *value* (or price) of another person's property. If A enters the labor or the marriage market, this may impair B's value in these markets. And if A changes his relative evaluation of beer and bread, or if A decides to become a brewer or a baker himself, this may change the property values of the—other—brewers and bakers. According to the view that *value*-impairments constitute rights violations it follows that A's actions may represent punishable offenses. Yet if A is *guilty*, then B and the brewers or bakers in turn must be entitled to *defend* themselves against A's actions. Their right to defend themselves can only consist in their (or their agent) being permitted to physically attack or restrict A and his property: B must be entitled to physically bar A from entering the labor or marriage market; and the brewers or bakers must be allowed to physically hinder A from spending

---

[1] See, for instance, Alchian (1977, pp. 131–32); notes Alchian

> although private property rights protect private property from physical changes chosen by other people, no immunity is implied for the exchange value of one's property. . . . Private property, as I understand it, does not imply that a person may use his property in any way he sees fit so long as no one else is "hurt." Instead, it seems to mean the right to use goods (or to transfer that right) in any way the owner wishes to so long as the physical attributes or uses of all other people's private property is unaffected. And that leaves plenty of room for disturbance and alienation of affections of other people.

[2] The idea of property-in-values underlies, for instance, John Rawls' "difference principle," i.e., the rule that all inequalities among people have to be expected to be to everyone's advantage—regardless of how they have come about (Rawls 1971, pp. 60, 75*n*, 83); and also Robert Nozick's claim that a "dominant protection agency" has the right to outlaw competitors regardless of their actual behavior, and his related claim that "nonproductive exchanges," in which one party would be better off if the other did not exist, may be outlawed—again regardless of whether or not such an exchange involved any physical invasion (Nozick 1974, pp. 55*n*, 83–86).

his own money as he pleases, e.g., from using his own possessions for the operation of a brewery or bakery. Based on this theory, the physical damaging or restricting of another person's property use obviously cannot be said to constitute a rights violation. Rather, physical attacks and physical restrictions on the use of private property then have to be classified as lawful defenses. On the other hand, suppose that physical attacks and physical property restrictions constitute rights violations. Then B and brewers or bakers are *not* allowed to defend themselves against A's actions.

For A's actions—his entering the labor or marriage market, his changed evaluation of beer and bread, and his opening of a brewery or bakery—neither affects B's bodily integrity nor the physical integrity of other brewers' or bakers' property. If they engage in physical resistance against A's actions nonetheless, then the right to defense rests with A. In this case, however, it cannot be considered a rights violation that a person's actions impair the *value* of another person's property. No other, third alternative exists.

These two theories of property are not only incompatible, however. The alternative view—that a person may own the *value* (or price) or scarce physical goods—is also "praxeologically" impossible,[3] i.e., it is a theory that we *cannot* put into effect even if we wanted to; as well, it is as argumentatively indefensible.

For while every person can, in principle, have control over whether or not his actions cause the *physical* attributes of other persons' property to change, control over whether or not his actions affect the *value* of other people's property rests with *other* people and their evaluations. Consequently, it would be impossible to ever know in advance if one's planned actions were permitted or not. One would have to interrogate the entire population to make sure that one's planned actions would not impair the value of anybody else's property; as well, one would have to reach a universal *agreement* on who was permitted to do what, with which goods. Mankind would be long dead before this was ever accomplished. Hence, the theory breaks down as nonoperational.

---

[3] On the concept of "praxeology," and the systematic reconstruction of economic theory as a "logic of action," see Mises (1966, 1985).

Moreover, the proposition that a person may own the value of a physical thing involves an internal contradiction. For simply in order to propose this theory it would have to be presupposed that its proponent is allowed to act. He must do so *prior* (and simultaneously) to making his proposition or seeking agreement for his proposal regarding how to protect property values from value-intrusive actions. He cannot wait, and suspend acting, *until* an agreement is reached; rather, he must be permitted to employ at least his own physical body (and its standing room) *immediately*. Otherwise he could not even *make* his proposal. Yet if one is permitted to assert a proposition—and no one could deny this without falling into a contradiction—then this is only possible because there exist *objective* (physical) borders of property.

Every person can recognize these borders as such on his own, without having to agree first with anyone else with respect to one's subjective system of values and evaluations. Prior to even beginning the intellectual endeavor of proposing property theories, then, as its very own praxeological foundation, there must be an acting (e.g., speaking) man, defined in terms of physical or human resources. Value of utility considerations, agreements or contracts—all things that contemporary political philosophers and economists typically regard as fundamental to their various theories of justice or property—already presuppose the existence of physically independent decision-making units. Also presupposed is a description of these units in terms of a person's property relations to definite physical resources—otherwise there would be no one to value or agree on anything, and nothing on which to agree or about which to make contracts. Anyone proposing anything other than a theory of property-in-physically-defined-resources would contradict the content of his proposition merely by making it. He could not even open his mouth if his theory were correct; and the fact that he does open it disproves his claim.[4]

3.

The notion of property-in-values is praxeologically *impossible* (nonoperational) if formulated as a theory of justice, i.e., as a system of rules

---

[4] See also Hoppe (1989, chap. 7; 1993, part II; 1990, esp. pp. 260–63; 2001).

that applies universally to each and every person alike. It becomes operational if—and only if—it is employed instead as a theory of exploitation. It is at least logically coherent as a system of rules that privileges *one* person or group of persons *at the expense* of *another*, underprivileged person or group. *No one* could act, if *everyone* owned the value attached to what he regarded as his.

Acting is possible, however, if B owns the value of the resources presently at his disposal and is entitled to determine what others, A, may or may not do with resources they control so as to not impair his, B's, property values. This would perforce include A's compensatory delivery to B of resources presently possessed by A. On the other hand, A is then entitled to own *neither* the value *nor* the physical integrity of his possessions and has no claim against B except that B allows him to do anything as long as it is to B's advantage. Although praxeologically possible, such a system of rules does not even qualify as a *potential* human ethic, because it fails to meet the universalizability criterion. By adopting this system, two distinct classes of persons are created—superhumans or exploiters such as B, and subhumans or the exploited such as A—to whom different "law" applies. Accordingly, it fails from the outset as a universal, human ethic. It is not—not even in principle—*universally* acceptable and thus cannot qualify as *law*. In order to be considered lawful, a rule must apply universally, for everyone *equally*. The idea of property-in-values, then, is not only praxeologically impossible—if universalized—but also inhumane—if not universalized.

4.

From this conclusion far-reaching consequences follow: (1) discrimination, (2) defamation and libel suits, (3) comparable worth, parity, and affirmative action policies, and (4) the notorious "ex-lover seeks compensation for no longer being loved" suits would then have to be regarded as scandalous if at times amusing perversions of law and justice. Likewise, institutions such as (5) licensing laws, (6) zoning regulations, (7) antitrust laws, (8) insider trading laws, etc., represent legal outgrowths of the property-in-value theory.

Ultimately, they all involve restricting A's control over specified resources by correspondingly expanding B's control over them. This holds true even though A had not physically damaged, and was not in the process of physically damaging, any of B's possessions in doing whatever A wants to do with the means presently at this own disposal. B's claim against A is based not on physical losses caused by A, but rests solely on B's assumption that A's actions, unless restricted, impose a *value*-loss on him. In this theory B owns the *value* of his property, and hence is entitled to reassure his value-integrity by imposing physical restrictions on A's actions. One party seeks material compensation from another for the crime of nonmaterial value damages suffered from having one's expectations regarding another's actions disappointed. Disappointed hopes, of which life offers an unlimited supply, are used by one person as a justification for trying to physically enrich himself at the expense of another.

Let us now illustrate the exploitative character of each of these legal practices in some more detail.

Discrimination

Strictly speaking discrimination is the refusal to deal with, trade with, live next to, buy from, sell to, engage in any commercial or noncommercial activity whatsoever, with another person. In discriminating against B, A undoubtedly reduces B's economic well-being, compared to what it would have been had A not so discriminated.[5] The value of B's physical property, as well as his "human capital"[6] falls below the level otherwise attainable. Nevertheless, since B *can* only own his person plus his physical property, he can have no just claim against A for shunning him.

There exists a categorical distinction between physical invasion and the refusal to deal with, or discrimination.[7] A's actions are that of a boycott, and do not constitute physical intrusion. But many commentators, unfortunately, fail to make this vital distinction. All too often it is thought, for example, that rape and discrimination against women are

---

[5] A reduces his own wealth, too, apart from the psychic income gains that accrue to him, which is the reason he indulges his preferences in this lmanner.

[6] Becker (1964).

[7] See Block (1992).

on a continuum. Or that lynching blacks is different only in degree to ignoring them. But a moment's reflection will show that these activities are night and day compared to each other. The physical assault of B on A (as "retaliation" against A's prior discriminatory action) always involves losses in value terms. But it also robs A temporarily or permanently of the very means to recover such losses. In contrast, while discrimination may likewise be unpleasant, in leaving B's physical possessions unimpaired, it strictly limits B's value losses. For example, if no one will hire ugly women to be secretaries, the wages they command will tend to decline. But at lower compensation levels, these females—their physical integrity and hence their job skills being unimpaired—will become more of a bargain in the labor market. This, presumably, will counter the negative effect of the initial discrimination. They will not be consigned to unemployment, the first result, but will rather find jobs, albeit at lower wages than absent discrimination. However, once on the payroll, they will be able to demonstrate their "true" productivity (perhaps even in excess of that of their more beauteous competitors) and can in this way recoup at least in part their initial salary losses. In sharp contrast, had physical invasion been directed against them (or, as a retaliatory action, against their more beautiful competitors), none of these ameliorative reactions could have come into play.[8]

Defamation and libel

Most commentators have argued that one has a legitimate ownership right to one's reputation. But this is not so. For the simple reason that one's reputation *consists* of the thoughts of *other* people.[9] That is, A's reputation consists solely of the thoughts of B, C, D, and B's reputation

---

[8] One must also distinguish between discrimination on the part of a private property owner and that engaged in by the State. In the former case, as we have seen, the law of private property assures that value losses may be recovered by the "victim." But this does not apply when government engages in discriminatory behavior. If the civil service shuns ugly secretaries, their wages will fall as a result. But this will not make them more attractive to the bureaucracy, since their access to coercive levies from the citizenry (e.g., taxes) shield them from any concern for profit. To the extent that the government engages in discrimination, then, the victims are in a far worse position than when this occurs in the private sector.

[9] See Rothbard (1970, 1978, 1982). See also Block (1976).

of those of A, C, D, . . . etc. But since no one can own the thoughts of
other people, one cannot, paradoxically, own one's own reputation.

While there can be no universal right to one's reputation, and libel
and defamation do not constitute exploitation *per se*, the right of a person
to engage in libelous or defamatory action is not unrestricted. For while
everyone has an unrestricted right concerning his thoughts, the right of
free speech is *not* absolute. For example, no one has the right to tell
another person "unless you hand over to me your wallet, I'll shoot you."
This sort of speech would be strictly forbidden in a private property
society. It is a threat to engage in initiatory violence. As well, no one,
including any of my detractors, has a right to come to my living room
to give me a speech or tell me what he thinks about me and when I tell
him to leave object on the ground of his right to freedom of speech. A
trespasser has no free speech rights whatsoever—on my property. Free
speech rights, so-called, are really but an instance of private property
rights. I can say anything I want on my property and so can anyone
else, including any libelous person, on his own property.

Comparative worth and parity policies

Most advocates of Equal Pay for Equal Work (EPFEW) or of Equal Pay
for Work of Equal Value (EPFWOEV) legislation maintain that these
enactments are necessary in order to combat employer discrimination
between males and females. Even were this the case, there would be
nothing that should be legally untoward in such a situation, for women
own only their labor power, not the price placed upon it by others. Did
they but have a right to the former, as we have seen, it would be impossible for anyone at all to engage in human action, lest they advertently
or inadvertently impact on the value of any women's effort.

But it is not at all the case that women earn less than men due to
employer discrimination. On the contrary, this state of affairs is due to the
asymmetrical effects of marriage: it enhances male wages and reduces that
of females. Due to unequal responsibilities in the average family for child
care, shopping, cleaning, laundering, cooking, and a whole host of other
such activities, the average wife earns only some 40 percent of her husband's
salary. In contrast, there is no pay gap at all between females and males

who have never been touched by the institution of marriage; the salaries of the never married are virtually identical. The much noted and reviled by feminists income ratio of 60 percent–75 percent is actually an amalgam of the experiences of these two very different groups of people.[10]

Contrary to the views of feminists, private property and markets are the institution, par excellence, which assures not only EPFEW, but EPFWOEV as well. Suppose, for example, that a man and a woman had equal productivity of $20/hour and that the man were paid this amount of compensation.[11] Suppose further that the women were paid only $12, 60 percent of the male wage, exemplifying the supposedly discriminatory "pay gap." This would set up the same irresistible profit opportunities as in the case of the male paid less than his productivity level. Any "male chauvinist" employer who hired the man at $20, rather than the equally productive woman at $12 would place himself at a serious competitive disadvantage. He would be a prime candidate for bankruptcy.

EPFEW and EPFWOEV, then, equate wages between equally productive males and females. The reason women earn only some 60 percent of what males do is because, on average (due, perhaps largely, to marriage asymmetries) they are only 60 percent as productive. So EPFEW and EPFWOEV have already been attained on the market. There is no discriminatory wage gap.

But this is not at all what the advocates of pay "equity" demand. Their view, predicated on the notion that people have a right not merely to their own persons and property but to the value thereof is, in effect, that males and females should receive the same compensation, *despite* differences in productivity. Imagine that their wish were granted. That

---

[10] See Sowell (1983). See also Block (1982, pp. 101–25; 1985); Levin (1987); Epstein (1992).

[11] That wages tend to equal productivity levels is one of the best established propositions in all of economics. This result can be illustrated in our example. If the man's productivity is $20 and his wage is higher than that, say $25, the firm employing him will lose $5/hour. If they persist in this behavior, and especially if they apply it to other workers as well, they will go bankrupt. On the other hand, if the wage is below this level, say at $12, then a profit opportunity of $8 exists. Any competitor would be glad to woo these workers away from his present employer for, say, $12.25. But if one company offers that amount, another will up the ante to $12.50. Where will this bidding process end? As close to the productivity level of $20 as search and transportation costs will allow.

is, suppose that the law requires a male with productivity of $20, and a female with productivity of $12, both to be paid the former amount. Now, incentives will all be turned around. Instead of having a financial interest in hiring the woman, the firm now will be led "as if by an invisible hand" to avoid her at all costs. The result will be greatly enhanced unemployment rates for women, a result which obtains whenever the legal system artificially prices factors of production out of the market.

Affirmative love

Most people can see through lawsuits seeking damage for alienation of affection. These are properly regarded as a scandal and a disgrace. People cannot own the love of others. The very notion is contradictory; true affection must be given voluntarily, while ownership implies the right to take it from another person, whether or not he is willing to bestow it. So these suits, too, are an instance of the confusion over physical ownership vs. property in values. An ex-lover seeking financial compensation from her no longer amorous suitor is really asserting that she has the right to control his feelings. If this were true his ownership right over his person would be null and void, since he could not even choose the object of his desires.

Licensing laws

This legislation is an attempt to restrict the actions of others so that the value of one's own property can be enhanced or stabilized. If entry into the industry of potential competitors can be precluded, one's wealth increases. Naturally, this motivation is disguised, hidden behind a plethora of "public interest" billingsgate. Accordingly, taxi license holders wax eloquent about the reduced traffic congestion afforded by this system, and members of the American Medical Association take pride in the enhanced quality of medical services thus engendered. But this is empty rhetoric. Taxi cab medallions sell for many thousands of dollars, attesting to the value of government-imposed monopoly, not to the ease of traffic flows. And the salary levels achieved by doctors has little to do with the nation's health; if anything, the very opposite is true.[12]

---

[12] See Friedman (1962, chap. 9); Hamowy (1984); Henderson (2001, chap. 15).

For example, consider the Viennese doctors—the best in the world at that time—who came to the U.S. to escape the ravages of National-Socialism in the 1930s. It was no coincidence that the AMA did everything in its power to hinder the process whereby they could practice their profession. They insisted on loyalty oaths, but this had nothing to do with patient care. They compelled familiarity with the English language—as if there were no German-speaking sick people, nor translators. They demanded residence periods, as if these were anything but a blatant attempt to forestall unwanted competition.[13]

But licensing laws do not even go far enough if the values of taxis, medical equipment, skills, are to be maintained and enhanced. Strictly speaking, there should also be requirements on the demand side as well. That is, the temporarily unemployed cabbies should be able to commandeer the man on the street, force him into the taxi, and drive him, if need be right back to the point of embarcation, so as to maintain revenues. And if ever revenues decline, doctors ought to be allowed to inflict diseases on innocent people—so that they can charge them for cures. After all, according to the property in values theory, people who do not get sick, and/or refuse to ride around in taxis, are really stealing from doctors and cabbies, respectively.

Zoning

Who has not yielded to the temptation—at least in thought—of wishing to maintain if not upgrade the value of his real estate holdings? One way to do this is through entrepreneurial action (including insurance). A person purchases a home in a large-scale condominium development, for instance, where all owners are precluded from any activity (painting a house with polka dots, ripping it down and putting in a cement factory) which might conceivably lower property values. Alternatively, a restrictive covenant can be signed with neighbors to the same end.

But this costs money, time and effort. There are "transaction" costs involved. Frequently it is much easier to rely on the political process. If a

---

[13] A similar situation took place with regard to Cuban doctors who fled Castro. The AMA placed obstacles in their way of attempting to practice medicine in the U.S. as well.

law is passed requiring a minimum one acre lot size for single family dwellings, hordes of "undesirables" can be kept out. For the only chance of the poor successfully bidding against wealthy people is in the form of multiple dwelling units. They can "gang up" on the rich by more intensive land settlement. But if this is precluded by zoning laws, that option is not available to them. Better yet, inaugurate the no-growth philosophy, ostensibly for environmental ends; this obstructs any new building, for whatever purpose, the better to maintain property values. Why rely on an "imperfect" market when legislative enactments can attain such ends?[14]

City planners (who owe employment to the existence of zoning laws) argue that this system keeps "incompatible" land uses separated from one another. But private property rights can achieve the same ends, without the use of force and compulsion.[15] The reason filling stations do not locate in cul-de-sacs is that there is too little traffic to support them there. Likewise, cement factories are prohibited by marketplace considerations from setting up shop in downtown areas. High real estate prices relegate them to the periphery. When land use bureaucrats err, they do so on a colossal, city-wide scale. They lose millions for the citizenry but not a penny of their own personal funds. The benefits of marketplace zoning, as is illustrated most drastically by the failure of the Soviet economic system, is that private investors, who risk their own money, tend to be more careful with it. The drawbacks of central planning apply to cities as well as to countries.

Anti-trust

Anti-trust laws serve many purposes. From the point of view of the expert in law and economics, for instance, they function as a full employment bill, calling forth millions of hours of highly paid expert testimony. From the perspective of the neo-classical economist it furnishes an opportunity to demonstrate manual dexterity with average and marginal cost and revenue curves, "dead weight losses" and "resource misallocations," the better to dazzle naïve students. For the political ideologue, the theory of

---

[14] See Tucker (1990).
[15] See Siegan (1972).

monopoly, upon which anti-trust laws are based, provides the "scientific legitimation" for the permanency of so-called "market failures"; it is a stick which can be used to beat up on the private property (capitalist) system.

For our purposes, anti-trust laws illustrate yet another instance of defining property in terms of values, not physical criteria. If company A sells a better product, or the same one at a lower price, how does it "hurt" its competitors? Only in value terms, not physical ones.

As in the case of witchcraft, or heresy during the period of the Inquisition, there is no defense against the charge of monopoly. Promotion of consumer welfare is no defense; indeed, it is part of the indictment. Selling at a price lower than competitors is *prima facie* evidence of cut-throat competition; selling at a higher price indicates monopolistic profiteering; selling at the same price as everyone else is evidence of collusion. Since there is no fourth alternative, any firm is theoretically guilty as charged, no matter what its behavior. Similarly with quantity sold. Too much is pre-emptive, too little is monopolistic withholding, and the same as others is collusive dividing up of the market. Heads the anti-trust division and the Federal Trade Commission win; tails, the business concern loses.[16]

Insider trading

The last instance of the property-in-value theory we shall discuss are laws prohibiting "insider trading." The complaint on the part of the advocates of such laws is that the knowledge possessed by someone, when acted upon in a commercial matter, is a violation of the rights of others. Previously we had asserted that "*no one* could act, if *everyone* owned the value attached to what he regarded as his." With insider trading we see a paradigm case of this.[17]

The legally established contention here is that a knowledgeable state of mind can convert what would otherwise be a legitimate purchase of stock into an illegitimate one, provided that the information relied upon is not homogeneously spread throughout the population. Since it never

---

[16] See Anderson *et al.* (2001, pp. 287–302).
[17] See Manne (1966a, 1966b). See also Block and McGee (1989, pp. 1–35).

is, virtually any commercial activity with regard to stocks and bonds can be deemed unlawful.

The situation is indeed worse than that. A rigorous pursuit of the "logic" of insider trading prohibitions could potentially be used to preclude any market transaction.

Did a woman buy an umbrella because she heard a newscast that it would rain tomorrow? Unless everyone tuned in to the same weather program, and listened as attentively as did she, this would give her an unfair advantage over other people. And what of the person who attended, horrors!, a course on the care and feeding of stocks and bonds? Such studies would surely give the student an "inside track" *vis-à-vis* those who had not attended the lectures. If the crime of excessive information[18] can be applied to umbrellas and stocks and bonds, it can be applied to anything: to real estate, to amenities, to human capital, to factors of production. Moreover, this doctrine calls into question the acquisition of any knowledge (unless, of course, it is evenly spread throughout the entire world community). Those particularly at risk include doctors, lawyers, economists, college professors, and Nobel Prize winners.

---

[18] Another "market failure" beloved by interventionists is "lack of perfect information." Let's see if we have this straight. Too little information is no good, because it violates the requirement of perfect information. Too much information is problematic, because it is incompatible with the strictures against insider trading. How about "the same amount of information as everyone else?" Aha. A lacuna in the theory. So far, to the best of knowledge of the present authors, this state of affairs has not been subjected to legal prohibition. But who knows? A theoretical breakthrough may be lurking in these intellectual thickets.

2 Toward a Universal Libertarian Theory of Gun (Weapon) Control: A Spatial and Geographical Analysis

(with Matthew Block)

No rational person can doubt that chemists must pick their way through an ethical minefield. The Nazi ovens owed their properties and attributes to members of this profession, directly or indirectly. Nor can it be denied that biologists are often faced with moral quandaries; genetic cloning and germ warfare spring readily to mind in this context. The same goes for doctors (Dr. Mengele and Dr. Kevorkian are cases in point),[1] veterinarians (just ask People for the Ethical Treatment of Animals) and physicists (the bomb).

However, what of geographers? Surely they are protected from this sort of risk? Not a bit of it. They, too, along with all these others, are exposed to the dangers implicit in ethical mis-steps in their professional capacities. For one thing, the Geographical Information Systems which emanate from this branch of knowledge are not at all irrelevant to the

Reprinted with kind permission of Taylor & Francis Group from *Ethics, Place and Environment* 3, no. 3 (2000): 289–98. Matthew Block graduated with honors from Simon Fraser University in British Columbia, Canada in 2001 with a major in computer science. He is now involved in the software industry, and has several patents in that area. He lives in Redmond, Washington.
[1] There is no implication here that both have acted improperly, only that their actions are fraught with moral implications. Indeed, according to libertarian principles (see below) the latter but not the former has acted in an entirely legitimate manner.

conduct of war. Indeed, the very opposite is the case. Surely, the spatial scientists who have helped develop such systems have acted in a manner intimately invested with ethical concerns. Some two millennia ago, Strabo (trans. 1949, p. 31) thus commented in this regard: "geography as a whole has a direct bearing upon the activities of commanders."[2]

For another thing, there is the topic of the present paper, which involves a spatial, political, environmental and geographical analysis of gun, and more generally weapon, control. Second amendment rights in the U.S. context certainly involve ethical issues, too. As we shall argue, the kinds of place, space, environmental and geographical assumptions employed in the analysis of gun control have a crucially important effect on the conclusions reached. In fact, given the political economic premises of libertarianism, on the basis of which we shall argue, there are virtually no other considerations involved than the geographical.

Libertarianism

Libertarianism is the political philosophy which would be beloved of the Occam of Occam's razor. It states, simply, that the one proscribed act is the use or the threat of force against a person or his legitimately held property. Property can justly be attained, first, through homesteading hitherto unowned property, and, second, through any noninvasive act such as trade or a gift (Spooner 1966; Rothbard 1970, 1978, 1982; Tannehill and Tannehill 1970; Woolridge 1970; Nozick 1974; Oppenheimer 1975; Machan 1982 1990; Benson 1989; Hoppe 1989, 1993; Block 1976, 1994; McGee 1991; Boaz 1997; Murray 1997). All the rest is elaboration, explication, implication, clarification and justification.

What is the libertarian position on the second amendment to the U.S. Constitution? At first blush, this philosophy is not compatible with any gun control legislation at all, since the mere ownership and possession of a rifle or pistol do not constitute an uninvited border crossing, or invasive violence. Nor do they even amount to a threat, for surely we must distinguish between the case of brandishing a weapon in a bellicose manner, on the one hand, and, on the other, with keeping one locked

---

[2] We owe this citation to an anonymous referee.

up in a drawer at home or in an auto, or with peaceably walking around with one safely holstered at the hip or even concealed, as in a shoulder harness. The former act violates the nonaggression axiom, while the latter two do not. Yes, there is a potential danger involved in private gun ownership and use,[3] but if we were to prohibit all such occurrences, we would have to ban autos, knives, scissors, letter openers, arms (for boxers) and legs (for karatekas), etc.

Then there is the slippery slope objection; that if a pistol is not a rights violator *per se,* then neither is a rifle, a machine gun, a bazooka, a howitzer, a tank, a battleship, a jet fighter plane; nor, for that matter, a nuclear bomb.

The libertarian response to this is predicated upon the issue of whether it is *possible* to use these weapons in a purely defensive manner; if so, there can be no objection to them *per se.* Consider a bazooka, for example. Can the power of this implement be confined to those at whom it is aimed? Yes. Therefore it can be used purely for purposes of self-defense, and its possession is not an *ipso facto* violation of the libertarian code. If it is not possible to limit, to its intended targets, the physical harm created by a weapon but, rather, this must necessarily spill over onto innocent parties, then such an implement must be eliminated from legitimate arsenals. When viewed in this manner, it is clear that all of the weapons mentioned above, except for the thermonuclear device, *do* allow for pinpointing,[4] namely for confining their destructive power to

---

[3] There is, of course, also a danger in public sector weapon ownership. However, since libertarianism in its pure form does not recognize a difference between the two spheres (there are only private individuals, some of whom illegitimately claim that their relationship with a "government" allows them special privileges not available to their private counterparts), we will not pursue this matter here.

[4] Some supposedly "smart" missiles have been anything but accurate under recent war-like conditions. Are they therefore illegitimate *per se?* Certainly, projectiles which cannot be aimed at all, that fall at totally random places in the geographical environment, could not be deemed licit in the libertarian philosophy. However, there is a continuum here. For no weapon at all—not pistols, not rifles, not baseball bats, not knives, not even fingernails—comes with a guarantee of perfect accuracy. Mistakes occur in all these cases. It would be a bit harsh to conclude that no defensive weapon may be used, because all of them are imperfect. In contrast, we are employing a far less restrictive criterion: as long as it is possible to aim a weapon, and thus at least in principle confine its negative impact to malefactors, then there can be no *per se*

the "bad guys." Therefore, it would be licit to own any of the former, but not the latter.[5]

This, then, is a fair summary of the consensus libertarian position on gun control, as it now exists. However, it is subject to criticism, when we take a wider perspective. Contemplate the possibility of meteors causing great damage to the Earth, and being blown up, defensively, by nuclear power, as in the movie *Armageddon,* or alien creatures attacking us, as in the book by Robert Heinlein (1959), *Starship Troopers,* and the movie of the same name. In this astronomical context, not limited to the Earth, the hydrogen bomb, or even many of them all together, *can* be used purely defensively, or appropriately, e.g., to blow up a meteor before it hits us, or to kill giant enemy alien bugs on distant planets, who have already attacked us.[6]

What, then, is the libertarian response to the critic who offers the specter of the nuclear weapon in someone's basement, located in the midst of a large city? This attempt at a *reductio ad absurdum* could perhaps have been defeated when the context was limited to the Earth;

---

objection to such an implement. We thank an anonymous referee for bringing this point to our attention.

[5] Libertarianism is a principled theory, not a consequentialist or utilitarian one. "Justice though the heavens fall" is an apt metaphor for this philosophy. Therefore, we are not concerned in this essay with the effects of gun control, only with its justification on pure libertarian grounds. For the utilitarian case against gun control, see Kates (1984, 1986, 1990, 1991, 1992), Kates *et al.* (1995), Barnett and Kates (1996), Halbrook (1995), Kleck (1991), Kleck and Patterson (1993), Mauser (1992), Mauser and Holmes (1992), Polsby and Kates (1998), Lott (1998), and Lott and Mustard (1997).

[6] Rothhard (1982, pp. 190–91) has anticipated this point. He writes:

> while the bow and arrow, and even the rifle, can be pinpointed, if the will be there, against actual criminals, modern nuclear weapons cannot. Here is a crucial difference in kind. Of course, the bow arid arrow could be used for aggressive purposes, but it could also be pinpointed to use only against aggressors. Nuclear weapons, even "conventional" aerial bombs, cannot be. These weapons are *ipso facto* engines of indiscriminate mass destruction. (The only exception would be the extremely rare case where a mass of people who were *all* criminals inhabited a vast geographical area.)

To this we have now, in effect, added only another exceptional case: where all of the bad guys occupy another planet.

here, at least by supposition, it is impossible to detonate an atom bomb without violating the rights of at least one other person.[7]

However, where extraterrestrial beings or meteors are concerned, the hydrogen bomb cannot be banned as intrinsically invasive. Now, it has, or at least can have, a defensive purpose. However, the idea of a Jeff Dahmer or a Ted Kaczynski in charge of one in a large city must give even a fanatical libertarian pause for thought. This is even more problematic given that the ability and knowledge needed for constructing these items are widely dispersed, and the cost of the raw materials, while expensive, is not prohibitive.

One possible answer to this conundrum is that the libertarian stance (nukes are prohibited because they are necessarily invasive) is quite sufficient for any reasonable scenario concerning the Earth; that meteors and unfriendly bug-eyed aliens, etc. are the stuff of science fiction, not reality; and that libertarianism can only concern itself with the former, not the latter. This perspective offers the following possible response:

> If the Earth were such a place as to be repeatedly threatened with meteors, our principles governing the legitimacy of nuclear weapons would be quite different. In *our* world, the view that such bombs are necessarily invasive, and hence should be prohibited, is the strongest. In another universe, it might be weaker. Another way of putting this point is that in the hypothetical world of Armageddon a nuclear weapon is not entirely and wholly offensive but serves a legitimate role in (planetary) self-defense.

The difficulty with this reply is that, at least ideally, libertarianism ought to be applicable as widely as possible: to all times, and to all places; to all possible universes. To the extent that this is not the case, this philosophy has less generalizability, and hence less validity than otherwise.

---

[7] On the other hand, if an extremely small "tactical" nuclear weapon were detonated in the Sahara or Nevada deserts, or underground, without rights violation, there would be no justified libertarian prohibition against keeping it in such a place.

Fortunately, however, there is a better defense available. The only way the nuclear bomb can be used defensively is for off-world activity.[8] Therefore, at the very least, the would-be stockpiler of this weapon must have at his disposal the wherewithal to launch it at an enemy planet or on-rushing meteor. Since rocketry of this sort costs billions of dollars, this consideration ought to be sufficient to preclude the specter of a nuclear device in numerous basements or attics.[9]

Let us reiterate. Libertarianism is in opposition to the prohibition of ordinary weapons since they do not *per se* violate its basic premise of nonaggression. When we focus only on earthly concerns, this philosophy favors the ban on nuclear weapons; since it is not possible to confine their force, their use must necessarily violate the libertarian axiom. However, when we incorporate the entire universe into our analysis, and science fiction considerations as well, then nukes cannot be banned, since a defensive purpose for them exists.

Proportionality

These considerations give rise to what might be called a geographical, spatial or proportionality thesis. We claim that there is an inverse relationship between population density and the power of a weapon that will be considered legitimate under libertarian law. Population density in the entire universe is extremely small, so armaments of mass destruction are legitimate in this context. On Earth, population density is relatively far higher; therefore, small arms would be allowed, but not atom bombs or worse. The key to legitimacy in both cases is the ability to pinpoint or limit destructive power. Other things equal, it is easier to do this, the lower the population density; hence the proportionality thesis.

---

[8]　We here abstract from Rothhard's "extremely rare case" of a "vast geographical area" occupied solely by criminals.

[9]　This holds, at least at present. In the far future, of course, it is possible, given that we rely upon free enterprise at such times, that new technology will enable most people to own interplanetary rockets. Then, the specter of too-numerous nuclear capability may once again return to haunt us. However, in such a high-tech world, it might also be that defensive capabilities would be enhanced, rendering this less of a problem.

Perhaps this point can be more easily made by use of a series of examples of decreasing population density. In the context of the entire universe, a person can own just about as many hydrogen bombs as desired since, given this vast arena, it is certainly possible for them all to be used defensively. Suppose that Jupiter were inhabited by only 1,000 people, evenly spaced throughout the planet. Here, it would appear reasonable for each of them to own the proverbial atom bomb, and keep it in their basements if they wished. Given the low population density involved, this device would no longer constitute a *reductio ad absurdum* of the libertarian position, for the explosive power, even including the fallout, could easily be confined to the enemy, or to the owner of the territory himself, thus not imposing any negative effects on innocent third parties. Since defensive use would thus be possible, there would be no necessary violation of the libertarian postulate. The next level down in population density might be places on Earth such as the Sahara, or Antarctica. There might be no libertarian justification for owning an atom bomb with fallout even in relatively empty areas such as these, for detonation would affect at least a few innocent people. However, one could, conceivably, own a "clean" atom bomb or a large amount of TNT in such deserted areas, but not in a more crowded venue.[10]

The proportionality thesis can be illustrated by use of a graph (Figure 1). On the y axis we plot the power of the weapon, with the hydrogen bomb at the top and fingernails at the bottom. On the x axis there is population density, with space the least populated and cities the most highly inhabited.

The relationship between these two could be depicted by any downward-sloping curve; this would indicate that the more crowded the situation, the less powerful the weapon that would pass muster under this libertarian criterion. If power and population density could be meaningfully integrated with one another (which is not being claimed here), the implication is that the downward-sloping curve would be a rectangular hyperbola, to indicate that the total of the two variables,

---

[10] This is the Rothbardian exceptional case scenario, given that regions of this sort are populated only by criminals.

when multiplied together, would yield the same sum, namely the amount of "force times population density" which would be on the dividing line between legitimacy and illegitimacy.

What of "cpb?" Depicted in this realm of the x axis is a world so crowded it would resemble a "crowded phone booth." What would be proper gun control policy under these extreme Malthusian assumptions? Again, contrary to what we have been calling traditional libertarian theory, the proportionality thesis yields a very different implication, namely the prohibition of firearms. However, the difference here is only with the conclusions that have previously been drawn on this topic, not with the underlying libertarian principle itself. In other words, we are putting forward the claim that proportionality theory leads to a more plumb-line libertarian position than previously achieved. That is because, paradoxically, it is *more* consistent with the premise that as long as a weapon's power can be confined to evildoers, that is, its purpose can be limited to defense against aggression, it is not *per se* invasive and thus must be legitimate.

Figure 1. The relation between geographical size and type of legal weaponry.

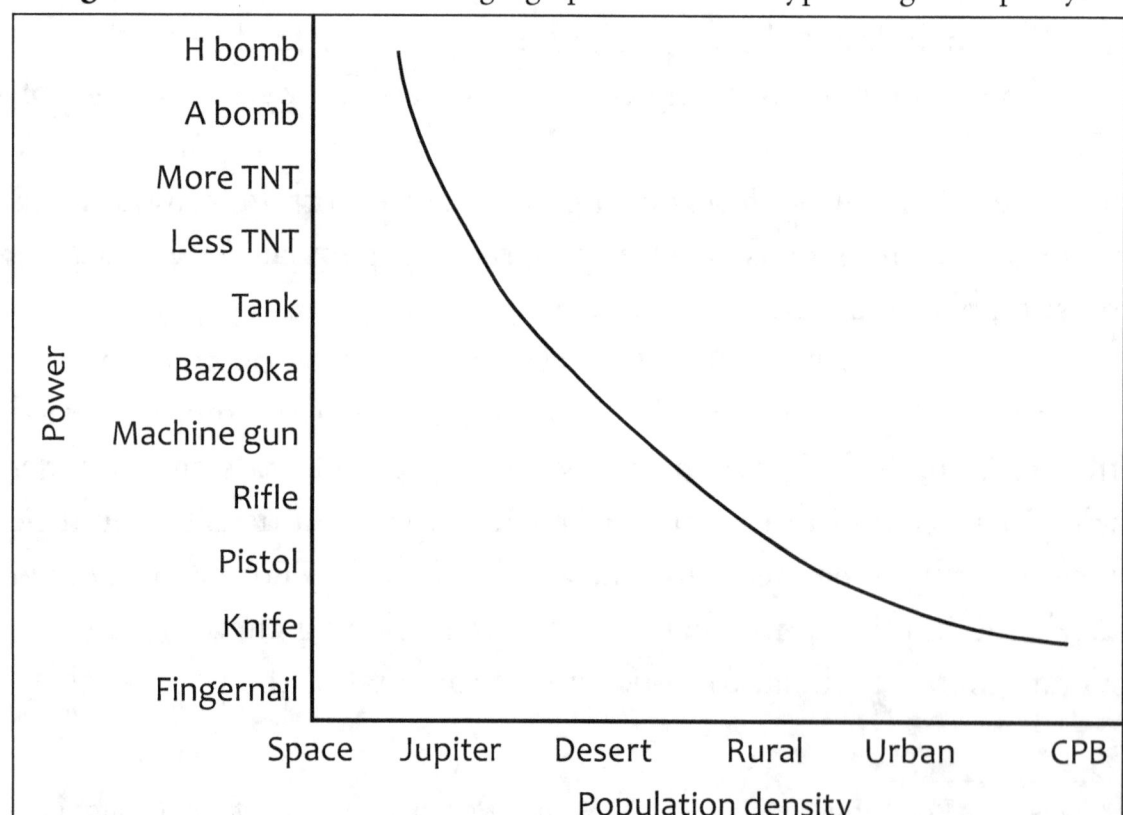

However, in the hypercrowded world,[11] not even a pistol, perhaps not even a knife, can possibly be used without impacting innocent people. If so, then it may be banned just as today we properly prohibit ownership of nukes in cities.

This new way of looking at the matter leads to new conclusions only at both ends of the population density continuum. At the low end, extensive space, it allows ownership of thermonuclear devices, when traditional libertarian theory would not. At the high end, the "crowded telephone booth" kind of world, it prohibits guns and knives, when traditional libertarian theory would legitimize these weapons. These changes are not the result of an alteration of libertarian theory; this remains the same. The different conclusions stem solely from very different assumptions about the world (or universe).

Objections

In closing, let us consider the objection to banning made by the person who wishes to possess a hydrogen bomb not for purposes of violence, but rather for contemplation, or for aesthetic or scientific reasons, or as a museum piece, etc. One answer is that the "artiste" could indeed locate a nuclear bomb in his city basement, but only the outer contours of it, that is, the shell casing alone, not the nuclear device. This ought to suffice for sheer artistic contemplation.

Suppose, however, that this will not create the necessary artistic "jolt." For that, only an armed device will do. Too bad, from the libertarian perspective. It is impossible to confine the harm done by such a weapon to the owner himself, or to a "bad guy."

In contrast, were a nuclear power station to blow up, its negative power could not be so confined either, and yet this is legitimate under libertarian law. What is the difference? The difference is that the one is

---

[11] A fictional reference to this assumption is the planet Gideon from the *Star Trek* episode "The Mark of Gideon." (We owe this example to Daniel L. Schmutter.) This, like the bug-eyed monster scenario of *Starship Troopers,* is not put forth as a likely scenario. Rather, as in that case, it is being considered only in order to trace libertarian theory to its ultimate conclusion. For rejoinders to the thesis that we are or are likely to ever become overcrowded, see Bauer (1987), Block (1989a), Block and Coffey (1999), and Simon (1981, 1989, 1990).

a weapon, the other not. Were we to ban all appliances whose power, under the worst possible scenario, could not be confined to the appropriate people and their holdings, we would have to prohibit all aircraft, and laboratories experimenting with deadly viruses, etc. This applies, even, to roofless baseball stadiums (an escaping home-run ball can break a window). The difference between all these others and the "artiste's" atom bomb is that the former is a weapon, the others not.

Rothbard (1990, p. 243) adumbrates the principles under which a just determination can be made in this regard:

> The basic libertarian principle is that everyone should be allowed to do whatever he is doing unless he is committing an overt act of aggression against someone else. But what about situations where it is unclear whether a person is committing aggression? In those cases, the only procedure consonant with libertarian principle is to do nothing; to lean over backwards to ensure that the judicial agency is not coercing an innocent man. . . . The presumption of every case . . . must be that every defendant is innocent until proven guilty, and the burden of proof must rest squarely upon the plaintiff.

So far, it sounds as if Rothbard is taking the side of the "artiste" who wishes to maintain for contemplative purposes an armed thermonuclear device in the basement of his home, located in the big city. However, this is merely a first approximation. Given that the burden of proof of criminal behavior is placed with this artiste's neighbors, how can these plaintiffs acquit their responsibilities?

States Rothbard (1990, p. 244):

> . . . the best standard for any proof of guilt is the one commonly used in criminal cases: proof "beyond a reasonable doubt." Obviously, some doubt will almost always persist in gauging people's actions, so that a standard such as "beyond a scintilla of doubt" would be hopelessly unrealistic. But the doubt must remain small enough that any "reasonable man" will be convinced of the defendant's guilt. Establishing guilt "beyond a reasonable doubt"

appears to be the standard most consonant with libertarian principle.[12]

An obvious rejoinder to this is that it conflicts with the Austrian economic notion of subjectivism (Rothbard 1962, 1973, 1977, 1989; Mises 1966; Buchanan 1969; Buchanan and Thirlby 1981). In this view, great weight is placed upon the subjective perceptions of the individual human actor: a hydrogen bomb may well be merely an object of historical contemplation, at least for some persons. The issue is, do we have to eschew Austrian subjectivism in order to argue, as libertarians, that the hydrogen bomb cannot legitimately be stored in a city art gallery?

Not at all, for under the libertarian code, to the extent that we accept the subjective evaluations of people regarding reality (as opposed to the "reasonable man" standard), it is the subjective evaluation of the threatened victim, not the perpetrator, which is determinative.

Suppose A comes rushing at B carrying a knife in the up-thrust position, while yelling "Kill!" in a blood-curdling manner, whereupon B draws his pistol and shoots A dead. Later, it turns out that A was merely an actor, practicing for a part, and that the knife was made of rubber, as are most stage props of that sort. Is B guilty of murder? Not a bit of it. Rather, B would properly be judged to have done no more than exercise his right of self-defense. Even the reasonable man would have so concluded.

In similar manner, were we to take any subjective considerations into account as a matter of libertarian law, it would not be those of the contemplator of the A bomb; rather, it would be those of his neighbors, who, presumably, take a very different view of this device.

What, then, of a possible *reductio* regarding airplanes? Every once in a while these devices crash, killing people on the ground who did not agree to bear this risk, as did the passengers. As we have seen, the victim of the knife attack, not the perpetrator, was allowed to determine the reality of the situation. Why do we not allow such possible victims of

---

[12] When it comes to standards of proof, we follow Rothbard in relying upon the "reasonable man" criterion. However, regarding innocence or guilt, we again follow Rothbard in eschewing the "reasonable man" standard in favor of strict liability. On the former, see Rothbard (1990).

airplane crashes to determine if these are invasive weapons (which they are, after the fact, from the perspective of those on the ground upon whom they crash). If such a determination were made, of course, it would spell the end of this industry.

The answer is that no reasonable person would ever come to any such conclusion. Yes, airplanes sometimes crash, but, apart from those used by Japanese kamikaze pilots in World War II, they cannot by any stretch of the imagination be considered as weapons. In contrast, the nuclear weapon located in the same geographical area as millions of innocent people, in any reasonable interpretation, would be understood as an armament, despite all the protestations of the contemplator to the contrary.

So far, we have looked at gun control from what we will call a macro-geographical perspective. In order to determine appropriate weapon restrictions, we must know the geographical context at large. If we are talking about the Earth, a "doomsday" thermonuclear device, able to blow up the entire planet and all the people who inhabit it, is *per se* offensive. Its power cannot possibly be confined to the guilty. Harboring such a weapon is thus an offense, and may properly be prohibited, but not in the vastness of space, an altogether different geographical domain. Similarly, a pistol must be banned from the super-crowded "phone booth" world, because, by stipulation, its offensive power cannot there be limited; in contrast, in our real world, revolvers would be allowed, since they most certainly can be pinpointed.

Now, in conclusion, we look at this issue from what might be called a micro-geographical perspective. Suppose there is a nuclear bomb which is at present able to explode, except for the fact that the trigger is located one mile away from the rest of the apparatus. Should this configuration be precluded by law in our real world, given our libertarian considerations? How about if the distance were 100 yards? Ten feet? One inch? One millimeter?[13] The problem, of course, is that if the trigger and the remainder of the bomb are very close to each other, the

---

[13] A similar consideration applies to the Smith and Wesson and its bullets in the "crowded phone booth" world. How far removed from one another must they be in order to be considered legal?

device can explode if someone as much as sneezes. This would tend to incline us to demand a reasonable distance between the constituent elements of a bomb which would, when assembled, be illegitimate. On the other hand, a distance of even one mile can be overcome easily by a determined evildoer. Further complicating the analysis is the fact that, at least nowadays, the different elements of a bomb (e.g., copper, zinc and uranium, etc.) can be assembled without too much difficulty, and if we want to prevent illegal atom bomb holding, we seem to be set on a slippery slope which will outlaw stockpiling all such elements, a manifest absurdity.

There is no real solution to this micro-geographical issue, since it is really a continuum problem. How far from B's nose does A's fist have to be before B is properly entitled to launch defensive forceful counter-measures? Again, there perhaps is no better answer than relying on context and the opinion of the "reasonable man." This may not be as satisfying philosophically as a more definitive answer, but, as the problem stems from the (continuous) nature of reality, this is the best answer that can be given.

3 Environmentalism and Economic Freedom: The Case for Private Property Rights

This paper shall attempt to reconcile environmentalism and economic freedom.

Before making this seemingly quixotic endeavor, we must be sure we are clear on both concepts. Environmentalism may be noncontroversially defined as a philosophy which sees great benefit in clean air and water, and to a lowered rate of species extinction. Environmentalists are particularly concerned with the survival and enhancement of endangered species such as trees, elephants, rhinos and whales, and with noise and dust pollution, oil spills, greenhouse effects and the dissipation of the ozone layer. Note, this version of environmentalism is a very moderate one. Moreover, it is purely goal directed. It implies no means to these ends whatsoever. In this perspective, environmentalism is, in principle, as much compatible with free enterprise as it is with its polar opposite, centralized governmental command and control.

Economic freedom also admits of a straightforward definition. It is the idea that people legitimately own themselves and the property they "capture" from nature by homesteading,[1] as well as the additional property

---

Reprinted with kind permission of Springer Science and Business Media from *Journal of Business Ethics* 17, no. 6 (1998): 1887–99.

[1] For a critique of homesteading, see Stroup (1988). For a rejoinder, see Block (1990a); for another defense of homesteading, see Hoppe (1993a).

they attain, further, by trading either their labor or their legitimately owned possessions.[2] Sometimes called libertarianism, in this view the only improper human activity is the initiation of threat or force against another or his property. This, too, is the only legitimate reason for law. To prevent murder, theft, rape, trespass, fraud, arson, etc., and all other such invasions is the only proper function of legal enactments.

At first glance the relationship between environmentalism and freedom would appear direct and straightforward: an increase in the one leads to a decrease in the other, and vice versa. And, indeed, there is strong evidence for an inverse relationship between the two.

For example, there is the Marxist and even communist background of some advocates of environmental concerns.[3] People like these come to the ecological movement with an axe to grind. Their real interest is with power: running the lives of others, whether for their own good, for the good of society, or for the good of the unstoppable "forces of history." They were doing pretty well on this score for decades in Russia and Eastern Europe. Thanks to them, this vast part of the globe was marching in lock step toward the Marxist vision of all power to the "proletarians." But then, in 1989, thanks to the inner contradictions of communism (Mises 1969a), their world turned topsy turvy. Some shifted their allegiances to the only fully communist systems remaining: Cuba, North Korea. As for the others, nothing daunted, they just switched horses on the same old wagon: instead of formal socialism, these people adopted environmentalism as a better means toward their unchanged ends. They can best be characterized as "watermelons," in that while they are green on the outside they are still red on the inside.

Then, there are the real greens. They see environmentalism not as a means toward an end, but as the very goal itself. The most radical of them are very forthright. They see man as the enemy of nature, and

---

[2] For a general explication of the private property-based free enterprise system, see Rothbard (1978), Hoppe (1989). For political economic perspectives that are sometimes confused with this vision, see Hayek (1973), Nozick (1974). For a rebuttal of these, see Rothbard (1982).

[3] Names which come to mind in this regard include Tom Hayden, Jane Fonda, Helen Caldicott, Jeremy Rifkin, Kirkpatrick Sale and E.F. Schumacher. For discussions of this phenomenon, see Horowitz (1991), Bramwell (1989), Rubin (1994) and Kaufman (1994).

would, if they could, destroy the former to save the latter. States Graber (1989, p. 9), who is a U.S. National Park Service research biologist: "Until such time as Homo sapiens should decide to rejoin nature, some of us can only hope for the right virus to come along." In the view of Foreman (1990, p. 48), who is co-founder of Earth First![4] and former lobbyist for the Wilderness Society, "We are a cancer on nature." And here is how Mills (1989, p. 106) describes the other members of her own species: "Debased human protoplasm."[5]

Some are only slightly less radical. They do not yearn for virtually the end of the human race. Instead, they merely hold that animals have rights, that trees have rights, that microscopic organisms have rights. It is reputed that Gandhi, for instance, sometimes went around wearing a surgical mask, so that he would not inadvertently kill a microorganism by inhaling it. If so, that practice would certainly be in keeping with this philosophy.

Stepping down a peg in the extremism of the ecologically concerned, there are those who merely blame markets, free enterprise, capitalism, for the ruination of the planet. In their view, what is needed is to curb these vicious appetites, and to return to a "kinder, gentler" version of governmental interventionism. For example, with regard to contaminated New York City beaches, the Commissioner of Health from the Big Apple stated on Canadian Public Television (30 July 1988):

> I think the motivation is greed, you know, noncaring about the planet, noncaring about the ocean, and not caring about the people who live on the planet and want to use the ocean—greed.

In the view of environmentalist Renate Kroisa regarding pulp mill operators (CTV Report, 15 March 1989):

> They would rather rape the environment and make a lot of money for themselves than not rape the environment, clean up, and later

---

[4] This is the group that urges tree spiking; placing a metal spike in trees so that when the chain saw of the lumberman encounters it, his injury or even death will result. Their rallying cry slogan is "Back to the Pleistocene."

[5] These views were cited in Goodman, Stroup *et al.* (1991, p. 3).

on . . . stay competitive. The mills are here to make a lot of profit, and they're making a lot of profit at the cost of our environment.[6]

And states Commoner,[7]

> The origin of the environmental crisis can be traced back to the capitalist precept that the choice of production technology is to be governed solely by private interest in profit maximization.

Other statements of this ilk include Porrit and Winner (1988, p. 11): "The danger lies not in the odd maverick polluting factory, industry or technology, but in . . . industrialism itself"; Bookchin (1970, p. 14): "The plundering of the human spirit by the marketplace is paralleled by the plundering of the Earth by capital"; and free markets "take the sacredness out of life, because there can be nothing sacred in something that has a price" (Schumacher 1973, p. 45).[8]

Then there are those who oppose not only market competition in general, but also want to ban particular products made possible by this system. For instance, there are calls to prohibit 747 airplanes (Rifkin 1980, p. 216), automobiles (Sale 1989, p. 33), eyeglasses (Mills 1989, p. 106), private washing machines (Bookchin 1989, p. 22), tailored clothing (Schumacher 1973, pp. 57–58), and toilet paper (Mills 1989, pp. 167–68).

Paradoxically, there is a very limited but possible sense in which it is rational to prefer the reds to the greens. True, the former, not the latter, killed millions upon millions of people (Conquest 1986, 1990). But at least their goal, their purpose, their aim, their end, was to help human beings. Yes, they picked a tragically erroneous way of going about this, a philosophy from which the entire world's peoples are still reeling. However, it must be conceded, they were not traitors to their species.[9]

---

[6] Reported in *On Balance* II, no. 9 (1989): 5.

[7] Cited in DiLorenzo (1990).

[8] Cited in Goodman, Stroup *et al.* (1991, p. 4).

[9] It is on this ground that the communists may be preferred to the Nazis. For apart from members of the Aryan nations, the Nazis actually did intend to, and actually succeed in, killing massive numbers of people. In terms of actual numbers of people killed, however, the reverse is the case.

This, unfortunately, cannot be said of some of the greens, particularly the more radical ones. Nor can it be denied that at least so far, with the exception of a few unfortunate loggers, the greens have not killed nor hurt very many people. But if their own publicly-articulated intentions are to be believed, given the power they might be a greater danger to the human race than even the communists.[10]

This, in short, is the case for believing there to be an inverse relationship between environmentalism and freedom. However, it is not a direct and straightforward one: an increase in the one does not always lead to a decrease in the other, and vice versa.

What are the exceptions? How can environmentalism and economic freedom be reconciled?[11] Simple. By showing that free enterprise is the best means toward the end of environmental protection. This appears a daunting task at the outset, given the emphasis placed by most environmentalists on socialism, and their hatred for capitalism. But a hint of the solution may be garnered by the fact that *laissez faire* capitalism, as adumbrated above, strenuously opposes invasions, or border crossings, and that many environmental tragedies, from air pollution to oil spills, may reasonably be interpreted in just such a manner. The reason for environmental damage, then, is the failure of government to protect property rights (omissions) and other state activity which either regulates private property, or which forbids it outright (commissions). Let us consider a few test cases.

Air Pollution

According to the mainstream economic analysis, libertarianism is wrong. The problem of airborne pollutants is not due to a failure of government to protect private property rights. Instead, this comes about because of "market failure," a basic flaw in free enterprise. Pigou (1912, p. 159) gives the classic statement of this view:

---

[10] Of course, actions speak louder than words, and on this basis the greens do not even deserve to be mentioned in the same breath. On the other hand, even though intentions are less important than actual deeds, the former are not morally irrelevant.

[11] For a book that attempts to do just this, see Block (1990a).

Smoke in large towns which inflicts a heavy loss on the community . . . comes about because there is no way to force private polluters to bear the social cost of their operations.

Samuelson (1956, 1970) conveys the same sentiment in terms of the divergence between private and social costs. Lange and Taylor (1938, p. 103) are yet additional socialists who make a complementary point:

A feature which distinguishes a socialist economy from one based on private enterprise is the comprehensiveness of the items entering into the socialist price system.

In other words, for some strange dark mysterious reason, capitalists, under *laissez faire*, are excused from even considering the physical harm they do to the property of others through the emissions of their smoke particles. Under socialism, in contrast, the central planner, of course, takes this into account, nipping the problem of pollution in the bud.

There is so much wrong with this scenario it is hard to know where to begin a refutation. Perhaps we may best start with an empirical observation. If this criticism of the market were true, one would expect that, even if the Soviets couldn't successfully run an economy, they could at least be trusted as far as the environment is concerned. In actual point of fact, nothing could be further from the truth.

Exhibit "A" is perhaps the disappearance of the Aral and Caspian Seas, due to massive and unchecked pollution, overcutting of trees, and consequent desertification. Then there is Chernobyl, which caused hundreds, if not thousands of deaths.[12] For ferry boats in the Volga River, it is forbidden to smoke cigarettes. This is not for intrusive paternalistic health reasons as in the West, but because this river is so polluted with oil and other flammable materials that there is a great fear that if a cigarette is tossed overboard, it will set the entire body of water on

---

[12] True, there is the U.S. counterpart nuclear meltdown at Three Mile Island. But a popular bumper sticker puts this into some sort of perspective. It stated: "More people died at Chappaquidick than at Three Mile Island." ("Chappaquidick" refers to the death of a single individual, Mary Jo Kopechne, while being driven by Senator Ted Kennedy.) The point is, of course, that no one, not a single solitary individual, lost his life at Three Mile Island.

fire. Further, under communism, there was little or no waste treatment of sewage in Poland, the gold roof in Cracow's Sigismund Chapel dissolved due to acid rain, there was a dark brown haze over much of East Germany, and the sulfur dioxide concentrations in Czechoslovakia were eight times levels common in the U.S. (DiLorenzo 1990).

Nor was it a matter merely of the absence of democracy in the U.S.S.R. The ecological record of the U.S. government, where democracy is the order of the day, is none too savory. The Department of Defense has dumped 400,000 tons of hazardous waste, more than the five largest chemical corporations combined. The Rocky Mountain Arsenal carelessly disposed of nerve gas, mustard shells, the anti-crop spray TX, and incendiary devices. And this is to say nothing of the infamous Yellowstone Park forest fire, which the authorities refused to put out, citing ecological considerations;[13] nor the TVA's 59 coal-fired power plants; nor the underpricing and overuse of land administered by the Bureau of Land Management; nor the fact that the government subsidizes forest overcutting by building logging roads.

These are not examples of market failure. Rather, they are instances of government failure: direct controls and inability or unwillingness to uphold private property rights.

But what of Pigou and Samuelson's charge of the misallocative effect of negative externalities, or external diseconomies? This, too, is erroneous.

Up to the 1820s and 1830s, the legal jurisprudence in Great Britain and the U.S. was more or less predicated upon the libertarian vision of noninvasiveness (Coase 1960; Horwitz 1977).

Typically, a farmer would complain that a railroad engine had emitted sparks which set ablaze his haystacks or other crops. Or a woman would accuse a factory of sending airborne pollutants to her property, which would dirty her clean laundry hanging on a clothesline. Or someone would object to the foreign matter imposed in one's lungs without permission. Almost invariably, the courts would take cognizance

---

[13] Forest fires, it turns out, are "natural," and nothing must be done which interferes with nature.

of this violation of plaintiff's rights.[14] The usual result during this epoch was injunctive relief, plus an award of damages.

Contrary to Pigou and Samuelson, manufacturers, foundries, railroads, etc., could not act in a vacuum, as if the costs they imposed on others were of no moment. There was a "way to force private polluters to bear the social cost of their operations:" sue them, make them pay for their past transgressions, and get a court order prohibiting them from such invasions in the future.

Upholding property rights in this manner had several salutary effects. First of all, there was an incentive to use clean-burning, but slightly more expensive anthracite coal rather than the cheaper but dirtier high sulfur content variety; less risk of lawsuits. Second, it paid to install scrubbers, and other techniques for reducing pollution output. Third there was an impetus to engage in research and development of new and better methods for the internalization of externalities: keeping one's pollutants to oneself. Fourth, there was a movement toward the use of better chimneys and other smoke-prevention devices. Fifth, an incipient forensic pollution industry was in the process of being developed.[15] Sixth, the locational decisions of manufacturing firms were intimately affected. The law implied that it would be more profitable to establish a plant in an area with very few people, or none at all; setting up shop in a residential area, for example, would subject the firm to debilitating lawsuits.[16]

But then, in the 1840s and 1850s, a new legal philosophy took hold. No longer were private property rights upheld. Now, there was an even more important consideration: the public good. And of what did the

---

[14] Called at the time "nuisance suits," we can with hindsight see them as environmental complaints.

[15] It is only because murder and rape were illegal that there was a call for a forensic industry, capable of determining guilt based on semen, blood, hair follicles, DNA, etc. If these activities were legal, these capabilities would not have developed. Similarly, when one can sue for pollution, it is of the utmost importance to determine guilt or innocence; hence, the establishment of environmental forensics.

[16] Of course, "coming to the nuisance" was not deemed acceptable. That is, one could not build a residential abode in an area first homesteaded by pollution emitters, and then sue for pollution. On this see Rothbard (1990).

public good consist in this new dispensation? The growth and progress of the U.S. economy. Toward this end it was decided that the jurisprudence of the 1820s and 1830s was a needless indulgence. Accordingly, when an environmental plaintiff came to court under this new system, he was given short shrift. He was told, in effect, that of course his private property rights were being violated; but that this was entirely proper, since there is something even more important that selfish, individualistic property rights. And this was the "public good" of encouraging manufacturing.[17]

Under this legal convention, all the economic incentives of the previous regime were turned around 180 degrees. Why use clean burning, but slightly more expensive, anthracite coal rather than the cheaper but dirtier high sulfur content variety? Why install scrubbers, and other techniques for reducing pollution output, or engage in environmental research and development, or use better chimneys and other smoke prevention devices, or make locational decisions so as to negatively impact as few people as possible? Needless to say, the incipient forensic pollution industry was rendered stillborn.

And what of the "green" manufacturer, who didn't want to foul the planet's atmosphere, or the libertarian, who refused to do this on the grounds that is was an unjustified invasion of other people's property? There is a name for such people, and it is called "bankrupt."[18] For to engage in environmentally sound business practices under a legal regime which no longer requires this is to impose on oneself a competitive disadvantage. Other things equal, this will guarantee bankruptcy.

---

[17] As a sop to the plaintiffs, the law and judicial practice was altered so as to require very high minimum heights for smokestacks. In this way the local perpetrator of invasive pollution no longer negatively impacted the local plaintiff. But of course this did no more than sweep the problem under the rug, or, rather, into the clouds. For if polluter A no longer affected complainant A, he affected others. And polluters B, C, D . . . who previously did not harm A, now began to do so.

[18] This is the exact opposite of Adam Smith's (1995) "invisible hand." Ordinarily, in *laissez faire* capitalism, selfish seeking of profit leads to the public good. For example, one invests in a good which is in very short supply, and hence most needed by the populace, and earns the greatest possible profit. Here, instead, if a person acts in an environmentally responsible manner, he goes broke.

From roughly 1850 to 1970, firms were able to pollute without penalty. *This* is why "there is no way to force private polluters to bear the social cost of their operations" à la Pigou; *this* is why there was a Samuelsonian "divergence of social and private costs." This was no failure of the market. It was a failure of the government to uphold free enterprise with a legal system protective of private property rights.

In the 1970s a "discovery" was made: the air quality was dangerous to human beings and other living creatures. Having caused the problem itself, the government now set out to cure it, with a whole host of regulations which only made things worse. There were demands for electric cars, for maximum mileage per gallon for gasoline, for subsidies to wind, water, solar and nuclear[19] power, for taxes on coal, oil, gas and other such fuels, for arbitrary cutbacks in the amount of pollutants into the air. The nationwide 55 mile per hour speed limit was not initially motivated by safety considerations, but rather by ecological ones. "Rent-seeking" played a role in the scramble, as Eastern (dirty-burning sulfur) coal interests prevailed over their Western (clean-burning anthracite) counterparts. The former wanted compulsory scrubbers, the latter wanted the mandated substitution of their own coal for that of their competitors.

And what was the view of the supposedly free market-oriented Chicago School? Instead of harking back to a system of private property rights, they urged the "more efficient" statist regulations. Instead of a command and control system, they urged the adoption of tradeable emissions rights (TERs). In this system (Hahn 1989; Hahn and Stavins 1991; Hahn and Hester 1989), instead of forcing each and every polluter to cut back by, say, one third, they would demand of all of them together that this goal be attained. Why is this beneficial? It might be difficult and expensive for some firms to reduce pollution from 150 to 100 tons, and easy and cheap for others. Under TERs, some could reduce the pollution levels by less than one-third (or even increase them), while they would, in effect, pay others to reduce theirs by more than this

---

[19] The Price Anderson Act—protecting firms from legal responsibility for accidents—is the most egregious case of the former.

amount. The means through which this would be accomplished would be a system of "rights to pollute," and an organized market through which these could be bought and sold.

The implications of this scheme for freedom are clear. States Anderson (1989):

> Fortunately, there is a simple, effective approach available—long appreciated but underused. An approach based solidly on . . . private property rights.
>
> At its root, all pollution is garbage disposal in one form or another. The essence of the problem is that our laws and the administration of justice have not kept up with the refuse produced by the exploding growth of industry, technology and science.
>
> If you took a bag of garbage and dropped it on your neighbor's lawn, we all know what would happen. Your neighbor would call the police and you would soon find out that the disposal of your garbage is your responsibility, and that it must be done in a way that does not violate anyone else's property rights.
>
> But if you took that same bag of garbage and burned it in a backyard incinerator, letting the sooty ash drift over the neighborhood, the problem gets more complicated. The violation of property rights is clear, but protecting them is more difficult. And when the garbage is invisible to the naked eye, as much air and water pollution is, the problem often seems insurmountable.
>
> We have tried many remedies in the past. We have tried to dissuade polluters with fines, with government programs whereby all pay to clean up the garbage produced by the few, with a myriad of detailed regulations to control the degree of pollution. Now some even seriously propose that we should have economic incentives, to charge polluters a fee for polluting—and the more they pollute the more they pay. But that is just like taxing burglars as an economic incentive to deter people from stealing your property, and just as unconscionable.
>
> The only effective way to eliminate serious pollution is to treat it exactly for what it is—garbage. Just as one does not have the

right to drop a bag of garbage on his neighbor's lawn, so does one not have the right to place any garbage in the air or the water or the Earth, if it in any way violates the property rights of others.

What we need are tougher, clearer environmental laws that are enforced—not with economic incentives—but with jail terms.

What the strict application of the idea of private property rights will do is to increase the cost of garbage disposal. That increased cost will be reflected in a higher cost for the products and services that resulted from the process that produced the garbage. And that is how it should be. Much of the cost of disposing of waste material is already incorporated in the price of the goods and services produced. All of it should be. Then only those who benefit from the garbage made will pay for its disposal.[20]

Economic freedom thus implies a movement back to the legal status of pollution in the earlier epoch. Nor need we fear undue economic hardship and dislocation because of adjustment problems. For apart from obvious and blatant pollution, which has already been curtailed through command and control regulations, it will take at least a few years for environmental forensics to develop to the point where industry will have to make more basic changes.

There are, of course, objections to "turning the clock back" to the 1820s. For one thing, there is the fear that if we allow anyone to sue anyone else for pollution, that will mean the end of industry altogether. And not only of industry and other accoutrements of modern civilized life. This would also bring the curtain down on life itself, as, strictly speaking, even exhaling (carbon dioxide) could be seen as a pollutant, and thus forbidden. Fortunately, this scenario is not tenable. First of all, although industry up to the 1830s was no great shakes compared to the modern era, it was not as nonexistent as implied by this objection either. Second, there is a reason for this: the burden of proof is on the plaintiff, so only the more egregious cases of pollution were, in effect, actionable,

---

[20] For another critique of tradeable emissions rights, see McGee and Block (1994).

and *de minimis* was in operation, so that frivolous lawsuits, or ones alleging only tiny amounts of pollution were disregarded.[21]

Another objection, a more reasonable one, is that if allowing pollution lawsuits again will not bring industry to a screeching halt, it will at least greatly disorganize it. Perhaps it might be better to allow for a ten-year waiting or warning period, so that industry could adjust, before imposing so draconian a set of measures.

This option does indeed sound more pragmatic, but there are problems with it. We have said that pollution amounts to an invasion. Suppose that someone had the authority to immediately end an invasion, say, for example, slavery, and refused to do so for ten years on the grounds that this would be too "disruptive" or "impractical." Say what you will about such a decision on pragmatic grounds, it cannot be maintained that it enhances freedom.

Fortunately, we can have our cake and eat it too in the present context. That is, we can allow environmental lawsuits immediately, but also have a "waiting period" of perhaps ten years or so in any case. This can be accomplished because of the 150-year gap, from approximately 1845 to 1995, when environmental forensics could have developed, but did not, thanks to a legal regime which was not conducive to it.[22] The point is, had environmental forensics been developing over these last 150 years, but for some reason not implemented, and we were to suddenly allow environmental lawsuits for the first time at present, this would indeed drive industry to an abrupt halt.[23] For the plaintiff's burden of proof would be easy to satisfy, under these assumptions. Moreover,

---

[21] On this see Rothbard (1990).

[22] From 1845 to 1970, approximately, polluters had a free run of the atmosphere, other people's property and their lungs. From roughly 1970 to 1995, and counting, there was concern for invasive air and water-borne pollutants, but only command and control (and in the last few years tradeable emissions rights schemes) regulations. Provision for environmental lawsuits is still, as of this 1995 writing, virtually nonexistent. See Horwitz (1977), Block (1990a, pp. 282–85).

[23] If a legal theory is to be a robust one, it must not rely on the accidents of time or place. That is, it must be applicable at any epoch in history. Since I claim that libertarianism fits this bill, it is incumbent upon me to show how it would apply not only when environmental concerns have been incorporated into the law, but also when they were not.

there would be plenty of invasive pollution around to find people guilty of perpetrating.

For with emissions strictly controlled (in the early period), development would have proceeded along nonpollution-intensive lines. In contrast, with *carte blanche* on emissions (the later period), industry would have developed in a pollution-intensive manner. Moving from a system where pollution was all but legal (1845–1970), to one where it was strictly controlled (as it was before 1845), would thus have called for a basic restructuring of industry.

Let me try to make this point in another way. There is a difficulty which the private property rights theory of environmental protection must wrestle with: if we institute such a system abruptly, especially if we did so, say, in the 1960s before these concerns had captured the public imagination, we ran the risk of halting industry dead in its tracks, something to be resisted at the very least on pragmatic grounds. On the other hand, if we offered, for example, a ten-year waiting period before environmental lawsuits could be undertaken, then we are complicit in violations of the libertarian code during this decade. Happily we can avoid this dilemma. First, we allow lawsuits as soon as we have the power to do so, thus escaping from the second (disrupting industry) horn of the dilemma. We escape from the first, too, because of the fact that for the plaintiff to be successful in his lawsuit he must prove beyond a reasonable doubt that a specific particular polluter is responsible for invading his person or property. But to do so, given the sad sorry state of environmental forensics at least at the time of this writing, will take time, plausibly, as much time as it will take for industry to end the error of its ways without any great disruption. That is, suppose it takes ten years for industry to adjust to the legal dispensation of the 1830s. This will not be as harmful to the economy as might be supposed because it might take a similar amount of time to figure out precisely who is polluting whom.[24]

---

[24] I am grateful to an anonymous referee for forcing me to clarify my presentation of this point.

Waste Disposal

The brou-ha-ha over paper vs. plastic and styrofoam wrappers also has implications for economic freedom.

In the late 1980s, a McDonald's restaurant opened its doors in Moscow. In some ways, this was no great shakes. Ray Kroc's burger emporia had by that time been doing business in hundreds of other countries. But in other ways, this was a very big deal indeed. For at that time Russia was still under the control of communism. Allowing a private firm to do business in the heart of the beast thus showed a weakness in the totalitarianism of the U.S.S.R. What could be a greater chink in the armor than a popular restaurant intimately tied to Western capitalism.

McDonald's is a reasonable example of a capitalist enterprise. It employs thousands of people, particularly young persons, minority members, and immigrants. It brings joy to millions of customers, and has sold, almost unbelievably, in the billions of burgers. It is an indication of quality. You can travel practically the world over, and be assured of the same kind of meal they serve in Kansas. This chain (and other imitators) has been a boon to the poor. Before its birth, it was difficult for the poor to enjoy a restaurant meal; thanks to this initiative, away from home dining has become a commonplace for those with modest means. All in all, McDonald's was not a poor choice as a chip in the high stakes gambling with the communists over the future of the world's political economy.

But at about the same time that Ronald McDonald was taking up residence behind the Iron Curtain, back at home, in "the land of the free and the home of the brave," he was running into entry restrictions and other barriers. Dozens of town councils, all across this great land of ours, were refusing to give McDonald's permission to open up new stores. Why? A takeover of Soviet fifth columnists? A communist revolution in the good old U.S. of A.? Not a bit of it. Instead, it was all due to left-wing environmentalism.

Why were the local greens so bitterly opposed to more quarter pounder outlets? Because they came wrapped in styrofoam and other plastic packaging, and if there is one thing practically guaranteed to drive an environmentalist to apoplexy, it is precisely these materials.

Let us assume, merely for the sake of argument, that everything any ecologist has ever said about plastic and styrofoam is true. That compared to paper, these substances are not environmentally friendly, they are not biodegradable, they are not recyclable, they are not reusable, they cannot be returned to nature. On the contrary, when buried in the ground, they come back to haunt us in the future as hazardous wastes. And that as a result, anyone foolish enough to dispose of them ruins his land for subsequent farming, housing, factories, shopping malls, etc.

Under these conditions, let us enquire into the ability of the marketplace to transmit this knowledge (paper, good; plastic, bad) so that it is taken into account by the economy. After all, this is precisely what the price system is presumably designed to do. Prices, after all, are like street signs. Just as the latter guide us around geographical space,[25] the former are supposed to impose direction on the economy.

At first glance it would appear that while prices might accomplish their task in the general economy, they are a dismal failure when it comes to environmental concerns. Picture yourself at the supermarket checkout counter. You have just selected your groceries, and the clerk has charged you for them. After paying, you are asked that inevitable, fateful $64,000 question: paper or plastic bag?

Under these circumstances, the only reason for picking the environmentally sound paper, and eschewing the toxic plastic, is benevolence. For let us assume that the cost to you is $0.01 for each. In some cases, this is explicit. You pay a penny for either one. In other cases, it is only implicit: you don't pay for the bag, paper or plastic; rather, it is included in the price of the groceries, in much the same manner as the lighting, or cleaning, or advertising of the store. Benevolence for the planet, or for your fellow creatures is your only possible motivation for choosing

---

[25] In the days of yore when a city was faced with a besieging army, one of the defensive measures they would take was to tear down the street signs. They did so on the ground that this would hardly much disaccommodate long time citizens, but would play havoc with the invader's ability to travel around town.

the paper; for by stipulation the economic considerations are equal. One penny for each.

But we all know what Smith (1776) said about benevolence. It is not from benevolence, but rather from a keen appreciation of self-interest, that the butcher, the baker and the candlestick maker share with us their wares. Given the evils of plastic, benevolence is a weak reed indeed upon which to base our hopes for its elimination. Nor is it a question of benevolence versus selfishness. Given the importance of ridding the planet of these noxious substances, it behooves us to mobilize both motivations, not just one of them.

Benevolence is far from sufficient. For suppose that half of all industrialists had the personality of a libertarian Mother Teresa, and refused to pollute, even though allowed to do so by law. What would happen to them? They would go bankrupt, for they would give themselves a competitive disadvantage. If all industrialists are roughly of equal ability, but some pollute and others spend money on smoke prevention devices, it is clear that the invisible hand will be choking us, not helping us. No, the only solution is to change the law to one which upholds property rights, so that trespassers do not continue to be privileged.

Why has the price system seemingly failed? Is this intrinsic to capitalism, one of the "market failures" that socialist economists are always prattling on about? Not at all. The failure stems not from *laissez faire*, but from state prohibition. Specifically, the government has nationalized, or municipalized, the industry of solid waste management.

Right now, we do not pay a red cent for garbage disposal. Instead, we are forced by government to disburse tax money for this purpose, and are then given these services for "free." In other words, this service is run along the lines of socialized medicine. There, too, services are provided for "free," courtesy of our tax dollars.

These systems have several disadvantages.[26] For one thing, there is the phenomenon of "moral hazard." Charge people a very low or zero price, and they will buy much more than at normal prices. Further,

---

[26] Apart, that is, from the immorality of forcing people, whether by democratic vote or no (Spooner 1966), to pay for things they have no desire to purchase.

they will "waste" the good or service.[27] This is seen in the fact that socialized medicine is a hypochondriac's dream come true, and that consumers purchase items which are promiscuously wrapped. Given that the housewife doesn't have to pay to dispose of package coverings, it is no wonder that the manufacturer has little incentive to economize on containers.[28]

How would a private market in garbage disposal function? Everything would be privatized. The trucks which make pickups from the homeowner as well as the dumpsites themselves. There would be no mandatory recycling nor bottle deposit requirements;[29] there would only be laws against trespassing: disgorging waste material onto other people's private property.

How would prices be established? Assume that burying inoffensive paper costs only a penny per bag, but that the plastic variety is so harmful that each one does $5.00 worth of damage[30] to the land in which it is placed. Given competition, no dumpsite owner will be able to charge more than $5.00 for burying a plastic bag, lest the additional profits earned thereby attract new entrants into the industry. In like manner the price cannot fall below this amount, since if it does, it will bankrupt all who agree to it. For example, if a private dumpsite owner were to accept $4.00 compensation for agreeing to permanently store a plastic

---

[27] If we ran a socialized milk program as we do garbage disposal and medical care, people would probably have "milk gun" (instead of water gun) fights, wash their cars with milk, and take milk baths.

[28] In addition to excessive amounts of wrappings, our zero price policy has also lead to the combination of different materials in them, such as paper, plastic, tin and other metals, cardboard, etc. All of this makes it more expensive to recycle.

[29] Which are but further infringements upon economic freedom.

[30] Science cannot at present precisely determine the amount of damage that might be caused. (I owe this point to an anonymous referee). However, this presents no philosophical challenge to entrepreneurship. Those dumpsite owners whose predictions are the closest to reality will prosper, at least compared to their colleagues furthest away, given *ceteris paribus* conditions. But make no mistake about it; given the assumptions on the basis of which we are now operating, storing paper most certainly *will* harm the dumpsite itself, at the very least in terms of economics. For, to reiterate, we are presuming that buried plastic and styrofoam has much the same effect as a toxic waste. Those dumpsite owners who allow storage of these items under their land will reduce its economic value after the landfill is complete, and alternative uses (housing, farms, etc.) are contemplated.

bag on his land, he would lose $1.00 on that transaction. Multiply this by a few truckloads of this substance, and he will no longer be able to continue in business.[31]

Now let us return to our supermarket checkout scenario. Only this time, under full privatization, we make an entirely different economic calculation than before.

	Purchase cost	Disposal cost	Total
Paper	$0.01	$0.01	$0.02
Plastic	$0.01	$5.00	$5.01

Previously, there was no impetus to choose either paper or plastic. Each cost $0.01, and that was the end of it. Now, however, matters are very different. For we are called upon not merely to purchase the bag material, but also to dispose of it later on at our own expense. Given disposal costs of one penny for paper and five dollars for plastic, our total costs are readily calculated: two cents for paper, and five dollars and one cent for plastic.

Is there any doubt that the whole problem would disappear in one fell swoop under these economic conditions? Virtually no consumer in his right mind would choose environmentally unfriendly plastic. The costs would simply be prohibitive. Everyone would "do the right environmental thing" and select paper.

This does not mean, of course, that plastic bags would be totally banned by economics. They would still be utilized, but only when their value to the user was greater than $5.01. For example, blood, intravenous solution and other medical fluids might still employ plastic containers.

Thus, thanks to the "magic of the market," we can again have our cake and eat it too. Under a full private property rights regime, there is no reason to legislatively ban McDonald's. If plastic and styrofoam are truly hazardous to the health of the planet, they will impose tremendous costs on dumpsite owners. These will be passed on to consumers. If

---

[31] I am here implicitly assuming that the present discounted (dis)value of burying a single plastic bag is $5.00. Obviously, to charge only $4.00 for this service would be to lose money on the deal.

McDonald's continued to insist upon use of plastic and styrofoam, this firm would lose out to other competitors (Burger King, Wendy's, Pizza Hut, Taco Bell, A&W, etc.) who were more greatly concerned for their customer's pocketbooks. Under present assumptions, there is simply no need to reduce freedom in order to protect the planet. The two work in tandem.

But it is now time to question our assumptions about the relative harm to the planet of plastic and styrofoam. According to "garbologist"[32] Rathje (1989), plastic is not so much a hazard to the globe as it is inert. If there is anything dangerous to the planet it is paper; not in the form of bags, but rather telephone books. After many years of burial, these release methane gas, and other dangerous substances. If so, perhaps paper and plastic will be able to compete with one another on a some-what more equal footing.

This is an empirical question, which cannot be decided on the basis of armchair economic theorizing. It may safely be left in the hands of the private dumpsite owning industry, for these entrepreneurs, unlike environmental bureaucrats, stand to lose their own personal fortunes if their prices are not consonant with actual harm to their property, and hence to the environment in general.

Conclusion

I have tried to show that in at least two cases, air pollution and waste disposal, the concerns of environmentalists and those who favor economic freedom can be reconciled. However, there might appear to be what one anonymous referee called a "basic structural flaw in the development of (my) argument" in that the public policy conclusions in each of these two cases appear to be very different. "On the one hand," continues this referee,

> [I] applaud . . . the existence of a pre-1850 legal system which enforced private property rights. But in (my) final argument for

---

[32] A garbologist is to mounds of waste material as is an archeologist to ancient ruins. Each yearns to "get to the bottom" of their respective subject matters. Each analyzes them from their own perspective.

letting the market control waste disposal there is no clear indication of what, *if any,* role environmental law would play.

I am tremendously grateful to this referee in that he has given me an opportunity to further explicate libertarian environmentalist theory. The seeming contradiction in how I handle the two ecological issues can be reconciled in this way. In the case of air pollution, the violation of economic freedom and private property rights was that polluters were allowed by law to, in effect, trespass on other people's land, to say nothing of their lungs. In the case of waste disposal, the breach of economic freedom and private property rights is no less apparent, although it takes an altogether different form.

Here, the infraction consists of the nationalization (e.g., municipalization) of what would otherwise be private dumpsites. But in both cases there is a transgression of the free enterprise ethic. Therefore, in each, the capitalist-oriented environmentalist will advocate a return to market principles. In the one case, this consists of an end to legal trespass; in the other, of privatization of garbage dumping. Thus, there is no "structural flaw," or indeed, any inconsistency whatever, in this analysis.

Let me make this point in a different way. Egalitarian socialists oppose both income disparities and private medicine. For the former they advocate wealth redistribution; for the latter, socialized medicine. Now these are two very distinct things. Seemingly, they are incompatible with one another. But not really, since both are aspects of an underlying vision.

It is the same in the present case. Laws prohibiting trespass of smoke particles, and privatizing dumpsites are superficially very different. In actual point of fact they are but opposite sides of the same coin, in that they both emanate from the same philosophical principle.

One last point. The typical way of treating pollution in the literature is as an "externality." By now it should be clear that I totally reject this approach. An external diseconomy is defined as a harm perpetrated by A on B, one for which B can neither collect damages nor halt through injunction. But *why* is B so powerless? It is my contention that the victim of pollution finds himself in this precarious position solely because of inadequacies in the law. Previous to 1850, for example, *there was no* pollution externality. This came about due to a "government failure" to uphold the law against trespass, not because of any alleged "market failure" such as externalities.

4 Enterprising Education: Doing Away with the Public School System

(with Andrew Young)

Besides national defense, no government-provided service enjoys as much exemption from scrutiny as the provision and subsidization of primary public education. Even presumed champions of the free market, such as Milton Friedman, support the government subsidization of education through high school:

> We have always been proud, and with good reason, of the widespread availability of schooling to all and the role that public schooling has played in fostering the assimilation of newcomers into our society, preventing fragmentation and divisiveness, and enabling people from different cultural and religious backgrounds to live together in harmony. (Friedman and Friedman 1979, pp. 140–41)

The very suggestion that government should be removed entirely from the realm of education is either taken as irrational and malicious

Reprinted with kind permission of Springer Science and Business Media from *International Journal of Value-Based Management* 12, no. 3 (1999): 195–207. Andrew T. Young graduated from College of the Holy Cross in Worcester, Mass., and holds a Ph.D. in Economics from Emory University in Atlanta, Ga. He is now Assistant Professor of Economics at University of Mississippi.

or viewed as foolhardy and quixotic. This seems very peculiar when considering that the critics of the present state of public education appear on both sides of the political spectrum. Still, the overwhelming sentiment, ubiquitous in both the general citizenry and academia, is that while public education may need to be reformed, it still should be guaranteed "free" to all by government.

This paper will advance the view that education, like any other service, cannot be provided more efficiently than via the market. Furthermore, unlike most modern arguments claiming to favor the "privatization" of schools, this paper will not view the government contracting of private companies, the issuance of government vouchers for payment of education, or the direct subsidization of private institutions through free market solutions.[1] Instead, the abolition of all governmental ties to primary education shall be explored.

First of all, let it be stated that primary education—i.e., that which begins in grammar school and continues up through high school—is a service like any other and can be allocated through the market and the price system. Parents, in general, would like to provide education for their children. Teachers, administrators, and owners of school buildings will provide this service to these children as long as they are compensated for their labors. When a parent approaches an institute of learning, he values the service offered. The school, drawn into the industry by the desire for profit,[2] incurs costs in providing its service. It will only accept a price greater than or equal to these costs. Likewise, the parent will only offer to pay a price less than or equal to his valuation of the education rendered. If a price is determined which is satisfactory to both

---

[1] For a discussion of these and other pseudo-privatization reforms, see Lieberman (1989, pp. 6–9).

[2] A point which is always overlooked by the market's critics and champions alike, though replete with practical applications in the workings of the market, is that profit need not be simply monetary; it can, as well, be emotional and/or psychological. Who profits more: the teacher who hates children and is paid $100 to teach a class, or a teacher who adores educating them but is only paid $75? It cannot be determined. True, in a market society love of one's fellow human being is not usually perceived as the dominating force behind economic activity. Still, to discount the goodness of much of humanity is to unjustly portray self-interest and the potential for benevolence in a market economy. For some interesting comments on this see Friedman (1978, chap. 3).

parties, an exchange will occur and the child will be provided with the service. In this straightforward way, familiar to every economist and intuitive to nearly everyone else, the market can provide primary education just as it provides hair styling, automotive repair, and the innumerable other services which people bargain to provide and receive.

Despite virtually omnipresent dogma, there is no simple explanation as to why government provision of primary education must be substituted for private alternatives.[3] Education is a service, and innumerable services are being provided by the market at any given moment. For society to hold to, and tax from individuals the resources for, government provision of primary education, there must be a justification. If it can be satisfactorily articulated, then, and only then, would government provision of primary education be legitimate.

What are the arguments in favor of government-provided primary education? They are as follows: (1) it is a necessary aspect of democracy and, paradoxically, the citizenry must be taxed for that system to secure their own freedom, (2) the market would not provide an equal opportunity for and quality of primary education to everyone, and (3) education is an example of an external economy; market provision would therefore be under-optimal. Let us consider each.

1. The view that primary education should be available to all through a public system has been made inseparable from the concept of a republican society over the years. Pierce (1964, pp. 3–4) provides a historical demonstration:

> Herein originated a new concern for education expressed by Thomas Jefferson in his belief that people could not govern themselves successfully unless they were educated. . . . This concept has gone through several stages of evolution—from Jefferson's

---

[3] Furthermore, there is no simple explanation as to why the certain and specific tasks which government has chosen to provide under the catch-all of "education" have come definitively to describe an education. Education also involves the innumerable experiences individuals live and learn from, e.g., reading books and newspapers, watching television, and speaking and debating other individuals. The classroom is a very limited exposure of learning. It is worth noting that the market is charged with provision of all other educational experiences.

idea that if people were to vote intelligently they must be educated as a means of survival in a world of competing ideologies.[4]

This view of education as catalyst for successful democratic government has metamorphosed through the passing of time into a view of education as a veritable necessary condition of freedom. For this expansion to occur, the meaning of freedom had to be modified. As Graham (1963, pp. 45–46) states, people might mistakenly, "interpret freedom in terms of their right to criticize and to choose their masters—the men for whom they work, the politicians who direct their public affairs, the newspapers, books, speeches, and television programs that influence their thinking." But a more correct definition, "for a democratic society would recognize the need for authority in any social group and equate freedom with the right to participate in power" (Graham 1963, pp. 45–46). To participate in the power (i.e., the representative nature of American government) citizens must have information, ergo to educate is a legitimate function of the state.[5]

This view of freedom is questionable though. Consider the view of liberty espoused by John Locke, one of, if not the, major philosophical influences of the American Revolution:

> The Freedom then of Man and Liberty of acting according to his own Will, is grounded on his having Reason, which is able to instruct him in the Law he is to govern himself by, and make

[4] It should be noted that, while Jefferson definitely valued education highly, it is questionable as to whether he would have approved of a public education system. Our second president was part of the drive in early America for very little if any government which was ultimately stalled by the federalists. For a description of the Jefferson influence in early America, see Rothbard (1978, p. 7).

[5] This paradoxical view that true freedom is achieved through coercion, albeit a coercion controlled by the representative citizenry, seems truer to many communist ideologies than to the liberal tradition usually associated with the founding of the United States. Compare Graham's concept of freedom with the statements of Peter Kropotkin, a czarist prince and proponent of anarchic communism:

> The people themselves will abolish private property . . . taking possession in the name of the whole community of all the wealth accumulated by the labor of past generations. . . . Never have men worked as they will on this day when labor becomes free and everything accomplished by the worker will be a source of well-being to the whole commune. (See Kropotkin 1970, p. 128)

him Know how far he is left to the freedom of his own will. (Locke 1960, p. 3)

Freedom is based primarily upon man's reason according to Locke. Because he possesses reason, man has the faculties and duty to rule himself. This Lockean concept of freedom was spread through early America in *Cato's Letters* (Rothbard 1978, p. 4). This concept of freedom was also that of John Stuart Mill, who wrote later on in the nineteenth century: ". . . the same reasons which show that opinions should be free, prove also that [an individual] should be allowed, without molestation, to carry his opinions into practice at his own cost" (Mill 1956, p. 23).[6]

Furthermore, while a cultivated citizenry might be more capable of exercising its influence in a republican government, there is something perverse in the state itself educating the citizenry on how to operate the state. As Lieberman (1989, p. 11) notes:

> Simply stated, public choice theory asserts that the behavior of politicians and bureaucrats can be explained by the same principles that govern behavior in private economic affairs. In the former, persons generally act so as to enhance their self-interest. . . . [Public officials] act either to get reelected or to enhance their pay, perquisites, and status.

If the purpose of providing public schooling is to create an informed citizenry capable of choosing those individuals who run the nation, then surely the power to determine what is taught and how should not be rested in the hands of the governing individuals.

As Boaz (1991, p. 19) observes: "Even in basic academic subjects there is a danger in having only one approach taught in all of the schools." The state-monopolistic nature of a public school system fosters undesirable conformity of curriculum. Williams (1978) correctly describes a public educational system as one which, "requires a collective decision on many attributes of [education]," and that education

---

[6] Though Graham's concept of freedom was not that which forged this nation, it has likely become the dominant concept. Fortunately, there have been recent explorations and expansions of basic ideas of liberty. For one of the most important, see Hayek (1960).

is offered to all, "whether or not [a parent] agrees with all the attributes or not."[7] The individuals entrenched in positions of power in the state are those with control over what children are taught concerning history, government, economics, and so forth. The result is a citizenry educated by operators of the state on how to choose the operators of the state! Of course, those government agents who plan and direct the curricula are most likely well-intentioned people,[8] but, as Ludwig von Mises (1952, p. 47) correctly notes: "No planner is ever shrewd enough to consider the possibility that the plan which the government will put into practice could differ from his own plan." In other words, no

---

[7] Brown (1992) has argued that conformity is actually what consumers of primary education want. He argues: "The comprehensive uniformity observed in schools can be accounted for in large part by the presence of uncertainty. . . . [P]eople will want to diversify in making their school choices by choosing schools that have comprehensive uniformity." Basically the argument is that the conventional school curriculum is a smattering of all fields (i.e., Math, History, English, Science, etc.) and that, considering the study of each subject as a separate investment, consumers are diversifying their educational portfolios. Therefore, regardless of whether or not the schools are public or private, conformity of curriculums will be present across schools. Brown cites the fact that private schools offer basically the same core curriculums and are forced to compete, rather, on secondary characteristics such as religious training. Brown errs in two ways, however. First, he ignores the fact that even though schools, both private and public, often offer the same basic subjects, private schools can and do compete on the margins of how and from which perspectives they teach the subjects, as well as the outcomes of the subjects taught (i.e., how well has the student learned). Second, Brown makes a dire mistake in stating the current curriculums of private schools as the market outcome when they are competing against a state monopoly which dominates via the ability to tax tuition (therefore rendering tuition to public schools a sunk cost to consumers).

[8] Of course, "most likely" does not mean "always." Consider The National School Lunch Act of 1946. Obviously there could be nothing but good intentions toward America's children behind such a piece of legislation. Actually, the act's purpose was twofold: first to "safeguard the health and well-being" of the children, and second to, "encourage the domestic consumption . . . of agricultural commodities." Who would have thought that behind such a seemingly benign act would be a subsidy for America's farmers? The school lunch program was supplemented in 1954 by the Agricultural Act, which was designed to increase the consumption of milk by reimbursing schools (with taxpayers' dollars, of course) for milk purchases. See Pierce (1964, p. 35). A further problem with this program is that it is an implicit attack on the family (this applies to latter school breakfast programs as well). The state properly sees the family as a competitive institution. Anything that weakens the latter strengthens the former, and vice versa (this is why the Soviet government encouraged children to "tattle" on their parents). What better way to wean youngsters from their parents and into the all-loving embrace of the state than to encourage a system where the very physical sustenance of the next generation is given over to the public sector?

matter how much such a person sincerely plans in the interests of others, ultimately the plans are still his own.

Furthermore, it should be realized that, for all the talk about the noble ideals of Thomas Jefferson, the foundation of America's government by the people, and the preservation of citizens' "freedom," the realization of public primary education in the United States was ushered in with quite ignoble motives. "[O]ne of the major motivations of the legion of mid-nineteenth-century American 'educational reformers' who established the modern public school system was precisely to use it to cripple the cultural and linguistic life of the waves of immigrants into America, and to mould them, as educational reformer Samuel Lewis stated, into 'one people'" (Rothbard 1978, p. 125). Particular targets of the American educational reformation were the Germans and the Irish. Monroe (1940, p. 224) articulates, with disarming benignity, the attitude toward these waves of immigrants and the cultures which they brought to America:

> More than a million and a half Irish and a similar number of Germans were added to the population. Great numbers of English and Welsh had also come, but the two former nationalities were sufficiently concentrated in location to cause their different racial temperaments and social customs to become new factors in our political, social, and economic life. . . . [These] elements as a whole made the educational problem more distinct, and by accentuating the tests to which our political and social structure must be subjected directed the attention of the native population to the significance of education.

Notice how the English and Welsh, with cultures more compatible with predominant American beliefs, are mentioned only in passing, while the more exotic Irish and Germans are elements to which "our political and social structure must be subjected," creating an "educational problem." Further, the individual liberties which America granted to its citizens and "led men to object to all form of governmental restraint caused such excesses that the success of self-government was seriously questioned. Much of the responsibility for this condition approaching anarchy was popularly attributed to the untrained and unbridled foreign element . . ." (Monroe 1940, pp. 223–24). Immigrant culture was seen as a cancer on the United States society, incompatible with American liberty. Paradoxically, the solution which would allow immigrants to enjoy liberty was to deny them freedom of education and instead force them to pay for public schools whether or not they wanted to attend.

A study of problems with the existing school system by the Secretary of the Connecticut School Board in 1846 noted numerous defects: "The tenth defect was the existence of numerous private schools" (Monroe 1940, p. 244). The existence of private schools was seen as especially troublesome with regards to the Irish Catholics. As Rothbard (1978, p. 125) writes: "It was the desire of the Anglo-Saxon majority to . . . smash the parochial school system of the Catholics." Taxing indiscriminately for education, thus forcing those individuals who would opt for private education to pay twice (once in taxes, and again in tuition to the private school), was one method for discouraging private education. Even more blunt was the attempt in Oregon during the 1920s to outlaw private schools (Rothbard 1978, p. 126). A law was passed making private primary education illegal and compelling all children to attend public schools. Fortunately, in *Pierce v. Society of Sisters* (1925), the Supreme Court found the law to be unconstitutional.

2. No matter what motives are revealed to have been behind the origin of a public system, however, there are those critics of the market who reply that presently government assures equal educational opportunity. The strongest of these critics even finds the lack of "free" public education to all to be unconstitutional (Pierce 1964, p. 12). The fact that market provision would not guarantee this service to each and every individual is undeniable. Under a market system, education is not a right. If one does not pay for it then one does not obtain it.[9] As long as one pays for it though, one will receive it.

---

[9] This statement would seem to preclude education as a gift of charity (e.g., scholarships) and, in regards to the price system, it does for the time being. Charity, of course, does exist, but for the sake of argument it is ignored here to show that even egoism in the coldest sense of the word is compatible with the proposal of this paper. Furthermore, as an aside, normally, scholarships (educational charity) are awarded for achievement of some sort. Therefore,

Therefore, to assist the market's critics for a moment, the real problem they are noting is not a lack of schooling for all. This is obvious because, under a market system of provision, all can afford some quality of tutelage, but they are not guaranteed a high quality service, nor one equal to that which all other individuals receive.[10] As the U.S. Department of Education claims: "Our Mission Is to Ensure Equal ACCESS to Education and Promote Educational EXCELLENCE throughout the Nation."[11]

This modified argument is still undeniable. A market system would not provide an egalitarian, high quality education for all; but in order to justify state provision it must be shown that state provision indeed provides a more egalitarian and higher quality education to all.

As far as egalitarian goals go, the state system does a horrible job. Even its most vehement supporters would scarcely claim that public schools offer equal quality of education across socioeconomic lines. Jencks (1985) declares, "the annual expenditure per pupil in a prosperous suburb is usually at least fifty percent more than in a slum in the same metropolitan area . . . taxpayers typically spend less than $5,000 [per pupil, per year] for the formal education of most slum children compared to more than $10,000 for many suburban children." Also, the statist system has failed to equalize primary education along racial lines. Coleman and Hoffer (1987, p. xxiv) found in private schools less racial segregation than their public counterparts.

---

recipients of scholarships have paid for their education in their dedication to prior academics, athletics, etc. The presenter of the scholarship, having deemed the demonstration of certain qualities pleasing enough to warrant giving out the educational service for free or at a reduced price, is also, in effect, paid for the education (i.e., psychic income). Perhaps there are examples where recipients of scholarships have done nothing to earn them, for instance there are scholarships based upon race or other ethnic backgrounds, but still the presenter is paid in the same sense as before noted and the recipient still "supplies" the characteristic valued by the scholarship provider, i.e., the correct skin color.

[10] The poorest of the poor under the present system could save enough from their welfare checks to buy four or five books a year for their children; or to pay some high school student to sit down and do basic math with them for an hour or so. Obviously this would be education of a very low quality, but it demonstrates that the problem is not simply that of education for all. It is, rather, an issue of quality and equality.

[11] U.S. Department of Education web site: www.ed.gov (3/31/97).

Furthermore, public education, even on average, is far from high quality. The National Assessment of Educational Progress reports that 50 percent of all high school seniors in America could not answer this question: "Which of the following is true about 87% of 10? (a) It is greater than 10, (b) It is less than 10, (c) It is equal to 10, (d) Can't tell" (Boaz 1991, p. 2). The NAEP also reported that a mere 7 percent of America's seventeen-year-old individuals, "have the prerequisite knowledge and skills thought to be needed to perform well in college-level science courses" (Boaz 1991, p. 3). Further, a 1989 National Endowment for the Humanities survey discovered that 54 percent of college seniors, the vast majority of whom came from the public school system, could not identify the half century during which the Civil War occurred, 58 percent could not name Plato as author of *The Republic,* and 23 percent made the mistake of placing Marx's "from each according to his ability, to each according to his need," in the text of the U.S. Constitution (Bacon 1989).

Not only is the quality of the public school system horrendous, but its cost is extraordinary. America's public primary schools spent $5,246 per pupil on average during 1989.[12] That is $130,000 for a classroom of twenty-five students.[13] Furthermore this is above that of many private schools. Of the approximately $212 million spent on education through high school in 1989,[14] only 40 percent went toward teachers' pay (West 1983).[15] Where did the other $100 billion-plus go? Far too much goes to administrators and bureaucrats. Boaz (1991, p. 17) writes:

---

[12] The socialist Richard Rothstein notes that in 1967 American schools spent only $687 per pupil on average. He then goes on to write: "It is probable, however, that the use of the CPI-U [to adjust the past and present expenditures into real measurements] causes an overstatement of school spending growth." In other words, America has not really embarked on a drastic increase in government spending on primary education since the 1960s (Rothstein 1996). However, the largely accepted opinion among economists is that the CPI-U overstates inflation by at least one percentage point (Belton 1996). So, in actuality, the use of the CPI-U understates the increase in educational expenditures by government.

[13] "1989 Back-to-School Forecast," Department of Education news release, August 24 (1989).

[14] *Ibid.*

[15] The actual statistics were 49.2 percent in 1970–1971 and 38.7 percent in 1980–1981. If the trend has continued, the percent could have been closer to 35 percent in 1989, but 40 percent is granting the benefit of the doubt.

Such massive bureaucracies divert scarce resources from real educational activities, deprive principals and teachers of any opportunity for authority and independence, and create an impenetrable bulwark against citizen efforts to change the school system.

Graham (1963, p. 57) claims that, "Modern education's chief contribution to preparing children for life in a democratic society is its emphasis upon cooperation in solving problems" (Graham 1963, p. 57), but when a system spends more than twice as much on bureaucrats than on the actual teachers, there cannot be much cooperation going on, and the problem that is not being solved is the unconscionable waste of taxpayer resources.

The solution to this massive waste of resources being thrown at goals which do not materialize, is the market. The public education system wastes resources because, like all socialistic endeavors, it cannot rationally calculate in the absence of prices and private property rights (Mises 1981; Hoppe 1989). Under a market system, businesses receive signals from consumers in the form of their choice to buy or not to buy. Public education, on the other hand, gets partial signals from consumers (as voters) electing some officials every few years. Furthermore the signals are muddled by the fact that voters elect officials based upon a plethora of issues other than education. On the other hand, consumers of a private service send a scintillatingly clear, immediate signal when they choose whether or not to enroll their children.

The clear, immediate signals which a market system provides are necessary for educational (or any other) firms to be motivated toward increased productivity. In a private system, teachers, principals and administrators are accountable to the consumers. Boaz (1991, p. 28) writes, "[in the public school system] no principal or teacher will get a raise for attracting more students to his or her school." Just as critical, principals and teachers are rarely fired or reprimanded for not providing education excellence in a public system. Lieberman (1989, p. 62) notes such in California:

> If a district wants to suspend a teacher for as little as one day, the procedure that must be followed is the same as for firing a tenured

teacher. The district and the employee each appoint someone to a three-member commission to conduct a hearing on the suspension. (The other member is a state-appointed hearing examiner.) If the school district loses, it must pay any compensation lost by the employee and the employee's hearing expenses as well. Not surprisingly, only about one teacher in 10,000 is suspended annually in California.

Civil servants lack both positive and negative incentives to educate children in a manner satisfactory to the parents who foot the bill (i.e., pay the taxes).

There is no automatic feedback mechanism encouraging government hirelings to design productive, cost-effective schooling which fits the distinct tastes of their "customers." For example, perhaps poor families would forgo the cost of hiring teachers for basic physical education and art classes which often consist of no more than the activities children pursue outside of school on their own time. Under the public system, however, administrators have no incentive to challenge predominant school structure. If they do, there is no immediate effect on the tax structure, so parents would only see their children as losing services with no decrease in the price of education; also there would be no increase in salary for the inventive administrator. Supporters of the public school system, once having abandoned market forces as schools' drive toward productivity, can only point at a district, state or federal bureaucracy to take their place.

There is only one way to restore the proper incentives toward a quality educational system. It is to take control away from the state. As Mises (1952, p. 45) observes, it is a question of either letting "individuals choose how they want to cooperate in the social division of labor and . . . what the enterprise should produce," or letting "the government alone choose and enforce its ruling by the apparatus of coercion and compulsion."

3. The final argument put forth in favor of government-provided primary education is that primary education is a public good. A public good is one that is nonexcludable and/or a collective-consumption good

(Holcombe 1997). Nonexcludability means that there are prohibitive costs to keeping people from consuming the good once it has already been produced. A collective-consumption good is one that, once it is produced for an individual, additional individuals can consume the good at no additional cost. Primary education, according to the public good argument, is nonexcludable. Externalities are associated with primary education, which cause benefits to be realized by individuals who are not the primary (i.e., paying) consumer of education.[16] Peterson (1991, pp. 345–46) writes:

> At the family level, the education of the parents should benefit the children. . . . Children of [educated] parents are more likely to attend college. . . . There is also a tendency for at least part of the knowledge gained by parents during their school years to be transmitted to their children. . . . At the community level, the education of individuals makes the community a better place to live for all. For example, one's chances of getting mugged are greater in neighborhoods where people are poorly educated and have low incomes than in places where the majority is highly educated and affluent. . . . An increase in the educational level of people also reduces the amount of fear and suspicion that people have of one another . . . it helps us become more tolerant of persons who are different than ourselves.

Because schooling is nonexcludable, it will be provided at a sub-optimal level. Individuals who benefit from the primary consumer of education free ride on the provider's (e.g., the school's) service. Since these free riders are not paying for the tutelage, educational providers are not receiving payment from the full scope of schooling demand. Ergo, educational providers will provide too little schooling. The solution,

---

[16] One should note that, if such nonexcludability is grounds for government provision, then the functions of government must be numerous indeed! For example, bakeries must be a proper function of government. There is almost no one who has not walked by a bakery and received pleasure, without paying, from the smell of freshly-baked bread. The costs to bakers of prohibiting passers-by from smelling the bread is almost surely prohibitive. Therefore, fresh bread is most certainly produced at a sub-optimal level.

according to the public good argument, is that free riders must be made to pay for primary education (i.e., citizens must be taxed for it) so that it is optimally provided for.

There are many problems with this public good argument. The most glaring problem that should be noted immediately is that, assuming that education indeed cannot be provided optimally by private means, what in the world would move someone to believe that government can better determine the optimal amount? Buchanan (1975a) correctly notes that many economists, as soon as they believe that they have diagnosed a public good, fail to consider critically the role which government can play: "It was as if the alternatives for public choice were assumed to be available independently from some external source; there was no problem concerning the behavior of [government] suppliers and producers." Furthermore, Tideman and Tullock (1976), who labored to design a process for social choice, admit that, "the process will not cure cancer, stop the tides, or, indeed, deal successfully with many other problems." Keeping that in mind, let us also ponder how many times the political process successfully translates economic theory into policy reality. In the political world of campaigns, interest groups and compromise, the answer is: very seldom if ever. Therefore, we cannot assume that government has the ability to determine efficient allocations.

Another problem with the public good argument—one which is not entirely independent from the above problem—is that it is doubtful that the only motive of the state in operating schools is one of concern for optimal provision. Above it has been demonstrated that public schools were founded as a means to attack the culture of certain immigrant groups. Also, as Holcombe (1997) observes:

> The government has the incentive to create the impression among its citizens that its actions are legitimate. . . . [It can do so by] creating propaganda that brainwashes citizens to respect government institutions and processes.

Government desires to educate because it can foster an obedient and loyal citizenry.

One has no trouble understanding why dictatorships demand government control over mass media, or why freedom of the press is viewed as a fundamental check on government's power. . . . Governments can still control the flow of ideas without controlling the mass media if they control the education system. (Holcombe 1997)

The public good argument for public schools lacks any strength when examined. It assumes that government can provide optimal levels of a service without any justification for such an assumption. Also, the argument assumes that the state is motivated solely by creating an optimal provision. However, government has ulterior motives which work against any presumed motive toward optimality.

Thus all the arguments in favor of a public provision of primary education prove to be unfounded and/or incorrect. The failure of the state to provide a high quality service to all (its explicit goal) has rendered public primary education illegitimate; and the immeasurable waste of resources and rejection of consumer desires has left public education borderline immoral. As well, if an educated citizenry is to be considered necessary for the operation of the republican government, then it is an inexcusable conflict of interest when elected officials are the ones in charge of providing that education. Furthermore, the argument of externalities and nonexcludability fails to buttress the case for socialist education. The only ethical, reasonable system for the provision of primary education is the free market.

5 Labor Relations, Unions and Collective Bargaining: A Political Economic Analysis

It is not difficult to document the fact that many segments of our society extol the virtues of unionism, as commonly practiced. Some people defend unions as a means of promoting employment. Others feel that "social justice" is a sufficient warrant for this curious institution. So deeply embedded in our folkways is the concept that unions are legitimate institutions that many mainline religious organizations have even gone so far as to invite them to organize their own church employees—on what they see as moral grounds. The simple fact is that in the minds of most pundits, unions have a legitimate role to play in our society. How else can we account for the fact that gangs of organized laborers who have engaged in violent strikes not only still remain at large, but are widely applauded for their courage and convictions? Were any other group of people to have interfered with the lives and property of others in a similar manner, they would have been summarily clapped into jail, and been considered proper objects of fear, loathing, ridicule and pity, the reaction elicited in most people by activities criminal.

Reprinted with kind permission of the Council for Social and Economic Studies from *Journal of Social, Political and Economic Studies* 16, no. 4 (1991): 477–507.

Complexity

Contrary to the popular notion, however, unionism is a complex phenomenon, which admits of a voluntary and a coercive aspect. The philosophy of free enterprise is fully consistent with voluntary unionism, but is diametrically opposed to coercive unionism. What do all varieties of unionism, both coercive and voluntary, have in common? Unions are associations of employees, organized with the purpose of bargaining with their employer in order to increase their wages.[1]

What, then, is the distinction between invasive and noninvasive unions? The latter obey the libertarian axiom of nonaggression against nonaggressors; the former do not. Legitimate unions, in other words, limit themselves to means of raising wages which do not violate the rights of others; illegitimate unions do not so inhibit themselves.

Some pundits have declared their "full support for the principle of free and voluntary association in labor unions." If this constitutes moral approval of voluntary unions, and condemnation of the coercive type, well and good. But if it is intended to apply to extant labor organizations, this statement is disingenuous. It is not even a rough approximation of how organized labor has operated—and still continues to operate—in the modern world.

Coercion

Let us be absolutely clear on this distinction, for it is at the root of any accurate assessment of unionism. There are those labor organizations which do all they can to raise their members' wages and working conditions—except violate the (negative) rights of other people by initiating violence against them. These can be properly called "voluntary unions."

---

[1] Since money wages are funds which the employees take home, and working conditions embody funds which are spent, at least in part, in behalf of the employees while on the job, there are really two desiderata here. One, the total of money wages and working conditions, and two, the allocation between them. On the free market, the employer has a great incentive to allocate these two sorts of wage expenditures in accordance with the desires of his employees. If, for example, the workers in his plant prefer most of their wages in the form of take-home pay, and very little in the form of expenditure for amenities on the job site, the employer who ignores this desire (or, equivalently, fails to ferret out this information) will suffer higher quit rates—or else he will have to increase his total wage package, in order to compete with other employers who are better able to discern employee tastes in this matter.

But then there are those which do all they can to promote their members' welfare both by legitimate nonrights-violative behavior as well as by the use of physical brutality aimed at nonaggressing individuals.

With regard to the activity of "coercive unions" defined in this manner, Ludwig von Mises has stated:

> Labor unions have actually acquired the privilege of violent action. The governments have abandoned in their favor the essential attribute of government, the exclusive power and right to resort to violent coercion and compulsion. Of course, the laws which make it a criminal offense for any citizen to resort—except in case of self-defense—to violent action have not been formally repealed or amended.
>
> However, actual labor union violence is tolerated within broad limits. The labor unions are practically free to prevent by force anybody from defying their orders concerning wage rates and other labor conditions. They are free to inflict with impunity bodily evils upon strikebreakers and upon entrepreneurs who employ strikebreakers. They are free to destroy property of such employers and even to injure customers patronizing their shops. The authorities, with the approval of public opinion, condone such acts. . . . In excessive cases, if the deeds of violence go too far, some lame and timid attempts at repression and prevention are ventured.
>
> But as a rule they fail. . . . What is euphemistically called collective bargaining by union leaders and "pro-labor" legislation is of a quite different character. It is bargaining at the point of a gun. It is bargaining between an armed party, ready to use its weapons, and an unarmed party under duress. It is not a market transaction. It is a dictate forced upon the employer. . . . It produces institutional unemployment.
>
> The treatment of the problems involved by public opinion and the vast number of pseudo-economic writings is utterly misleading. The issue is not the right to form associations. It is whether or not any association of private citizens should be granted the privilege of resorting with impunity to violent action.

Neither is it correct to look upon the matter from the point of view of a "right to strike." The problem is not the right to strike, but the right—by intimidation or violence—to force other people to strike, and the further right to prevent anybody from working in a shop in which a union has called a strike. (Mises 1966, pp. 777–79.)

And in the view of Friedrich Hayek:

It cannot be stressed enough that the coercion which unions have been permitted to exercise contrary to all principles of freedom under the law is primarily the coercion of fellow workers. Whatever true coercive power unions may be able to wield over employers is a consequence of this primary power of coercing other workers; the coercion of employers would lose most of its objectionable character if unions were deprived of this power to exact unwilling support. Neither the right of voluntary agreement between workers nor even their right to withhold their services in concert is in question. (F. A. von Hayek 1960, p. 269)[2]

Given that there are legitimate and illegitimate forms of labor organization, it follows that sound public policy consists of defending the former and eliminating the latter. In legal terminology, this reduces to a call for the repeal of legislation that promotes invasive action, and for an expansion of the legal protections for noninvasive ones. In the just society, a union may do anything that individual citizens have a right to do, and must refrain from all activities prohibited to other citizens. The labor code, in other words, ought be nothing more than the ordinary rule of law (Hayek 1973; Leoni 1961, pp. 59–76), applied to management-labor relations.

This leads us to the $64,000 question. Which arrows in the quiver of organized labor are invasive, and which are not? Let us start off by

---

[2] Says Reynolds (1984, p. 50): "Hitting a person over the head with a baseball bat is much less likely to be treated as criminal if the person wielding the bat is an organized (i.e., unionized) worker in a labor dispute." See also Hutt (1989).

mentioning several legitimate techniques utilized by organized labor, and then look at the panoply of illegitimate actions engaged in by unions.

Legitimate Unionism

Mass walkout

First is the mass walkout: threatening, or organizing, a mass walkout, unless wage demands are met.[3] This is not an infringement of anyone's rights, since the employer, in the absence of a contract, cannot compel people to work for him at wages they deem too low. Nor is it any valid objection to this procedure that the workers are acting in concert, or in unison, or in collusion, or in "conspiracy." Of course they are. But if it is proper for one worker to quit his job, then all workers, together,[4] have every right to do so, *en masse.*[5] All conspiracy laws ought to be repealed, provided only that the agreement is to do something that would be legal when undertaken by a single individual.

There are numerous conservatives, as opposed to libertarians, who take the view that anti-trust and anti-combines law ought to be applied to unions.[6] Thus, even what we have been describing as voluntary unions would be for them illegitimate, because they claim that "collusive actions" on the part of unions "'exploit' the community as a whole,"[7] in their

---

[3] This is on the assumption that there is no valid employment contract in effect at this time which prohibits such an act.

[4] This follows directly from a defense of voluntary socialism, *vis-à-vis* coercive voluntary unionism is merely one facet of the former. For an elaboration of this point, see Block (1990c).

[5] This is not a violation of the law of composition, or an instance of this fallacy. The only serious challenge to the textual statement is the case where harms can be additive. For example, the scenario where if one person touches another, slightly, it is not a rights violation, because no harm is done, whereas if a million persons do so, the victim can indeed be harmed, and thus here is a rights violation. The difficulty with this line of argument, though, is that even the first slight touching, done by only one person, is an illicit act, even though the harm is slight, or even nonexistent, provided only that the victims person has been interfered with.

[6] In contrast, libertarians take the view that anti-trust and anti-combines legislation ought not be applied to anyone, neither unions nor business firms. See Armentano (1972, 1982).

[7] Hutt (1973, p. 3; 1989); Schmidt (1973); Simons (1948). In sharp distinction, for a libertarian analysis which defends the right of organized labor to threaten or to quit in unison, see Petro (1957); Reynolds (1984).

violation of consumers' sovereignty.[8] But this only shows that there is all the world of difference between economists who support the system of *laissez faire* capitalism, on the one hand, and those who favor a system of national or state capitalism on the other.

Back to work legislation

Again, libertarians would disagree with many "right-wing" conservatives on the question as to whether it is improper for governments to enact legislation forcing unions back to work where a union strike threatens to disrupt broad segments of the economy and to harm innocent parties not involved in the dispute. The libertarian viewpoint holds that the government does not have such a right, and that this follows from the basic libertarian premise of self-ownership. In the words of Murray Rothbard (1978, pp. 83–84):

> On October 4, 1971, President Nixon invoked the Taft-Hartley Act to obtain a court injunction forcing the suspension of a dock strike for eighty days; . . . It is no doubt convenient for a long-suffering public to be spared the disruptions of a strike. Yet the "solution" imposed was forced labor, pure and simple: the workers were coerced, against their will, into going back to work. There is no moral excuse, in a society claiming to be opposed to slavery, and in a country which has outlawed involuntary servitude, for any legal or judicial action prohibiting strikes—or jailing union leaders who fail to comply.

Conventional conservatives tend to place the national good above the good of individuals, so there is a basic disagreement between right-wing conservatives and libertarians on this issue.

Boycott

Another activity held to be legitimate by libertarians is the boycott, whether primary or secondary. A boycott is simply the refusal of one

---

[8] For a critique of Hutt, see Rothbard (1970, pp. 561–66).

person to deal with another.[9] All interaction in a free society must be on a mutual basis, but there is no presumption that any particular interaction must take place. It is part and parcel of the law of free association that any one person may refuse to associate with another for any reason that seems sufficient to him. Since a boycott is merely an organized refusal to deal with another, and each person has a right to so act, then people may act in this way in concert. A "hot edict," whereby a union declares the handling of certain products to be prohibited by organized labor, is a special case of the boycott.

Provided that there is no contract in force which is incompatible with such a declaration, it, too, is an entirely legitimate activity. Says Rothbard (1982, p. 131) in this regard:

> A boycott is an attempt to persuade other people to have nothing to do with some particular person or firm—either socially or in agreeing not to purchase the firm's product. Morally, a boycott may be used for absurd, reprehensible, laudatory or neutral goals. It may be used, for example, to attempt to persuade people not to buy nonunion grapes *or* not to buy union grapes. From our point of view, the important thing about the boycott is that it is purely voluntary, an act of attempted persuasion, and therefore that it is a perfectly legal and licit instrument of action . . . a boycott may well diminish a firm's customers and therefore cut into its property values; but such an act is still a perfectly legitimate exercise of free speech and property rights. Whether we wish any particular boycott well or ill depends on our moral values and on our attitudes toward the concrete goal or activity. But a boycott is legitimate per se. If we feel a given boycott to be morally reprehensible, then it is within the rights of those who feel this way to organize a counter-boycott to persuade the consumers otherwise,

---

[9] Thus, all anti-discriminatory laws are incompatible with the libertarian legal code. For an analysis which shows that such legislation is itself a rights violation, and that the free marketplace is the best protector of liberties, see Friedman (1985), Sowell (1983), Williams (1982b). It is logically inconsistent to maintain that people do not have the right to discriminate against one another, and that they do have the right to boycott, since the boycott is merely an orchestrated discrimination against certain individuals or groups of people.

or to boycott the boycotters. All this is part of the process of dissemination of information and opinion within the framework of the rights of private property.

Furthermore, "secondary" boycotts are also legitimate, despite their outlawry under our current labor laws. In a secondary boycott, labor unions try to persuade consumers not to buy from firms who deal with nonunion (primary boycotted) firms. Again, in a free society, it should be their right to try such persuasion, just as it is the right of their opponents to counter with an opposing boycott.

Sorenson

An illustration of this principle took place in Canada. Alderman Bill Sorenson of North Vancouver City had voted to contract out the municipal garbage collection services to private enterprise. And, to add insult to injury—at least in the eyes of Local 389 of the Canadian Union of Public Employees (CUPE)—he also voted for a wage freeze covering all city employees.

The union didn't take long to strike back.

As it happens, Sorenson was the operations manager for the North Shore Community Credit Union, a local banking facility. As it also happens, Local 389 of CUPE holds deposits with this credit union. In response to Alderman Sorenson's votes on the city council, the Union withdrew $25,000 of its funds from the bank which employed Sorenson.

Now this decision to withdraw funds was no mere coincidence. It was motivated by spite—an attempt to get back at a part-time politician by attacking him in his capacity as a private citizen.

As a result of this act, Mr. Sorenson resigned his seat on the city council—it isn't clear whether he was forced to do this to keep his job.

According to pundits, this sorry spectacle was a threat to democracy. Said one editorialist, "It was a mean, cheap tactic on the part of a trade union, and no credit to the labor movement as a whole."

Mean? Yes. Cheap? Yes. Petty? Again, yes. But let's put things into perspective. The union, and all other depositors for that matter, have every right in the world to withdraw funds at any time they wish, for whatever reason seems sufficient to them. That, after all, is the meaning of a demand deposit. Such an arrangement is the embodiment of a contract between two mutually consenting parties, the depositor and the lending institution. In choosing to withdraw $25,000, even for this spiteful reason, CUPE Local 389 was thus completely within its moral and legal rights. The $25,000 is owned by the union. It and it alone has the sole right to determine its place of investment. Neither Mr. Sorenson nor the credit union for which he works has any right to determine where, how or whether this money shall be invested. Certainly their rights have not been abridged by the decision of the proper owners[10] to withdraw the money from the care of the bank.

Not only has the union every right to withdraw its funds for this reason, but other groups in society act in the same way—without the wailing and gnashing of teeth visited upon CUPE.

Does anyone really doubt that corporations deposit and withdraw their funds in accordance with what they perceive as their own best interests? Certainly, church groups and others have publicly withdrawn holdings from banks which have invested in South Africa, or which support firms which are not "ecologically sound." And do not consumers continually pick and choose amongst the stores they will patronize, partially on the basis of boycotting merchants who displease them, sometimes on the most subjective of grounds? Why should unions be singled out for opprobrium for stewardship of their own money?

Then there is the difficulty of legally prohibiting such behavior. How could government stop this practice without dictating how to spend and invest private property? Any attempt to stop such practices would surely involve us in the scenario warned against so eloquently by George Orwell, in his book *Nineteen Eighty-Four*.

Contrary to the political commentators, this act of boycott was a moderate response by the union, certainly when compared to the acts which are customary to organized labor. Canadian unions, and also

---

[10] We are assuming for the moment, in effect, that CUPE is a legitimate or noncoercive union organization. Unfortunately, this is not at all the case. Their illegitimacy stems, however, not from their decision to boycott Sorenson's bank; it is a result of their failure to renounce initiatory violence as a means of conducting business.

those in the U.S., as a matter of institutional arrangement are commonly allowed to invoke the coercive power of government in order to pursue their own commercial goals. This is their defining characteristic, for organized labor is one of the few institutions in our society permitted to use the threat of fines and/or jail sentences to prohibit competition.

This is a reference, of course, to the manner in which nonunion workers who compete with unions for jobs are treated. They are branded as scabs and pariahs. Canadian law forces the employer to "bargain fairly" with the union, and thus prohibits him from dealing with those who would compete for the jobs of organized workers. Even though mutually agreeable contracts could be made between employers and "scabs" for the jobs and pay scales rejected by striking workers, labor legislation forbids such an occurrence.

So there we have it. On the one hand, a union boycott which violates no rights, but which is roundly condemned by commentators. On the other hand, the union practice of restricting entry to employment which is a patent violation of the rights of every nonunion would-be competitor for these jobs. And yet this immoral practice is condemned by practically no one, and even enjoys the prestige and protection of modern law.

A greater travesty of justice can scarcely be imagined.

Illegitimate Unionism

Picketing

Now let us consider several illegitimate union activities. These are acts which coercive unions engage in, but which noncoercive unions totally eschew. Picketing, for example, is morally illicit, and therefore should be outlawed, because it is equivalent to a threat or an initiation of physical force.[11] This activity must be clearly distinguished from a boycott. In picketing, the object is to coerce and often physically prevent people who would like to deal with the struck employer (suppliers, customers,

---

[11] In the typical legal analysis of this subject, only secondary picketing (which is not directly aimed at the employer, but rather at third parties, in order to in this way more effectively impact the employer) is even discussed. Implicit in this analysis is the understanding that primary picketing is a legitimate activity. See, for example, Gall (1984).

competing laborers—"scabs," or strikebreakers) from so doing. In a boycott, in contrast, the aim is to mobilize those who already agree with the strike to refrain from making the relevant purchases. True, one may try to convince neutral parties, but in a boycott the means of doing so are strictly limited to noninvasive techniques. Once physical encroachments are resorted to, a boycott becomes converted into picketing.

There are those who characterize picketing as merely "informational." In order to see the problematic nature of such a claim, try to imagine what our response would be were McDonald's to send its agents, hundreds of them, carrying big sticks with signs attached to them (picket signs), to surround the premises of Burger King, or Wendy's, in order to give "information" to their customers or suppliers. In like manner, we do not allow Hertz to picket Avis, or General Motors to picket Ford. There is absolutely no doubt that such activities would be interpreted, and properly so, as an attempt to intimidate. If these firms wish to convey information, they have other avenues open to them: advertising, direct mail, contests, giveaways, bargains, etc. And the same applies to a union. If it wishes to communicate, it must restrict itself to these activities. Nevertheless, it is continually asserted that the pickets are only at a job site in order to impart the information that a strike is in progress; however, it is "conceded" that the picketers become enraged if they see anyone engaging in commercial endeavors with the struck employer. The attempt, here, is to claim that these "interferences" (people going about their ordinary business, attempting to ignore the strike) are responsible for the violence which is endemic on a picket line. But one cannot have it both ways. Either there is only knowledge being given out, or there is not. If there is, then how do we account for the typicality with which violence arises on the picket line? Are its members particularly "sensitive?" But this is all beside the point. Even if violence was never associated with picket lines, this would only prove they were so successful in their intimidation that none was necessary. The libertarian nonaggression axiom precludes both the actual initiation of violence as well as the threat thereof; thus, even picketing which is (so far) nonviolent is a threat to all would-be crossers of the picket line.

A more accurate interpretation of picketing (whether primary or secondary) is as a nuisance or harassment. This is precisely how it would be regarded were it to take place in any other commercial or personal arena.

Suppose, that is, that a person vacates the premises of landlord A, and patronizes landlord B instead. Surely the courts would cast a baleful eye on A, if he, together with his family, cronies, and business associates, began to picket the tenant for being "unfair." Or take another case. Suppose that a man divorces his spouse, and then along with all his friends "pickets" the home of his ex-wife, warning off possible suitors. Would this be considered an informational exercise in free-speech rights? Hardly. On the contrary, it would be clearly seen for the harassment it is, and be summarily prohibited by any court in the land.

Can we afford any less rigorous a definition of justice in labor-management relations?

There is one complication, however. It concerns the legal status of the area on which the picketing occurs. If the picket line operates on private property, the analysis from the libertarian perspective is clear and straightforward: this activity may properly occur only with the permission of the owner. Otherwise, as we have seen, it must be interpreted as oppressive. Unfortunately, in a series of cases concerning the right of picketing and leafletting, the courts have undermined the private property status of streets and thoroughfares in shopping malls, by a finding that these areas are "public places." But they were privately built, are privately operated and maintained, and therefore ought to be considered as part of the private sector—their use to be determined by their owners.

It is far more difficult to determine the proper use of public streets and sidewalks. For the libertarian theorist, these areas are a conundrum. Given that it is morally improper and economically inefficient for the government to have nationalized them in the first place (Block 1979), it is difficult to determine whether or not picketing should be allowed on the public sidewalk, for example, right in front of the employer's premises. The determination of whether to allow any public assembly (e.g., a parade) to disrupt the normal traffic patterns on government streets is essentially an arbitrary one. It depends upon public pull, not on philosophically determined rights. Perhaps the best course of action in this moral vacuum is to treat the picketers as if they were merely offering information, as they so vociferously claim. In this case, the best analogy is the man who walks up and down the street with sandwich board placards advertising for a local merchant. Would the court allow one or even two such moving billboards? Certainly, provided that they kept some distance between themselves, and did not interfere with passersby. Would the court allow dozens of tightly packed sandwich board carriers who impeded the normal traffic flow? Certainly not. We conclude from these considerations that striking unionists who use "public property" should be treated exactly like any other group of people attempting to advertise information. If the courts would allow one or two sandwich boarders the use of the public sidewalk, they should extend the same right to informational union picketers. And where they would deny this right to dozens or hundreds of sandwich boarders, they must act in the same way with regard to organized labor.

Scabs

Who are the innocent persons against whom coercive union violence is commonly directed? These are the people at the bottom of the employment ladder; the least, last, and lost of us, the individuals after whose welfare we should take particular concern if we have any regard for the poor. They are, in a word, "scabs."

Now scabs have had a very bad press. Even the appellation ascribed to them is one of derogation. But when all the loose and inaccurate verbiage is stripped away, the scab is no more than a poor person, oft-times unskilled, uneducated, under- or unemployed, perhaps a member of a minority group, who seeks nothing more than to compete in the labor market, and there to offer his services to the highest bidder.

In fact, it is no exaggeration to consider the scab the economic equivalent of the leper. And we all know the treatment with regard to lepers urged upon us by moral and ecclesiastical authorities.

In their pro- (coercive) union stance, defenders of organized labor expose themselves as untrue to the morally axiomatic principle of the preferential option of the poor, which was adumbrated by both the U.S. and Canadian Conferences of Catholic Bishops.[12] The "poor," in this case, are not the princes of labor, organized into gigantic, powerful and coercive unions. Rather, they are the despised, downtrodden and denigrated scabs.[13]

Violence

A strange adventure recently befell Patrick McDermott, the twenty-seven-year-old son of Canadian Labor Congress president Dennis McDermott. Young Patrick was innocently riding a bus in suburban North York, in Ontario, when he witnessed a beating in the street. Dianne McIntyre, aged forty-two, was being assaulted by a man—whereupon our hero jumped off the bus, came to the rescue of the damsel in distress, and for his pains was wrestled to the ground by four other men, colleagues of the hoodlum battering Mrs. McIntyre, and was kicked and punched while he was down.

"No big deal" you say? "Happens every day?" Well, yes, unfortunately; street violence seems to be part and parcel of modern day life, not only in the U.S., but increasingly in Canada as well. But this case was exceptional. The victimized woman was crossing a picket line at the main Visa credit card center for the Imperial Bank of Commerce, and the five bully boys were bank workers, engaged in a labor strike against this financial institution. What a position to be in for Patrick McDermott, a staunch union supporter in his own right, and son of the outgoing president of the C.L.C.!

Mr. McDermott the younger tried to remain loyal to his principles. That is, to both of them: chivalry and defense of innocent persons against assault and battery on the one hand, and unionism on the other. Although suffering from an arm injury, bruised ribs and a split lip in his confrontation with the minions of organized labor, he stated that he still believes "in the strike and the cause, but when it comes to goons hitting

---

[12] For a critique of these documents, see Block (1983, 1986).

[13] Nothing said here mitigates against the legitimacy of voluntary unions, those which restrict themselves to mass walkouts and other noninvasive activity. The only difficulty is that at present, such entities are nonexistent, at least in North America, to the best of the present author's knowledge.

defenseless women, it's got to stop. That guy should be thrown out of the union."

This, however, is too facile, by half. Unionism as practiced in the Western democracies is intrinsically a violent, confrontational and physically aggressive institution. Young Mr. McDermott cannot have it both ways. He must either renounce the "cause," or give up on his principle that goons should not be able to beat up innocent persons.

Why is this? How can it be that a widely respected institution, organized labor, necessarily initiates violence against nonaggressing people?

The reason is straightforward. Actual union practice, and the labor codes of the land which underlay it, are predicated on the assumption that competition, no matter how well it works elsewhere in the economy, is simply inappropriate for the labor market. And not only inappropriate, but deserving of legal penalties as well. Labor enactments commonly mandate that the employer "bargain fairly" with a union, when what he may want to do most of all is ignore his striking employees entirely, and hire competing workers (i.e., "scabs") in their place. Some Canadian provinces (e.g., Quebec) prevent management from hiring temporary replacements for the duration of the labor dispute; others allow this, but insist that the firm not deal more favorably with these laborers than with its unionized work force. If the employer declines to be bound by these restrictions, he is liable to fines or even jail sentences—which is certainly equivalent to visiting violence against a person, the employer, for doing no more than encouraging competition in the labor market. It is perhaps for this reason that the police and courts turn a blind eye—or even a sympathetic one—to situations where union violence is directed against the employer, or, in the case of Mrs. McIntyre, against those who support scab workers by crossing picket lines. "If the government will physically prohibit labor market competition anyway, why penalize organized labor for doing the same thing?" seems to be the prevailing opinion.

A moment's reflection will convince us that this practice—union violence *or* government violence practiced against employers and/or scabs—is completely unjustified. The nonemployed competing workers (scabs) have every bit as much right as the striking unionists to compete for jobs offered by the employer. Any other conclusion would set up two classes of people—unionists and scabs—with different types of rights. But all people have the same human rights to compete for employment, without being victimized by physical violence, whether from unionists *or* policemen.

As for the assault and battery perpetrated on Patrick McDermott and Dianne McIntyre, a union spokesman termed the incident "minor," and said there were no plans for disciplinary action against the pickets who injured them! And, of course, the police did nothing to quell this violence in our streets, even though they and all citizens would have been outraged had this situation occurred in any context other than that of a labor strike.

Breakdown of Law and Order

One way to understand this phenomenon of the widespread acceptability of union violence is to focus on the role of the police. They are, after all, supposedly society's fail-safe mechanism against violence. The problem, however, is that this institution, too, has been beset by the virus of accepting unions as legitimate.[14]

According to Mr. Bob Stewart, chief of police of Vancouver, one of Canada's largest cities, the use of violence by his constables is inappropriate in a labor dispute. Happily, this man is not a complete pacifist; this view only applies, it would appear, with regard to union unrest. Addressing a meeting of the Atlantic Police Chiefs, he stated "the role of the police officer is to maintain peace and order and not be seen as partisan."[15] The reason for this low profile, it was contended, is that a labor dispute is really a contract dispute between two parties, and not a dispute with police. It is easy to understand the motivation behind this stance. Canada sees itself as a very stable, polite and civil society, and union-management confrontations are potential tinder boxes. The

---

[14] For a moral and religious defense of unionism, see Novak (1984), U.S. Bishops (1984); for a critique, see Block (1986).
[15] *Vancouver Sun*, July 8, 1987.

last thing desired is to fan the flames of violence that have so unfortunately erupted in other corners of the globe.

Nevertheless, there are grave flaws in such a view. Were it to have come from someone else, who did not occupy such an exalted place in the country's law enforcement hierarchy, it could be easily dismissed. But when it is stated by a high-ranking police official, it has great capacity to do harm. First of all, there is the danger that strikes will become more violent, not less. If the police announce beforehand that they will not energetically quell labor violence, this may encourage hotheads to give vent to their more base instincts. Second, it is the very rare case indeed when a person picks a fight directly with a policeman (except, perhaps, when the officer of the law is disguised). Typically, the services of the police officer are called upon when there is a dispute between two parties, neither of whom is engaged in a direct altercation with the police. But when two men are fighting in a public street, or when one is assaulting and battering another, we expect the policeman to intervene, with force if necessary, even if the dispute does not directly concern him. After all, we the citizens supposedly pay taxes for police protection, and we expect these services when we are attacked, not only when they are. Third, this philosophical position is woefully ignorant of what actually takes place during a strike. Superficially, it is a confrontation between employer and union, who are, or in some cases once were, parties to a labor contract. But it is only in the race instance that the unionized workers attack their employer's plant, or their employer; after all, they work there, and when the dispute is solved, they typically prefer to have a plant in which to return back to work. On the contrary, a strike is almost always a dispute between parties who are unrelated by contract. That is, between organized labor and replacement workers, or strikebreakers. The union brands these individuals as "scabs," and then initiates violence against people who are guilty only of daring to bid for the jobs currently claimed by the unionists.

Further, it is not really important whether or not the two disputants are contractually linked. Even if they are, it is still the sworn duty of the police to stop—by force if necessary—either side from initiating violence against the other.

That a Canadian police chief purposefully wishes to take a "low profile" under such circumstances only indicates he does not really understand the purpose or significance of his job.

Job Ownership

Another defense of picketing and attendant violence concedes that this is a physically aggressive activity, but asserts that it is not an initiation of coercion, but rather a defense of private property rights, namely the jobs of the striking unionists. There is a certain superficial plausibility in this rejoinder. However, the "scab" is not stealing the job of the striking coercive unionist. A job, by its very nature, cannot be owned by any one person.

Rather, it is the embodiment of an agreement between two consenting parties. In the case of the strike, organized labor is unsatisfied with the offer of the employer. It is publicly renouncing this offer. It therefore cannot be said that these workers still "have" these jobs.[16] Under *laissez faire*, all people are allowed to compete for jobs in a free labor market. It is a vestige of the guild system to think that there are two groups of people with regard to employment at any given plant: the coercive unionists, who own the jobs, or have a right to them, and all other people, who must refrain from bidding for them.

To some extent we are fooled by the very language we use in order to describe this situation. We speak of "my" job, or "your" job, or "his" job, or "her" job; this use of the possessive pronoun does seem to indicate real possession, or ownership.

We also speak of "my" tailor, or "my" employee, or "my" customer, and yet it would be nothing short of grotesque to assign ownership rights to any of these relationships. All of them are based on mutuality, not ownership on the part of either person. This use of the term "my" does not imply ownership. If it did I could forbid "my" employee from quitting his job. If it were "my" customer, I could prevent him from taking

---

[16] We must assume that there is no longer a valid employment contract in force between the employer and employees. If there is, then the workers do indeed "own" these jobs, but only because of the contract (assuming that it was initially agreed upon without duress), not because of any superior status they may claim as members of the union caste.

his business elsewhere, to a competitor. And if it were "my" tailor, it would be a violation of my rights if he moved to another city, retired, or entered a new occupation.

A job is an embodiment of an agreement between two consenting parties—employee and employer. It cannot be the possession of only one of them. A worker no more owns "his" job than does a husband own "his" wife. A striking union which forcibly prevents the employer from hiring a replacement is like a husband who divorces his wife—and then threatens to beat her up, and any prospective new suitor as well—if she tries to remarry. Just as one spouse may now divorce the other for any reason or for none at all, the employer should be able to fire an employee without being compelled to show "cause." Our laws do not force the worker to justify a decision to quit his job, and the employee-employer relationship should be an entirely symmetric one.

Sweat Shops

What of the claim that without picketing, coercive unions would be rendered virtually powerless, and in the absence of strong coercive labor organizations, the working people would be forced back into the "sweat shops." First of all, even if this claim were true, picketing would still be unjustified, and a violation of the basic libertarian premise against the initiation of violence. Second, even if coercive unions were all that stood between the sweat shop and present living conditions for their members, it still does not follow that the lot of working people would be improved by picketing. For this activity is aimed not so much at the employer as at the competing worker, the strikebreaker. The major aim of the picket line, as we have seen, is to prevent alternative workers from attaining access to the job site. Indeed, the very terminology employed by coercive unionists to describe him, "scab," is indicative of the extreme denigration in which he is held. But these people are working people too. Further, as we have noted, they are almost always poorer[17] than the striking coercive unionists. This is seen by the fact that the "scabs" are usually

---

[17] The Canadian and U.S. bishops are on record as supporting the "preferential option for the poor." Yet, inconsistently, they support coercive unionism as against the "scabs," who are their major victims. However, the scab may be considered as the economic equivalent of the

more than happy to take the offer spurned by the strikers. So if there is anyone who needs to be protected from the specter of the "sweat shop," it is not the coercive unionist, but the scab. Third, it is profoundly mistaken to believe that the modern level of wages depends upon coercive union activity. As any introductory economic textbook makes clear,[18] wages depend, to the contrary, on the productivity of labor. If wages are bid above productivity levels, bankruptcy and consequent unemployment will tend to result.[19] If wages somehow find themselves below the rate of marginal revenue productivity, other employers can earn profits from bidding these workers away from their present employers—by continually improving the job offer until wages and productivity levels come to be equated.

There is abundant evidence to support the view that coercive unionism cannot be credited with the explosion of wages and living standards. For one thing, the modern coercive labor movement has only been with us in this century, and only gained much of its power (in the U.S.) with the advent of special legislation in the 1930s, when its share of the labor force rose from 5 percent to 20 percent (Rothbard 1978, p. 84). And yet wages, welfare and standards of living have been on the increase for hundreds of years before that. For another, the economies of countries of Southeast Asia such as South Korea, Taiwan, Hong Kong, Singapore, have been burgeoning in the last several decades, in the virtual absence of unionism, coercive or voluntary (Novak 1986). As well, there have been sharp wage increases in industries—within countries with a strong labor movement—which are completely unorganized. Examples include banking, computers, even housecleaners.

The comparison between the U.S. and Canada is also instructive. In 1960, the (coercively) unionized sector in both countries was about 30 percent; by 1988, labor organizations represented over 40 percent of

---

leper. But the ecclesiastical and biblical authorities urge upon us the kindest of treatment with regard to lepers. Therefore, their own analysis of the scab is illogical.

[18] Even those written by authors who are far from sympathetic to the free enterprise system. See, for example, Samuelson (1970, chap. 29).

[19] This was the fate of West Virginia, which fell victim to the activities of John L. Lewis, and organized labor in the coal fields.

the Canadian work force, but less than 15 percent in the U.S. If the union-as-the-source-of-all-prosperity hypothesis were correct, we would have noted a slippage toward sweat shop labor conditions in the U.S., and an era of extreme affluence in Canada. Needless to say, that has not at all been the case.[20]

Homework

A man's home may be his castle, but not as far as working there is concerned—at least according to legislation which restricts commercial activity in one's own domicile. Originally, such laws were placed on the books in order to support legislation concerning child labor and compulsory minimum wages. As well, the unions protested vociferously that homeworkers would be very difficult to organize, and the result would be a return to sweatshop conditions.

In the modern era, however, the people who wish to work at home are more likely to be reasonably well off women who wish to earn a bit of extra pin money. For example, there was a "kerfluffle" over several hundred women in the New England states who were knitting snow mittens and ski caps, and who justified this practice on the grounds of "freedom of enterprise." And, as if to show that politics does make strange bedfellows, they also defended themselves on the basis of womens' liberation. Being able to work at home was the only way that many of them could work at all—while continuing to watch over their children.

The debate over home knitters is really only a tempest in a teapot. At most, it involves several thousand seamstresses in an industry that has

---

[20] Grubel and Bonnici (1986, pp. 40–43). As well as the differing unionization rates, the two countries also experienced widely divergent unemployment insurance policies. In 1970, the U.S. and Canada both spent about 0.9 percent of their G.N.P. on unemployment insurance benefits: by 1983, the U.S. had maintained its previous level of 0.9 percent, but Canada's had risen to 3.4 percent, an increase of 277 percent! (pp. 44–47). These two events had a profound effect upon the unemployment rates of the two North American neighbors. Traditionally, U.S. and Canadian unemployment rates have moved together within a narrow range. In 1963, for example, they were both slightly less than 6 percent. But as the disparate unionization and unemployment policies began to take effect, the Canadian rate began to exceed that for the U.S. In the early 1980s a gap of some 4 percent opened up (p. 2).

been on the verge of being supplanted by technology for many years now. Of far greater statistical significance will be the likely move of clerical workers from office to home. This is now just beginning to be made possible by technological breakthroughs in computers and word processors, and has thus so far amounted to only a trickle. If present trends continue, however, it is possible that this small stream could turn into a tidal wave.

If this occurs, the union argument that cottage industry is synonymous with sweat shop conditions will be given even wider publicity. It is incorrect, and public policy based on its truth will, as a result, be counterproductive. We can no longer countenance the idea that unionization is all that stands between the laborer and the sweat shop. Thus, there is simply no case for interfering with the institution of homework, no matter how big it becomes.

And there is every moral reason for allowing this new form of industrial organization. People have a natural right to do whatever they please, provided only that their actions do not infringe on the rights of others to do exactly the same. Those who favor both unionism and women's liberation will have to make a choice: one or the other. As this example shows, they cannot have it both ways.

Unequal Bargaining Power

A major reason given by some commentators for their unseemly support of unionism is that employers frequently possess greater bargaining power than do employees in the negotiation of wage agreements. Such unequal power may press workers into a choice between an inadequate wage and no wage at all, it is alleged.

But this rather seriously misconstrues the process of wage determination. In a free labor market, wages are basically set by the marginal revenue productivity of the employee—not on the basis of bargaining power, scale of enterprises, or size of labor units. Were the bargaining power explanation for wage rates correct, remuneration would be negatively correlated with the concentration ratio; that is, industries with fewer employers would pay lower wages than ones with many—and pay would be unrelated to measures of productivity such as educational attainment. Needless to say, no evidence for this contention exists.

The typical reason for supposing that there is unequal bargaining power[21] is that there are more employees than employers.[22] If so, this is hardly sufficient to establish the case. Let us assume that bargaining power is defined in such a way that when there is a difference of opinion over wages, or a dispute about them, the person with the greater bargaining power is more likely to attain his goal than is the person with the lesser bargaining power.[23] But in actual point of fact, the likelihood of attaining one's goal in a bargaining situation depends almost entirely on whether the wage is above, below, or equal to equilibrium, e.g., productivity levels (Hutt 1973, chap. 5). In the first case, the employer will have more "bargaining power," as wages will tend to fall in any case; in the second case, the employee will have more "bargaining power," as the market will dictate an increase in wages. One may say, if one wishes, that in the third case "bargaining power" is equal, since wages will tend not to change. But on the basis of Occam's razor it would be more scientific to dispense with the concept of bargaining power[24] entirely, and confine our purview to basic supply and demand analysis of the labor market.

---

[21] For a particularly unsophisticated version of this view, see Weiler (1980, p. 96), who states:

> workers realized that they had no real leverage in dealing with their employer on an individual basis. True, any one employee might threaten to quit if her pay was not raised. But any sizable employer, let alone a national bank, could always get along without that single employee, whose ability and contribution is fungible and who is easily replaced if and when she makes her exit. By contrast the employee will find that she cannot make do without her employer, since she needs a job to earn a living, and jobs may not be too plentiful.

[22] Other attempted justifications of this thesis are that employers are typically more wealthy than employees, and that it is easier for the former to replace the latter than the inverse.

[23] To define bargaining power in the opposite manner (so that the person or group with greater bargaining power would tend to lose disputes over wages) would be to render the argument ludicrous.

[24] There are more customers than merchants (and more whites than blacks, more right-handed persons than southpaws, more brunettes than blondes). Does this mean that the former have more "bargaining power" than the latter whenever the two are embroiled in competition, or in a dispute over the terms of trade? Not a bit of it. Customers have more "bargaining power" than merchants when prices are presently above equilibrium, that is, when goods are in surplus, because prices tend to fall in such cases. Likewise, merchants have more "bargaining power" than consumers when prices are below equilibrium, i.e., when there is a shortage of the good in question because prices tend to rise in such cases.

The bargaining power notion is also erroneous in that it disregards the basic economic tenet that in a free market wages tend to be equated with productivity levels. If wages are higher than worker productivity, the enterprise tends to become bankrupt; if lower, the firm suffers a high quit rate, as employees are enticed away by other employers. It is only when wages and productivity are equal that there is no automatic market impetus for change (Hazlitt 1979).

Weiler sneeringly rejects this as "sophisticated economic analysis," and thus a "somewhat romantic notion," that is somehow out of step with what "has always seemed intuitively clear to workers—and to their employers." Continues Weiler (1980, pp. 26–27):

> In real life, labour markets are notoriously imperfect. There is no central clearinghouse to set an auction price for labour. Workers are poorly informed about alternative jobs and comparative compensation. Once the average employee has invested a significant part of his working career in a single job, he faces tangible and psychological barriers to moving on. Thus employers have the effective ability to quote the price they will pay for labour and to make that price stick.

On closer inspection this latter statement sounds more like the ravings of a Marxist than the sober commentary of a scholar of labor markets. Weiler goes on to assert that "typically, employers (do not) set those wage rates at exploitative levels," but this only compounds the fallacy. Why, if they have the power to do so, do supposedly profit-maximizing firms refrain from "exploiting" labor?

Nor do the other parts of this analysis withstand scrutiny. No central clearinghouse for labor is necessary for the smooth functioning of labor markets, nor is worker information required. As long as there is competition between employers, and knowledge of wages on at least one side of the market—for example, that of the employer—the market operates inexorably to equate compensation and productivity levels. And further, to the extent that long-term employees face psychological costs in job switching, they are earning psychic profits by remaining with their present employer. If they are reluctant to leave, this is because they are earning nonmonetary income over and above their actual salaries by remaining precisely where they are.[25]

Labor Legislation

It follows from our analysis of coercive unionism that much of our present labor legislation is mischievous and misguided. If voluntary association and mutual consent are the only legitimate foundations of employment; if it should be strictly forbidden for one group of workers to forcibly prevent another ("scabs") from competing for jobs; then it follows that government-made laws which are inconsistent with these principles are incompatible as well with the libertarian legal code. For example, there should be no laws which compel the employer to "bargain in good faith" with any one set of employees; he should be allowed to deal with anyone he wishes. Further, all legislation prohibiting an employer from firing striking workers, and hiring replacements on a permanent basis, should be repealed. Says Rothbard (1978, pp. 84–85):

> It is true that the strike is a peculiar form of work stoppage. The strikers do not merely quit their jobs; they also assert that somehow, in some metaphysical sense, they still "own" their jobs and are entitled to them, and intend to return to them when the issues are resolved. But the remedy for this self-contradictory policy, as well as for the disruptive power of labor unions, is not to pass laws outlawing strikes; the remedy is to remove the substantial body of law, federal, state, and local, that confers special governmental privileges on labor unions. All that is needed, both for libertarian principle and for a healthy economy, is to remove and abolish these special privileges.

---

[25] Weiler (1980, p. 27), maintains, without benefit of citation, that "empirical investigation of labour markets in the absence of collective bargaining discloses a remarkable dispersion of wage rates paid to workers with comparable skills in comparable jobs and in comparable industries and regions—all contrary to the hypothesis of competitive markets, which are supposedly marred by trade unionism." But how large is "remarkable?" Who is to determine that the skills, industries and regions are truly comparable? Ivory tower researchers? Nor can these unnamed studies take into account nonmonetary psychic on-the-job earning, attained, as Weiler himself postulates, by long tenure on the job.

These privileges have been enshrined in federal law—especially in the Wagner-Taft-Hartley Act, passed originally in 1935, and the Norris-LaGuardia Act of 1931. The former prohibits the courts from issuing injunctions in cases of imminent union violence; the latter compels employers to bargain "in good faith" with any union that wins the votes of the majority of a work unit arbitrarily defined by the federal government—and also prohibits employers from discriminating against union organizers. . . . Furthermore, local and state laws often protect unions from being sued, and they place restrictions on the employers' hiring of strikebreaking labor; and police are often instructed not to interfere in the use of violence against strikebreakers by union pickets. Take away these special privileges. . . .

It is characteristic of our statist trend that, when general indignation against unions led to the Taft-Hartley Act of 1947, the government did not repeal any of these special privileges. Instead, it added special restrictions upon unions to limit the power which the government itself had created. . . . The government's seemingly contradictory policy on unions serves, first, to aggrandize the power of government over labor relations, and second, to foster a suitably integrated and establishment-minded unionism as junior partner in government's role over the economy.

Conclusion

It is an important aspect of public policymaking to examine extant labor codes with a view to revising them. In the past, such attempts have been superficial; they have placed bubble gum, band aid, and scotch tape solutions on a corpus in need of major surgery. Our legislative representatives must go to the heart of the matter this time out, for economic justice, the rule of law and the health of the economy depend upon it. In the field of labor relations, the most important issue is the strike. Actually, this is misnomer, as it refers not to one act, but to two. A strike is, first, a withdrawal of labor in unison from an employer, on the part of the relevant organized employees. To this, there can be no objection. If a single individual has a right to withdraw labor services, or to quit a job, he does not lose it merely because others choose to exercise their rights simultaneously.

There is a second aspect of the strike, however. This element is pernicious, insidious and entirely improper: the union practice of making it impossible for the struck employer to deal with alternative sources of labor, who are anxious to compete for the jobs the strikers have just vacated.

A properly revised labor code, then, would allow strikes in the sense of mass refusals to work, or quits in unison. It would entrench this behavior, as a basic element of the rights of free men. But it would *limit* union activity to this one option. It would thus prohibit, to the full extent of the law, any and all interferences with the rights of alternative employees ("scabs") to compete for jobs held by union members. It would end, forevermore, all picketing, and other such forms of threatened or actual violence.

Although many people think that pickets are aimed at the struck employer, they are actually an attack on competing workers ("scabs"). And just as our laws should not allow business firms to picket the premises of suppliers, competitors or customers, no group of workers should be able, by picketing, to forcibly prohibit another group of workers—almost always poorer—from bidding for jobs. A proper labor code would thus define a "legitimate union" as one which strictly limited its actions to organizing mass resignations. A "legitimate union" would eschew picketing, violence, and all other special advantages—legislative or otherwise—*vis-à-vis* its nonunionized competitors. This would end, once and for all, the legal fiction that workers who have left their job can yet retain any right to employment status in those positions.

We must conclude that the key distinction in any analysis of unions is between those that engage in coercion—whether directly or through the intermediation of unjust laws. And that sound public policy, in the first, best sense, consists not of allowing illegitimate union activities, coupled with restricting them by the imposition of secret ballots, etc., but rather of stripping them of all coercive powers. The only just unions are those which limit their activities to boycotts, mass walkouts and other such activities that any one person has a right to engage in. When labor organizations transcend these limitations, they must be reined in, if economic justice is to prevail.

6 Is There a Right To Unionize?

I resist the notion that we have a "right to unionize" or that unionization is akin, or, worse, an implication of, the right to freely associate. Yes, theoretically, a labor organization *could* limit itself to organizing a mass quit unless they got what they wanted. That would indeed be an implication of the law of free association.

But every union with which I am familiar reserves the right to employ violence (that is, to initiate violence) against competing workers, e.g., scabs, whether in a "blue collar way" by beating them up, or in a "white collar way" by getting laws passed compelling employers to deal with them, and not with the scabs. (Does anyone know of a counter-example to this? If you know of any, I'd be glad to hear of it. I once thought I had found one: The Christian Labor Association of Canada. But based on an interview with them I can say that while they eschew "blue collar" aggression, they support the "white collar" version).

But what of the fact that there are many counter-examples: unions that have not actually engaged in the initiation of violence? Moreover, there are even people associated for many years with organized labor who have never witnessed the outbreak of actual violence.

Printed with kind permission of Mr. Llewellyn H. Rockwell, Jr. This article was initially posted on http://www.lewrockwell.com website.

Let me clarify my position. My opposition is not merely to violence, but, rather, to "violence, *or* the threat of violence." My position is that, often, no actual violence is needed, if the threat is serious enough, which, I contend, always obtains under unionism, at least as practiced in the U.S. and Canada.

Probably, the IRS never engaged in the actual use of physical violence in its entire history. (It is mostly composed of nerds, not physically aggressive people.) This is because it relies on the courts-police of the U.S. government who have overwhelming power. But it would be superficial to contend that the IRS does not engage in "violence, or the threat of violence." This holds true also for the state trooper who stops you and gives you a ticket. They are, and are trained to be, exceedingly polite. Yet, "violence, or the threat of violence" permeates their entire relationship with you.

I do not deny, moreover, that sometimes, management also engages in "violence, or the threat of violence." My only contention is that it is possible to point to numerous cases where they do *not*, while the same is impossible for organized labor, at least in the countries I am discussing.

In my view, the threat emanating from unions is objective, not subjective. It is the threat, in the old blue collar days, that any competing worker, a "scab," would be beat up if he tried to cross a picket line, and, in the modern white collar days, that any employer who fires a striking employee union member and substitutes for him a replacement worker as a permanent hire, will be found in violation of various labor laws. (Why, by the way, is it not "discriminatory," and "hateful," to describe workers willing to take less pay, and to compete with unionized labor, as "scabs?" Should not this be considered on a par with using the "N" word for blacks, or the "K" word for Jews?)

Suppose a small scrawny hold-up man confronts a big burly football player-type guy and demands his money, threatening that if the big guy does not give it up, the little guy will kick his butt. I call this an objective threat, and I don't care if the big guy laughs himself silly in reaction. Second scenario. Same as the first, only this time the little guy whips out a pistol, and threatens to shoot the big guy unless he hands over his money.

Now, there are two kinds of big guys. One will feel threatened, and hand over his money. The second will attack the little guy (in self-defense, I contend). Perhaps he is feeling omnipotent. Perhaps he is wearing a bullet-proof vest. It does not matter. The threat is a threat is a threat, regardless of the reaction of the big guy, regardless of his inner psychological response.

Now let us return to labor-management relations. The union objectively threatens scabs, and employers who hire them. This, nowadays, is purely a matter of law, not psychological feelings on anyone's part. In contrast, while it cannot be denied that sometimes employers initiate violence against workers, they need not *necessarily* do it, *qua* employer. (Often, however, such violence is in self-defense.)

This is similar to the point I made about the pimp in my book *Defending the Undefendable:* For this purpose, I don't care if each and every pimp has in fact initiated violence. Nor does it matter if they do it every hour on the hour. This is not a *necessary* characteristic of being a pimp. Even if there are no nonviolent pimps in existence, we can still imagine one such. Even if all employers always initiated violence against employees, still, we can *imagine* employers who do not. In very sharp contrast indeed, because of labor legislation they all support, we cannot even imagine unionized labor that does not threaten the initiation of violence.

Murray N. Rothbard was bitterly opposed to unions. This emanated from two sources. First, as a libertarian theoretician, because organized labor necessarily threatens violence.[1] Second, based on personal harm suffered at their hands by his family.[2]

We must never succumb to the siren song of union thuggery.

---

[1] See Rothbard (1962, pp. 620–32).
[2] See Raimondo (2000, pp. 59–61).

7 Free Market Transportation: Denationalizing the Roads

Were a government to demand the sacrifice of 46,700 citizens[1] each year, there is no doubt that an outraged public would revolt. If an organized religion were to plan the immolation of 523,335 of the faithful in a decade,[2] there is no question that it would be toppled. Were there a Manson-type cult that murdered 790 people to celebrate Memorial Day, 770 to usher in the Fourth of July, 915 to commemorate Labor Day, 960 at Thanksgiving, and solemnized Christmas with 355 more deaths,[3] surely *The New York Times* would wax eloquent about the carnage, calling for the greatest manhunt this nation has ever seen. If Dr. Spock were to learn of a disease that killed 2,077 children[4] under the age of five each year, or were New York City's Andrew Stein to uncover a nursing home that allowed 7,346 elderly people to die annually,[5] there would be

---

Reprinted with kind permission of the Ludwig von Mises Institute from *Journal of Libertarian Studies* 3, no. 2 (1979): 209–38.

[1] The number of people who were victims of motor vehicle accidents in 1976, in National Safety Council (1977, p. 13).

[2] The number of road and highway deaths in the decade 1967–1976, in *ibid*.

[3] Data for 1968, in *ibid*., p. 57.

[4] Data far 1969, in *ibid*., p. 60.

[5] Statement by Charles M. Noble, distinguished traffic engineer who served as director of the Ohio Department of Highways, chief engineer of the New Jersey Turnpike, and recipient of the Matson Memorial Award for Outstanding Contributions to the Advancement of Traffic Engineering. "Highway Design and Construction Related to Traffic Operations and Safety," *Traffic Quarterly* (November 1971, p. 534).

no stone unturned in their efforts to combat the enemy. To compound the horror, were private *enterprise* responsible for this butchery, a cataclysmic reaction would ensue: investigation panels would be appointed, the justice department would seek out antitrust violations, company executives would be jailed, and an outraged hue and cry for nationalization would follow.

The reality, however, is that the government is responsible for such slaughter—the toll taken on our nation's roadways. Whether at the local, state, regional, or national level, it is government that builds, runs, manages, administers, repairs, and plans for the roadway network. There is no need for the government to take over; it is already fully in charge, and with a vengeance. I believe there is a better way: the marketplace. Explaining how a free market can serve to provide road and highway service, as it has furnished us with practically every other good and service at our disposal, is the objective of this article.

Before dismissing the idea as impossible, consider the grisly tale of government road management. Every year since 1925 has seen the death of more than 20,000 people. Since 1929, the yearly toll has never dropped below 30,000 per year. In 1962, motor vehicle deaths first reached the 40,000 plateau and have not since receded below that level. To give just a hint of the callous disregard in which human life is held by the highway authorities, consider the following statement about the early days of government highway design and planning:

> The immediate need was to get the country out of the mud, to get a connected paved road system that would connect all county seats and population centers with mudless, dustless roads. These were the pioneering years. *Safety, volume, and traffic operations were not considered a problem.* But by the middle thirties there was an awakening and a recognition that these elements were vital to efficient and safe operation of the highway system. [Emphasis added][6]

---

[6] National Safety Council (1977, p. 13).

By the "middle thirties," indeed, nearly one-half million people had fallen victim to traffic fatalities.[7]

Rather than invoking indignation on the part of the public, government management of the roads and highways is an accepted given. Apart from a Ralph Nader, who only inveighs against unsafe vehicles (only a limited part of the problem), there is scarcely a voice raised in opposition.

The government seems to have escaped opprobrium because most people blame traffic accidents on a host of factors other than governmental mismanagement: drunkenness, speeding, lack of caution, mechanical failures, etc. Typical is the treatment undertaken by Sam Peltzman,[8] who lists no less than thirteen possible causes of accident rates without even once mentioning the fact of government ownership and management.

> Vehicle speed . . . alcohol consumption . . . the number of young drivers . . . changes in drivers' incomes . . . the money costs of accidents . . . the average age of cars . . . the ratio of new cars to all cars (because it has been suggested that while drivers familiarize themselves with their new cars, accident risk may increase) . . . traffic density . . . expenditures on traffic-law enforcement by state highway patrols . . . expenditures on roads . . . the ratio of imports to total cars (because there is evidence that small cars are more lethal than large cars if an accident occurs) . . . education of the population . . . and the availability of hospital care (which might reduce deaths if injury occurs).

Further, David M. Winch cites another reason for public apathy: the belief that "[m]any persons killed on the roads are partly to blame for their death."[9] True, many victims of road accidents are partly responsible. But this in no way explains public apathy toward their deaths. For people killed in New York City's Central Park during the late evening

---

[7] *Regulation and Automobile Safety* (1975, pp. 8–9).

[8] Winch (1963, p. 87).

[9] Strictly speaking, this is far from the truth. Before the nineteenth century, most roads and bridges in England and the U.S. were built by quasi-private stock companies.

hours, are also at least partially to blame for their own deaths; it takes a monumental indifference, feeling of omnipotence, absentmindedness or ignorance to embark upon such a stroll. Yet the victims are pitied, more police are demanded, and protests are commonly made.

The explanation of apathy toward highway mismanagement that seems most reasonable is that people simply do not see any alternative to government ownership. Just as no one "opposes" or "protests" a volcano, which is believed to be beyond the control of man, there are very few who oppose governmental roadway control. Along with death and taxes, state highway management seems to have become an immutable, if unstated, fact. The institution of government has planned, built, managed and maintained our highway network for so long that few people can imagine any other workable possibility. While Peltzman puts his finger on the proximate causes of highway accidents, such as excessive speed and alcohol, he has ignored the agency, government, which has set itself up as the manager of the roadway apparatus. This is akin to blaming a snafu in a restaurant on the fact that the oven went out, or that the waiter fell on a slippery floor with a loaded tray. *Of course* the proximate causes of customer dissatisfaction are uncooked meat or food in their laps. Yet how can these factors be blamed, while the part of restaurant management is ignored? It is the restaurant manager's job to insure that the ovens are performing satisfactorily, and that the floors are properly maintained. If he fails, the blame rests on his shoulders, not on the ovens or floors. We hold the trigger man responsible for murder, not the bullet.

The same holds true with highways. It may well be that speed and alcohol are deleterious to safe driving; but it is the road manager's task to ascertain that the proper standards are maintained with regard to these aspects of safety. If unsafe conditions prevail in a private, multistory parking lot, or in a shopping mall, or in the aisles of a department store, the entrepreneur in question is held accountable. It is he who loses revenue unless and until the situation is cleared up. It is logically fallacious to place the blame for accidents on unsafe conditions, while ignoring the manager whose responsibility it is to ameliorate these factors. It is my contention that all that is needed to virtually eliminate highway deaths is a nonutopian change, in the sense that it could take place now, even given our present state of knowledge, if only society would change what it can control: the institutional arrangements that govern the nation's highways.

Answering the Charge "Impossible"

Before I explain how a fully free market in roads might function, it appears appropriate to discuss the reasons why such a treatment is likely not to receive a fair hearing.

A fully private market in roads, streets, and highways is likely to be rejected out of hand, first, because of psychological reasons. The initial response of most people goes something as follows:

> Why, that's impossible. You just can't do it. There would be millions of people killed in traffic accidents; traffic jams the likes of which have never been seen would be an everyday occurrence; motorists would have to stop every twenty-five feet and put one-hundredth of a penny in each little old lady's toll box. Without eminent domain, there would be all sorts of obstructionists setting up roadblocks in the oddest places. Chaos, anarchy, would reign. Traffic would grind to a screeching halt, as the entire fabric of the economy fell about our ears.

If we were to divide such a statement into its cognitive and psychological (or emotive) elements, it must be stated right at the outset that there is nothing at all reprehensible about the intellectual challenge. Far from it. Indeed, if these charges cannot be satisfactorily answered, the whole idea of private roads shall have to be considered a failure.

But there is also an emotive element which is responsible, perhaps, not for the *content* of the objection, but for the hysterical manner in which it is usually couched and the unwillingness, even, to consider the case. The psychological component stems from a feeling that government road management is *inevitable* and that any other alternative is therefore unthinkable. It is this emotional factor that must be flatly rejected.

We must realize that just because the government has always[10] built and managed the roadway network, this is not necessarily inevitable, the most efficient procedure, nor even justifiable. On the contrary, the state of affairs that has characterized the past is, logically, almost entirely irrelevant. Just because "we have 'always' exorcised devils with broomsticks in order to cure disease" does not mean that this is the best way.

We must ever struggle to throw off the thralldom of the status quo. To help escape "the blinds of history" consider this statement by William C. Wooldridge:

> Several years ago I was a student at St. Andrews University in Scotland, and I found that placing a telephone call constituted one of the environment's greatest challenges. Private phones were too expensive to be commonplace, so a prospective telephoner first had to accumulate four pennies for each call he desired to make, a project complicated by the absence of any nearby commercial establishment open beyond the hour of six or seven. Next, the attention of an operator had to be engaged, in itself a sometimes frustrating undertaking, whether because of inadequate manpower or inadequate enthusiasm on the switchboard I never knew. Finally, since the landward side of town apparently boasted no more telephones than the seaward, a long wait frequently followed even a successful connection, while whoever had answered the phone searched out the party for whom the call was intended. A few repetitions of this routine broke my telephone habit altogether, and I joined my fellow students in communicating in person or by message when it was feasible, and not communicating at all when it was not.
>
> Nevertheless, the experience rankled, so I raised the subject one night in the cellar of a former bishop's residence, which now accommodates the student union's beer bar. Why were the telephones socialized? Why weren't they a privately owned utility, since there was so little to lose in the way of service by denationalization?

---

[10] Wooldridge (1970, pp. 7–9).

The reaction was not, as might be expected, in the least defensive, but instead positively condescending. It should be self-evident to even a chauvinistic American that as important a service as the telephone system could not be entrusted to private business. It was inconceivable to operate it for any other than the public interest. Who ever had heard of a private telephone company?

That incredulity slackened only slightly after a sketchy introduction to Mother Bell (then younger and less rheumatic than today), but at least the American company's example demonstrated that socialized telephone service was not an invariable given in the equation of the universe. My friends still considered the private telephone idea theoretically misbegotten and politically preposterous, but no longer could it remain literally inconceivable, for there we all were sitting around a table in the bishop's basement talking about it. It had been done. It might—heaven forfend—be done again. The talk necessarily shifted from possibility to desirability, to what lawyers call the merits of the case.

Like the St. Andrews students, Americans show a disposition to accept our government's customary functions as necessarily the exclusive province of government; when city hall has always done something, it is difficult to imagine anyone else doing it.

When an activity is being undertaken for the first time, the operation of the Telstar communications satellite, for instance, people keenly feel and sharply debate their option for public or private ownership. Discussion of the costs and advantages of each alternative accompanies the final choice. But once the choice is made and a little time passes, an aura of inevitability envelops the status quo, and consciousness of any alternative seeps away with time.

Today, most Americans probably feel the telegraph naturally belongs within the private sphere, and few doubt the post office should naturally be a public monopoly. "Naturally," however, in such a context means only that's-the-way-it's-been-for-as-long-as-we-can-remember, an Americanized version of Pope's declaration that "Whatever is right." Yet few could think of a convincing *a priori* rationale for distinguishing the postal from the telegraphic mode of communication. At least one postmaster general could not: in 1845 his annual report prophesied intolerable competition from the telegraph and suggested it might appropriately be committed to the government. At that early stage in its history, the telegraph might conceivably have become a government monopoly for the same reasons the post office already was, but the mere passage of time has obliterated any consideration of whether they were good reasons or bad reasons.[11]

In advocating a free market in roads, on one level, we shall be merely arguing that there is nothing unique about transportation; that the economic principles we accept as a matter of course in practically every other arena of human experience are applicable here, too. Or at the very least, we cannot suppose that ordinary economic laws are *not* apropos in road transportation until after the matter has been considered in some detail.

Says Gabriel Roth:

---

[11] Roth (1967, p. 16). See also:

> The highway situation can be improved substantially by visualizing the similarities between the highway problem and a host of comparable problems to which economists have applied some rather ancient ideas: namely, those of "good old supply and demand analysis." (Brownlee and Heller 1956, p. 233)

> The provision of highways involves basically the same problems as any other economic activity. Scarce resources must be used to satisfy human wants by the provision of goods and services, and decisions must be made as to how much of our resources will be devoted to one particular service, and who is going to make the necessary sacrifice. (Winch, p. 141)

> Many of the characteristics that are held to make transportation "different" are in fact found in other industries as well, and . . . the same forms of analysis that are applicable in other industries can be utilized as well for transportation. Thus complementarity, or joint production, as between forward and back hauls, has its counterpart in the joint production of hides and meat from the same animal. Perishability is greater than from fresh produce, but less, in many cases, than for a newspaper. Congestion occurs in supermarkets, and externalities or "neighborhood effects" are pervasive. Customer time cost is involved in getting a haircut. (Vickrey, unpublished manuscript)

There is a[n] approach to the problem of traffic congestion—the economic approach—which offers a rational and practical solution. . . . The first step is to recognize that road space is a scarce resource. The second, to apply to it the economic principles that we find helpful in the manufacture and distribution of other scarce resources, such as electricity or motor cars or petrol. There is nothing new or unusual about these principles, nor are they particularly difficult. *What is difficult is to apply them to roads, probably because we have all been brought up to regard roads as community assets freely available to all comers.* The difficulty does not lie so much in the technicalities of the matter, but rather in the idea that roads can usefully be regarded as chunks of real estate. [Emphasis added][12]

Unfortunately, even those economists who, like Roth, call explicitly for a consideration of the similarities between roads and other goods are unwilling to carry the analogy through to its logical conclusion: free enterprise highways and streets. Instead, they limit themselves to advocacy of *road pricing*, but to be administered, always, by governmental authorities.

What *reasons* are there for advocating the free market approach for the highway industry? First and foremost is the fact that the present government ownership and management has failed. The death toll, the suffocation during urban rush hours, and the poor state of repair of the highway stock, are all eloquent testimony to the lack of success which has marked the reign of government control. Second, and perhaps even more important, is a *reason* for this state of affairs. It is by no means an accident that government operation has proven to be a debacle, and that private enterprise can succeed where government has failed.

It is not only that government has been staffed with incompetents. The roads authorities are staffed, sometimes, with able management. Nor can it be denied that at least some who have achieved high rank in the world of private business have been incompetent. The advantage

---

[12] The present author wishes to express a debt of gratitude to the two trailblazers into this subject: Wollstein (1974), and Rothbard (1978, pp. 202–18).

enjoyed by the market is the automatic reward and penalty system imposed by profits and losses. When customers are pleased, they continue patronizing those merchants who have served them well. These businesses are thus allowed to earn a profit. They can prosper and expand. Entrepreneurs who fail to satisfy, on the other hand, are soon driven to bankruptcy.

This is a continual process repeated day in, day out. There is always a tendency in the market for the reward of the able, and the deterrence of those who are not efficient. Nothing like perfection is ever reached, but the continual grinding down of the ineffective, and rewarding of the competent, brings about a level of managerial skill unmatched by any other system. Whatever may be said of the political arena, it is one which completely lacks this market process. Although there are cases where capability rises to the fore, there is no continual process which promotes this.

Because this is well known, even elementary, we have entrusted the market to produce the bulk of our consumer goods and capital equipment. What is difficult to see is that this analysis applies to the provision of roads no less than to fountain pens, frisbees, or fishsticks.

A Free Market in Roads

Let us now turn to a consideration of how a free market in roads might operate.[13] Along the way, we will note and counter the intellectual objections to such a system. *All* transport thoroughfares would be privately owned: not only the vehicles, buses, trains, automobiles, trolleys, etc., that travel upon them, but the very roads, highways, byways, streets, sidewalks, bridges, tunnels, crosswalks themselves upon which journeys take place. The transit corridors would be as privately owned as is our fast food industry.

As such, all the usual benefits and responsibilities that are incumbent upon private enterprise would affect roads. The reason a company or individual would want to build or buy an already existing road would be the same as in any other business—to earn a profit. The necessary

---

[13] Vickrey (1963, p. 452; 1974, p. 24).

funds would be raised in a similar manner—by floating an issue of stock, by borrowing, or from past savings of the owner. The risks would be the same—attracting customers and prospering, or failing to do so and going bankrupt. Likewise for the pricing policy; just as private enterprise rarely gives burgers away for free, use of road space would require payment. A road enterprise would face virtually all of the problems shared by other businesses: attracting a labor force, subcontracting, keeping customers satisfied, meeting the price of competitors, innovating, borrowing money, expanding, etc. Thus, a highway or street owner would be a businessman as any other, with much the same problems, opportunities, and risks.

In addition, just as in other businesses, there would be facets peculiar to this particular industry. The road entrepreneur would have to try to contain congestion, reduce traffic accidents, plan and design new facilities in coordination with already existing highways, as well as with the plans of others for new expansion. He would have to set up the "rules of the road" so as best to accomplish these and other goals. The road industry would be expected to carry on each and every one of the tasks now undertaken by public roads authorities: fill potholes, install road signs, guardrails, maintain lane markings, repair traffic signals, and so on for the myriad of "road furniture" that keeps traffic moving.

Applying the concepts of profit and loss to the road industry, we can see why privatization would almost certainly mean a gain compared to the present nationalized system of road management.

As far as safety is concerned, presently there is no road manager who loses financially if the accident rate on "his" turnpike increases, or is higher than other comparable avenues of transportation. A civil servant draws his annual salary regardless of the accident toll piled up under his domain. But if he were a *private* owner of the road in question, in competition with numerous other highway companies (as well as other modes of transit such as airlines, trains, boats, etc.), completely dependent for financial sustenance on the voluntary payments of satisfied customers, then he would indeed lose out if his road compiled a poor safety record (assuming that customers desire, and are willing to pay for, safety). He would, then, have every incentive to try to reduce accidents, whether by technological innovations, better rules of the road, improved methods of selecting out drunken and other undesirable drivers, etc. If he failed, or did less well than his competition, he eventually would be removed from his position of responsibility. Just as we now expect better mouse-traps from a private enterprise system which rewards success and penalizes failure, so could we count on a private ownership setup to improve highway safety. Thus, as a partial answer to the challenge that private ownership would mean the deaths of millions of people in traffic accidents, we reply, "There are, at *present*, millions of people who have been slaughtered on our nation's highways; a changeover to the enterprise system would lead to a precipitous *decline* in the death and injury rate, due to the forces of competition."

Another common objection to private roads is the spectre of having to halt every few feet and toss a coin into a tollbox. This simply would not occur on the market. To see why not, imagine a commercial golf course operating on a similar procedure: forcing the golfers to wait in line at every hole, or demanding payment every time they took a swipe at the ball. It is easy to see what would happen to the cretinous management of such an enterprise: it would very rapidly lose customers and go broke.

If roads were privately owned, the same process would occur. Any road with say, 500 toll booths per mile, would be avoided like the plague by customers, who would happily patronize a road with fewer obstructions, even at a higher money cost per mile. This would be a classical case of economies of scale, where it would pay entrepreneurs to buy the toll collection rights from the millions of holders, in order to rationalize the system into one in which fewer toll gates blocked the roads. Streets that could be so organized would prosper as thoroughfares; others would not. So even if the system somehow began in this patchwork manner, market forces would come to bear, mitigating the extreme inefficiency.

There is no reason, however, to begin the market experiment in this way. Instead of arbitrarily assigning each house on the block a share of the road equal to its frontage multiplied by one-half the width of the street in front of it (the way in which the previous example was presumably generated in someone's nightmare vision), there are other methods more in line with historical reality and with the libertarian theory of homesteading property rights.

One scenario would follow the shopping center model: a single owner-builder would buy a section of territory, build roads, and (fronting them) houses. Just as many shopping center builders maintain control over parking lots, malls, and other "in common" areas, the entrepreneur would continue the operation of common areas such as the roads, sidewalks, etc. Primarily residential streets might be built in a meandering, roundabout manner replete with cul-de-sacs, to discourage through travel. Tolls for residents, guests, and deliveries might be pegged at low levels, or be entirely lacking (as in the case of modern shopping centers), while through traffic might be charged at prohibitive rates. Standing in the wings, ensuring that the owner effectively discharges his responsibilities, would be the profit and loss system.

Consider now a road whose main function is to facilitate through traffic. If it is owned by one person or company, who either built it or bought the rights of passage from the previous owners, it would be foolish for him to install dozens of toll gates per mile. In fact, toll gates would probably not be the means of collection employed by a road owner at all. There now exist highly inexpensive electrical devices[14] which can register the passage of an automobile past any fixed point on a road. Were suitable identifying electronic tapes attached to the surface of each road vehicle, there would be no need for a time-wasting, labor costly system of toll collection points. Rather, as the vehicle passes the checkpoint, the electrical impulse set up can be transmitted to a computer which can produce one monthly bill for all roads used, and even mail it out automatically. Road payments could be facilitated in as unobtrusive a manner as utility bills are now.

---

[14] Says Rothbard (1978, p. 205):

> The answer is that everyone, in purchasing homes or street service in a libertarian society, would make sure that the purchase or lease contract provides full access for whatever term of years is specified. With this sort of "easement" provided in advance by contract, no such sudden blockade would be allowed, since it would be an invasion of the property right of the landowner.

Then there is the eminent domain challenge: the allegation that roads could not be efficiently constructed without the intermediation of government-imposed eminent domain laws which are not at the disposal of private enterprise. The argument is without merit.

We must first realize that even with eminent domain, and under the system of government road construction, there are *still* limits as to where a new road may be placed. Not even a government could last long if it decided to tear down all the skyscrapers in Chicago's Loop in order to make way for yet another highway. The logic of this limitation is obvious: it would cost billions of dollars to replace these magnificent structures; a new highway near these buildings, but one which did not necessitate their destruction, might well be equally valuable, but at an infinitesimal fraction of the cost.

With or without eminent domain, then, such a road could not be built. Private enterprise could not afford to do so, because the gains in siting the road over carcasses of valuable buildings would not be worthwhile; nor could the government accomplish this task, while there was still some modicum of common sense prohibiting it from operating completely outside of any economic bounds.

It is true that owners of land generally thought worthless by other people would be able to ask otherwise exorbitant prices from a developer intent upon building a straight road. Some of these landowners would demand high prices because of psychic attachment (e.g., the treasured old homestead); others solely because they knew that building plans called for their particular parcels, and they were determined to obtain the maximum income possible.

But the private road developer is not without defenses, all of which will tend to lower the price he must pay. First, there is no necessity for an absolutely straight road, nor even for one that follows the natural contours of the land. Although one may prefer, on technical grounds, path A, it is usually possible to utilize path B . . . Z, all at variously higher costs. If so, then the cheapest of these alternatives provides an upper limit to what the owners along path A may charge for their properties. For example, it may be cheaper to blast through an uninhabited mountain rather than pay the exorbitant price of the farmer in the valley; this fact tends to put a limit upon the asking price of the valley farmer.

Second, the road developer, knowing that he will be satisfied with any of five trajectories, can purchase options to buy the land along each site. If a recalcitrant holdout materializes on any one route, he can shift to his second, third, fourth or fifth choice. The competition between owners along each of these passageways will tend to keep the price down.

Third, in the rare case of a holdout who possesses an absolutely essential plot, it is always possible to build a bridge *over* this land or to tunnel underneath. Ownership of land does not consist of property rights up to the sky or down to the core of the Earth; the owner cannot forbid planes from passing overhead, nor can he prohibit a bridge over his land, as long as it does not interfere with the use of his land. Although vastly more expensive than a surface road, these options again put an upper bound on the price the holdout can insist upon.

There is also the fact that land values are usually influenced by their neighborhood. What contributes to the value of a residence is the existence of neighboring homes, which supply neighbors, friends, companionship. Similarly, the value of a commercial enterprise is enhanced by the proximity of other businesses, customers, contacts, even competitors. In New York City, the juxtaposition of stock brokerage firms, flower wholesalers, a jewelry exchange, a garment district, etc., all attest to the value of being located near competitors. If a road 150 feet wide sweeps through, completely disrupting this "neighborliness," much of the value of the stubborn landowner's property is dissipated. The risk of being isolated again puts limitations upon the price which may be demanded.

In an out-of-the-way, rural setting, a projected road may not be expected to attract the large number of cash customers necessary to underwrite lavish expenditures on the property of holdouts. However, it will be easier to find alternative routes in a sparsely settled area. Urban locations present the opposite problem: it will be more difficult to find low-cost alternatives, but the expected gains from a road which is expected to carry millions of passengers may justify higher payments for the initial assemblage.

Of course, eminent domain is a great facilitator; it eases the process of land purchase. Seemingly, pieces of land are joined together at an exceedingly low cost. But the *real* costs of assemblage are thereby concealed. Landowners are forced to give up their property at prices determined to be "fair" by the federal bureaucracy, not at prices to which they voluntarily agree. While it appears that private enterprise would have to pay more than the government, this is incorrect. The market will have to pay the full, voluntary price, but this will, paradoxically, be less than the government's real payment (its money payments plus the values it has forcibly taken from the original owners). This is true because the profit incentive to reduce costs is completely lacking in state "enterprise." Furthermore, the extra costs undergone by the government in the form of bribes, rigged bidding, cost-plus contracts, etc., often would bloat even limited government money outlays past the full costs of private road developers.

Another objection against a system of private roads is the danger of being isolated. The typical nightmare vision runs somewhat as follows:

> A man buys a piece of land. He builds a house on it. He stocks it with food, and then brings his family to join him. When they are all happily ensconced, they learn that the road fronting their little cottage has been purchased by an unscrupulous street-owning corporation, which will not allow him or his family the use of the road at any but an indefinitely high price. The family may "live happily ever after", but only as long as they keep to their own house. Since the family is too poor to afford a helicopter, the scheming road owner has the family completely in his power. He may starve them into submission, if he so desires.

This does indeed appear frightening, but only because we are not accustomed to dealing with such a problem. It could not exist under the present system, so it is difficult to see how it could be solved by free market institutions. Yet, the answer is simple: no one would buy any plot of land without first insuring that he had the right to enter and leave at will.[15]

---

[15] Hayek (1960, p. 160).

Similar contracts are now commonplace on the market, and they give rise to no such blockade problems. Flea markets often rent out tables to separate merchandisers; gold and diamond exchanges usually sublet booths to individual, small merchants; desk space is sometimes available to people who cannot afford an entire office of their own. The suggestion that these contracts are unworkable or unfeasible, on the grounds that the owner of the property might prohibit access to his subtenant, could only be considered ludicrous. Any lawyer who allowed a client to sign a lease which did not specify the rights of access in advance would be summarily fired, if not disbarred. This is true in the present, and would also apply in an era of private roads.

It is virtually impossible to predict the exact future contour of an industry that does not presently exist. The task is roughly comparable to foretelling the makeup of the airline industry immediately after the Wright Brothers' experiments at Kitty Hawk. How many companies would there be? How many aircraft would each one own? Where would they land? Who would train the pilots? Where could tickets be purchased? Would food and movies be provided in flight? What kinds of uniforms would be worn by the stewardesses? Where would the financing come from? These are all questions not only impossible to have answered at that time, but ones that could hardly have arisen. Were an early advocate of a "private airline industry" pressed to point out, in minute detail, all the answers in order to defend the proposition that his idea was sound, he would have had to fail.

In like manner, advocates of free market roads are in no position to set up *the* blueprint for a future private market in transport. They cannot tell how many road owners there will be, what kind of rules of the road they will set up, how much it will cost per mile, how the entrepreneurs will seek to reduce traffic accidents, whether road shoulders will be wider or narrower, or which steps will be taken in order to reduce congestion. Nor can we answer many of the thousands of such questions that are likely to arise.

For one thing, these are not the *kinds* of questions that can be answered in advance with any degree of precision, and not only in transportation. The same limitations would have faced early attempts to specify industrial setups in computers, televisions, or any other industry. It is impossible to foretell the future of industrial events because, given a free market situation, they are the result of the actions of an entire cooperating economy, even though these actions may not be intended by any individual actor.[16] Each person bases his actions on the limited knowledge at his disposal.

Nevertheless, we shall attempt a scenario, though not for the purpose of mapping out, forevermore, the shape of the road market of the future. We realize that such patterns must arise out of the actions of millions of market participants, and will be unknown to any of them in advance. Yet if we are to consider objections to a road market intelligently, we must present a general outline of how such a market *might* function. We will now consider some problems that might arise for a road market, and some possible solutions.

Who will decide upon the rules of the road?

This question seems important because we are accustomed to governments determining the rules of the road. Some people even go so far as to *justify* the very existence of government on the ground that *someone* has to fashion highway rules, and that government seems to be the only candidate.

In the free market, each road owner will decide upon the rules his customers are to follow, just as nowadays rules for proper behavior in some locations are, to a great extent, determined by the owner of the property in question. Thus, roller- and ice-skating emporia decide when and where their patrons may wander, with or without skates. Bowling alleys usually require special bowling shoes, and prohibit going past a certain line in order to knock down the pins. Restaurants demand that diners communicate with their waiter and busboy, and not go marching into the kitchen to consult with the chef.

There are no "God-given" rules of the road. While it might have been convenient had Moses been given a list of the ten best rules for the road, he was not. Nor have legislators been given any special

---

[16] I owe this point to David Ramsay Steele, of the Department of Sociology, University of Hull.

dispensations from on high. It is therefore man's lot to *discover* what rules can best minimize costs and accidents, and maximize speed and comfort. There is no better means of such discovery than the competitive process. Mr. Glumph of the Glumph Highway Company decides upon a set of rules. Each of his competitors decides upon a (slightly) different version. Then the consumer, by his choice to patronize or not, supports one or the other. To the extent that he patronizes Glumph and avoids his competitors, he underwrites and supports Glumph's original decisions. If Glumph loses too many customers, he will be forced to change his rules (or other practices) or face bankruptcy. In this way the forces of the market will be unleashed to do their share in aiding the discovery process. We may never reach the all-perfect set of rules that maximizes the attainment of all conceivable goals, but the *tendency* toward this end will always operate.

If a free market in roads is allowed and bankruptcies occur, what will be done about the havoc created for the people dependent upon them?

Bankrupt road companies may well result from the operations of the market. There are insolvencies in every area of the economy, and it would be unlikely for this curse to pass by the road sector. Far from a calamity, however, bankruptcies are paradoxically a sign of a *healthy* economy.

Bankruptcies have a *function*. Stemming from managerial error in the face of changing circumstances, bankruptcies have several beneficial effects. They may be a signal that consumers can no longer achieve maximum benefit from a stretch of land used as a highway; there may be an alternative use that is ranked higher. Although the subject might never arise under public stewardship, surely *sometime* in the past ten centuries there were roads constructed which (from the vantage point of the present) should not have been built; or, even if they were worth building originally, have long since outlasted their usefulness. We *want* a capacity in our system to acknowledge mistakes, *and then act so as to correct them.* The system of public ownership is deficient, in comparison, precisely because bankruptcy and conversion to a more valuable use never exists as a serious alternative. The mistakes are, rather, "frozen in concrete," never to be changed.

Would we really want to apply the present nonbankruptcy system now prevailing in government road management to any other industry? Would it be more efficient to maintain every single grocery store, once built, forevermore? Of course not. It is part of the *health* of the grocery industry that stores no longer needed are allowed to pass on, making room for those in greater demand. No less is true of the roadway industry. Just as it is important for the functioning of the body that dead cells be allowed to disappear, making way for new life, so is it necessary for the proper functioning of our roadway network that some roads be allowed to pass away.

Bankruptcy may serve a second purpose. A business may fail not because there is no longer any need for the road, but because private management is so inept that it cannot attract and hold enough passengers to meet all its costs. In this case, the function served by bankruptcy proceedings would be to relieve the ineffective owners of the road, put it into the hands of the creditors and, subsequently, into the hands of better management.

How would traffic snarls be countered in the free market?

If the roads in an entire section of town (e.g., the Upper East Side of Manhattan), or all of the streets in a small city were completely under the control of one company, traffic congestion would present no new problem. The only difference between this and the present arrangement would be that a private company, not the government road authority, would be in charge. As such, we could only expect the forces of competition to improve matters.

For example, one frequent blocker of traffic, and one which in no way aids the overall movement of motorists, is the automobile caught in an intersection when the light has changed. This situation arises from entering an intersecting cross street, in the hope of making it across so that, when the light changes, one will be ahead of vehicles turning off that street. In the accompanying diagram 1 (see below) a motorist is traveling west along the Side Street. Although the Side Street west of

Main Street is chock full of cars, he nevertheless enters the intersection between Main Street and Side Street; he hopes that, by the time Main Street again enjoys the green light, the cars ahead of him will move forward, leaving room for him to leave the intersection.

Diagram 1

	Main Street	(North)
Side Street		

All too often, however, what happens is that traffic ahead of him on Side Street remains stationary, and the motorist gets caught in the middle of the intersection. Then, even when the traffic is signaled to move north on Main Street, it cannot; because of the impatience of our motorist, he and his fellows are now stuck in the intersection, blocking northbound traffic. If this process is repeated on the four intersections surrounding one city block (see diagram 2) it can (and does) bring traffic in the entire surrounding area to a virtual standstill.

Diagram 2

Broadway	Main Street	
		Side Street
		Maple Street

Currently, government regulations prohibit entering an intersection when there is no room on the other side. This rule is beside the point. The question is not whether a traffic system legally *calls* for certain actions, but whether this rule *succeeds* or not. If the mere passage of a law could suffice, all that would be needed to return to the Garden of Eden would be "enabling legislation." What is called for, in addition to the proper rules of the road, is the actual attainment of motorists' conformity with those rules. As far as *this* problem is concerned, private road companies have a comparative advantage over governments. For, as we have seen, if a government fails in this kind of mission, there is no process whereby it is relieved of its duties; whereas, let a private enterprise fail and retribution, in the form of bankruptcy, will be swift and total. Another street company, and still another, if needed, will evolve through the market process, to improve matters.

It is impossible to tell, in advance, what means the private street companies will employ to rid their territories of this threat.

Just as private universities, athletic stadiums, etc., now enforce rules whose purpose is the smooth functioning of the facility, so might road owners levy fines to ensure obedience to rules. For example, automobiles stuck in an intersection could be registered by the road's computer-monitoring system, and charged an extra amount for this driving infraction, on an itemized bill.[17]

What problems would ensue of each street owned by a separate company, or individual?

It might appear that the problems are insoluble. For each owner would seem to have an incentive to *encourage* motorists on his own street to try as hard as they can to get to the next block, to the total disregard of traffic on the cross street. (The more vehicles passing through, the greater the charges that can be levied.) Main Street, in this scenario, would urge its patrons, traveling north, to get into the intersection between it and Side Street, so as to pass on when the next light changed. The Side Street management would do the same: embolden the drivers heading west to try to cross over Main Street, regardless whether there was room on the other side. Each street owner would, in this view, take an extremely narrow stance; he would try to maximize his own profits, and not overly concern himself with imposing costs on the others.

The answer to this dilemma is that it could never occur in a free market, based on specified individual private property rights. For in such a system, *all* aspects of the roadway are owned, including the *intersection itself*. In the nature of things, in a full private property system,

---

[17] We assume away here the presence of psychic income phenomena. See Block (1977, p. 111).

the intersection must be owned either by the Main Street Company, the Side Street Company, or by some third party. As soon as the property rights to the intersection between the two streets are fully specified (in whichever of these three ways) all such problems and dilemmas cease.

Suppose the Main Street Company had been the first on the scene. It is then the full owner of an unbroken chain of property, known as Main Street. Soon after, the Side Street Company contemplates building. Now the former company knows full well that *all* of Main Street is private property. Building a cross street to run over the property of Main Street cannot be justified. The Main Street Company, however, has every incentive to welcome a Side Street, if not to build one itself, for the new street will enhance its own property if patrons can use it to arrive at other places. A city street that has no cross street options does not really function as an access route; it would be more like a limited access highway in the middle of a city. The two companies shall have to arrive at a mutually satisfactory arrangement. Presumably, the Side Street Company will have to *pay* for the right to build a cross street. On the other hand, if the owners of Main Street intend to use it as a limited access highway, then the Side Street Company shall have to build over it, under it, or around it, but not across it. (As part of the contract between the two parties, there would have to be an agreement concerning automobiles getting stuck in the intersection. Presumably this would be prohibited.)

Since original ownership by the Side Street Company would be the same analytically as the case we have just considered, but with the names of the companies reversed, we may pass on to a consideration of ownership by a third party.

If the intersection of the two streets is owned by an outsider, then it is he who decides conflicts between the two road companies. Since his interests would best be served by smoothly flowing traffic, the presumption is that the owner of the intersection would act so as to minimize the chances of motorists from either street being isolated in the intersection as the traffic light changed.

This analysis of the ownership situation concerning cross streets and their intersections will enable us to answer several other possibly perplexing problems.

How would green light time be parceled out under free enterprise?

Of course, most street owners, if they had their choice, would prefer the green light for their street 100 percent of the time. Yet, this would be tantamount to a limited access highway. If it is to be a city street, a road must content itself with less. What proportion of red and green lights shall be allotted to each street?

If all the streets in one neighborhood are owned by one company, then it decides this question, presumably with the intention of maximizing its profits. Again, and for the same reasons, we can expect a more effective job from such a "private" owner, than from a city government apparatus.

In the case of intersection ownership by a third party, the two cross street owners will *bid* for the green light time. *Ceteris paribus,* the presumption is that the owner of the street with the larger volume of street traffic will succeed in bidding for more of the green light time. If the owner of the larger volume street refused to bid for a high proportion of green light time, his customers would tend to patronize competitors—who could offer more green lights, and hence a faster trip.

A similar result would take place with two street owners, no matter what the property dispersal.[18] It is easy to see this if the larger street company owns the intersections. The larger company would simply keep a high proportion (two-thirds, three-quarters, or perhaps even four-fifths) of green light time for itself, selling only the remaining small fraction to the intersecting side street. But much the same result would ensue if the smaller road owned the common intersections! Although the relatively lightly traveled road company might like to keep the lion's share of the green lights for itself, it will find that it cannot afford to do so. The more heavily traveled street, representing a clientele willing and able in the aggregate to pay far more for green light privileges, will make it extremely tempting for the small street owner to accept a heavy payment, in order to relinquish most of its green light time. In other words, the customers of the main street, through indirect payments via the main street owner, will bid time away from the smaller number of customers using the minor street. This principle is well established in

---

[18] Smerk (1965a, p. 228).

business, and is illustrated every time a firm sublets space, which it could have used to satisfy its own customers, because it receives more income subletting than retaining the premises for its own use.

The provision of staggered traffic lights (the lights continually turn green, for example, as an auto proceeding at twenty-five miles per hour approaches them) may present some conceptual difficulties but, again, they are easily overcome. Of course, there are virtually no problems if either one company owns all the roads, or if the main road (the one to be staggered) is continuously owned. The only question arises when the *side* streets are continuously owned, and it is the main avenues which are to receive the staggered lights. (We are assuming that staggering cannot efficiently be instituted for both north-south *and* intersecting east-west streets, and that staggering is better placed on the main roads than the side ones.)

Under these conditions, there are several possible solutions. For one, the main avenues, being able to make better use of the staggering system, may simply purchase (or rent) the rights to program the lights so that staggering takes place on the main roads. The side roads, even as owners of the intersections, would only be interested in the proportion of each minute that their lights could remain green; they would be indifferent to the necessity of staggering. Since this is precisely what the main roads desire, it seems that some mutually advantageous agreement could feasibly be made.

Another possibility is that the main roads, better able to utilize the staggering capabilities which intersection ownership confers (and perhaps better able to utilize the other advantages bestowed upon their owners) will simply arrange to purchase the intersections outright. If so, the pattern would change from one where the side street corporations owned the intersections to one in which these came under the possession of the main street companies.

Still another alternative would be integration of ownership. We have no idea as to the optimal size of the road firm (single block, single road, continuous road, small city, etc.), so thoughts in this direction can only be considered speculative. With regard to the ease of coordinating staggered light systems, however, it may well be that larger is better. If so, there will be a market tendency for merger, until these economies are exhausted.

Let us recapitulate. We have begun by indicating the present mismanagement of roads by government. We have claimed that improvements, given the status quo of government management, are not likely to suffice. We have briefly explored an alternative—the free market in road ownership and management—and shown how it might deal with a series of problems, and rejected some unsophisticated objections. We are now ready to examine in some detail how private road owners actually might compete in the market place.

How Private Road Owners Might Compete

On the rare occasions when the feasibility of private road ownership has been considered by mainstream economists, it has been summarily rejected, based on the impossibility of competition among private road owners. Seeing this point as almost intuitively obvious, economists have not embarked on lengthy chains of reasoning in refutation. Thus, says Smerk, rather curtly, "Highways could not very well be supplied on a competitive basis, hence they are provided by the various levels of government."[19]

Economists, however, are willing to expound, at great length, upon the need for the conditions of perfect competition, if efficiency is to prevail in the private sector. One of the main reasons the idea of private enterprise for roads has not been accepted is the claim that perfect competition cannot exist in this sphere.

A typical example of this kind of thinking is that of Haveman.[20] Says he:

> A number of conditions must be met if the private sector of the economy—the market system—is to function efficiently. Indeed, these conditions are essential if the private sector is to perform in

---

[19] Haveman (1970, p. 23). For a telling criticism of the "control over price" confusion, see Rothbard (1962, pp. 87–90).

[20] Cf. Kirzner (1973).

the public interest. . . . It is the absence of these conditions which often gives rise to demands for public sector [government] action.

These conditions of perfect competition are widely known: numerous buyers and sellers, so that no one of them is big enough to "affect price;" a homogeneous good; and perfect information. One problem with the strict requirement that an industry meet these conditions, or else be consigned to government operation, is that there is virtually no industry in a real-life economy that would remain in the private sector! Almost every industry would have to be nationalized, were the implicit program of Haveman followed. This is easy to see, once we realize how truly restrictive are these conditions. The homogeneity requirement, by itself, would be enough to bar most goods and services in a modern, complex economy. Except for thumb tacks, rubber bands, paper clips, and several others of this kind, there are hardly any commodities which do not differ, even slightly, in the eyes of most consumers. Perfect information bars even the farm staples from inclusion in the rubric of perfect competition. This can be seen in a healthy, functioning Chicago mercantile exchange. If there were full information available to all and sundry, there could be no such commodities market.

Not "affecting price" also presents difficulties. No matter how small a part of the total market a single individual may be, he can always hold out for a price slightly higher than that commonly prevailing. Given a lack of perfect information, there will usually (but not always) be someone willing to purchase at the higher price.

Therefore, the objection to private roads on the ground that they are inconsistent with perfect competition cannot be sustained. It is true that this industry could not maintain the rigid standards required for perfect competition, but neither can most. In pointing out that *perfect competition* cannot apply to roads, we have by no means conceded that *competition* between the various road owners would not be a vigorous, rivalrous process. On the contrary, were we to allow that perfect competition *could* apply to roads, we would then have to retract our claim that vigorous competition could also ensue. For perfect competition, and competition in the ordinary sense of that word (implying rivalry, attempts to entice customers away from one another) are *opposites*, and inconsistent with each other.[21]

In the perfectly competitive model, each seller can sell all he wants, at the given market price. (This is the assumption that each perfect competitor faces a perfectly elastic demand curve.) A typical rendition of this point of view is furnished by Stonier and Hague:[22]

> The shape of the revenue curve [demand curve] of the individual firm will depend on conditions in the market in which the firm sells its product. Broadly speaking, the keener the competition of its rivals and the greater the number of fairly close substitutes for its product, the more elastic will a firm's average revenue curve be. As usual, it is possible to be precise about limiting cases. One limiting case will occur when there are so many competitors producing such close substitutes [the perfectly competitive model] that the demand for the product of each individual firm is infinitely elastic and its average revenue curve is a horizontal straight line. This will mean that the firm can sell as much of its product as it wishes at the ruling market price. If the firm raises its price, then, owing to the ease with which the same, or a very similar, product can be bought from competitors, it will lose all its customers. If the firm were to lower its price, it would be swamped by orders from customers wishing to take advantage of its price reduction. The demand—and the elasticity of demand—for its product would be infinite.

Under these conditions, competition in the usual sense of opposition, contention, rivalry, etc. would be completely lacking. Where is the need to attract the customers of other firms to oneself if each so-called "competitor" can "sell as much of its product as it wishes at the ruling market price?" Why go out and compete if one is guaranteed all the customers one could possibly want? If "competition" is supposed to indicate rivalrous behavior, one would think that "perfect competition" would denote a sort of super-contentiousness. Instead, through dint of

---

[21] Stonier and Hague (1964, p. 104).
[22] See Robbins (1932).

misleading definition, it means the very opposite: a highly passive existence, where firms do not have to go out and actively seek customers.

Again, we can see that rejecting the possibility of perfect competition for a roads industry is by no means equivalent to conceding that there can be no rivalrous competition between the different road owners. Paradoxically, only if perfect competition were applicable to roads, might we have to consider the possibility that the process of competition might not be adaptable to highways.

In contrast to the passive notion of perfect competition, which has held center stage in the economics profession for the last few decades, there is a new comprehension of competition, in the *market process* sense, that is now drawing increasing attention.

Instead of concentrating on the maximization of ends, assuming given scarce means, as does the Robbinsian[23] notion of perfect competition, the market process view makes the realistic assumption that the means, although scarce, are in no way given; rather, knowledge of them must actively be sought out. The allocation of scarce means among competing ends is a passive procedure when the means and the ends are known. All that need be done can be accomplished by a suitably programmed computer. But the active seeking out of the ends and the means in the first place is a task that can be accomplished only by entrepreneurial talent; active, not passive. The entrepreneur, denied his crucial role in the perfectly competitive world-view, takes center stage in the market process conception.

Instead of merely economizing, the entrepreneur seeks new and hitherto unknown profit opportunities; not content to allocate given means to already selected ends, the businessman blazes new trails, continually on the lookout for new ends, and different means. States Israel Kirzner,[24] one of the pathbreakers in this way of looking at our economy:

We have seen that the market proceeds through entrepreneurial competition. In this process market participants become aware of opportunities for profit: they perceive price discrepancies (either

---

[23] Kirzner (1973, pp. 122–23).
[24] Brookings Institution (1956, p. 119).

between the prices offered and asked by buyers and sellers of the same good or between the price offered by buyers for a product and that asked by sellers for the necessary resources) and move to capture the difference for themselves through their entrepreneurial buying and selling. Competition, in this process, consists of perceiving possibilities of offering opportunities to other market participants which are more attractive than those currently being made available. It is an essentially *rivalrous* process . . . [which] . . . consists not so much in the regards decisionmakers have for the likely future reactions of their competitors as in their awareness that in making their present decisions they themselves are in a position to do better for the market than their rivals are prepared to do; it consists not of market participants' reacting passively to given conditions, but of their actively grasping profit opportunities by positively changing the existing conditions.

It is this *competitive market process* that can apply to the road industry. Highway entrepreneurs can continually seek newer and better ways of providing services to their customers. There is no reason why street corporations should not actively compete with other such firms for the continued and increased tolls of their patrons. There may not be millions of buyers and sellers of road transport service at each and every conceivable location (nor is there for *any* industry) but this does not preclude vigorous rivalry among the market participants, however many.

How might this work?

Let us consider, for the sake of simplicity, a town laid out into sixty-four blocks, as in a checkerboard (see diagram 3). We can conveniently label the north-south or vertical avenues A through I, and the east-west or horizontal streets first through ninth. If a person wants to travel from the junction of First Street and Avenue A to Ninth Street and Avenue I, there are several paths he may take. He might go east along First Street to Avenue I, and then north along Avenue I, to Ninth Street, a horizontal and then a vertical trip. Or he may first go north to Ninth Street, and then east along Ninth Street to Avenue I. Alternatively, he may follow any number of zig-zag paths: east along First Street to Avenue B; north

Diagram 3

North

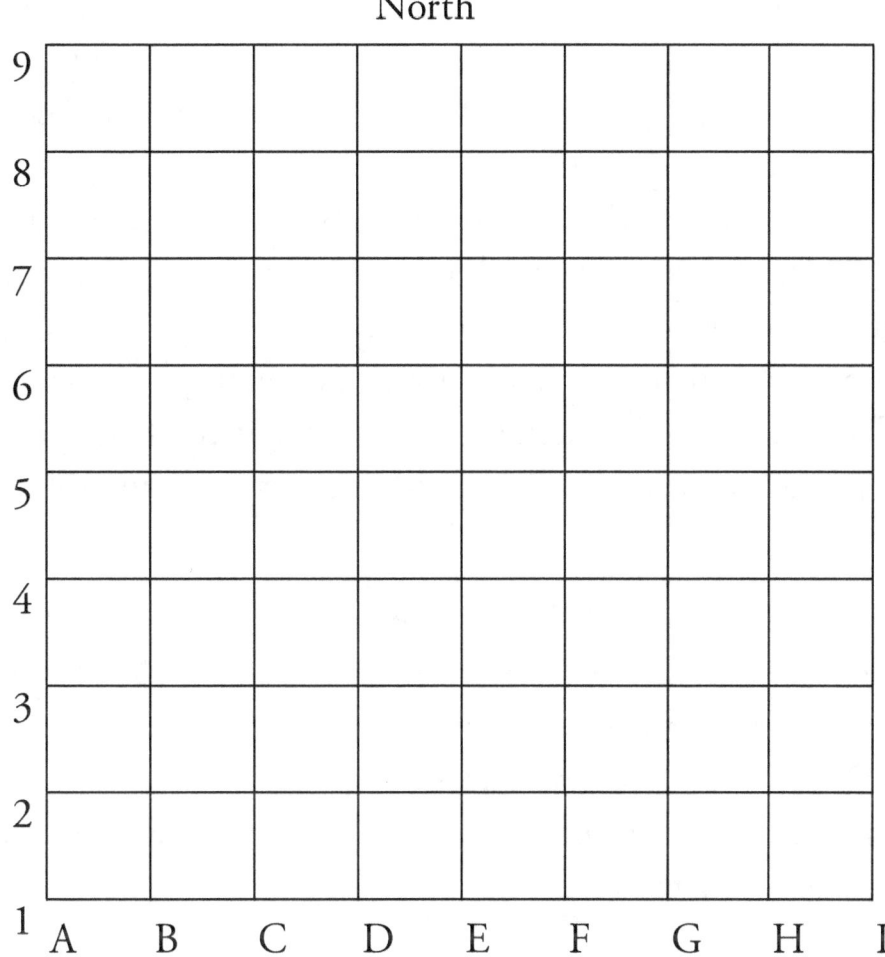

along Avenue B to Second Street; east again, along Second Street to Avenue C; north on C to Third Street . . . etc. Additionally, there are numerous intermediate paths between the pure zig-zag and the one turn.

These possibilities do not open an indefinitely large number of paths, as might be required by the dictates of perfect competition. However, they are sufficiently numerous to serve as the basis for rivalrous competition, where one road entrepreneur, or set of entrepreneurs, seeks to offer better and cheaper channels for transportation than others.

Let us consider the traffic that wishes to go from the junction of First Street and Avenue D to Ninth Street and Avenue D. (Intersections can be seen as whole towns or cities, and streets as actual or potential highways.) If Avenue D is owned by one firm, it might be thought that here, no competition is possible. For the best route is obviously right up Avenue D from First to Ninth Street. Even though this is true, there is still potential competition from Avenues C and E (and even from B and F). If the Avenue D Corporation charges outrageous prices, the customer can use the alternative paths of C or E (or, in a pinch, to B or F, or even A or G, if need be). A second source of potential competition derives, as we have seen, from the possibility of building another road above the road in question, or tunneling beneath it. Consider again, the management of Avenue D, which is charging an outrageously high price. In addition to the competition provided by nearby roads, competition may also be provided by double-, triple-, or quadruple-decking the road.

The transportation literature is not unaware of the possibility of double-decking roads, tunneling, or adding overhead ramps. For example, Wilfred Owens[25] tells us:

> The Port of New York Authority Bus Terminal helps relieve mid-Manhattan traffic congestion. Approximately 90% of intercity bus departures and intercity bus passengers from mid-Manhattan originate at this terminal. The diversion of this traffic on overhead ramps from the terminal to the Lincoln Tunnel has been equivalent to adding three cross-town streets.

John Burchard lauds double-decking as follows:

> On one short span of East River Drive [in New York City] there are grassed terraces carried over the traffic lanes right out to the edge of the East River, a special boon for nearby apartment dwellers. The solution was perhaps triggered by the fact that space between the established building lines and the river was so narrow as to force the *superposition of the north and south lanes*. But this did not do more than suggest the opportunity. Applause goes to those who grasped it, but none to those who with the good example in view so consistently ignored it thereafter. [Emphasis added][26]

From Burchard's limited perspective, it is indeed a mystery that some should have taken this step and that, once it was taken and proven

---

[25] Burchard (1970, p. 245).
[26] Noble (1971, pp. 546–47).

successful, it should not have been emulated. From the vantage point of a market in roads, the mystery disappears: one bureaucrat stumbled, out of necessity, onto a good plan. Having no financial incentive toward cost minimization, no others saw fit to expand this innovation. *On the market,* given that it is economical to double-deck, there will be powerful forces tending toward this result: the profit and loss system.

An authoritative reference to double-decking was made by Charles M. Noble, former Director of the Ohio Department of Highways and chief engineer of the New Jersey Turnpike Authority:

> It seems clear that, ultimately, many urban freeways will become double- or triple-deck facilities, with upper decks carrying the longer distance volumes, possibly with reversible lanes, and probably operating with new interchanges to avoid flooding of existing interchanges and connecting streets.[27]

It is impossible to foretell exactly how this competition via multiple decking might work out in the real world. Perhaps one company would undertake to build and maintain the roads, as well as the bridgework supporting all the different decks. In this scenario, the road deck owner might sublease each individual deck, much in the same way as the builder of a shopping center does not himself run any of the stores, preferring to sublet them to others. Alternatively, the main owner-builder might decide to keep one road for himself, renting out the other levels to different road companies. This would follow the pattern of the shopping center which builds a large facility for itself, but leases out the remainder of the space.

Whatever the pattern of ownership, there would be several, not just one road company in the same "place;" they could compete with each other. If Avenue D, as in our previous example, becomes multiple decked, then traveling from First Street and Avenue D to Ninth Street and Avenue D need not call for a trip along Avenue C or E, in order to take advantage of competition. One might also have the choice between *levels* w, x, y, z, all running over Avenue D!

---

[27] Haritos (1974, p. 57).

Let us consider the objections of Z. Haritos:

> There is joint road consumption by consumers with different demand functions. The road is not as good as steel which may be produced to different specifications of quality and dimensions. The economic characteristics necessitate the production of one kind of road for all users at any given place.[28]

This statement is at odds with what we have just been saying. In our view, the double- or triple-decking of roads *allows* for the production of at least several kinds of road along any given roadway. We would then be forced to reject Haritos's contention. One point of dispute is the equivocation in his use of the word "place."

For in one sense, Haritos is correct. If we *define* "place" as the entity within which two different things cannot possibly exist, then logic forces us to conclude that two different roads cannot exist in the same place. But by the same token, this applies to steel as well. Contrary to Haritos, a road occupies the same logical position as steel. If roads cannot be produced to different specifications of quality and dimensions at any given place, then neither can steel.

But if we reverse matters, and use the word "place" in such a way that two different things (two different pieces of steel, with different specifications) *can* exist in one place (side by side, or close to each other) then steel may indeed be produced to different specifications at any given place, but so may roads! For many different roads, through the technique of multiple decking, can flow along the same pathway, or exist in the same "place."

Another objection charges that competition among roadway entrepreneurs would involve wasteful duplication. Says George M. Smerk: "Competition between public transport companies, particularly public transit firms with fixed facilities, would require an expensive and undesirable duplication of plant."[29]

---

[28] Smerk (1965a, p. 228).

[29] Even if someone intends, for some reason, to purposefully invest in a "losing" proposition, we would still deny, *ex ante*, that he intends to worsen his position. That people act in order to benefit themselves is an axiom of economics. If a person intends to lose *money* through

This is a popular objection to market competition in many areas; railroad "overbuilding," in particular, has received its share of criticism on this score. However, it is fallacious and misdirected.

We must first of all distinguish between investment *ex ante* and *ex post*. In the *ex ante* sense, *all* investment is undertaken with the purpose of earning a profit. Wasteful overbuilding or needless duplication *cannot* exist in the *ex ante* sense; no one intends, at the outset of his investment, that it should be wasteful or unprofitable.[30] *Ex ante* investment must of necessity, be nonwasteful.

Ex post perspective is another matter. The plain fact of our existence is that plans are often met by failure; investments often go awry. From the vantage point of history, an investment may very often be judged unwise, wasteful and needlessly duplicative. But this hardly constitutes a valid argument against private roads! For the point is that *all* investors are liable to error. Unless it is contended that government enterprise is somehow *less* likely to commit error than entrepreneurs who have been continuously tested by the market process of profit and loss, the argument makes little sense. (There are few, indeed, who would be so bold as to make the claim that the government bureaucrat is a better entrepreneur than the private businessman.)

Very often criticisms of the market, such as the charge of wasteful duplication on the part of road owners, stems from a preoccupation with the perfectly competitive model. Looking at the world from this vantage point can be extremely disappointing. The model posits full and perfect information, and in a world of perfect knowledge there of course can be no such thing as wasteful duplication. *Ex post* decisions would be as successful as those *ex ante*. By comparison, in this respect, the real world comes off a distant second best. It is perhaps understandable that a person viewing the real world through perfectly competitive-tinged sunglasses should experience a profound unhappiness with actual investments that turn out to be unwise, or needlessly duplicative.

---

his investment, it could only be because, by so doing, he thinks he will increase his *psychic income* by enough to more than compensate himself for his loss of money. In short, he is engaging in charity.

[30] Roth (1967, p. 63).

Such disappointment, however, is not a valid objection to the road market. What must be rejected is not the sometimes mistaken investment of a private road firm, but rather the perfectly competitive model which has no room in it for human error.

An intermediate position on the possibility of road competition is taken by Gabriel Roth. He states:

> While it is possible to envisage competition in the provision of roads connecting points at great distances apart—as occurred on the railways in the early days—it is not possible to envisage competition in the provision of access roads in towns and villages, for most places are served by one road only. A highway authority is in practice in a monopoly position. If any of its roads were to make large profits, we could not expect other road suppliers to rush in to fill the gap. If losses are made on some roads, there are no road suppliers to close them down and transfer their resources to other sectors of the economy.[31]

Here we find several issues of contention. First, it is a rare small town or village that is served by *only one* road, path, or cattle track. Most places have at least several. But even allowing that in many rural communities there is only one serviceable road, let us note the discrepancy in Roth between roads and other services. Most local towns and villages are also served by only one grocer, butcher, baker, etc. Yet Roth would hardly contend that competition cannot thereby exist in these areas. He knows that, even though there is only one grocer in town, there is potential, if not actual competition from the grocer down the road, or in the next town.

The situation is identical with roads. As we have seen, there is always the likelihood of building another road next to the first, if the established one proves highly popular and profitable. There is also the possibility of building another road above, or tunneling beneath the first road. In addition, competition is also brought in through other transportation *industries.* There may be a trolley line, railroad or subway linking this

---

[31] Mahring (1965, p. 240).

town with the outside world. If there is not, and the first established road is very profitable, such competition is always open in a free market.

Finally, we come to the statement, "If losses are made on some roads, there are no road suppliers to close them down and transfer their resources to other sectors of the economy." We agree, because a road is generally fixed, geographically. An entrepreneur would no more "move" a no longer profitable road, than he would physically move an equivalently unprofitable farm or forest. More importantly, even if it were somehow economically feasible to "move" an unprofitable road to a better locale, there *are* no such road suppliers simply because private road ownership is now *prohibited.*

With Roth's statement, we also come to the spectre of monopoly, and to claims that a private road market must function monopolistically. Why are such claims made? There are two reasons usually given. First, indivisibilities—the fact that many factors of production cannot be efficiently utilized at low levels of output. A steel mill or automobile factory cannot be chopped in half and then be asked to produce one-half of the output it had previously been producing.

Says Mohring, "But indivisibilities do exist in the provision of transportation facilities. Each railroad track must have two rails, and each highway or country road must be at least as wide as the vehicles that use it."[32] In similar vein, says Haritos, "To get from A to B, you need a whole lane, not just half, for the full distance, not half of it."[33] And, in the words of Winch, "indivisibility of highways make it impractical to have competing systems of roads, and the responsible authority must therefore be a monopoly."[34]

We do not believe that the existence of indivisibilities is enough to guarantee monopoly, defined by many as a situation in which there is a single seller of a commodity. There are indivisibilities in *every* industry, and in all walks of life. Hammers and nails, bicycles and wheelbarrows,

---

[32] Haritos (1974, p. 56).

[33] Winch (1963, p. 3).

[34] For an explanation of "monopoly" as a government grant of exclusive privilege, see Rothbard (1962, pp. 586–619).

locomotives and elevators, tractors and steel mills, professors and podiatrists, ballet dancers and bricklayers, musicians and motorists, ships and slippers, buckets and broomsticks, none of them can be chopped in half (costlessly) and be expected to produce just half of what they had been producing before. A railroad needs *two* rails (with the exception, of course, of the monorail), not one, or any fraction thereof. Also, in order to connect points A and B, it must stretch completely from one point to the other. It may not end halfway between them, and offer the likelihood of transportation between the two points.

Does this establish the need for government takeover of railroads? Of course not. Yet they exhibit the concept of indivisibilities just as do roads and highways. If indivisibilities justify government involvement in roadways, then they should justify it in *all* other cases wherein indivisibilities can be found. Since the advocates of the indivisibility argument are not willing to extend it to broomsticks, slippers, steel mills, and practically every other good and commodity under the sun, logic compels them to retract it in the case of highways.

Conclusion

So what do we conclude? Having debunked the notion that private ownership of the roads is not "impossible," and that, in fact, it may offer a variety of exciting alternatives to the present system, we return to the question of why should it even be considered. There we come face-to-face again with the problem of safety. A worse job than that which is presently being done by the government road managers is difficult to envision. We need only consider what transpires when safety is questioned in other forms of transportation to see a corollary. When an airline experiences an accident, it often experiences a notable dropping off of passengers. Airlines with excellent safety records, who have conducted surveys, have found that the public is aware of safety and will make choices based upon it.

Similarly, private road owners will be in a position to establish regulations and practices to assure safety on their roads. They can impact on the driver, the vehicle, and the road—the key elements of highway safety. They can react more quickly than the government bureaucracy in banning such vehicles as "exploding Pintos." The overriding problem with the National Highway Traffic Safety Administration, and with all similar governmental systems of insuring against vehicle defects, for example, is that there is no competition allowed. Again, in a free market system, opportunities would open up for innovative approaches to safety problems. Should stiffer penalties be shown unsuccessful in reducing unsafe vehicles and practices, an incentive system may be the answer. We cannot paint all the details of the future from our present vantage point. But we do know that "there has to be a better way."

8 Public Goods and Externalities: The Case of Roads

When government monopolization of the roadways is discussed by economists, the "externalities" argument is usually raised. The argument is said to be simple, clear, and irrefutable. In fact, none of these terms really apply. Let us consider the argument closely.

The externalities argument is based upon a distinction between private goods and services, the use of which benefits only the consumer in question, and public or collective goods, consumption of which necessarily affects the welfare of third or "external" parties. For example, externalities are said to exist when Mr. A paints his house and neighboring householders benefit as a result.[1] Housepainting is contrasted with completely private goods such as bread, which adds to the well-being of only those who purchase and consume it.

The distinction is often made in terms of excludability: in the case of private goods, the consumer is able to exclude all others from the benefits; in the case of public goods, he is not, and so some of the benefits

---

Reprinted with kind permission of the Ludwig von Mises Institute from *Journal of Libertarian Studies* 7, no. 1 (1983): 1–34.

[1] Externalities are usually separated into external economies (positive externalities) and external diseconomies (negative externalities). Although considered by most economists as virtually the same (i.e., as merely opposite sides of the same coin), in our view positive and negative externalities are conceptually different and in need of separate treatment. See Rothbard (1990, pp. 55–99).

"spill over" onto third parties. A typical textbook makes the point in the following way:

> For a good, service, or factor to be "exclusive," everyone but the buyer of the good must be excluded from the satisfaction it provides. A pair of socks, for example, is a good which is consistent with the exclusion principle. When you buy the socks, it is you alone who gets the satisfaction from wearing them, no one else. On the other hand, a shot for diphtheria is a "commodity" which is not subject to the exclusion principle. While the person inoculated surely get(s) benefits from having the shot, the benefit is not exclusively his. Having become immune to the disease, he can't communicate it to other people. They cannot be excluded from the benefit of the shot even though they do not pay for it and even though the person receiving the shot cannot charge them for it.[2]

Even at this introductory level an objection must be made. There are any number of external economies, neighborhood effects, spillovers, benefits to third parties, which flow from the purchase and use of supposedly private goods. Take, for example, the paradigm case of a private good, socks. First, there is a health question. People who do not wear socks are liable to colds, sore feet, blisters, and possibly pneumonia. And sickness means lost days of work and lost production; it means possible contagion (as in the diphtheria case); it may result in rising doctor bills and increased health insurance premiums for other policyholders. Increased demand for doctors' time and energy will result in reduced medical attention for others. There is, in addition, an aesthetic problem: many people take umbrage at socklessness. Restaurants often forbid bare feet, presumably in the interests of retaining their more sensitive customers. Not wearing socks is also interpreted by some as a disturbing political statement, like flag or

---

2 Haveman (1970, p. 25), Bish and Warren (1972, pp. 97–122) define public goods in terms of excludability: "Public or collective goods in economic terminology are 'nonpackageable;' that is, in principle, no one can be excluded from consuming them."

draft-card burning. Many mothers—a third party, if ever there was one—rejoice when their "hip" sons finally don footwear. That benefits of sock-wearing "spill over" to these mothers cannot be denied.

The problem is by no means limited to the socks example, for all so-called private goods affect second or third parties in some way. The reader is challenged to think of any item the use and purchase of which is not affected with a public interest, i.e., which does not similarly have spill-over effects on other people.

Misguided though the definition may be, the externalities argument still has strong influence. Many economists continue to claim that to the extent that externalities are present, "market imperfections" are created and government action is justified to remedy the situation.

External Economies

Leaving aside these objections for the time being, let us consider the externalities argument as it applies to roadways. The argument assumes that roadways are an instance of positive externalities. Any entrepreneur who constructs a road will have to bear all the costs (of labor, materials, etc.), just as in any business, but since highways are an external economy, he will be unable to reap rewards proportional to the benefits provided. For example, benefits would spill over to those who own land near the highways, in the form of increased value (i.e., the road builder cannot charge the beneficiaries for these gains). Other benefits would be enjoyed, for free, by people who simply prefer more and more highways. Nor could the road owner exclude from increased benefits those who gain from the resulting cheaper transport in the form of lower prices for shipped merchandise.

The claim is that private road builders, responsible for all of the costs but only partially compensated (through fee charges) for providing the benefits, would underinvest. The marginal dollar, therefore, would have a higher return in highway investment (were all benefits to be considered) than it would in alternative outlets.

This argument is sometimes put forth in terms of social and private returns. Private returns—the difference between the outlay and revenue which accrue entirely to the individual entrepreneur—are said to be lower than social returns—the difference between the costs and the benefits for society as a whole. In both cases, the builder—whether an individual business or society as a whole—must pay the full costs of the highway; but it is possible only for society as a whole to derive the full benefits. The entrepreneur, being limited to the tolls he can collect, is unable to capture the gains in terms of increased land values, etc., which spill over onto the remainder of the population.

Given this alleged tendency of the market to underinvest in highways, the argument from externalities concludes that it is the government's obligation to correct matters by subsidizing road building, or, more likely, by building roads itself. Consider the following argument made by Bonavia:

> The extreme *laissez faire* doctrine of noninterference by the State depends upon the assumption that social and private net returns are identical—that self-interest is equated with the common weal.
>
> We are only concerned here with one aspect of positive intervention by the State—namely, through investment in transport. It is clear . . . that the object of State investment is to secure output of a kind whose private net returns are lower than its social net returns, and which accordingly tends to be less than it would be under ideal conditions. A railway, for example, may yield high prospective social returns, and yet, in a community chronically short of capital, offer lower private returns than other industries. The State may then find it advisable to invest the communities' resources in railway construction.[3]

This argument is erroneous, for its conclusion does not follow from its premises. Even if we accept the view that private road ownership will indeed result in underinvestment, it does not logically follow that government must step into the breach and make up the deficit.

---

[3] Bonavia (1954, pp. 48–49). Consider also this statement: "Transportation almost always involves rather strong . . . externalities of one sort or another, so that unsubsidized private operation involves necessarily higher prices, in order to break even, than would be conducive to the most efficient utilization of the facilities" (private correspondence, September 6 1977, from William Vickrey to the present author).

The contention that government should involve itself with the private economy is a moral conclusion, one that can be reached only if there are ethical arguments in the premises. But the science of economics must of necessity be value-free.[4] Therefore, no strictly economic argument can ever establish the legitimacy of government intervention into the economic sphere.

Can we interpret the argument as leading to the conclusion that, since the market will underinvest, given externalities, government action will correct the misallocation of resources by adding to the mileage of road construction? This will not work either. On the one hand, the addition of government investment in roads may decrease the amount of private investment,[5] so that the total amount of road building, private plus public, may fall below the previously established market level and thus worsen the so-called original underinvestment in roads. On the other hand, government, unshackled by any market test of profitability, may so expand the scope of road building that a resultant overinvestment may ensue. If so, a new misallocation will emerge, with an overinvestment substituted for an underinvestment. Further, even if government action results in the correct amount of total road mileage, government management of its domain may be so inept as to erase any allocation gains. If any of these eventualities obtains, and there is little reason to think not, then the argument fails.

There is another flaw in Bonavia's view: his notion of a "chronic shortage of capital." Economies are always short of capital in the sense that people would prefer to have more; this is because capital is an economic good. If capital is not in short supply, it becomes a free good, or a general condition of human welfare, and thus is not amenable to economic analysis. If, however, "chronic shortage of capital" is meant to distinguish poor from wealthy economics, then it is irrelevant to the issue of externalities. The presence of neighborhood spill-overs has to

---

[4] See Rothbard (1962, p. 883). Also Block (1975).

[5] Whenever government competes in the market, it has a chilling effect on private investment in that area, for the government can underwrite its losses out of tax proceeds, and a market enterprise cannot. In this paper we assume the plausibility of a private market in road building. For further explication, see Block (1979, pp. 209–38).

do only with whether third parties are affected, and they will occur or fail to occur regardless of the wealth of a society.

The externalities argument for governmental roads, although widely acclaimed in the modern era, is by no means recent. On the contrary, it is a hoary tradition. Jackman, writing of England in the mid-1830s, referred to the argument "that [only] those who used the roads should [financially] sustain them," saying:

> But the fact is that it was not alone the carriers, but the public as a whole, that reaped the benefits from good roads, and therefore the upkeep of the roads should not be a charge upon those who used the road, but upon the public treasury, for all derived the advantages from them. It was, therefore, inevitable that in time the turnpike gates should be taken down and a more equitable method adopted to secure the end desired.[6]

The American Henry Clay wrote that it is

> very possible that the capitalist who should invest his money in [turnpikes] might not be reimbursed three per cent annually upon it; and yet society, in its various forms, might actually reap fifteen or twenty percent. The benefit resulting from a turnpike road made by private associations is divided between the capitalist who receives his toll, the land through which it passes, and which is augmented in its value, and the commodities whose value is enhanced by the diminished expense of transportation.[7]

The major flaw in the externalities argument is, as we have seen, the fact that it is vulnerable to a *reductio ad absurdum*, for indeed there is precious little (if anything) that is not an example of an externality. And unless we are willing to follow the internal logic of the argument and hold that government is justified in taking control of practically every aspect of our economy, we must, perforce, pull back from the conclusions of the argument from neighborhood effects.

---

[6] Jackman (1916, p. 261).
[7] Cited in Wooldridge (1970, p. 129).

Gabriel Roth wrote the following concerning external economies:

It is sometimes suggested that roads should not be charged for because they provide "external economies," that is, benefits to the community which cannot in principle be recouped from road users. For example, it is said that the construction of the Severn Bridge will stimulate economic activity in South Wales, that the benefits from this increased activity cannot be reflected in the tolls collected on the bridge, and that therefore there is no point in charging a toll.

While this argument is good as far as it goes, it applies in the case of all intermediate goods and services. There is no reason to suppose that the benefit to the community from a new or improved means of transport is greater than the benefit from an improved supply of electricity or steel. Unless it can be shown that roads are a special case, the "external economies" argument ... in the case of roads becomes a general argument for subsidizing *all intermediate goods and services.*[8,9]

Shorey Peterson is another economist who seems to understand this point, though he is reluctant to accept its full implications:

Actually it is easy to endow much of private industry with great collective significance, if one is so inclined. There is no greater social interest than in having the population well fed and housed.

---

[8] Roth (1967, pp. 20–21).

[9] Roth unfortunately contradicts himself several pages later. Even though he is unwilling to accept the implication that government becomes involved in the production of all "intermediate goods and services," he states: "As roads benefit nonmotorists by providing facilities for pedestrians and cyclists, and access to properties of different kinds, there is a logical case for charging nonmotorists for the use of the roads" (p. 43). There would be no problem for Roth if the nonmotorist he advocated as liable for tolls were limited to cyclists and pedestrians. Although they are certainly nonmotorists, it is no less sure that these two groups do use the roads. This interpretation will not do, however, for Roth raises this point specifically in order to justify property taxes as a source of road funding. But property taxes are paid by landowners, who are not to be confused with motorists, pedestrians, or cyclists (although there is obviously an overlap). In basing road charges on property ownership, Roth is using the very externality argument which he had earlier seemed to reject.

The steel industry is vital to national defense. Railroads perform the specific social functions credited to highways. The point is that, in a society such as ours in which an individualistic economic organization is generally approved, it is usually deemed sufficient that an industry should develop in response to the demands of specific beneficiaries, and that the social benefits should be accepted as a sort of byproduct. If the steel industry, spurred by ordinary demand, expands sufficiently for defense purposes, further development because of the defense aspect would be wasteful . . .

Thus if highways, when developed simply in response to traffic needs, serve adequately the several general interests mentioned above, no additional outlay because of these interests is warranted.[10]

On one hand this is a very welcome statement, for it clearly sets forth the thesis that the externalities argument for government intervention into the highway industry must be opposed. If we were to allow state takeovers in all areas with "great collective significance," there would scarcely be any private enterprise left in our "individualistic economic" system.

On the other hand, Peterson seems unable to carry through his own logic. In the sentence omitted from the above quote, he states: "But if, as in the case of the American merchant marine, the ordinary demand is not believed to bring forth what some collective purpose requires, additional investment on the former account is indicated." He thus denies practically everything he stated before, for there will always be some "collective purpose" which "requires" additional investment on the part of the state because of externalities. If additional state investments in the American merchant marine are indeed indicated for "collective purposes," even though it is now as large as voluntary payments

---

[10] Peterson (1950, p. 196). See also Mohring (1965). Mohring states that "the aesthetic, humanitarian, and other 'nonmarket benefit' arguments that are often used to justify subsidies to such areas as education, research, and the arts seem to apply little to transportation" (pp. 231–32).

from satisfied customers would make it, then why is not a governmental takeover of the food and housing industries warranted? After all, there is no question, as Peterson himself has pointed out, that food and housing are imbued with the public, collective interest.

William Baumol is one who does not seem to be aware of this problem. In fact he carries the externality argument to almost ludicrous lengths in contending that population growth, of and by itself, is a justification for increasing the scope of government operations because of the neighborhood effects it brings in its wake.

> Thus, increasing population adds to the significance and degree of diffusion of the external effects of the actions of all inhabitants of the metropolis, and thereby requires increasing intervention by the public sector to assure that social wants are supplied and that externalities do not lead to extremely adverse effects on the community's welfare.
>
> Indeed, the very growth of population itself involves external effects. New residents usually require the provision of additional services and facilities—water, sewage, disposal, road paving, etc., and this is likely to be paid for in part out of the general municipal budget.[11]

The obvious question that cries out for an answer is: Why should we single out government services tinged with externalities, such as water, sewage, and road paving, as examples of areas requiring growth, given population increases? Why not also include services and goods that are usually forthcoming on private markets? As we have learned from Peterson, "There is no greater social interest than in having the population well fed and housed." It surely cannot be denied that a lack of food and shelter will create all sorts of negative externalities. Were a population to be deprived of these necessities, disease, famine, and death would soon appear, commerce would grind to a halt, and the economy, indeed the very society, out of which all external benefits flow, would soon end. How can it be, then, that an increase in population does not

---

[11] Baumol (1963, p. 8).

create the need for government takeovers of the farming and housing industries, to mention only two, even before the stepped-up and continued nationalization of such paltry things as sewage and paving, as called for by Baumol? Can it be because we have all witnessed the doubling, redoubling, and doubling again of the U.S. population, since the level attained in the 1770s, with no apparent harm to the nation's farms or construction firms, externalities notwithstanding? Can it be that we are simply unused to the idea of a market in road paving, water, and sewage? Such shall be our contention.[12]

The unique power of the *reductio ad absurdum* is that it casts doubts on the externalities argument, as used by Baumol, Roth, and Peterson. If a nationalized industry can be justified on the basis of externalities, but this phenomenon applies as well to areas where no one wants to see the spread of government enterprise, then one may question just how seriously its advocates take their own argument. They cannot have it both ways. Either externalities justify state enterprise on roads and in practically every other industry as well, or they justify it in no case. It is completely illogical to apply an argument in one case and to fail to apply it in all other cases in which it is just as relevant.[13]

---

[12] For the same logical error, although presented with a slight variation of emphasis, see Smerk (1965a), where he states:

> External economies abound from the provision of transport. In other words, there are many gains and costs which are not realized in pecuniary terms by the enterprise in question, since by its very nature transport confers substantial benefits upon nonusers. Assuming operation of public transport to reflect the general interests of the public, transport output therefore seems most justifiably geared to a point of equality between social costs and benefits rather than strict and sole adherence to the forces of the market as expressed in purely pecuniary terms. (p. 63)

Assuming, however, operation of merry-go-rounds to reflect the general interests of the public, and assuming also, as is the case, that these mechanisms, too, are replete with external benefits, does it follow that merry-go-round output therefore seems most justifiably geared to public rather than private enterprise? If so, then it would seem that there is nothing that cannot be claimed for government operation.

[13] It would be consistent, although nonsensical, to accept the externality argument in favor of government road monopoly—and nationalization of all other industries wherein externalities obtain—as well. For opposing positions, however, the reader might consult Hayek's *The Road to Serfdom* and *Collectivist Economic Planning*, and three books by Ludwig von Mises, *Bureaucracy*, *Planning for Freedom*, and *Human Action*.

External Diseconomies

One phenomenon that particularly infuriates those who see externalities as a justification for intervention is the fact that, under congested road conditions, each additional motorist imposes extra costs on all others, costs which he does not take fully into account, resulting in uneconomic use of resources. Roth states the problem as follows:

> The level of traffic flow will depend on decisions taken by individuals taking account of the costs and benefits to them associated with road use. But from the point of view of the traffic as a whole this is an unsatisfactory state of affairs, for the individual road user when making his decision does not—indeed he cannot—take into account the costs imposed by him on others. He assesses his private costs but ignores the road use, congestions and community costs. It follows that so long as the volume of traffic in conditions of congestion is determined by each road user considering only his own costs and benefits, traffic volumes will be larger, and costs higher, than is socially desirable.[14]

And A.A. Walters expresses it this way:

> Under congested conditions an additional vehicle journey will add to the congestion. The vehicle will get in the way of other vehicles using the road and will cause their costs to increase as they waste more time in traffic jams and incur higher maintenance costs per mile in the dense traffic. Thus the decision by a vehicle owner to use a congested highway involves all other users in increased operating costs.[15]

---

[14] Roth (1967, p. 34). Haveman (1970, p. 34) writes the following:

> When the next semi-truck pulls onto the freeway with the effect of delaying your arrival and that of all other freeway motorists, you and your fellow drivers are the objects of a spill-over cost. It is characteristic that . . . the person harmed bears identifiable "costs" for which he is not compensated. Moreover . . . this person would be willing to pay something to avoid bearing the spill-over cost.

[15] Walters (1968, p. 11).

Unquestionably, under present conditions motorists do indeed ignore the costs they impose on other drivers with respect to overcrowding. Frequently a driver takes account of congestion costs imposed on him by others in that he tries to avoid being ensnared in tie-ups if possible. But to suggest that a commuter would refrain from traveling out of fear of slowing down others is ludicrous. The traffic jams endemic to urban rush hours are eloquent testimony to this fact.

Why does such antisocial behavior take place on our highways, and not in other areas where it might be expected? The reason is that our roadway network is in a state of chaotic nonownership, run by the government, while other settings in which such behavior might be expected, but does not appear, are run by private enterprise.

We can ask, for example, why it is that economists of the Roth-Walters-Haveman stamp never spare a worry about moviegoers who impose crowding costs on others? Why do not the "externality economists" wax eloquent in describing the individual moviegoer (or opera patron, punk rock devotee, supermarket shopper, hotel patron, department store customer, airplane traveler, or indeed any person who utilizes a resource which is actively sought by many others at the same time) who shows callous disregard for the costs he imposes on others?

One reason is that the institution of private property[16] is allowed to function in these other areas, so that the so-called externalities can be internalized. Externalities are said to be internalized when A, the source of the externality, and B, the recipient, interact on privately owned property, and can be appropriately penalized or compensated for the externalities through fees imposed by C, the owner. In the case of nonownership of the roads, which presently obtains, each additional driver, A, imposes congestion costs on all other drivers, B, and there is little or no reason for A to desist. But if the road were privately owned, then it would be possible (and indeed profitable) for the owner, C, to reduce negative externalities such as crowding, by raising charges for rush-hour

---

[16] If the government charged a price for highway use, such a user fee might deter congestion and lead motorists, in effect, to take account of the congestion costs they impose on others. For an analysis of why a privately owned road system is preferable even to a government pricing mechanism, see Block (1979).

use. C's profit potentialities are in direct proportion to the smooth functioning of the roads, and the fewer the negative externalities, the more attractive will his place of business be, and the more he can charge for additional amenities.

This relation may be difficult to perceive in the case of roads, for we are not accustomed to thinking of roads in terms of private ownership. Let us consider, then, an example which will make the process clearer. A loudmouthed swaggering drunkard is an external diseconomy on a public (unowned) street. He frightens passers-by, but as long as he does not violate any law, no incentive to forbear is placed upon him. Let this same worthy put in an appearance in a nightclub, however, and he is no longer an external effect on his fellow customers. He no longer can adversely affect them and expect to be free of countersanctions. He has now been transformed into an "internal" financial liability to the night-club owner. It is no longer true that A can act without "tak[ing] into account these costs imposed by him on others," for C, as the owner of the premises, has the lawful right to force A to take account of these impositions, by throwing him off the premises if need be. In the private club, the victims (B) of A's unsavory actions cease to bear the complete burden. Though they are the initial sufferers of A's excesses, it is the work of a moment to depart for greener nightclub pastures. The real loser is C, who stands to lose not only revenue, but his entire investment, should his nightclub become known as one that tolerates the likes of A. The existence of bouncers and private guards shows that nightclub owners take seriously the threat of external diseconomies offered by the drunkards of the world.

The drive-in movie furnishes us with a case in which external economies were successfully internalized. When pornographic films were first shown at outdoor theaters adjacent to highways, they created quite a stir. Row after row of tractor-trailers were seen parked at the shoulders of roads, their operators perched atop their cabs to view without paying admission. These spectators, B, received the positive externality (namely, the view of the screen) from A, the theater owners. Had this situation been permitted to continue, it might have created an under-investment in outdoor theaters, compared with the case in which all spectators were forced to pay admission. Needless to say, it did not long continue. In quite short order the owners in question erected higher fences, forcing all those who valued the view to pay for it. No longer was A conferring a benefit on B, unable to charge him for it. With the advent of the fence, the truck drivers' free view was cut off. The choice open to B was to see the movie and pay for it, or to not pay and not watch. If nonexcludability is the hallmark of the externality, then the ability to exclude nonpayers from the benefits, as here afforded by the fence, is the key to the internalization.

The objection has been raised that a private market in roads would result in underinvestment because the private developers would not be able to reap benefits of their efforts associated with increased land values and lowered costs of transporting goods. Rejecting free enterprise, most economists call instead for increased property taxes on the increased site value of land abutting a highway by the amount of gain attributable to the increased benefits conferred on the property by the road.[17] As we have seen, however, this argument is without merit. External benefits do not lead to underinvestment. On the contrary, the prospective road builder can recoup the gains by internalizing the potential externality. The ease with which this can be done is evident when we reflect upon the fact that, before the actual building process begins, the entrepreneur is the only one who knows where the road is scheduled to be located (or even that a road is intended to be built at all). All the prospective builder need do is buy up territory likely to gain in value from his road at the old, low prices, which do not reflect the increased values likely to be imparted by the highway.[18]

The logic of this argument is not lost upon mainstream economists. For example, Cooper perceptively states:

---

[17] Winch (1963, p. 130), for example, calls for "taxes aimed to recoup from property owners the costs of the road attributable to the traffic which has conferred benefits on that property."

[18] He may not be able or even willing to purchase all of the land that may conceivably be benefited from his construction, but this will not affect the viability of private roads any more than will the advent of helicopters, able to see over even the highest of fences, win the possibility of a private market in outdoor movies.

In the immediate vicinity of a transportation corridor, urban land values tend to increase at a much higher rate from the beginning of facility construction until some time after the facility is in operation. Increases that are more than double or even triple the prevailing growth rate are common. A strong rationale exists for public rather than private realization of this increase in land value. It is argued that, because the taxpayers' money earned the increment, the taxpayers should receive the return. This rationale could justify the purchase of a right of way somewhat wider than needed for actual facility construction, thereby achieving greater flexibility with respect to mode choice and design.[19]

The only problem with this statement, from our point of view, is that Cooper ignores the possibility that the capitalist, too, could purchase "a right of way somewhat wider than needed for actual facility construction." If there is any question about which institution, private enterprise or government, would be better able to predict which land would benefit, and to keep plans in secret until the actual purchase was made, etc., there seems little doubt that the market would win hands down. The profit and loss test alone should ensure this.

However, the problem goes deeper. It is widely claimed that the market cannot function, given external economies. It is then argued that the government could act so as to dispel the positive externalities. *A fortiori*, we must conclude, the market can also internalize these externalities, and more effectively to boot.

The "Evil" Free Rider

The indictment against private ownership of roads is sometimes reversed. Instead of the highway owner being accused of not building enough, the nonhighway-user who benefits without cost is castigated as a "free rider" who "refuses" to pay for the benefits he receives. But certainly he has not asked for these benefits, and in no case can it be alleged that he has contracted for them.

---

[19] Cooper (1971, p. 23).

Let us now consider the gains imparted to the consumers of final goods who benefit because goods can now be more easily shipped. If too large a proportion of the benefits created by the highway are provided free of charge, consumers will gain from lower-priced goods, but a private concern may be unable to cover its costs. But through the advent of externality internalization, the road owner will receive payment for the benefits he is providing. The process is simple. All that the road owner need do is charge a price for highway usage roughly conformable to the savings in transport fees created by the facility. The road will still benefit its users (the shippers) and their customers (the final consumers), but there will be no benefits seeping out, or spilling over, as it were, for "free." Such benefits will be paid for, given a price that makes it still profitable for a trucker to use the road. This point is made by Brownlee and Heller as follows:

> That highways may cut transportation costs undoubtedly is true; but this truth does not warrant special taxes for highways purpose levied against persons who do not use the highways. Insofar as truckers pay for using the highways, those persons not directly using the highways can help pay highway costs indirectly through the price system. If appropriate charges for highway use were levied against the military, nonusers would also pay indirectly for the highways from general tax funds spent by them for highway services. The alleged benefits of highways to those who do not use them directly are primarily illusions arising from failure to charge highway users appropriately for the services provided by the highway system.[20]

Without this insight, one might assume that highways necessarily involve the creation of an external benefit by the road-building company to the advantage of the rest of the public. According to this reasoning, to the extent that highways are important for the national defense effort, the population at large gains a measure of security from them. But the Brownlee-Heller statement shows this argument to be false, for if the military, like anyone else, were required to pay for (potential) road use,

---

[20] Brownlee and Heller (1956, p. 236).

then roads would be no more of a positive externality than shoes, lead, paper, or any other material used by the army.

The Hrownlee-Heller statement has not gone unchallenged, however, in the economic literature. According to William D. Ross:

> The highway users cannot theoretically or practically be assessed the fill cost of providing low traffic volume connecting highways and access roads and streets. Some of the benefits of such roads are realized in forms other than the direct use of these roads, but the benefits are more than "illusions arising from failure to charge highway users appropriately for the services provided by the highway system." Some nonhighway-user revenues are necessary if adequate support for highway improvements is to be provided.[21]

But Ross's response is unsatisfactory. He fails to cite any theoretical reason why the overwhelming majority of benefits (or at least enough to make road building profitable) cannot be captured in revenue to the private road owner. We have seen how the entrepreneur would be able to capture the increased values of land by purchase at the old, lower prices. And the same principle can be applied to other important sources of externalities. Nor has Ross succeeded in countering the Brownlee-Heller contention that a price charged for highway use would end the free benefits provided to those who use roads indirectly. Indeed, he ignores this point.

Ross does point out a practical problem:

> As a practical matter, utility of service or value of service cannot be used as a basis for pricing highway services to the highway user except in the very limited case of toll roads. But modern innovations in electronic counting mechanisms and computers have taken the force out of this argument, if it was ever valid. We must conclude that the external benefits in this case are, in the words of Brownlee and Heller, "illusions arising from failure to charge highway users appropriately for the services provided by the highway system."

---

[21] Ross, *ibid.*, p. 257.

Let us take a quite different case. An attractive woman sauntering down the street in a miniskirt provides an external benefit.[22] She is a delight to other pedestrians, yet she is unable to charge them for these viewing pleasures.[23] The recipients, according to the theory, however, are the "free riders," who benefit without paying their "fair share" of the costs. Ought they to be forced to pay? Although examples cited by the advocates of the view that free riders ought to be made to pay for benefits received are usually far more sober, the miniskirt case is perfectly analogous. In all cases, the so-called free rider's benefits come to him unsolicited. If it is ludicrous to insist that he pay for an uninvited view of a woman's legs, it is equally so to insist that he be charged, via tax payments, for the losses accompanying "transport of all types."[24] And to call such forced payment "justified," as is often done, is to be guilty of a clear violation of "wertfrei" or value-free economics. No value judgments whatsoever logically follow from strictly economic postulates. Since we are here concerned only with what economics, not ethics, can teach us, we do not consider the question of what, if anything, would justify the extraction of coercive payments from free riders. We must content ourselves with the observation that the receipt of unsolicited services certainly cannot do so.

If the free-rider argument were really valid, it would open up a Pandora's box of truly monumental proportions. For example, a hoodlum could approach anyone walking along some street, smile at him,[25] and then ask the recipient of the smile for a payment of any arbitrary

---

[22] To most males, that is. In the eyes of competitive women, homosexuals, perhaps, and strict, fundamentalist clergymen, presumably, she is anything but. (We deal on page 177 with the question of one man's meat being another's poison.)

[23] Even such an externality can be internalized by the ever watchful and vigilant marketplace. For an account of how this is accomplished by the management of Maxwell's Plum restaurant, in New York City, see *New York* magazine. March 1978, and for a similar account involving Sardi's restaurant, see *United* magazine, November 1982.

[24] Smerk (1965a, p. 230) writes: "As the general public benefits from an increased supply of transport of all types, tax receipts from the general public may with justice be used to make up losses."

[25] Or do anything else, whatsoever, that could theoretically be interpreted as being of benefit to the free rider. Remember, it has not been proven that the free rider must admit to being a beneficiary. Smerk and other writers have been willing merely to assume that the general public benefits from an increased supply of transport.

amount (for the value of the benefit that the free rider supposedly enjoys has not been established by any proponent of this view). If the honest burgher refuses to pay, the hoodlum has as much (or as little) right to force him to do so as does Smerk, or his agents, the government, to compel the average citizen to pay for the benefits he receives from "transport of all types."

The so-called free-rider problem would not be limited, however, to such fanciful examples, for our lives are riddled with such phenomena. As Murray Rothbard has written:

> The difficulty with this argument is that it proves far too much. For which one of us would earn anything like our present real income were it not for external benefits that we derive from the actions of others? Specifically, the great modern accumulation of capital goods is an inheritance from all the net savings of our ancestors. Without them, we would, regardless of the quality of our own moral character, be living in a primitive jungle. The inheritance of money capital from our ancestors is, of course, simply inheritance of shares in this capital structure. *We are all, therefore, free riders on the past. We are also free riders on the present*, because we benefit from the continuing investment of our fellow men and from their specialized skills on the market. Certainly the vast bulk of our wages, if they could be so imputed, would be due to this heritage on which we are free riders. The landowner has no more of an unearned increment than any one of us. Are all of us to suffer confiscation, therefore, and to be taxed for our happiness? And who then is to receive the loot? Our dead ancestors who were our benefactors in investing the capital?[26] [Emphasis added]

Public Goods

Another line of attack on the possibility of a free market in roads is that centered around the concept of "public" or "collective" goods. A pure public good is defined by Haritos as one, such as an outdoor circus, or

---

[26] Rothbard (1962, pp. 888–89).

national defense, "which all enjoy in common in the sense that each individual's consumption of such goods leads to no subtraction from any other individual's consumption of that good."[27] The polar opposite of this is the pure "private consumption good, like bread, whose total can be parcelled out among two or more persons, with one man having a loaf less if another gets a loaf more."[28]

Samuelson acknowledges the polar aspects of this partition of goods: "Obviously I am introducing a strong polar case. . . . The careful empiricist will recognize that many—though not all—of the realistic cases of government activity can be fruitfully analyzed as some kind of a blend of these two extreme polar cases"[29] As we saw in the case of the socks, there is no clear dividing line between the two categories and, furthermore, no criteria by which the disinterested observer can objectively distinguish between a private good, a public good, and a blend of the two. Let us consider three examples.

First, to the extent that bread is a source of external economies it is a public good, rather than a private one, since these external benefits are "enjoyed by all in common." In other words, while the bread itself may be a private good in that if one person has more, someone else necessarily has less, the bread plus its inseparable neighborhood effects is a collective good, since the externalities from the bread that benefit Mr. D do not in any way subtract from those enjoyed by Mr. E. Mr. D's gain from the externalities, again in Haritos's words, "leads to no subtraction from any other individual's consumption of that good."

Second, contrary to what might be assumed, an outdoor circus need not be a collective good at all. If a fence is placed around the festivities and a charge is levied for admission, the external benefits will no longer seep out onto the general public. In addition, if no one in the neighborhood likes circuses, then it is not a good at all. However, if so many people like circuses that crowding results, then it will not be true that one person's enjoyment of the spectacle will not detract from another's.

---

[27] Haritos (1974, p. 54).

[28] Samuelson (1955, p. 350).

[29] *Ibid.*

Rather, in the press for a good view, one person's good position will necessarily entail a poor one, or none at all, for another.[30]

A third case, national defense, is one of the reddest of red herrings. This case is of such wide renown and so hoary with tradition that it has gone almost completely unchallenged. But, in fact, national defense does not fit well with the definition of a public good. One problem stems from differing tastes: not everyone views national defense in the same light. In the words of Rothbard, "an absolute pacifist, a believer in total nonviolence, living in the [sheltered] area, would not consider himself protected . . . or [as] receiving defense service."[31] Far from being a collective good, so-called defense would be considered a liability. Furthermore, defense protection is supplied through the intermediation of physical tangible goods and services which are very certainly limited in supply—if one person or locale has more of them, another must have less. According to Rothbard: "A ring of defense bases around New York, for example, cuts down the amount possibly available around San Francisco."[32]

Furthermore, contrary to the definition of public goods, the positive external effects of national defense can be largely internalized. While it might not be possible to exclude all nonpayers from protection, there is no evidence indicating that internalization could not be made to work reasonably well.

How might this work? We might divide the country into sections according to the alacrity with which most people in an area are likely to welcome a private defense agency dedicated to their protection from foreign enemies. Thus, Orange County, California, parts of Arizona, the far West, and the old South might be considered highly interested in safeguarding their liberties in such manner. Mid-Pennsylvania, home of the pacifistic Mennonites, Amish, and other Pennsylvania Dutch peoples, along with the Upper West Side of Manhattan, and Ann Arbor, Michigan, strongholds of liberalism and anti-war sentiment, would very

---

[30] On this point, see Enke (1955, pp. 131–33), Margolis (1955, pp. 247–49), and Tiebout (1956, p. 417).

[31] Rothbard (1962, p. 884).

[32] *Ibid.*, p. 885.

likely be lukewarm in their reception of such an enterprise. The rest of the country would fall somewhere in between these two extremes.

One manner of internalization of the externalities, on what we might call the "macro level," would be the use of restrictive covenants. People could simply refuse to sell their homes (or rent their apartments) to those who would not agree, and also hold all future owners to agree, to a contract calling for payments to a defense company. Although there might be a few holdouts and recluses, most people in these areas would soon find it in their interest to subscribe. And in the same manner, the areas of the country with a less developed preference for such services would tend to have commensurately less defense provision.

On what might be called the "micro level," the defense company might at some point announce that those who had not paid for service would no longer be protected by its personnel. The company would, of course, continue to protect their own dues-paying members, and indiscriminate attacks on the neighborhood would be repelled. Any attacks which interfered with paying customers would be liable to retaliation from the defense company. But, of course, an attack pinpointed against nonpayers, which did not at all interfere with customers, would be ignored by the company. Given these conditions, the provision of defense service loses most of its qualities of being a public good.[33] People who paid for the service would receive it; others would not. As in so many other cases, the notion of a collective or public good is an illusion created by the absence of an actual market. Effective operation of the market depends on excludability. But the important point is that *excludability is not an inherent characteristic of goods*. Rather, the ability to exclude nonpayers from benefits is something that can be *learned*, that *must* be learned, if the market is to operate. We cannot first prohibit the operation of the market (by government pre-emption), and then conclude that a market could not function, because of its inability to exclude beneficiaries who do not pay. Of course it would be very difficult for a market which hitherto has been prohibited to suddenly begin effective

---

[33] This is not meant as an exhaustive brief for a free market in defense services. Such treatment would take us far beyond the scope of this paper, but the interested reader can consult Rothbard (1978, chaps. 11, 13; 1970, chap. 1), as well as Wooldridge (1970, chap. 6).

operation (and it is much more difficult, as we have seen, to envision the operation of such a market). But this difficulty is not the result of anything intrinsic. It is because the erection of bigger and better fences, the creation of more sophisticated jamming devices, etc., can come only with practice; if there is no market in operation, there is no chance for the experimentation with the skills, institutions, and management requisite to its development.

Bish and Warren assert that all "public or collective goods . . . are 'nonpackageable'; that is, in principle, no one can be excluded from consuming them."[34] But they are incorrect. As we have seen, even in the case of national defense, the paradigm case of the collective good, there exist potential methods and institutions for excluding nonpayers.[35] There is nothing in principle to prevent excludability—there is only a lack of a past history of market operation in this area and the limited powers of imagination on the part of economists.

An interesting sidelight on the definitional problem of using national defense as an example of a public good is considered by Charles M. Tiebout. Tiebout contrasts national defense with radio broadcasting, which he holds is not a collective good.

> There seems to be a problem connected with the external economies aspect of public goods. Surely a radio broadcast, like national defense, has the attribute that A's enjoyment leaves B no worse off; yet this does not imply that broadcasting should, in a normative sense, be a public good. . . . The difference between defense and broadcasting is subtle but important. In both cases there is a problem of determining the optimal level of outputs and the corresponding level of benefits taxes. In the broadcasting case, however, A may be quite willing to pay more taxes than B, even if both have the same "ability to pay" (assuming that the benefits are determinate). Defense is another question. Here A is not content that B should pay less. A makes the *social judgment* that B's preference *should* be the same. A's preference, expressed as an

---

[34] Bish and Warren (1972, p. 100).
[35] For examples of excludability of road users, see Haritos (1974, pp. 55–56).

annual defense expenditure such as $42.7 billion and representing the majority view, thus determines the level of defense. Here the A's may feel that the B's *should pay* the same amount of benefits tax.[36] [Emphasis added]

Troubling and puzzling is the importation of value judgments into the analysis. It would appear that the concept of "public good" was offered in a scientific, not a normative sense. What, then, are we to make of the statement, "Broadcasting should, in a normative sense, be a public good." In the spirit of the definitions offered, one would have thought that broadcasting (or any other service or good) either is or is not a public good, and that normative judgments were beside the point. This is not the case, however, for later in the quote we learn that A's "social judgment" is all that is necessary to justify that B "should pay" for national defense. But what is a "social judgment" as opposed to, for example, a "private judgment?" And by what authority can A, a mere individual, make a "social judgment," whatever that is? Suppose that it is A's considered "social judgment" that B should, through taxes, pay for can openers. Does that judgment automatically convert these implements into collective goods? Moreover, why need we assume that A is content that B pay less taxes for radio, but not for defense? May we not reverse this and assume that although A is willing that B pay less for defense, he is not so inclined when it comes to radio? Is there anything intrinsic to the goods "radio" and "defense" that precludes this reversal? And if A's preferences were indeed reversed, would this prove that radio, rather than defense, is a "true" collective good?

Perhaps we should reckon with the institution of "democracy," for Tiebout cites majority support for A's preference. It is majoritarianism, then, that puts the winning side in a position to label its view a "social judgment." But this is very far indeed from the initial definition of a collective good. If this is all his argument amounts to, Tiebout might just as well have spared us all the rigmarole about externalities, public goods, and the fact that A's enjoyment leaves B no worse off. All he need have said is that, if and when, for whatever reason, a majority of the

---

[36] Tiebout (1956, p. 417).

eligible voters decides that any particular good ought to be provided by the government, why then, so be it.

Signposts and "Free" Goods

If classifying a good as "public" implies that one person's utilization of that good does not detract from another's, then defining roads as a "public good" presents another problem. If, on congested highways, any one motorist imposes costs on all others, the classification of roads as a public good fails. Conversely, if roads really are an example of a public good, then, by definition (but contrary to evidence), one motorist cannot impose costs on others in overcrowded conditions.

According to Samuelson, "no decentralized pricing system can serve to determine optimally [the] levels of collective consumption." And why is this so? "It is the selfish interest of each person to give false signals, to pretend to have less interest in a given collective consumption activity than he really has."[37] It is for this reason that Savas holds that "public goods are properly paid for by the public at large, for their benefits cannot be charged to individual consumers or small collective groups."[38]

For a more elaborate rendition of this point of view, we turn to Haveman:

> The posting of signs on a highway, for example, is a public good. The benefits cannot be denied to anyone who travels the road. Similarly, when a society provides national defense, the benefits accrue to all of its citizens. Because it is so costly to ration the system of city streets once it has been put into place, they, too, are public goods.
>
> Because one cannot economically be excluded from the benefits of a public good once it has been provided, private firms have no incentive to produce and market these commodities. Any potential buyer would refuse to pay anything like what the commodity is worth to him. Indeed, he would be likely to express an unwillingness to pay anything at all for it. He would reason: "If

---

[37] Samuelson (1954, pp. 388–89).
[38] Savas (1974, p. 483).

I simply sit tight and refuse to pay, I may get the benefit of the good anyway, if someone down the line provides it for himself—after all, it's a public good." However, if each buyer reasons this way (and presumably he will), the good will not be provided. Public goods will only be provided if collective action, usually through a government, is taken. Only through collective action can the availability of worthwhile public goods be assured.[39]

Needless to say, there are many compelling problems with this argument. As we have seen, highway sign-posting is a public good only when private ownership is forbidden and no price is charged. It becomes a private good just as soon as the externalities are internalized by the market. It is easy to see this point. No one, after all, would call signs in a privately owned department store public goods. Yet the benefits of the signs, usually posted on each floor as well as on elevators and escalators, indicating the departments located on the various floors, "cannot be denied to anyone who travels" in the store. Is there a case, by analogy, for making government responsible for informing people where dresses, sportswear, and household utensils can be found?

Let us turn now to the doctrine of revealed preference. It, too, has serious flaws. It is our contention that, government interferences into the market apart, *all* external benefits, spill-overs, etc. will tend to cease to exist, provided they are significant enough to make it profitable for private enterprise to internalize them. For example, if the costs of building a tall fence around the drive-in theater are lower than the (discounted) value of the additional receipts the owner expects to receive as a result of its construction, then he will build it. If the costs exceed the benefits derivable, he will not build the fence. But if the benefits to be received are so low, then the externalities and spill-overs are not likely to discourage the businessman from providing the service in the first place.

It has been objected that the government can provide the internalization for free and may thus be more efficient than the market (profit and loss incentives notwithstanding). Let us construct an example.

---

[39] Haveman (1970, pp. 42–43).

Suppose that in a society of 100 people each would benefit from the provision of a "public good" to the extent of $10. And let us also suppose that the cost of providing the good, in terms of alternatives foregone, is only $50. Thus, with a total benefit of $1,000, less a cost of $50, there would be a $950 profit in this enterprise. The only problem is that, while each of the 100 people would indubitably benefit to the tune of $10, we must also consider the cost—let us assume, $1,000,000— of erecting a fence sufficient to exclude these people from enjoying the benefits for free. Therefore, it cannot be a paying proposition for free enterprise. But what will government do? Rather than wastefully spend the $1,000,000 on the fence, the state simply recoups the $50 cost by taxing $.50 from each of the 100 people, and then provides the service to all comers "for free."

Can we, as strictly value-free economists, conclude that the government will maximize utility by so acting? I submit that we cannot. We cannot, unless, in addition to all the facts heretofore presented, we assume that none of the 100 people will resent being forced to contribute to the scheme via compulsory taxes. And this we have no reason to do. In other words, even while maintaining the assumption that each person values his benefits from the project at $10, and that each realizes that the government's plan will cost him (as well as everyone else) only $.50, it is still conceivable that a person will so resent being forced to do something, even "for his own good," that the costs to him will vastly exceed the $9.50 gain he stands to capture.

To deny this possibility is to make an implicit assumption of the validity of interpersonal comparisons of utility. In order to justify government action on utility grounds in this case, one has to assume either that all 100 people are identical, as far as utility is concerned, or, at the very least, that the benefits derived by the ninety-nine outweigh the psychic income losses of the one malcontent. In fact, the assumption of interpersonal utility comparison is not merely implicit in the thinking of mainstream economists. Samuelson, for example, speaks of a "social welfare function that renders interpersonal judgements,"[40] and then

---

[40] Samuelson (1955, p. 351).

proceeds to draw an indifference curve map encompassing the utilities of two or more different people.[41]

This procedure is scientifically invalid, however, as there are no units with which to measure or compare happiness or utility. We may, in ordinary discourse, say that one child likes pickles more than another and that therefore, should any temporary household shortage arise, the "pickle lover" should get first crack. But in so speaking we do not have in mind any units of happiness. We do not imagine that one child loves pickles to a degree of, let us say, 48.2 happiness units, the other child only 24.1 units, and that therefore the first child likes pickles exactly twice as much as the other.

Rothbard tells us that

> There is never any possibility of measuring increases or decreases in happiness or satisfaction. Not only is it impossible to measure or compare changes in the satisfaction of different people; it is not possible to measure changes in the happiness of any given person. In order for any measurement to be possible, there must be an eternally fixed and objectively given unit with which other units may be compared. There is no such objective unit in the field of human evaluation. The individual must determine subjectively for himself whether he is better or worse off as a result of any change. His preference can only be expressed in terms of simple choice, or rank. Thus, he can say, "I am better off" or "I am happier" because he went to a concert instead of playing bridge, . . . but it would be completely meaningless for him to try to assign units to his preference and say: "I am two and a half times happier because of this choice than I would have been playing bridge." Two and a half times what? There is no possible unit of happiness that can be used for purposes of comparison, and hence of addition or multiplication. Thus, values cannot be measured. . . . They can only be ranked as better or worse.[42]

---

[41] *Ibid.*, p. 352.

[42] Rothbard (1962, pp. 15–16). See also Krutilla (1963, p. 227), and Renshaw (1962, p. 374). Winch (1963, p. 38) writes that "unless we make some assumption about interpersonal comparisons of utility, economics can offer no help in problems of policy such as that of highway planning."

If, then, it is impossible to make interpersonal utility comparisons, we cannot, as scientific economists, conclude that government intervention in "public goods" production will unambiguously lead to an increase in welfare.

Measuring the Unmeasurable

In order to avoid these difficulties, the neighborhood effects economists have attempted to measure externalities. Large numbers of impressive statistics have not been forthcoming however. Rather the work of these economists has been sort of a "meta-measurement," a prolegomenon to any future measurement; benefit measures have been developed and discussed, but no one has, as yet, offered any definite findings which purport to gauge external benefits received with any degree of exactitude. Mohring, in a typical statement, writes: "the benefit measures developed in this paper ignore externalities—plus or minus, pecuniary or technological. My basic excuse for this shortcoming is the conventional one: the data required to place dollar values on externalities are lacking."[43]

There is indeed a lack of data placing dollar values on externalities. The problem would appear to be, judging from the above quote, a mere accident: economists have, for some (implicitly) unimportant reason, not yet begun the actual measuring. But in this age of statistics, this is indeed puzzling. Surely a few economists should have taken time out to measure such important data.

Actually, of course, the problem is far more intractable. What is being proposed by those who would attempt to measure the value of externalities is simply the measure of utility. But as we have seen, such an undertaking is impossible and hence doomed to failure. Utility is a subjective phenomenon, rooted in individual preference. There are no units with which to measure utility, a fact that appears to be no more than a slight annoyance to those who would measure it.

In a second attempt, Mohring and Harwitz inform us that in questions of highway benefits "reliance is placed entirely on the body of theory that

---

[43] Mohring (1965, p. 231).

would likely be used by an economist in attempting to place a value on a dam, a steel mill, or any other productive investment."[44] But this, too, fails. First, the economist, *qua* economist, simply has no special aptitude as an appraiser of real estate, factories, or any capital good. This is the job, rather, of the businessman, or entrepreneur, whose success depends on his acuity in making such determinations. No theoretical economist, empirical economist, historical economist, nor any other kind of economist, *qua* economist, has any practical training or experience as an appraiser. Second, there is no "body of theory" that can be used by an economist (or by anyone else) in determining the value of a capital asset. The value the market places on an asset depends upon what people plan to do with it, with its complements and substitutes, upon the reactions consumers are expected to have toward the finished product; it depends upon the course of new discoveries and inventions, upon wars, famines, storms, and so forth. Some people are better able to anticipate the future course of the market than others; but such people are successful entrepreneurs, not economists or other social scientists. But Smerk nevertheless suggests in his book on urban transport:

> External costs and benefits, many of them of a nonpecuniary nature, should be weighed along with the pecuniary costs and revenues internal to the project. Some of the external factors to be considered will be: 1. Overall freedom of movement; 2. Gains or losses to central city businesses in terms of customer traffic; 3. Gains or losses in travel time for subway riders, public transport riders in general, and motorists; 4. Gains or losses in real estate values; 5. Effects on air pollution and other amenities.[45]

As a statement of the measurement task, Smerk's is par for the course. It is really no more than an exhortation that measurement be undertaken, and a specification of some of the facets to be measured. But it does not help us to overcome any of the problems involved. Indeed, it underscores them. How, for example, would we approach a calculation of the value of increasing "overall freedom of movement?" Even if we

---

[44] Mohring and Harwitz (1962, p. 7).
[45] Smerk (1965a, p. 236).

choose to ignore the lack of a unit of pleasure and the problem of inter-personal comparisons of utility, the task is insurmountable. Nor is his specific suggestion for measuring the benefits of a belt highway in terms of "the resulting increase in sales"[46] of much use. Smerk seems to be saying that we can measure the external benefits of a belt highway by noting the sales of the relevant stores before and after its construction and simply attribute the difference to the road. But there is no constancy in human affairs, and other factors may well have intervened between the first measurement and the second. Tastes and fashions, consumer knowledge concerning alternatives, the prices of substitutes and complements, zoning laws, the alacrity with which laws are enforced—all of these might have changed in the interim. Thus, to ascribe all measured change to the belt highway would be illegitimate. Moreover, the use of econometric techniques, which are commonly employed for purposes of this sort, are unsuitable.[47] Perhaps their most important drawback is that they rely on the facile assumption that discrete, unique, nonrepeatable events (e.g., a presidential election, or the economic effects of opening a mall at a particular time and place) can be abstracted from to produce a series of random events (i.e., all presidential elections, all road openings). This assumption is necessary for econometric equations; but if applicable anywhere, they are applicable only to truly random events such as flipping a coin or tossing dice.

Revealed Preferences

We now return to our second criticism of the Samuelson-Savas-Haveman assertion that the market will fail, in the case of public goods, because economic actors will fail to register their true preferences. The basic drawback of this approach to the question of "revealed preference" is the vantage point from which the decision-maker is viewed. Let us, then, focus our attention on how these economists view market participants who refuse to voluntarily purchase the public good on the market. Under their theory a market actor would have as his constant refrain, "Let

---

[46] *Ibid.*, p. 241.
[47] See Leoni and Frola (1977, pp. 101–10), Mises (1966, pp. 107–15, 350–52), and Rothbard (1962, pp. 277–80).

George do it." Unwilling to spend his own money on a good which he may enjoy through the payment of others, this person contributes to the unlikelihood of private provision of that good.

An embarrassing question arises: How does the economist propose to determine the preference scales of market participants? It might be suggested that each individual knows his own preference ranking by introspection, and that the rest of us come to know it by simply asking him. Both, however, are incorrect. The former, the questionnaire method, may easily be dismissed. The empirical unreliability of questionnaires and public opinion polls alone should give us pause for thought. Furthermore, the fact that people lie clearly invalidates this method as a good foundation for scientific economics.

It might be argued nevertheless that the individual himself surely knows his own preferences by introspection. Our answer, once again, is no. The evidence of impulsive buying is overwhelming. How many of us have walked down the street with nothing further from our minds than the purchase of an ice cream cone, only to find ourselves, seemingly without any conscious volition, plunging hand into pocket, relinquishing the required sum, and avidly eating away? Is it that we "really" or "unconsciously" were thinking of ice cream? While that could be true, it need not be. Regardless, however, of the exact psychological mechanics involved, it is clear that, before the purchase, introspection might well have failed to reveal the hidden desire. We must therefore conclude that, in at least some cases, the individual economic actor may not know his own value scales. Motivational advertising, to the extent that it is efficacious, is further evidence of the fact that introspection will not necessarily dredge up the true preferences of the individual. The buyer may think he knows what he wants, but in reality, according to this argument, some of his tastes are at the beck and call of Madison Avenue, and not amenable to his own consciousness.

If true value-rankings can be scientifically discovered neither by introspection nor by questionnaire surveys, how can they be? The answer is through market purchases and sales, or more generally, through observation of human action.[48] Ludwig von Mises expressed this idea as follows:

> It is customary to say that acting man has a scale of wants or values in his mind when he arranges his actions. On the basis of such a scale he satisfies what is of higher value, i.e., his more urgent wants, and leaves unsatisfied what is of lower value, i.e., what is a less urgent want. There is no objection to such a presentation of the state of affairs. However, one must not forget that the scale of values or wants manifests itself only in the reality of action. These scales have no independent existence apart from the actual behavior of individuals. The only source from which our knowledge concerning these scales is derived is the observation of a man's actions. Every action is always in perfect agreement with the scale of values or wants because these scales are nothing but an instrument for the interpretation of a man's acting.[49]

In our previous example, all the prior introspection and questionnaires in the world would not have ineluctably established that the buyer valued ice cream over the money it cost. It was his action alone, in making the purchase, which established that, at least at the time of purchase, the buyer actually valued the ice cream more than the money spent.[50]

Let us consider a possible challenge to this view. Suppose the ice cream buyer is actually an economist intent upon proving Mises's argument false. Suppose, further, that he hates chocolate and that to refute Mises's theory he goes to the candy store and purchases chocolate. Would he then have demonstrated Mises's theory as wrong by virtue of its

---

[48] Mises (1966, pp. 107, 110).

[49] *Ibid.,* pp. 94–95.

[50] Rothbard (1962, p. 890) asks

> by what mysterious process the critics know that the recipients [of external benefits] would have liked to purchase the "benefit." Our only way of knowing the content of preference scales is to see them revealed in concrete choices. Since the choice concretely was *not* to buy the benefit, there is no justification for outsiders to assert that B's preference scale was "really" different from what was revealed in his actions.

implication that he valued the hated chocolate more highly than the money paid for it?

There is more than one way to handle this challenge. First, we might deny that the purchaser really hates chocolate. Following a strict interpretation of Mises, we can reason that whatever his past relationship with this particular treat, his present purchase reveals either that he has changed his taste or that at least he prefers it to the money he exchanged for it. His action has spoken, in this interpretation, louder than all his protestations to the contrary.

Second, and perhaps in the present scenario more straightforwardly, we can reinterpret the good that was actually purchased. What was really bought was not only chocolate, but chocolate plus the pleasure of "proving Mises wrong." If it had been a question of the chocolate alone, a true chocolate hater would not have purchased it perhaps at any positive price. It was the compensatory pleasure of attempting to disprove the thesis (that only human action establishes value orderings) that more than made up for the disutility of the chocolate. And if the person went so far as to eat the hated chocolate in order to prove his point, our interpretation would still apply and would be fully consistent with the Misesian view.

The trouble with the revealed preference doctrine put forth by Samuelson, Savas, and Haveman is that it assumes a preference ordering on the part of the general public which is completely divorced from actual choices and actions. There is no room in scientific economics for "true preferences" which are not embodied in action. Samuelson may contend that "it is in the selfish interest of each person to give false signals"—i.e., signals which underestimate that person's true value for the collective good—but he cannot show that his interpretation has any scientific validity. This is not to say that his statement is meaningless. Indeed, in the ordinary discourse that has room for measured and interpersonal utility comparisons, it is perfectly sensible. But if we are to remain true to the strict discipline of economics, we shall have to relinquish such loose talk from our vocabulary. There is simply no action that anyone can take which would demonstrate the truth of Samuelson's contention. Samuelson might reply, with an admission that he is citing inaction, not action; a refusal to purchase, not an actual purchase. The problem, though, is that (temporary) nonaction is consistent with all too many other things. No one can logically reason from the fact that a person is not buying something (a "public good") to the conclusion that he really relishes the service in question and is seeking a "free ride." It may be that he simply does not want it. We can speculate at length about the different reasons people have for not buying something (distaste, ignorance, the desire to "free ride"), but we cannot as scientific economists conclude from the fact of nonpurchase that the person "really" values the good.

If we could legitimately reason in this manner, the sky would be the limit. Once we leave the solid foundations of preferences revealed in market action, the imagination is left free. Some contend that parks, roads, and national defense are public goods and would receive underinvestments in a free market. But using the same reasoning, one might hold that Edsels, pickle-flavored ice cream, and kerosene lamps are presently victims of vicious underinvestment because people are secretly waiting for everyone else to buy first, so that they can be free riders. All of these claims have the same logical status. Each is conceivable and expressible in ordinary discourse. But none is supported by demonstrated preference. We must regard all of them as scientifically invalid.

Isolability

Another argument for government provision of roads, closely allied to the externalities argument, might be called the isolability condition. According to this line of thought, a good or service comes properly under the province of the marketplace only if its benefits can be isolated and imputed to specific individuals. Otherwise its benefits are said to be "diffused," and the good in question must then be supplied by government. As stated by one advocate of this position: "If it were agreed that the benefits from highway improvements are so diffused among inhabitants of a state that it is impossible to isolate individual beneficiaries, . . . [then] highways should be supported from the general fund."[51]

---

[51] Netzer (1952, p. 109).

One problem with this reasoning is that if there is really no one person willing to step forward and declare himself a beneficiary, then there remains a serious question as to whether there really are any beneficiaries. As we have seen in the discussion on revealed preference, the only secure evidence of actual benefits is market action—the actual payment by consumers for goods delivered or services rendered. If payment is not forthcoming, then it is only idle speculation to suppose that there are hordes of beneficiaries who are unwilling to reveal their interests through market action.

Second, if one is free to justify government waste on this ground, then one is free to defend any state action on the same ground: "X really benefits the masses, although no one person will exemplify this through voluntary payments; the problem is that the gains are diffuse, so that no one beneficiary can be isolated. Therefore government involvement in the provision of X is justified." We would not for a moment accept this argument were it applied to any good or service that the government is not now engaged in supplying. As a defense of the status quo, however, its defects are more difficult to see.

This argument can also be attacked on a third ground. Most contemporary economists are comfortable with the phenomenon of continuity in economics. For example, revenue curves and cost curves are usually drawn as smoothly continuous, presumably depicting economic action as taking place in a series of infinitely small steps. The doctrine of "diffused benefits" is entirely in keeping with this tradition, for here, too, an infinitesimal benefit, so small as to not even be noticeable to the presumed beneficiary, is regarded as "real"; indeed, it is seen as justifying government involvement in the economy.

It is true that such a conception of the universe is exceedingly helpful in the employment of the mathematical tools of analysis, especially differential calculus. This no doubt explains, at least in part, the popularity of smooth curves, and the acceptability of diffuse, infinitely small gains. However, as Rothbard states, "we must never let reality be falsified in order to fit the niceties of mathematics. In fact, production (and, similarly, benefits from the actions of others or of oneself) is a series of discrete alternatives, as all human action is discrete, and cannot be smoothly continuous, i.e., move in infinitely small steps from one . . . level to another."[52] Strictly speaking, either a gain is noticeable to the presumed beneficiary, or it is not part of his realm of human action at all. If a person makes no notice of something, then for him it is not an element that can affect his choices. And if it cannot enter into his economic decision making, it is irrelevant.

An implicit justification for government activity here is that, while the benefits to any one person in a group are indefinitely small, once their benefits are added up they become substantial. This may work, under some assumptions, in physics and other natural sciences. But in economics, where human action is the touchstone, it is nonsense to posit that a phenomenon which is of no benefit to any one individual can be of substantial importance to a group of such individuals. If no one person can be shown to gain from these "diffuse benefits," it cannot be claimed that the whole group somehow gains.

One Man's Meat is Another's Poison

Let us consider now a shortcoming, previously alluded to, in the public good view: that tastes differ and that what may be viewed as a benefit by one person may be seen as something to be avoided by another. Samuelson replies to this objection as follows:

> Even though a public good is being compared with a private good, the indifference curves are drawn with the usual convexity to the origin. This assumption could be relaxed without hurting the theory. Indeed, we could recognize the possible case where one man's circus is another man's poison, by permitting indifference curves to bend forward. This would not affect the analysis but would answer a critic's minor objection.[53]

---

[52] Rothbard (1962, p. 643).

[53] Samuelson (1955, pp. 350–51). Neither will Tiebout's attempted reformulation do: "A definitive alternative to Samuelson's might be simply that a public good is one which should be produced, but for which there is no feasible method of charging the consumers" (p. 417). We can ask Tiebout (and Samuelson, too) how we can know that consumers really value a good for which they have no way of registering a demand. If there is no feasible method of charging a consumer, then he can never make his desires known.

While it is true that, in a formalistic sense, indifference curves could be drawn as concave to the origin to represent disutility, garbage, or negative feelings toward the "good" in question,[54] this answer will not suffice. When we reflect on the fact that Samuelson's use of the concept of public goods to justify government takeovers is based on the assumption that such takeovers will maximize everyone's welfare, we can see the weakness of this answer. A person for whom a good or its presumed external benefits are in fact disadvantageous will actually lose by its subsidization. To the confirmed pacifist, for example, the expenditure of ever more billions of dollars for military purposes leads to increased disutility. And to add insult to injury, Samuelson's argument is used to justify taxing the pacifist, supposedly for his own benefit, to cover the costs of those increasing expenditures. What we have, then, is a situation which forces a person to pay for the provision of a good that he regards as a "poison."

No minor rearrangement of an indifference curve can erase the harm done to a man so confronted. At best, Samuelson's suggestion of permitting the indifference curve to bend forward provides a means of representing the problem—a geometrical way of stating the dilemma—but hardly a solution to it. It is as if, in response to a complaint that the economy is constantly in a state of disequilibrium, Samuelson were to offer to draw supply and demand curves, showing price to be other than at their intersection. Such a drawing would be an illustration of the difficulty, not a solution to it. It cannot seriously be maintained that a man's lot will be bettered by forcibly extracting his money in taxes, if it is intended that these funds be spent on a good that for him is detrimental. The objection cannot be dissolved by pointing out that the situation where one man's circus is another man's poison can adequately be *portrayed* by forward falling indifference curves.

---

[54] This is not the time to expound on the general difficulties of indifference curve analysis. It is worth noting, however, that it is impossible to reveal indifference through the usual market procedures of buying or selling. Thus, an economics based on the view that preference orderings are seen only in human action must entirely reject indifference curve analysis. For a full exposition of this point, and a general discreditation of indifference as an economic category, see Rothbard (1962, pp. 265–67), and Block (1980, pp. 422–37).

Is Group Action Irrational?

We next consider a version of the public good argument put forth by Mancur Olson. It is his contention that "unless the number of individuals in a group is quite small, or unless there is coercion or some other special device to make individuals act in their common interest, rational, self-interested individuals will not act to achieve their common or group interests." And, as a corollary, only "groups composed of either altruistic individuals or irrational individuals may sometimes act in common for group interests . . . even when there is unanimous agreement in a group about the common good and the methods of achieving it."[55]

Olson limits his analysis to groups whose avowed purpose is the furtherance of the economic well-being of their membership: "The kinds of organizations that are the focus of this study are expected to further the interests of their members."[56] A group such as a "lobbying organization, or indeed a labor union or any other organization, working in the interest of a large group of firms or workers in some industry, would get no assistance from the rational, self-interested individuals in that industry."[57] Olson accounts for this situation by invoking neighborhood effects and public goods. He writes:

> Some goods and services . . . are of such a nature that all of the members of the relevant groups must get them if anyone in the group is to get them. These sorts of services are inherently unsuited to the market mechanism, and will be produced only if everyone is forced to pay his assigned share. Clearly, many governmental services are of this kind.
>
> It would obviously not be feasible, if indeed it were possible, to deny the protection provided by the military services, the police, and the courts to those who did not voluntarily pay their share of the costs of government, and taxation is accordingly necessary . . . A common, collective, or public good is here defined as any good such that, if any person X_i in a group $x_1 . . . x_i, . . . x_n$

---

[55] Olson (1965, p. 2).
[56] *Ibid.,* p. 6.
[57] *Ibid.,* p. 11.

consumes it, it cannot feasibly be withheld from the others in that group.[58]

And further:

> To be sure, for some collective goods it is physically possible to practice exclusion. But . . . it is not necessary that exclusion be technically impossible; it is only necessary that it be infeasible or uneconomic.[59]

We have already touched upon the case of unfeasible excludability in our numerical example (page 165). There, we concluded that the value-free economists could not justifiably deduce that government action, albeit "cheaper," would unambiguously increase utility. Now we must consider Olson's assertion that economic rationality and market action are incompatible. We must ask whether market action in the case of collective goods can function only if the economic actors are altruistic or irrational. We must ask if a large group of individuals can collaborate in the provision of a good whose benefits, once created, cannot feasibly be limited to cooperating members.

In fact, there are literally hundreds of groups now in existence which meet Olson's definition. Labor unions, charities, businessmen's associations, and civic organizations are numerous. Contributions to artistic and musical societies are in abundance. As I write this, a local nonprofit radio station is featuring "160 uninterrupted hours of J.S. Bach" and asking for funds. If contributors respond generously, such programming can continue to exist. But each potential contributor may reason that, if many others give, he himself will not be excluded from the benefits. And the same applies for the Society for the Prevention of Cruelty to Animals, the N.A.A.C.P., disease research foundations, etc.

In a recent year, the United Way charity alone raised $1,039,000,000 for such purposes as individual and family services, hospitals and health, social adjustment, and community organization. The American National Red Cross reported donations received totaling $248,700,000,

---

[58] *Ibid.*, p. 94.
[59] *Ibid.*, p. 14.

as well as the involvement of 4,262,000 participants in its blood donor programs. And, in this era of government assumption of increasing numbers of functions previously in the private domain, private philanthropy funds were in a recent year as follows: individuals, $21.4 billion; foundations, $2 billion; business corporations, $1.2 billion; and charitable bequests, $2.2 billion.[60] One might want to discount some of the corporate giving as motivated by tax incentives, which no doubt did play a role. But the generous financial outpourings from concerned individuals provide ample evidence of the charitable impulses of many of the American people.

Are we to assume, on Olson's theory, that no rational, self-interested persons are involved in these enterprises? I think not. Rather, it seems clear that Olson is guilty of a stipulative re-definition of some rather slippery words such as "rationality," "self-interest," "altruism," and so on. Specifically it would be inconsistent with his theory to suggest that a rational, self-interested person might be interested in the welfare of others to that extent that he derived pleasure from an increase in theirs. But why should this suggestion be considered unreasonable? Olson has definitionally precluded such motives from the realm of the rational.

It might appear that Olson is on firmer ground in using the term "self-interested." Dickens's Scrooge, after all, was not known for his charitable instincts. But on consideration, it does not seem correct to so restrict the word "self-interested" to those who take only their own happiness into account, and no one else's. Surely the word is sufficiently elastic to include as "self-interested" a person who includes the welfare of others around him, such as the members of his immediate family, in his own utility calculations. Doesn't Papa Scrooge ever worry about how Li'l Scrooge is making out?

If we are wrong in this contention, and it is somehow shown that true self-interest is limited to consideration of one's own pleasure and no one else's, then Olson's view is, of course, correct. But even then, Olson's position is much less powerful than he seems to believe, for all we are left with is the argument that those individuals who are strictly

---

[60] U.S. Bureau of the Census (1976).

self-interested will be unable to coalesce into groups which can work for common ends. But since there cannot be more than a minute proportion of people who really take into account no one's happiness but their own, this would seem to be but a slight impediment to the smooth functioning of cooperative groups.

Another problem with Olson's hypothesis is that it ignores the role of the entrepreneur.[61] To be sure, it is difficult to rouse large numbers of individuals for collective action. And it is difficult to convince people to contribute to the production of any good whose benefits they will receive whether they contribute or not. The entrepreneur is not faced with this problem, however. If the entrepreneur sees an opportunity for profit, he seizes it, presenting *a fait accompli* to the consumers. In the case of a "public good," of course, the businessman will first have to take steps to ensure that there will be sufficient funds forthcoming to defray expenses and leave a profit. Olson argues that in the case of public goods, if one person in a group consumes the service, then it cannot feasibly be withheld from others. The entrepreneur will strive to deal with this challenge by lowering the costs of exclusion of nonpayers to the point at which potential revenues warrant investment. The feasibility or unfeasibility of exclusion is not predetermined, but rather a function of market operation. If hitherto government-monopolized markets were suddenly opened to the domain of the entrepreneur, the number of goods and services to which Olson's definition applies would be sharply reduced.

Indeed, the key to excludability may be as cheap as it is obvious. We have seen how a simple announcement of discontinuance of protection for noncontributors might work in the case of defense. Fire protection would probably fall into the same mold. Let just one house burn down, with the private fire department and its apparatus on the scene but refusing to quench the flames—all because the owner not only did not keep the company on retainer, but also refused to meet a "special, emergency price"—and let this event be widely reported by the media,

---

[61] For an excellent exegesis of the importance of the entrepreneur, see Kirzner (1973).

and fire protection would probably cease, from that moment on, to be an example of Olson's public goods.

The History of Private Roads

Perhaps the most telling argument against the externality and collective goods thesis as applied to the provision of roads is the sheer weight of historical experience to the contrary. Roads are nowadays generally considered a paradigm case of public goods, for the very possibility of privately operated roads is dismissed. Yet, prior to the former part of the nineteenth century, private roads, highways, turnpikes, etc. played an important role in world commerce.

Privately owned and operated turnpikes were the backbone of the highway network in England in the eighteenth and nineteenth centuries. Exact statistics for this time period are unfortunately difficult to come by. However, since the formation of each new turnpike required a specific Act of Parliament, the number of such acts provides "a fairly reliable, though rough, estimate of the progress that was taking place."[62] According to Jackman, the number of such parliamentary acts throughout England in the two decades from 1751 to 1770 was twice as great as the number passed during the previous fifty years. In the north midland counties, the number rose from fifty-five in the earlier time period, to 189 in the former. And from the first half of the eighteenth century to the forty-year period after the mid-century mark, there was a 388 percent increase in the number of such acts passed.[63] And if the percentage increase figures are impressive, the base is no less so. Says Sir Alker Tripp, "it is computed that more than a thousand Turnpike Acts were passed between 1785 and 1810, and that in all there were more than four thousand acts of this character."[64]

---

[62] Jackman (1916, p. 233).

[63] *Ibid.*, pp. 233–34.

[64] Tripp (1950, p. 43). According to Sidney and Beatrice Webb (1922, pp. 155–59), toll roads, or turnpikes, were in operation as early as 1662 and 1670 but did not achieve a modest frequency until 1691. The earliest historical example on record, however, seems to be much earlier: "Authority seems to have been given in 1267 to levy a toll in Gloucestershire Manor" (*ibid.*, p. 157).

From the perspective of history, it is difficult to avoid the conclusion that private turnpikes were the norm. For example, in the view of Shorey Peterson:

> But history shows, if two notable instances establish a rule, that when highways come to play a major part in transportation, the view of them in strict collective terms breaks down both in theory and in practice. This was true in the 18th and early 19th centuries when the growing commerce of the Industrial Revolution turned to the public roads for accelerated and cheapened movement. The local governments were unable to take care of the traffic; and turnpike trusts of a quasi-private nature were set up to exploit the discoveries of Telford and McAdam on a business basis. Toll gates might seem offensive by customary usage, but there was effective logic in the idea that highway service, unlike other basic government activities, might be developed by ordinary investment standards and financed by specific beneficiaries, rather than the general public.[65]

If every dirt track, muddy path, narrow passageway, and winding route were counted, of course, the actual mileage of public highways was far in excess of the turnpikes. Jackman, citing two historical reports, calculates that in 1820, "out of a total length of about 125,000 miles of road, only a little over 20,000 miles, or roughly, one-sixth of the whole, was turnpike; and even by 1838 there was only 22,000 miles of turnpike, while the amount of ordinary highway was computed as not less than 104,770 miles."[66]

These statistics are, however, misleading in terms of the actual importance played by the turnpike system, for highway mileage is not

---

[65] Peterson (1950, pp. 192–93).

[66] Jackman (1916, p. 234). The two reports he cites are "Report from the Committee of the House of Commons to Consider Acts Regarding Turnpikes, Roads, and Highways, 1821" and "Report of the Royal Commission on the State of the Roads, 1840." Webb and Webb (1922, p. 152) give rough support to these estimates in stating that 23,000 miles of roads were administered by the Turnpike Trusts in 1835. They add the fact that, in the same year, 1,100 Turnpike Companies collectively levied an annual revenue of more than 1.5 million sterling and had a debt of £7 million.

a homogeneous commodity. Miles cannot be equated one to another. On the contrary, some mileage is more strategically placed, is of better quality, and supports more important and valuable traffic. And in each of these respects the (quasi-) private turnpikes surpassed the public highway system. In terms of strategic location, for example, Jackman tells us that "the greatest industrial and commercial centres at this time [1838] were linked up by practically continuous turnpike roads."[67] In comparison, the less industrialized areas of the country were served by the parish highways. Although these served "large and important sections" of the country, the typical rate of industrialization and commercialization was lower there. Further, the parish, or public highways, in comparison with the turnpikes "were generally in a bad state."[68] And, as for the quality of traffic, "turnpike roads were constantly treated by the legislature on the assumption that the traffic upon them was more important than the traffic upon an ordinary highway."[69]

The early American experience of private road building was entirely in keeping with that of England.[70] Replying to the view that individual investment in roads would have to make way for societal or public investment, Wooldridge had this to say:

> Exactly the opposite situation prevailed for most of the important roads of the nineteenth century. From 1800 to 1830 private investment poured into thousands of miles of turnpikes in the United States, notwithstanding the miniscule return the capital earned, and hundreds of turnpike companies built roads that carried the rivers of emigration to the old Northwest and the products of the newly settled states back to the seaboard. For the first third of the century, constructing the roads that were the only means of transportation to and communication with most parts of the West remained a function of private capital. An

---

[67] Jackman (1916, p. 234).
[68] Brit. Mus., T. 1157 (4), "Highways Improved," p. 2, quoted in *ibid.*
[69] Scholefield and Cockburn (1932, p. 467), quoted in Tripp (1950, p. 43).
[70] See also Bonavia (1954, p. 53), concerning the Italian experience with private roads, or *autostrade*.

occasional exception, like the famous National Road going west from Cumberland, Maryland, was a deviation from the norm.

The history of the grandfather of all the turnpike companies, the Philadelphia and Lancaster Turnpike Corporation, chartered in 1792, has much in common with all the rest. Pennsylvania had no desire on principle to commit its program of road building to private enterprise, and in fact had resorted unsuccessfully to several other expedients before chartering its first turnpike company. That was the pattern in most of the states where the companies later flourished; in the late 1700s, the states tried lotteries, forced road service from local landowners, grants-in-aid to localities, and even offers of large acreages to contractors if they would build roads to the interior. All these measures failed, as well as the routine expedient of levying taxes and spending them on the highways of the states. None of the states' financing schemes could begin to supply the volume of capital necessary for the improvements the people were more and more vociferously demanding as they in ever larger numbers pushed to the West. An economist might have told the states that if the people needed roads that badly, it ought to be a simple matter to levy sufficient taxes to pay for them, but then as now political reality was not always conducive to economic models, particularly when the people using the roads were often using them to leave the states. *In view of the durable consensus on the necessity of publicly financed roads that developed well before the end of the nineteenth century, it is a little ironic that the private road companies should have been chartered only because it proved impossible for the states themselves to raise enough capital to build the roads everyone seemed to want.*[71] [Emphasis added]

Although the early part of the nineteenth century was the heyday of private road construction, similar efforts are to be found much later on. The Lincoln Highway, for example, was built in the twentieth cen-

---

[71] Wooldridge (1970, pp. 129–30).

tury.[72] Although not privately owned, its impetus, and much of its financing, came from private sources. The idea for a road across the United States was first presented by Carl Fisher in 1912 to a body of automobile and allied businessmen, who, as we can imagine, had an immediate and pressing interest in the construction of highway mileage. And there were dozens of private contributions, including $300,000 from Goodyear and $150,000 from Packard, although these were given to various state governments for actual construction.

Furthermore, if the existence of externalities are held to be an impediment to the private construction of roads, then the existence of private railroads throughout American history must be counted as evidence to the contrary, for the external effects are virtually the same in the two cases. Yet the existence of externalities has never acted as a barrier to private railroad construction. Indeed, as of 1950, there were some 224,000 miles of railroad track in operation,[73] virtually all of it privately owned; this is truly ample testimony to the fact that the existence of claimed externalities has not interfered with the construction of substantial railroad mileage.

Conclusion

Finally, even if the externality–public good argument for government intervention were correct, it would be problematic because it can so easily lead to abuses. All sorts of state activities could, on the same grounds, be demanded by those who advocate an ever larger role for government. Baumol warns of this when he says:

"The presence of external effects and other grounds for increased governmental intervention need not constitute a license for petty bureaucrats and others to impose their view of virtue and good living on a recalcitrant public."[74]

The problem is, of course, that many governmental operations, supposedly justified on public goods grounds, do not really involve

---

[72] See Lincoln Highway Association (1935).
[73] U.S. Bureau of the Census (1976, p. 604).
[74] Baumol (1963, p. 14).

externalities, even in the view of the proponents of this view. Says Peterson, for example:

> But government does not limit itself to activities which are purely of this type [collective or public goods], or, necessarily, even approximately of this type. For a variety of reasons, it may, and often does, enter fields where the principles of the private economy can and do operate, wholly or in considerable degree. This happens when a government undertakes to supply water or gas or electricity or street railway or bus service, when it markets forest or mineral products from the public domain, or even when it provides postal service.[75]

Peterson might well have included the provision of highways in this regard. Savas makes a different but related point:

> Public goods are properly paid for by the public at large, for their benefits cannot be charged to individual consumers or small collective groups. However, from this reasonable arrangement, it is easy to leap to the unwarranted implication that public goods paid for by the public through payments to the public tax collector must be provided to the public by a public agency through public employees. There is no logical reason for the mode of payment to bear any relation to the ultimate mode of delivery of collective goods.[76]

Here, again, we find the government, seemingly basing its actions on the "scientific" arguments from externalities, somehow overstepping these bounds. And we know that this trend is widespread. Modern government has undertaken a myriad of tasks unrelated to the collective good argument (or any other arguments we have discussed here), as Peterson has indicated. As Savas suggests, even when the collective goods argument does apply, the ensuing state involvement monumentally oversteps the bounds set by it. In how many cases does the government

---

[75] Peterson (1950, p. 192).
[76] Savas (1974, p. 483).

limit its activities merely to ensuring that the good is produced? Quite to the contrary, in the transportation sector, as in many others, the government has undertaken the direct provision of the service by a public agency, through public employees.

Given this state of affairs, it behooves us to question the role played by the collective goods argument. Is it, as is implicitly maintained by its adherents, an intellectually sound defense of government activities? Or is it no more than an apologetic for programs which would have been embarked upon regardless of the availability of the argument—and which were actually begun long before the argument was conceived?

9 The Gold Standard: A Critique of Friedman, Mundell, Hayek and Greenspan from the Free Enterprise Perspective

This is an essay which takes as its jumping off point the free enterprise system. It then attempts to evaluate the contributions of four distinguished scholars to monetary theory in general, and to an evaluation of the gold standard in particular. I take for granted the general case for markets, competition, economic freedom.[1] The four individuals mentioned in the title have been chosen because they are widely believed to be exemplars of this limited government, free market, political philosophy—and are also opponents of the gold standard. It is one of the purposes of the present contribution to test that very proposition. To wit, it is an attempt to see how consistent with their otherwise expressed principles of free enterprise are their contributions to monetary theory.

Which monetary regime is consistent with the free enterprise philosophy? In order to answer that, we must first be clear on what is meant by this political economic theory. *Laissez faire* capitalism implies economic freedom and private property rights. As long as these are respected, a person may do whatever he wishes; there are no economic regulations,

---

Reprinted with kind permission of Emerald from *Managerial Finance* 25, no. 5 (1999): 15–33.
[1]   For a defense of this position, see Friedman (1962, 1979); Mises (1966); Rothbard (1962).

and government is limited to protecting persons and property through courts, armies and police. People are "free to choose" (Friedman and Friedman 1980) within these legal constraints.

My argument is that the gold standard is the only financial arrangement compatible with such a vision (Mises 1966, pp. 471–78). This is because all that is meant by a gold standard are those monetary arrangements which are arrived at by freely-choosing individuals. However, it is a matter of historical fact that whenever societies have been "free to choose" in this regard (Menger 1950, pp. 257–85), they have always evolved to gold.[2] It is for this reason that an actual misnomer has arisen within the field of economics: although "gold standard" would appear to imply that the yellow metal has something to do with monetary arrangements, this is not strictly true. In actual point of fact, the phrase "gold standard" now denotes whichever commodity emerges as money from the free interplay of market forces. For example, if silver, or platinum, or some other commodity were to have arisen as the money as a result of free market forces, there is not one advocate of the "gold standard" who would be disappointed; this is the case, because, literally, that is how the phase functions in our language: it refers to free market money, whatever its chemical properties.

This makes our quest at once more difficult and easier too. It is now simplicity itself to be able to declare that all those who oppose the gold standard (as defined above) cannot possibly advocate free enterprise, at least in this one field. This follows from the very definition. If all that gold standard *means* is marketplace money, and one opposes the gold standard, then one cannot without pain of contradiction assert that he favors the free operation of markets. But it is more difficult, too, if only for psychological reasons; opponents of this thesis will feel victimized by sharp practice; they will charge definitional legerdemain.

But there is no way out of this contradiction. The gold standard advocate means no more by this term than "free market money." The proof of this is in his warm embrace of any other metal (or commodity)

---

[2]   And sometimes to silver, for smaller denominations.

which comes to be used as the money medium in the absence of any government compulsion. To be fair to the critics, however, we now turn to a careful consideration of their several objections to our thesis. We do not take up those emanating from Marxists, Keynesians, or other self-avowed enemies of economic freedom. Rather, we look at the critiques penned by scholars who are associated with this very same perspective. And not only are the four scholars mentioned above associated with it: they are seen by all and sundry as leading advocates, as foremost spokesmen, for economic liberty. All the more disappointing, then, that all four have rejected the market's choice in this regard, in favor of a panoply of idiosyncratic interventionist monetary schemes.

Milton Friedman

Friedman (1960, p. 4) starts out on a high note, fully justifying his leadership role in this field. He states:

> The (classical) liberal is suspicious of assigning to government any functions that can be performed through the market, both because this *substitutes coercion for voluntary cooperation*, in the area in question and because, by giving government an increased role, it threatens freedom in other areas. Control over monetary and banking arrangements is a particularly dangerous power to entrust to government because of its far-reaching effects on economic activity at large—as numerous episodes from ancient times to the present and over the whole of the globe tragically demonstrate. [Emphasis added]

After ringing this glowing endorsement for monetary freedom, one could almost infer that he favors the gold standard. After all, he extols the virtues of the market and of free competition, and as we know, it was through this very process that gold "beat out" all other competitors. He forthrightly distinguishes between voluntary cooperation and coercion,[3] and this, too, implies the gold standard, the only monetary

---

[3] The most important distinction in all of political economy, one which, unfortunately, escapes the notice of many commentators in this field.

system which arose through the voluntary cooperation of the market.[4] Not content with merely a theoretical account of the virtues of the gold standard, Friedman seemingly buttresses his case with an empirical historical note, attesting to the tragic history of governmental (e.g., nongold standard) control. What more could be said on behalf of gold in so short a statement? Nothing at all.

In the event, however, we are sadly disappointed. For after so promising a beginning, our reasonable expectations that this is just the preliminary to a clarion call for market money is dashed to pieces. Says Friedman (1962, p. 40):

> The fundamental defect of a commodity standard (read gold standard) from the point of view of the *society as a whole,* is that it requires the use of real resources to add to the stock of money. People must work hard to dig gold out of the ground in South Africa—in order to rebury it in Fort Knox or some similar place. The necessity of using real resources for the operation of a commodity standard establishes a *strong incentive for people* to find ways to achieve the same result without employing these resources. If people *will accept* as money pieces of paper on which is printed "I promise to pay ___ units of the commodity standard," these pieces of paper can perform the same function as the physical pieces of gold or silver, and they require very much less in resources to produce. [Emphasis added]

This is very disappointing, to say the least. The argument as presented here in the two quotes above amounts to the following syllogism:

(1) a ringing endorsement of freedom
(2) a realization that this freedom will cost real resources
(3) the conclusion that we should not indulge in such freedom after all, since it costs something; instead, there is an option made on behalf of coercion, and we are, in effect, told to forget all about "substituting voluntary cooperation for coercion."

---

[4] See Mises (1981) for the view that fiat currency *must* arise through coercion.

Let us assume for a moment, with Friedman, that freedom costs real resources, at least in the monetary field. This still does not logically imply anything like (3) the conclusion of his argument. For there are very different alternative resolutions of these propositions, which make at least as much sense as his own. For example, what about "justice though the heavens fall?" What has become of "our lives, our fortunes, and our sacred honor?" And where has gone "millions for defense, not a penny for tribute?" These, too, are equally valid as conclusions of the Friedmanite premises. That he has not taken up any of them is irrelevant to his skills as a positive economist, but speaks volumes in terms of his ranking of the importance of premises (1) and (2).

Nor need we resort only to philosophical notions of freedom. Even without these arguments, it still does not follow that just because a gold standard costs something, it is not worth it and should therefore be eschewed. Cars, houses and sailing boats all cost "real resources." Does this mean we should never buy them? Not at all. The usual ways such matters are settled is to consider their costs as well as their benefits.

What, then, are the values of gold as a money? Why should people pick it when they are "free to choose?"[5] Why should this be their choice when it "costs real resources," and there are all these cheap substitutes potentially available? To ask the question in this way is practically to answer it. They choose gold, they have always chosen gold, because even though it is more expensive,[6] the credits derived more than make up for the debits. The advantages provided by gold *vis-à-vis* other commodity standards (malleability, portability, high value per unit weight and volume, etc.) are only the tip of the iceberg. Of far greater importance is its superiority when compared to fiat paper. And here the record is clear. Throughout history, and even in the modern era, millions of people have been victimized by governmental fiat currency inflation,[7] even as Friedman has himself stated above.

---

[5] This is a phrase paradoxically popularized by Milton Friedman. Paradoxically, in that he refuses to apply it to the field of money.

[6] We shall challenge this assumption, or stipulation, below.

[7] The German hyperinflation of the 1920s was perhaps only the most egregious example. See Friedman and Schwartz (1963), Mises (1966), Rothbard (1983), and Hoppe (1993b).

The point is, gold is like an insurance policy. Just as locks, fences and doors are used to preclude losses from theft—even though they come only at the expense of real resources, so, too does the costly use of gold attain something desirable, namely, protection from statist monetary depredations.[8]

So far, we have been assuming the truth of (2). It is now time to call this assumption into question. Much to the contrary of Friedman's assertion, it is simply not true that a gold standard will be a debit, even in financial terms. Digging gold in South Africa and elsewhere, and burying it in Fort Knox or similar places takes place *anyway*, whether or not gold is the money medium.[9] This metal is a valuable commodity, and will be sought after whether or not it is used as money.[10]

Let us now address ourselves to several other problems with Friedman's analysis. First, from whose perspective is the choice of monetary medium to be made? Friedman presumably speaks "from the point of view of society as a whole." The obvious retort here is that from the economic perspective, only individuals choose, not societies as a whole, and whenever individuals have been free to choose, they have selected

---

[8] Is our line of reasoning guilty of violating the fallacy of composition? An objection to the thesis adumbrated here might be posed as follows:

> Yes, yes, you have shown that the gold standard has real benefits as an insurance policy against government monetary profligacy, which has unfortunately characterized the history of virtually all nations. However, that is a matter of macroeconomics. Society as a *whole* would be better off with a gold standard. But as far as each *individual* is concerned, he has no such reason to favor the "barbarous relic." On the contrary, the typical economic actor rationally prefers fiat paper to commodity gold.

The reply is very straightforward. If this charge were true, the market would never have originally migrated to a gold standard. Instead, we would have moved directly to fiat currency.

[9] I owe this point to Roger Garrison.

[10] True, as a medium of exchange will increase its value over and above what it would have been for purely metallic use (jewelry, dentistry, etc.). But this cannot be used to deny the proposition that vast amounts of the yellow metal will still be dug up and then reburied, whether or not it is used as money. This assumes not only that gold is not used as money, but also that it is not expected in the future to be used for this purpose. Further, it is highly probable that were gold's "moneyness" to be ended entirely, there would be at least a temporary end to the mining of this metal, as the some 135,000 tonnes now above ground could be used for other purposes. (I owe these latter two points to Lawrence M. Parks.)

gold from amongst all market possibilities. Fiat currency, to be sure, has been *imposed* on societies, but never freely chosen.

The only interpretation of Friedman's remarks that is logically coherent is that it is not from the *economic perspective* that the choosing of a monetary system is to be attained, but rather from the political. If this is the correct meaning, then the truth of his statement cannot be denied. We did indeed choose paper money through the political system; it is undeniable that our democratically elected representatives chose to rescind the market choice of gold, and impose fiat currency in its place. But what does this have to do with freedom? Just because a majority of the people elected representatives who choose a certain path does not mean that this path enhances liberty. Indeed, one might go so far as to defend the very opposite thesis: that if a democratically elected government made a given decision—of any kind, type or variety—it was probably counterproductive to freedom.

Second, Friedman asserts that there is "a strong incentive for people" to find substitutes for gold money, since it costs real resources. We have seen the fallacy of the former part of this claim, but the former is problematic as well. It implies that the masses of the people, through markets, prefer greenbacks to gold. In actual point of fact, though, such a decision was never made in this manner; on the contrary, this was imposed from above, politically.

Third, he talks of "people *accepting* as money pieces of paper on which is printed 'I promise to pay ___ units of the commodity standard'." But this is entirely ingenuous. Of course, they will accept a statist medium of exchange after legal tender laws require this, and after gold has been, in effect, outlawed as a money. But this is an entirely different matter than the one addressed by Friedman in the first (1960) quote above. There, he talks in terms of substituting coercion for voluntary cooperation, presumably allowing the decision as to the money substance to emanate from markets; here, he speaks of "accepting" paper as payment under a political regime which compels such behavior and prohibits alternatives.

Even more egregious, this statement is entirely compatible with the gold standard! For no one defines this institutional arrangement in such a way as to preclude people from carrying around in their wallets ware-house receipts for specific amounts of this metal. E.g., under a full robust 100 percent gold standard, people could still conduct business with checks, plastic credit cards, or folding money, or any other convenient substitute. The point is, all of these transactions would be *in terms of* gold; this metal would *underlay* all commercial interactions, even if its actual use is mainly implicit. Under this interpretation, Friedman is incomprehensibly attacking the gold standard by praising one particular aspect of it.[11] Thus, if all that is on his mind is the saving of resources, our economic freedom need not be pillaged in order to accomplish this task. All we need do is reinaugurate the gold standard, and content ourselves with the fact that various money substitutes will undoubtedly be employed as attributes of it, thus obviating the need for digging up excessive amounts of gold.

In addition to the fame he has garnered as an opponent of the gold standard, Friedman has taken a high profile in support of flexible exchange rates between different currencies.

In contrast, a full, worldwide gold standard implies fixed exchange rates. In this scenario, the names of the national currencies indicate, merely, the different numbers of grams of the precious metal embodied in them. For example, the pound might be four grams of gold, the dollar two grams, and the yen one gram. If so, there is an unambiguous, totally "fixed" exchange rate between them all: the ratio of 4:2:1. That is, the pound is twice as valuable as the dollar, which in turn is worth two yen; and, of course, four yen trade for one pound.

It is sometimes objected that this would be akin to price control, where the price of one commodity is "fixed" in terms of another, or of money. But nothing could be further from the truth. The reason for the "fixity" in price controls is due to legislative enactments. If silver must exchange for gold at the rate of 16 to 1, this is because of unwise and invasive law, not any natural requirement. But a fixed gold exchange rate comes about for entirely different reasons. It is because the various

---

[11] To be fair to him, it must be conceded that the use of substitutes is compatible with practically *any* monetary regime. But it cannot be denied that this also applies to gold.

national currencies are simply the names of different amounts of gold; the fixity, here, is engendered by this fact, not man-made law. It is as natural as the fact that nickels, dimes and quarters trade at fixed rates with one another, that feet, yards and miles are all inextricably tied up with one another in fixed proportions. The former is clearly a violation of market freedom; not so the latter.

One problem with flexible exchange rates, therefore, is that they cannot be made compatible with a worldwide gold standard, which requires fixity, not flexibility. Another is that they lower the barriers against inflation. Gold, of course, is the inflation fighter *par excellence*. Since it is virtually impossible to counterfeit this metal, at least in the modern era, the stock of money under this standard is fixed, apart from new mine production. This holds true apart from this consideration. Even in the absence of a pure gold standard, fixed exchange rates provide some insurance against inflation which is not forthcoming from the flexible system. Under fixity, if one country inflates, it falls victim to a balance of payment crisis. If and when it runs out of foreign exchange holdings, it must devalue, a relatively difficult process, fraught with danger for the political leaders involved. Under flexibility, in contrast, inflation brings about no balance of payment crisis, nor any need for a politically embarrassing devaluation. Instead, there is a relatively painless depreciation of the home (or inflationary) currency against its foreign counterparts.[12]

Robert Mundell

How does Robert Mundell fit into the gold standard picture? Strictly speaking, he does not fit in at all. He is not particularly known for his views on this subject, and spends little of his intellectual capital on it. This is not to say he eschews it totally; on the contrary, his views in this regard are typical of most mainstream economists: he rejects the monetization of gold, contenting himself with attempts to bring greater accountability to a system that has long since been wrenched out of the hands of the market, and given over to the tender mercies of the political

---

[12] True, this also has its political and economic costs, particularly for those who see a connection between the prestige of a country and the value of its currency in foreign exchange markets. These costs, however, are not sharp and painful; they do not constitute a "crisis."

system. In his particular case he advocates the "gold price rule" which is similar, in effect and in intention, to Friedman's 3 percent "rule" for the Fed. That is, it is an attempt to obviate government's natural tendency to inflate, without setting up a separation of money and state, as would exist under a pure gold standard. If this were all there was to it, he would not have been included in the present work.

The reason he is worthy of this dubious honor—apart from the fact that like the other three, he is noted for a general stance on behalf of economic freedom—is his work in the theory of optimal currency areas (Mundell 1961).[13] That is, the question of what geographical zone is appropriate for each type of money.

In his view, the "optimal currency area" is not the whole world. On the contrary, it encompasses far less territory than that. Right off the bat, that puts him in conflict with the gold standard view, which, of course, sees the optimal currency area for gold as the entire globe. Thus, not only should not the world be on the gold standard for Mundell, it should not operate on the basis of any one currency, no matter what it is, whether or not it is gold. We need, in his analysis, many currencies. But not competing ones, the Hayekian perspective. Instead, each one should be supreme, within its own area.

How does he arrive at this conclusion? He starts off with an initial assumption of full employment and equilibrium in the balance of payments. Then he posits a shift in demand, say from country B to country A (Mundell 1961, p. 658). In his Keynesian model, this causes unemployment in B and inflation in A.[14] As a result, there will be a flow of funds from B to A; B will be in balance of payments deficit, A in surplus.

To correct unemployment in B, there should be an increase in its money supply.[15] But this would aggravate inflation in A. So slower or

---

[13] His purpose here was to criticize flexible exchange rates, not the gold standard, but his analysis is nonetheless germane to our present concerns.

[14] For a critique of the Keynesian system, see Hazlitt (1959).

[15] Objections might be leveled at the claim that this is Keynesian and not "monetarist." Although most debates on this and related topics in the professional literature have been between these two purported schools of thought, nothing of the kind is true. But both monetarists and fiscalists employ the Keynesian model of aggregate demand. Therefore, these controversies are more of an internecine battle than a disagreement between two separate

zero monetary growth is indicated there. Or, best of all, a fall in the value of B's currency, and a rise in that of A's.

To the unreconstructed Keynesian, this represents no problem at all. With their keen insights into the workings of macroeconomics, money manipulation, fine-tuning, flexible exchange rates, all is solved.

Now suppose that the world consisted of only the U.S. and Canada (Mundell 1961, p. 659). Again, Mundell posits a situation of initial full employment, and balance of payment equilibrium, this time between the different regions of the two countries. As before, he then assumes a shift in demand. This is not from one country to another, but rather from goods produced in the Western part of both countries to goods produced in the East.

The analysis flows along familiar channels: as a result of this demand shift, there will be unemployment in the West, and inflation in the East. There will be a flow of bank reserves from West to East. The West will be in (internal) balance of payments deficit, the East in surplus. To correct unemployment in the West, an increase in the money supply would be called for. But this would just exacerbate the inflation in the East. Unlike the previous case, there is no solution for Mundell. Except, that is, if currency is tailored to regions which are economically significant, not nations, which need not always be. To wit, there is a solution if the East and the Western zones each have their own separate currencies. Then, the twin scourges of unemployment and inflation can be solved as they were before, through the use of monetary and fiscal policy and flexible exchange rates.

---

philosophies. As Friedman himself says, "we are all Keynesians now" (cited in Samuelson 1970, p. 193).

As it happens, Friedman objects that he has been quoted out of context (personal correspondence). His full statement on this matter as follows: "If by Keynesianism you mean public policy prescriptions of big government budgets, deficit spending, etc., then there are great differences between we monetarists and the Keynesians; but if you mean utilization of the same tools of economic analysis, then we are all Keynesians now" (paraphrase, based on personal conversation). For some purposes, one is inclined to take the Friedman side in his altercation with Samuelson. But for our public policy purposes, the alternative view has its attractions.

Having presented this model, let us now consider a few of its drawbacks. First, how is the region to be defined? Mundell does this in terms of a place within which there is factor mobility, and outside of which there is none. But regions so defined continually change.[16]

That is, relative prices, new discoveries, innovations, the supply and demand of complements and substitutes are in a continual flux in the real world. If there are to be separate currencies for each region, and the regions keep changing, the implication would appear to be that the currencies, too, should continually be altered. This, however, appears more as a recipe for chaos than a serious suggestion for a new monetary policy.

Further, in one sense government is the main or only source of factor immobility. The state, with its regulations, required specifications, "buy local" requirements, licensing arrangements—to say nothing of explicit interferences with trade—is the prime reason why factors of production are less mobile than they would otherwise be. In a bygone era the costs of transportation would have been the chief explanation, but what with all the technological progress achieved here, this is far less important in our modern "shrinking world." If this is so, then under *laissez faire* capitalism, there would be virtually no factor immobility. Given even the approximate truth of these assumptions, the Mundellian region then becomes the entire globe—precisely as it would be under the gold standard. (Here factor immobility is being defined as essentially government prohibition on trade.)

There is an entirely different sense of factor mobility, however. Lying at the opposite end of the spectrum from the previous one, here it consists of the fact that costs (mainly transportation costs) render factors immobile, geographically. Based on this assumption, each individual person would have to be defined as a separate region. This is so because by

---

[16] Mundell (1961, p. 662) sees this as a problem, but contents himself with an appeal to "common sense." One problem with his analysis is that the decision as to how many "regions" there are, and hence how many currencies would be in existence, is not one to be made by the market. Rather, the unspoken implication is that it would be made by Mundell, or a band of economists, or politicians, or perhaps by the entire economics profession. It is likely that if the choice came down to a market or political decision, Mundell would opt for the former.

definition he is the region within which there is mobility, and outside of which there is none. What is the implication of this second model? If there are supposed to be as many different types of currencies as regions, and if each person is a region, then there would have to be as many currencies as there are people—a separate type of money for each person. The problem with this, of course, is that it would be the end of money as we know it. A world with six billion different currencies is, in effect, a world with no money at all. Under these conditions we would fall back to a situation of barter.

Mundell himself sees this problem.[17] But rather than shrinking in horror from either scenario (especially the former) he proposes what all economists in good standing in the neoclassical school would propose—a cost-benefit analysis. If the primary goal is economic stability, then the number of currencies should be larger; if it is the use of money as a medium of exchange, then the fewer the different numbers of currencies the better. So, what *is* the optimal number of currencies for the world? Mundell does not vouchsafe us a specific answer to this rather important question. Reading between the lines, one gets the feeling that this number should lie for Mundell somewhere in between several dozen to a few hundred, but as he never specifies, this is at best an educated guess.

So far, we have accepted the stability argument; the quaint Keynesian notion that monetary and fiscal policy can lead us to the promised land. Actually, however, the charge that Keynesianism is dead from the neck up is hard to resist. And that it was killed off by the spectre of inflationary recession. For in this world-view, the antidote to inflation is to draw down expenditure, whether by fiscal or monetary policy. The cure for unemployment, on the other hand, is to increase general spending. What happens if there is *both* unemployment and inflation in the system? Stepping on the gas will solve the latter problem, but aggravate the former; hitting the brakes will have the opposite effect. The wonder of the matter is not that Keynesianism has foundered on this particular set of shoals, but that it continues to enjoy a ghoulish existence despite

---

[17] States Mundell (1961, p. 660), "the concept of optimum currency areas helps us to see that the conflict . . . between Meade, who sees the need for more currencies, and Scitovsky, who sees the need for fewer . . . reduces to an empirical rather than a theoretical question."

the foregoing. With the best will in the world, monetary and fiscal policy are just not up to the job. Rather than anticyclical, bureaucratic interference with the market has been *pro*-cyclical.[18] Nor can we rely on the best will in the world, as the Public Choice School (Buchanan 1975b; Buchanan and Tullock 1971) has so valiantly taught us. For civil servants, not only private entrepreneurs, can be expected to indulge in "rent-seeking"[19] at the expense of the public good.

A further problem with the Mundell model is that it is open to a possible *reductio ad absurdum* rejoinder. At present, no one worries about a "balance of payments" problem between New York State and New Jersey. Nor between California and Maine, nor Oregon and Florida. But with the advent of the Mundellian perspective, this would no longer be true. Now, we can add this worry to all the rest which plague mankind.

Friedrich Hayek

Hayek (1976) opposes the gold standard. This, indeed, is puzzling, since he has several good things to say about this system:

> Significantly, it was only during the rise of the prosperous modern industrial systems and *during the rule of the gold standard*, that over a period of about two hundred years . . . prices were at the end about where they had been at the beginning. [Emphasis added] (1976, p. 9)
>
> With the exception only of the 200-year period of the gold standard, practically all governments of history have used their exclusive power to issue money in order to defraud and plunder the people. (1976, p. 16)

Why this rejection? It would appear that this is out of a counsel of despair. It is not that he specifically opposes such a system, so much, as

---

[18] It was for this reason that Friedman penned his famous aphorism, "rules, not authority, in monetary policy" as part of his public policy suggestion that the Fed be limited to increasing the money supply by 3 percent annually. See also Simons (1936).

[19] See Krueger (1974); Posner (1975); Tullock (1967, 1980).

it is based on a fear that it would not be allowed to function due to the political realities:

> I do not believe we can now remedy this position by *constructing* some new international monetary order, . . . or even an international agreement to adopt a particular mechanism or system of policy, such as the classical gold standard. I am fairly convinced that any attempt now to reinstate the gold standard by international agreement would break down within a short time and merely discredit the ideal of an international gold standard for even longer. (1976, p. 15)

Unfortunately, Hayek does not realize that the political impossibility of a gold standard—due in part to a rent-seeking desire for inflationary policies—would tend to apply to any other scheme addressed to this end, and for the same reasons. To wit, if the politically powerful desire inflation, and are able to quell the gold standard on this ground, then they would likely be able to obviate any other system, such as the one now proposed by Hayek, which had the same effect.

Another problem is that Hayek does not appreciate the fact that if those such as himself who would advocate gold (but for its expected political impossibility) refrain from doing so on this ground, then they themselves render such an occurrence less likely.

Hayek (1976) repudiates gold for these reasons which, perhaps, may best be characterized as psychological. That is, he implies that there is something problematic about "discredit(ing) the ideal of an international gold standard," and that it would only break down due to lack of widespread appreciation for it.

But in his 1990 work he rejects gold on more sharp and forceful grounds: the government cannot be trusted to run the system, and it is not worthy of being run in the first place. He states (1990, p. 110):

> Most people therefore now believe that relief can come only from returning to a metallic (or other commodity) standard. But not only is a metallic money also exposed to the risks of fraud by government; even at its best it would never be as good a money

as one issued by an agency whose whole business rested on its success in providing a money the public preferred to other kinds. Though gold is an anchor—and any anchor is better than a money left to the discretion of government—it is a very wobbly anchor. It certainly could not bear the strain if the majority of countries tried to run their own gold standard. There just is not enough gold about.

There are several problems with this analysis. First, while it is undoubtedly true that "a metallic money (is) also exposed to the risks of fraud by government,"[20] we should also recognize that metallic money is in far *less* danger of debasement than anything else—particularly Hayek's own suggestion of a market basket of fiat currencies. Debasement might have worked for the king several centuries ago, but what with the modern science of metallurgy, the treasury will likely be in a straight-jacket as far as this scam is concerned.

Second, Hayek is wrong in implying that gold is *not* "issued by an agency whose whole business rested on its success in providing a money the public preferred to other kinds." Our Nobel Laureate presumably supposes that a gold standard must be administered by government. Nothing, however, could be further from the truth. While it can, of course, not be denied that historically the state has indeed achieved control over what passed for a gold standard, this is by no means necessary. That is, it is entirely possible, and plausible, for the whole industry—from mining to minting, from banking to warehousing, from certification to providing brand names—to be run privately. And this is precisely the public policy alternative to his "competing money" system.

Third, there is no minimal requirement with regard to the number of gold ounces available to serve as the money. There is thus no "strain" that "could not be borne," if not only the majority of countries, but the entire world, with Mars and Venus tossed in for good measure, decided to embrace the gold standard. All that would occur is that the value of

---

[20] It would seem that *nothing* is free of this particular risk.

each gold ounce would rise in value, until, in equilibrium, the monetary needs of the entire community could be satisfied.

Instead of the gold standard, Hayek proposes[21] the elimination of legal tender laws (1976, pp. 17–19), coupled with competition between the present statist currencies, and a new one to be called the "ducat" (1990, p. 46).

No one who favors freedom in the monetary area can disagree with Hayek's call to end legal tender laws. These are an affront to our rights to contract. If I purchase a cow from you, and promise to pay you two ounces of gold, under this enactment I may break our agreement, and force you to accept instead some fiat coins of the realm, which are legal tender for all debts public and private. Under strict legal tender laws, you have no right to insist that I honor our contract and pay you back in gold.[22]

But this step is only necessary for monetary liberty, not sufficient. And, as it happens, accomplishing it will do very little for the ultimate goal. Why is this? It is because this public policy recommendation fails to incorporate the insights of Mises's (1912) regression theorem.[23] In that view, money must originally have been a commodity, highly valued for reasons other than its ability to transact business. It was initially accepted as a money in return for goods other than its ability to transact business. It was initially accepted as a money in return for goods or services only because of the well-founded expectation that when the recipient wished to turn around and buy other items with the good he has just received, he would be able to do just that. Without this assurance, no one would accept the item in payment for parting with the good or service in question in the first place. And what explains this pattern of trust, or acceptability? The fact that the (soon to be money)

---

[21] See also Hayek (1948).

[22] From time to time gold clauses become legal, as do futures contracts which allow for gold delivery. This complicates the situation somewhat. (I owe this point to Lawrence M. Parks).

[23] For critiques of this theorem, see Patinkin (1965), Anderson (1917), and Ellis (1934); for replies, see Mises (1966, pp. 405–19) and Rothbard (1991).

commodity was in wide use on the basis of its own merits as a consumption item.[24]

States Rothbard (1981–1982, p. 9):

> Hayek's plan ignores the most fundamental part of Mises' regression theorem: that nothing ever becomes money out of the blue; that it can only emerge as money as a unit of weight of a useful market-produced commodity; almost always either gold or silver. Once the public becomes accustomed to the dollar or pound as a unit of weight of gold, *then* the government can sever the accustomed name from its base in the market-produced commodity, and seize the monopoly of supplying it as a fiat currency—with results that we know all too well in the 20th century.

The key element of money ("moneyness") is this pattern of trust, or acceptability. Without it, nothing can be money, be it ever so attractive, and imbued with the figures of no matter how many princes or presidents. With it, practically *anything*[25] can be money, no matter how modest and unassuming. Once this faith or credence has been established, it is very hard to break it.[26]

Legal tender and other statist laws were undoubtedly instrumental in the past in breaking the link between the commodity gold and the "moneyness" it once had. But it does not follow that rescinding this law now will succeed in turning back the clock. On the contrary, once acceptability of a fiat currency has been attained in this way, legal tender laws are no longer necessary to maintain it. Money has a life of its own in this respect, barring extraordinary circumstances, such as hyperinflation.

The reason we all accept U.S. currency today is *not* due to the legal tender law. It is because of its present "moneyness:" we all have the firm conviction that if we accept it, others will, too, when it comes time for

---

[24] This is why early monies typically consisted of salt, or sugar, or dried fish or some such. For a discussion of this process see Menger (1950, pp. 257–85).

[25] Radford (1945) tells of cigarettes being used as money in prisoner of war camps.

[26] Hyperinflations may sometimes be sufficient to wean an economy away from its money, but little else can.

us to spend it. If the legal tender law were rescinded tomorrow, U.S. currency would likely still circulate as a money.

Let us now consider the second aspect of Hayek's proposal, competition between fiat currencies, up to and including the "ducat," a basket of other fiat currencies. There is, to be sure, nothing wrong with competition. If anything, there is far too little of this precious activity, and more can well be preferred to less. But what is needed is *market* competition, not competition between fiat currencies. For economic liberty consists of private individuals competing against one another; it has nothing to do with rivalry between states, or statist institutions such as fiat currency.

States Rothbard (1981–1982, p. 9):

[Here is] the major flaw in Hayek's scheme: Not just that no one would pay any attention to these currencies, but that the scheme leaves the really important current moneys, dollars, pounds, etc., in the hands of monopoly government. Hayek's "denationalized" money may allow for freedom to produce such trivial paper tickets as "Hayeks" and "Rothbards," ("Ducats") but it would disastrously leave real money: dollars, pounds, etc. safely nationalized and monopolized in the hands of government. And so inflation would proceed unchecked upon its way.

It cannot be denied that the Catholic notion of subsidiarity, or decentralism, or federalism, has a role to play; but only within *political* institutions. That is to say, for any given level of governmental intervention, it is better that it take place at the local than at the central level. This is because people can always "vote with their feet" if a city or state becomes abusive, but find it far more difficult to move to a different country if victimized at that level.

For example, it would enhance liberty by not one whit should the government create a second wholly-owned post office, to compete with the first. Customers may possibly receive better service, but that is an entirely different matter. The same applies to a school voucher program whose only effect is to promote competition within the public school system. Again, there might conceivably be a gain in efficiency from such an enterprise, but this can have nothing to do with free markets, since by definition such institutions are in no way involved.

Hayek's suggestion is subject to much the same criticism as were flexible exchange rates. The similarity is that in both cases trade and competition are supported. But these phenomena are only necessary, not sufficient, for a free market. Also required is an underlying set of legitimate property rights. One might as well advocate trade in stolen goods. This, too, would increase utility in the sense that this term is used in welfare economics. But it would not augment liberty. On the contrary, heightened efficiency would reduce it; for if there must be theft in this world, at least it should be allowed to be as *in*efficient as possible. The point is, fiat currencies are not themselves aspects of markets; they are not derived, nor deriveable, from voluntary choices of consenting economic actors. They are, rather, imposed from above by the political system. As such, trade in them, no matter how salutary on other grounds, cannot be counted as an aspect of economic freedom.

Hayek's competitive ducat system may in some practical ways be preferable to present institutional arrangements. It will not increase freedom, but it may enhance consumer satisfaction. But clearly it is inferior to gold on both counts. This metal was chosen, not imposed by fiat; it is therefore compatible with free enterprise. And the fact that gold passed the market test of competition—something that cannot be said on behalf of any of these other alternatives—suggests that it is preferable on merely pragmatic grounds as well.

Alan Greenspan

This economist presents the greatest challenge to our thesis: that the four scholars named in the title of this paper do not consistently maintain their adherence to free market principles, at least when it comes to gold. The reason for the difficulty is that Greenspan (1966) is, seemingly, an enthusiastic supporter of the gold standard. Based on direct citations, he is as good on gold as it is possible to be, at least from a strictly economic perspective. It is worth quoting him at great length on this point, to show just how keen is his appreciation of the gold standard, and of its connection between gold and liberty:

An almost hysterical antagonism toward the gold standard is one issue which unites statists of all persuasions. They seem to sense—perhaps more clearly and subtly than many consistent defenders of *laissez faire*—that gold and economic freedom are inseparable, that the gold standard is an instrument of *laissez faire* and that each implies and requires the other. (p. 96)

When gold is accepted as the medium of exchange by most or all nations, an unhampered free international gold standard serves to foster a worldwide division of labor and the broadest international trade. Even though the units of exchange (the dollar, the pound, the franc, etc.) differ from country to country, when all are defined in terms of gold the economies of the different countries act as one—so long as there are no restraints on trade or on the movement of capital. (p. 98)

But the opposition to the gold standard in any form—from a growing number of welfare state advocates—was prompted by a much subtler insight: the realization that the gold standard is incompatible with chronic deficit spending (the hallmark of the welfare state). (p. 100)

This is the shabby secret of the welfare statist's tirades against gold. Deficit spending is simply a scheme for the "hidden" confiscation of wealth. Gold stands in the way of this insidious process. It stands as a protector of property rights. If one grasps this, one has no difficulty in understanding the statist's antagonism toward the gold standard. (p. 101)

It might be possible to find a more ringing endorsement of the gold standard, and in particular a tighter linkage between it and economic freedom, but one would have to delve deep into the literature to find it. For our purposes, we may take his statements as quite definitive: the gold standard enhances economic well-being, is necessary for economic freedom, and is cordially hated and detested by people who oppose liberty and prosperity, and for those very reasons.

How, then, can we account for the fact that Greenspan has been Chairman of the Federal Reserve System for many years, and not only do we not yet have a gold standard, we have absolutely no movement in that direction?[27]

In this context Rothbard's (1987) analysis of this puzzling situation has the ring of truth to it. In his view, Greenspan *does* favor gold and *laissez faire* capitalism, but only on a high philosophical level where he does not have to *do* anything about it; in contrast, he does not champion it as a practical matter, for then he would be called upon at least to show some evidence of his beliefs. States Rothbard (p. 3):

> Greenspan's real qualification is that he can be trusted never to rock the Establishment's boat. He has long positioned himself in the very middle of the economic spectrum. He is, like most other longtime Republican economists, a conservative Keynesian, which in these days is almost indistinguishable from the liberal Keynesians in the Democratic camp. . . . Which means that he wants moderate deficits and tax increases, and will loudly worry about inflation as he pours on increases in the money supply.
>
>   There is one thing, however, that makes Greenspan unique, and that sets him off from (the) Establishment. . . . And that is that he is a follower of Ayn Rand, and therefore "philosophically" believes in *laissez faire* and even the gold standard. But as *The New York Times* and other important media hastened to assure us, Alan only believes in *laissez faire* "on the high philosophical level." In *practice* in the policies he advocates, he is a centrist like everyone else because he is a "pragmatist." . . .
>
>   Thus, Greenspan is only in favor of the gold standard if all conditions are right: if the budget is balanced, trade is free, inflation is licked, everyone has the right philosophy, etc. In the same way, he might say he only favors free trade if all conditions are right:

---

[27] To be fair to Greenspan, he has spoken publicly in favor of the gold standard. For example, see his speech at Catholic University, Leuven, Belgium, on January 14, 1997. (For a commentary on this see Parks 1998.) But efforts such as these are hardly consistent with serious public policy support for this system. Surely a strong advocate of a free market gold standard would make this a centerpiece of his administration; perhaps even go so far as to threaten to resign were it not implemented, let alone seriously studied with a view toward implementation.

if the budget is balanced, unions are weak, we have a gold standard, the right philosophy, etc. In short, *never* are one's "high philosophical principles" applied to one's actions. It becomes almost piquant for the Establishment to have this man in its camp.

Of course, there are other possible explanations of this phenomenon: Greenspan has changed his mind about the efficacy of gold (but then, why not share his new reasoning with the world?); he still advocates this monetary standard, but deems it so politically incorrect as to not be feasible even to attempt to implement it (but who better than the Chairman of the Fed to do this?); he has fallen under the sway of the inside the beltway types; he regards his early flirtation with gold as a youthful indiscretion. But all of this is speculation. Perhaps his autobiography will one day clarify this matter.

Conclusion

We have considered the views of four economists usually associated with the free enterprise system. We have found that despite this background, none of them have consistently applied that theory to the question of the money medium. That is, all have rejected the gold standard—on one level or another.

Before calling into question their positions, we must address ourselves to one additional issue: have *any* erstwhile champions of capitalism seen their way clear to applying these principles to money? If not, then the failure of these four is perhaps more understandable; perhaps there is something about gold which renders the usual capitalist principles somehow inapplicable.

Unfortunately for this thesis, there are indeed economists who have championed the market in other areas, and nonetheless carried through consistently with regard to monetary policy. They have supported it, and not as a theoretical curiosity, but rather as a living, breathing vital aspect of political economy.

Part Two:
HUMAN RIGHTS

10 The Nonaggression Axiom of Libertarianism

The nonaggression axiom is the lynchpin of the philosophy of libertarianism. It states, simply, that it shall be legal for anyone to do anything he wants, provided only that he not initiate (or threaten) violence against the person or legitimately owned property of another. That is, in the free society, one has the right to manufacture, buy or sell any good or service at any mutually agreeable terms. Thus, there would be no victimless crime prohibitions, price controls, government regulation of the economy, etc.

If the nonaggression axiom is the basic building block of libertarianism, private property rights based on (Lockean and Rothbardian) homesteading principles are the foundation. For if A reaches into B's pocket, pulls out his wallet and runs away with it, we cannot know that A is the aggressor and B the victim. It may be that A is merely repossessing his own wallet, the one B stole from him yesterday. But given a correct grounding in property rights, the nonaggression axiom is a very powerful tool in the war of ideas. For most individuals believe, and fervently so, that it is wrong to invade other people or their property. Who, after all, favors theft, murder or rape? With this as an entering

Printed with kind permission of Mr. Llewellyn H. Rockwell, Jr. This article was initially posted on http://www.lewrockwell.com website.

wedge, libertarians are free to apply this axiom to all of human action, including, radically, to unions, taxes, and even government itself.

The nonaggression axiom and private property rights theory which underlies it have recently come under furious attack, amazingly, from commentators actually calling themselves libertarians. Let us consider two cases posed by these people.

First, you are standing on the balcony of a twenty-fifth-story high-rise apartment when, much to your dismay, you lose your footing and fall out. Happily, in your downward descent, you manage to grab onto a flagpole protruding from the fifteenth floor of the balcony of another apartment, ten floors below. Unhappily, the owner of this apartment comes out to her balcony, states that you are protesting by holding on to her flag pole, and demands that you let go (e.g., drop another fifteen floors to your death). You protest that you only want to hand-walk your way down the flag pole, into her apartment, and then right out of it, but she is adamant. As a libertarian, are you bound to obey her?

Second case. You are lost in the woods, freezing, with no food. You will die without shelter and a meal. Fortunately, you come upon a warm cabin stocked with staples. You intend to eat, stay the night, leave your business card, and pay double any reasonable price that could be asked. Unfortunately, the cabin has a sign posted on the door: "Warning. Private Property. No Trespassing." Do you tamely go off into the woods and die?

Opponents of the nonaggression axiom maintain that you have no obligation to die in either of these cases, much less in the name of private property rights. In their view these concepts have been adopted to *promote* human life and well-being, which, ordinarily, they do, and superlatively so. But in these exceptional cases, where the nonaggression standard would be contrary to utilitarian principles, it should be jettisoned. The nonaggression principle, for them, is a good rule of thumb, which sometimes, rarely, should be ignored.

There are several grave problems with these critiques of the nonaggression axiom.

1. They misunderstand the nature of libertarianism. These arguments implicitly assume that libertarianism is a moral philosophy, a

guide to proper behavior, as it were. Should the flagpole hanger let go? Should the hiker go off and die? But libertarianism is a theory concerned with the justified use of aggression, or violence, based on property rights, not morality. Therefore, the only proper questions which can be addressed in this philosophy are of the sort: if the flagpole hanger attempts to come into the apartment, and the occupant shoots him for trespassing, would the forces of law and order punish the home owner? Or, if the owner of the cabin in the woods sets up a booby trap, such that when someone forces his way into his property he gets a face full of buckshot, would he be guilty of a law violation? When put in this way, the answer is clear. The owner in each case is in the right, and the trespasser in the wrong. If force is used to protect property rights, even deadly force, the owner is not guilty of the violation of any licit law.

2. These examples purposefully try to place us in the mind of the criminal perpetrator of the crime of trespass. We are invited, that is, to empathize with the flagpole hanger, and the hiker, not the respective property owners. But let us reverse this perspective. Suppose the owner of the apartment on the fifteenth floor has recently been victimized by a rape, perpetrated upon her by a member of the same ethnic or racial group as the person now hand-walking his way down her flag pole, soon to uninvitedly enter her apartment. May she not shoot him in self-defense before he enters her premises? Or, suppose that the owner of the cabin in the woods has been victimized by several break-ins in the past few months, and has finally decided to do something in defense of his property. Or, suppose that the owner, himself, views his cabin as his own life preserver. Then, may he not take steps to safeguard his property? To ask these questions is to answer them, at least for the consistent libertarian.

3. The criticisms of libertarian property rights theory base their views on the philosophy of emergencies. The nonaggression axiom is all well and good in ordinary circumstances, but when there are lifeboat situations, all bets are off. The problem, however, with violating libertarian law for special exigencies is that these occurrences are more commonplace than supposed. Right now, there are numerous people dying of starvation in poor parts of the world. Some are suffering from illnesses

which could be cured cheaply, e.g., by penicillin. We have all read those advertisements placed by aid agencies: "Here is little Maria. You can save her, and her entire village, by sending us some modest amount of money each month."

In point of fact, many so-called libertarians who have attacked the nonaggression axiom on these emergency grounds live in housing of a middle class level or better; drive late model cars; eat well; have jewelry; send their children to pricey colleges. If they truly believed in their critiques, none of this would be true. For if the cabin owner and the apartment dweller are to give up their property rights to save the hiker and the flagpole hanger, then *they* must give up their comfortable middle class life styles in behalf of all the easily cured sick and starving people in the world. That they have not done so shows they do not even take their own arguments seriously.

The logical implication of their coercive welfarist argument is far worse than merely being required to give a few dollars a month to a relief agency. For suppose they do this. Their standard of living will *still* be far greater than those on the verge of death from straightened circumstances. No, as long as these relatively rich "libertarians" have enough money to keep themselves from dying from poverty, the logic of their argument compels them to give every penny they own over and above that level to alleviate the plight of the endangered poor.

11 Libertarianism, Positive Obligations and Property Abandonment: Children's Rights

A basic premise of libertarianism (Cuzán 1979; de Jasay 1985, 1997; Friedman 1978; Hoppe 1989; Hummel 1990; Kinsella 1996a; Morriss 1998; Rothbard 1978, 1982; Skoble 1995; Sechrest 1999; Stringham 1998; Tinsley 1998) is that there are no positive obligations. No one is forced to contribute to charity. Good Samaritan laws mandating that people come to the aid of those in trouble (say, an unconscious person) are incompatible with libertarianism. To take an extreme case, there would be no law against refusing to toss a life preserver to a drowning man even if one could do so with minimal effort, and his death would occur otherwise. In this political philosophy, there are only negative obligations.[1] It is prohibited, and a punishable criminal offense, to initiate or even threaten violence against anyone or his justly acquired property.

As such, libertarianism is a deontological theory of law. Proper legal enactments are those that support this basic premise (e.g., prohibitions

Reprinted with kind permission of Emerald from *International Journal of Social Economics* 31, no. 3 (2004): 275–86.

[1] Rothbard (1982, p. 100) states:

> The very concept of "rights" is a "negative" one, demarcating the areas of a person's action that no man may properly interfere with. No man can therefore have a "right" to compel someone to do a positive act, for in that case the compulsion violates the right of person or property of the individual being coerced.

of murder, rape, theft, fraud, etc.) and improper ones are those in conflict with it (e.g., Good Samaritan laws, seat belt requirements, mandates that the rich be forced to help the poor through programs such as Aid to Dependent Children, welfare, subsidies to the poverty stricken, etc).

However, libertarianism also claims to be at least broadly utilitarian that is, at least in the view of its proponents; following this philosophy tends to lead to happiness for mankind, and to a greater degree than any other perspective, even those explicitly utilitarian. How can it be argued that the libertarian nonaggression axiom will help people, when the paradigm cases (allowing people to drown, not helping an unconscious man) appear to move in precisely the opposite direction? We rely upon two things. First, the invisible hand insight of Adam Smith (1776/1965) that self-interest, not public spiritedness, best promotes the common weal. And second, the fact that there are no legitimate interpersonal comparisons of utility on the basis of which one could scientifically conclude even that the interest of the drowning man in staying alive is more important than that of the passerby who refuses to spend but a moment on saving him (Rothbard 1977).

The purpose of the present paper is to test this premise of no positive obligations against a challenging critique that can be made of it. To wit, abandonment of babies. That is, does the mother who abandons her baby have the positive obligation to at least place it "on the church steps," e.g., notify all other potential caregivers of the fact that unless one of them comes forward with an offer to take in the infant, it will die? If so, then there is at least one positive obligation in the libertarian philosophy; if not, then, at least at the outset, the libertarian claim to be generally utilitarian must be greatly attenuated. At best, there would now be an exception to the previously impermeable principle of no positive obligations; at worst, one exception tends to lead to another, posing the risk that the premise will be fatally compromised, which can undermine the entire philosophical edifice.

Property rights

In order to analyze the case of the mother abandoning her infant, we must hark back to the issue of property (for in the libertarian view babies are but a form of property[2]), how it gets to be owned in the first place, how it can be transferred, and how it can be abandoned. That is, since libertarianism defends "justly acquired property," not any old property rights, if we are to be thorough we must first delve into the theory of how man attains property in the first place. We will trace down the implications of property theory for children's rights in general, and then apply these to the question of abandoning children without notification.

The proper premise, we contend, is based on the Lockean-Rothbardian-Hoppean (see Locke 1955, 1960; Rothbard 1982; Hoppe 1989, 1993a) labor theory[3] of acquisition. Land, to start with the most basic element of nonhuman property, is justly won by mixing one's labor with it: farming it, cutting logs on it, clearing away debris, putting in improvements such as paths, lighting, fences, etc. It is by imprinting one's personality on the land, in effect, that we come to own it; we do this through "blood, sweat and tears," sometimes, but mainly the middle bodily secretion just mentioned.

There are, of course, questions about the precise meaning of "mixing your labor with the land." How intensive does the farming have to be? One plant every square foot, yard, meter, acre, mile? How many crops must be planted before ownership obtains? The answer that emanates from this perspective is whatever is the usual practice in land of that sort. For example, in the relatively irrigated land east of the Mississippi, the farming must be more intensive; in the more arid land west of this river, less intensive. As to how long the homesteading process must take before full property rights are vested, this, too, is a social and cultural matter.

---

[2] Or, more exactly, states Rothbard (1982, p. 100), ". . . even from birth, the parental ownership is not absolute but (that) of a 'trustee' or guardian." It is important to emphasize that the property right the parent has is not over the baby, itself, but rather over the right to continue to raise it. As I am forcefully reminded by my Loyola University New Orleans colleague Bill Barnett, if this were not the case, then the parent would have the right to dispose of his "property" in any way he wished, up to and including killing it, or harvesting its "kidneys or liver or heart" (personal correspondence dated May 17, 2001). Needless to say, this is not at all what the libertarian means by property rights in children.

[3] This should not be confused with the Marxian labor theory of "value."

A similar process occurs with regard to people's ownership of themselves, of their own bodies, as it were. In early babyhood, before consciousness arrives, we can hardly be said to own ourselves in any meaningful way; certainly, we have not yet "homesteaded" ourselves. But at around age two, and increasingly as time goes on, the baby gets a sense of its ownership over itself. It asserts this by, for example, refusing to be any longer kissed by loving parents whenever the former wish to do so.[4]

Yes, the homesteading justification for property ownership is not an apodictic airtight one. It is forced to rely upon local practice, the rulings of judges, etc., to buttress itself as to these specific details. In like manner, its answer to the question of how one comes to own virgin land whose main value lies in contemplation of it as is, cannot be accorded synthetic *a priori* status. For example, how does Niagara Falls pass from unowned to owned status? Any attempt to "mix one's labor" with it would decrease its value.[5] The answer is that the owner would place paths around it, enabling tourists and those who appreciate the beauties of nature to better enjoy this amenity. The thing itself remains unchanged, but, through the actions of the homesteader, he and perhaps more people are now able to enjoy it.

But if homesteading theory is not without its slight deviation from absolute perfection, these are as nothing compared to the alternatives to it. Rothbard (1978, p. 34) explains:

> If the land is to be used at all as a resource in any sort of efficient manner, it must be owned or controlled by someone or some group, as we are . . . faced with . . . three alternatives: either the land belongs to the first user, the man who first brings it into production; or it belongs to a group of others; or it belongs to the world as a whole, with every individual owning a quotal part of every acre of land.

The second alternative may be dismissed out of hand: why should a group of "others" have any rights to the land brought into an economic

---

[4] Things go downhill quickly when the baby learns the word "no."
[5] But see text accompanying footnote 16 below.

relation by the first user of it? Be these others the state, or passers-by, or random thugs, the argument in behalf of their ownership of the land in question is clearly inferior to that of its first possessor. And, as to the third alternative, if there are six billion people, we would then each own one six billionth of every acre on Earth. But this is nothing short of a recipe for absolute disaster, ending in the virtual starvation of everyone. Nothing could be done with any land, for it would be "difficult" in the extreme, to get six billion owners to agree to anything. The holdout problems, for one thing, would be insurmountable.[6]

Rothbard (1978, p. 35) puts this matter into perspective:

> . . . if a producer is not entitled to the fruits of his labor, who is? It is difficult to see why a newborn Pakistani baby should have a moral claim to a quotal share of ownership of a piece of Iowa land that someone has just transformed into a wheatfield—and vice versa, of course, for an Iowan baby and a Pakistani farm.

There is actually a fourth possibility, in addition to the first three categories mentioned by Rothbard. That is, rather than one, the homesteader owning the land, or two, other people, people other than the homesteader controlling it, or, even, three, that all of us possessing everything communally, there is the scenario where no one is able to attain it, thanks to the action of what we will now call the "forestaller."

Suppose that a person does not homestead a stretch of land but instead places a fence around it. In this scenario we stipulate that he "mixes his labor" only with that narrow strip of land upon which the fence rests, but to a sufficient degree in order to come to own it. What he has done, then, is to take possession of a narrow perimeter of land, surrounding property which he does not own, nor claim. In other words,

---

6   The objection might be that all the owners would vote over the use of each parcel of land, the decision going to the majority in each case. This alone would constitute a practical difficulty of such enormity as to render the Earth uninhabitable. Moreover, why should the present author, the duly constituted part owner of one six-billionth of all land on Earth, agree to be bound by any majority? Another difficulty with this position is that it is impossible to vote for this or for anything else without standing on any land. But if the vote is to settle land ownership in the first place, then, all the voters, standing on presently unowned land, are acting illegitimately, and their ballots must be considered null and void.

he homesteads a very thin donut-shaped parcel of land, which encircles property he neither owns nor claims. It is the contention of the present paper that this is not a legitimate homesteading scenario. The whole purpose of homesteading is to bring hitherto unowned virgin territory into private property ownership. A circle appearing on a globe divides the former into not one but two parcels of land: that lying inside of the donut-shaped area, and that lying outside of it. In the present case, we are assuming a perimeter that surrounds an area of one square mile. This would mean that the fenced land divides the Earth into two parts, one, this square mile, and the other, the entire remainder of the Earth's surface apart from this one little area. As far as homesteading theory is concerned, the person who owns the donut-shaped area has as much claim to the land on the one side of it as the other: namely, none at all. He has no claim to the land lying inside or outside of his fenced parcel, since, by stipulation, he did not mix his labor with any of it.

One implication of the foregoing is that the donut owner cannot prevent others from crossing his property (in order to have access to the land he is, in effect, blockading). That is, under the donut configuration assumption, even though the owner has duly homesteaded every square inch of his holdings, he still cannot claim full ownership to it in its entirety; for him to be able to do so would imply that the land lying inside (or outside!) of this area can forever remain unowned. Just as physical reality abhors a vacuum, so to does libertarian homesteading theory abhor land which cannot be claimed nor owned because of the land ownership pattern of the forestaller. This means that the owner of the donut-shaped land must allow people at least a path across it so as to be able to homestead, on their own account, land that the forestaller has left unoccupied and unowned.[7]

But does the owner of the donut-shaped area have to notify others of the fact that there is a parcel of unowned land lying right in the middle

---

[7] This should be sharply distinguished from the squatter who cuts a path across someone's land, with his permission, and then later claims the right to continue using this path even over the objections of the owner. Under the libertarian legal code, the owner would not lose rights to his land in their entirety even though he gave permission to passers-by to cut across a corner of his land.

of his own holdings? No. For to place this requirement upon the owner of the donut-shaped land would be to impose upon him a positive obligation, and this, as libertarians, we are prohibited from doing.

Abandonment

Let us take another crack at this donut-shaped land scenario from a somewhat different perspective. This time, we will assume not that the owner homesteads only a donut-shaped parcel, surrounding unowned land, but rather, say, a solid holding of five square miles. Now, however, he wishes to abandon an interior area of one square mile, and to retain ownership rights over only the remaining donut-shaped parcel. As we have seen from the previous analysis, he must now allow access through[8] the land he still owns; this follows from the fact that he has abandoned the central piece of his land, and if this is truly to be abandoned, it must now be homesteadable. If it is not, this violates the libertarian axiom to the effect that all land must, in principle, be available for ownership. Nor can the nonowner be prevented from reaching ownership status through forestalling. But this interior piece of land can only be homesteadable if the owner of the donut-shaped parcel allows other would-be owners of his abandoned land access to this interior territory. If he does not allow them this access, he is guilty of the crime of forestalling.

What about notification? Must the man who wishes to abandon the interior portion of his land notify others of his act? Yes. And this follows not from any positive obligation whatsoever, but rather from the logical implication of what it means to abandon something. You cannot (logically) abandon something if you do not notify others of its availability for their own ownership.[9] At most, if you do not undertake any notification, you have not abandoned it, but rather are simply the absentee

---

[8] We are assuming away the possibility of tunneling under, or building a bridge over, this donut-shaped parcel of land in order to have access to it for homesteading purposes. On this latter phenomenon, see Block and Block (1996), and Block (1998).

[9] According to the *Talmud*, before property can be considered abandoned, a public avowal to this effect must be made, either to a Bet Din (court) or to two qualified witnesses. See on this *Encyclopedia Talmudit* (1976, pp. 58–59). For the general concept of Hefker, or abandonment, or disowning, see *Encyclopedia Talmudit* (1976, pp. 49–98). See also Maimonides, Mishna, Nidarini, chap. 2, Halakha, 15. I owe this citation to Rabbi Lipa Dubrawski.

owner over it. Suppose you leave your old sweater in your closet. You never wear it anymore. But you do not give it to the local Goodwill organization, nor do you sell it, nor do you do anything with it except possibly contemplate it from time to time. Have you (truly) abandoned it? You have not. Instead, you are still the owner of it, and are (temporarily, for the moment, even for the rest of your life) not using it anymore. You have, in a word, not yet succeeded in abandoning it. In other words, abandoning property is not something you can attain merely by wishing for it;[10] merely by no longer using it; merely by no longer exercising the traditional ownership rights over it. No. In order to succeed in fully or truly abandoning your property, you must take two steps: first, you must notify others that you have indeed abandoned your property, and second, you must not set up roadblocks preventing others from homesteading your now-abandoned property. If you do not accord your actions with both of these requirements, it cannot be said of you that you have successfully engaged in an abandonment of your property.

The whole point of the exercise is to get virgin territory into the hands of people so that it can be used. The former is ever so much more important than the latter, so much so that as long as the former does not undermine the latter,[11] it is no exaggeration to say that it almost doesn't matter how this is accomplished, as long as it is accomplished.

Abandoning land or goods without telling anyone about it is thus an undermining of this goal. For what is the point of having a theory of the process of converting unowned into owned property if it can all be made null and void through a choice such as abandonment. Therefore, just as forestalling is illegitimate since it undermines the process, so does

---

[10] Property abandonment is, in effect, an honorific; it is not as easy as falling off a log. A person can try to abandon something, and not succeed in this task, unless he notifies people. How many people? This is a continuum problem, and libertarianism has no comparative advantage in answering this question. The *Talmud* calls for "two witnesses." But these people would have to spread the word to many others, if not to the entire community, if the libertarian maxim is to be satisfied. Alternatively, only one person need be notified, for example, if he is the editor of the newspaper or radio station which then broadcasts this information to all and sundry.

[11] Rothbard (1982) gives the example of the king of Ruritania who illegitimately and "arbitrarily parcels out the entire land area of his kingdom to the 'ownership' of himself and his relatives." This would be a paradigm case in point.

this apply to abandoning property without notification. This is not a positive obligation. Rather, it is part and parcel of the rights/responsibilities of owning property in the first place. Just as the owner of the land donut has to allow physical egress through what would otherwise be considered his property since he would otherwise be engaged in land forestalling, so must he allow "mental egress" through the miasma of lack of information—e.g., he must notify someone (e.g., a land registry, title search [see Rothbard 1982] company) that he is abandoning land.

Babies

With this introduction, we are now ready to focus on the proper libertarian relationship between babies and parents. In effect, the mother "homesteads" the baby within her body, with a little initial help from the father.[12] Babies, of course, cannot be owned in the same manner as applies to land, or to domesticated animals. Instead, what can be "owned" is merely the right to continue to homestead the baby, e.g., feed and care for it and raise it.[13]

States Rothbard (1982) in this regard:

> . . . the parents—or rather the mother, who is the only certain and visible parent—as the creators of the baby become its owners. A newborn baby cannot be an existent self-owner in any sense. Therefore, either the mother or some other party or parties may

---

[12] The implication of this is that the mother's rights far exceed those of the father, in any dispute between them as to the right to "own" the child, e.g., bring it up. In times of yore, the mother of the baby was evident to all concerned; not so the father. With the advent of genetic testing, this situation no longer obtains. Nevertheless, the homesteading theory would still give primacy to the mother, not the father, in that she did far more of the "work" of gestating the baby than did the father. Under the libertarian legal code, the "best interests" of the baby would not be paramount in determining custody. Even if it were somehow determined that the best interests of the baby consisted of being brought up by the rich father, not the poor mother, this factor would be ignored, in justice, due to her priority in homesteading. The only time the mother would not be given the baby to raise in a disputed custody battle would be if she were pronounced unfit to raise it (e.g., she was a child abuser, etc.).

[13] Child abuse would, of course, constitute the very opposite of "raising" a baby, and would be met by loss of what would otherwise be the continual right to bring up the child until maturity. The precise definition of child abuse opens one up to continuum problems, the solution of which libertarianism has no comparative advantage *vis-à-vis* other positions.

be the baby's owner, but to assert that a third party can claim his "ownership" over the baby would give that person the right to seize the baby by force from its natural or "homesteading" owner, its mother.

Suppose, now, that the mother, or both parents, wish to abandon their baby.[14] Several options are open to them, consistent with libertarian theory.[15] For one thing, they can give their child up for adoption. They can do so for no financial compensation, or for pecuniary gain (Landes and Posner 1978). But since they cannot give up more with regard to the baby than they did in fact own, it would be illegitimate for the new parents to mistreat the baby; had the original parents done so, they would have lost the rights to continue parenting it. For the only way to attain homestead rights to the child after giving birth to it is to bring it up in a reasonable manner. Were the parents to instead abuse their child, this would not at all be compatible with homesteading it. If so, they would lose all rights to continue to keep the child.

Here, it might be thought there is another disanalogy between homesteading land, or animals on the one hand, and children on the other. In the former cases, it might be argued, one can attain ownership through abuse, or by decreasing the value of it. That is, a man may come to own a deer by killing it, or a tract of land by burning down all of the trees on it. And, to some people, a live animal is worth more than a dead one, and wooded acreage more than the denuded version. But a basic premise of Austrian subjectivist economics (Barnett 1989; Buchanan and Thirlby 1981; Buchanan 1969; Mises 1966; Rothbard 1962) is that man acts so as to substitute a more preferred state of affairs for a less satisfactory one. If he burns woods, and kills a deer, we have no warrant to interpret this as anything but an improvement, despite the possible evaluations to the contrary of an outside observer.

---

[14] For a brilliant libertarian defense of the right of the mother to abandon her baby see Evers (n.d.). See also Evers (1978).

[15] For a libertarian analysis of abandoning the fetus, e.g., abortion, see Rothbard (1982). See also Block (1978, 2005).

For another thing, they could abandon the baby without choosing adoptive parents. That is, as long as they notify all and sundry of their intention to give up their rights to the baby, and do not prevent anyone else from homesteading the child, they have no positive obligation to keep it, or even to ensure that the baby is taken up by others.

Would it ever be possible, under libertarian law, for a baby to be abandoned by its parents, for there to be no other adult willing to care and feed it, and the baby be relegated to death? Yes. However, this could occur only under the condition where the entire world, in effect, was notified of this homesteading opportunity, no roadblocks were placed against new adoptive parents taking over, but not a single solitary adult stepped forward to take on this responsibility.[16] Since there are no positive obligations in the libertarian lexicon[17] it is logically possible for such a sad state of events to take place.[18]

We now arrive at more intellectually challenging scenarios. First, suppose that the parents are willing to notify others of their impending abandonment of their baby, but set up roadblocks against anyone else taking over care of it. For example, they announce to the world that they are trying to set up a *reductio* to embarrass the libertarian philosophy. To this end they are going to leave the baby in his crib, and not feed or diaper him. To those who wish to adopt this baby they say: "The baby is in his crib. The crib is in our house. This house is private property: you cannot have access to it." Picture hundreds of would-be caretakers surrounding these parent's house, all of them willing to adopt the

---

[16] This is, of course, exceedingly unlikely, at least in the economically developed nations, since there are numerous churches, orphanages, adoptive agencies, who stand ready to support all unwanted children they cannot place with families.

[17] The Canadian Robert Latimer killed his severely handicapped (Cerebral Palsy) daughter, Tracy, twelve, by carbon monoxide poisoning (see *Report Newsmagazine* 2001; *Vancouver Sun* 2001). He was properly sentenced to prison insofar as he did not first determine that no other person on Earth was willing to take on the trusteeship of this child.

[18] An interesting question arises. Suppose there are no people willing to care for a baby. No one in the entire world. There are only two options: a quick mercy killing (which, we posit, someone is willing to do), or allowing it to die a lingering painful death. The libertarian position is clear: killing a human being without his permission is murder. This baby is too young to give any such permission. Killing it would thus be murder. As libertarians, we have no positive obligations to keep it alive, but may not kill it either. However, this would be a very special case, and, presumably, leniency could be accorded such a mercy killer.

baby, but she insists, based upon her property rights in this dwelling, that all of them stay out while the baby dies of starvation.

Does this *reductio* succeed? Not at all. Apart from the pragmatic fact that most others in society would severely boycott such a couple, there is the point that they would be guilty of forestalling the homesteading of property (e.g., the baby) which is no longer owned. This would be in direct and blatant contradiction to the libertarian homesteading theory which oversees the bringing in to ownership of virgin territory, not the shielding of it from those who wish to homestead it.

Ordinarily, in the case of forestalling new ownership of land which has been abandoned, not allowing newcomers access to one's own property (the donut) for this purpose would be equivalent to land theft, and punished accordingly. But in the present case what is being shielded from homesteading is not land, but rather a baby. This would be equivalent to murder, and those responsible for it treated very severely.[19]

Second, take the case where the parents who are abandoning the baby place no physical barriers against the entry of would-be homesteaders of it to their home, but instead fail to notify anyone of their intention. Again, a similar result applies: the parents are guilty of murder.

Their position is an intellectually incoherent one.[20] They claim to be abandoning the baby, but, as we have seen from the case of the sweater considered above, they have succeeded in doing no such thing. Rather, they are in a situation with regard to the baby where it is still in their care, but they are not caring for it. That is the paradigm case of child abuse, a serious crime indeed, and if it persists until the death of the child they are guilty of murder also.

In order to be thorough and exhaustive, we may briefly mention the third option, where these "parents" both fail to notify of their baby abandonment, and also attempt to physically prevent others from taking over this job. Since either of these actions on its own would merit severe penalties, this would surely apply to the combination of both of them.

---

[19] On libertarian punishment theory, see Benson (2001), Bidinotto (1994), Evers (1996), Kinsella (1996 a,b, 1998/1999) and Rothbard (1982).

[20] To employ Kinsellian language, they are "estopped" from doing any such thing. See on this Kinsella (1996 a,b, 1998/1999).

Conclusion

The libertarian argument is that baby abandoners do not have a positive obligation to notify others of their act; rather, this stems from what it means to abandon property, any property. The essence of the libertarian rejection of the *reductio*, when applied to physical property, is as follows: If you have a sweater in your closet, even one you don't use anymore, you haven't abandoned it. If you have abandoned it, really abandoned it (are not just an absentee owner, or a stockpiler, or a packrat) then you have to (you are compelled by the laws of logic to):

- notify someone who will spread the word about this; and
- refrain from preventing others from homesteading it (e.g., setting up a blockade against their doing so).

This is a logical have to. That is, it is an apodictic certainty that upon pain of self-contradiction you cannot really abandon property if you: tell no one of it; and prevent others from homesteading it. If you move away, without renouncing your claim, like the "tar baby" it sticks with you. If you return, even after an absence of decades, only to find "squatters" who have been using your land in the interim, you still do not lose title. Absentee ownership is not an oxymoron in the libertarian lexicon.

This applies to babies no less than to sweaters or to land.[21]

---

[21] If it came to it, I would rather concoct an implicit contractual obligation that arises out of land ownership to notify of abandonment, than to concede that there is a positive obligation to notify, and I would prefer to do either than allow it to be legal that the mother could starve the baby without notification. Happily, it does not come down to this. As has been shown, libertarianism has a perfectly rational objection to the *reductio* against it launched by those who wish to embarrass this philosophy by demanding of it either that it agree to the legality of starving babies, or acquiesce in the notion of positive obligations.

12 Social Justice

On many university campuses, there is a push on to promote social justice. There are two ways to define "social justice."

First, this concept may be defined substantively. Here, it is typically associated with left-wing or socialist analyses, policies and prescriptions. For example, poverty is caused by unbridled capitalism; the solution is to heavily regulate markets, or ban them outright. Racism and sexism account for the relative plight of racial minorities and women; laws should be passed prohibiting their exercise. Greater reliance on government is required as the solution of all sorts of social problems. The planet is in great danger from environmental despoliation, due to an unjustified reliance on private property rights. Taxes are too low; they should be raised. Charity is an insult to the poor, who must obtain more revenues by right, not condescension. Diversity is the *sine qua non* of the fair society. Discrimination is one of the greatest evils to have ever beset mankind. Use of terminology such as "mankind" is sexist, and constitutes hate speech.

Second, social justice may be seen *not* as a particular viewpoint on such issues, but rather as a concern with studying them with no

Printed with kind permission of Mr. Llewellyn H. Rockwell, Jr. This article was initially posted on http://www.lewrockwell.com website.

preconceived notions. In this perspective, no particular stance is taken on issues of poverty, capitalism, socialism, discrimination, government regulation of the economy, free enterprise, environmentalism, taxation, charity, diversity, etc. Rather, the only claim is that such topics are important for a liberal arts education, and that any institution of higher learning that ignores them does so at peril to its own mission.

So that we may be crystal clear on this distinction, a social justice advocate of the first variety might claim that businesses are *per se* improper, while one who pursued this undertaking in the second sense would content himself by merely asserting that the status of business is an important one to study.

Should a university dedicate itself to the promotion of social justice? It would be a disaster to do so in the first sense of this term, and it is unnecessary in the second. Let us consider each option in turn.

Should an institution of higher learning demand of its faculty that they support social justice in the substantive left-wing sense, it would at one fell swoop lose all academic credibility. For it would, in effect, be demanding that its professors espouse socialism. But this is totally incompatible with academic freedom: the right to pursue knowledge with an open mind, and to come to conclusions based on research, empirical evidence, logic, etc., instead of working with blinders, being obligated to arrive only at one point of view on all such issues.

This would mean, for example, in economics, the area with which I am most familiar, to be constrained to conclude that the minimum wage law is the last best hope for the unskilled, and that continually raising it is both just and expeditious; that free trade is pernicious and exploitative. It is more than passing curious that those in the university community who are most heavily addicted to diversity cannot tolerate it when it comes to divergence of opinions, conclusions, public policy prescriptions, etc.

What about promoting social justice in the second sense; not to enforce conclusions on researchers but merely to urge that questions of this sort be studied?

This is either misguided, or unnecessary.

It is misguided in disciplines such as mathematics, physics, chemistry, music, accounting, statistics, etc., since these callings do not typically address issues related to social justice. There is no "just" or "unjust" way to deal with a "T" account, a quadratic equation or an econometric regression; there are only correct and incorrect ways to go about these enterprises. To ask, let alone to demand, that professors in these fields concern themselves with poverty, economic development, wage gaps or air pollution is to take them far out of their areas of expertise. It is just as silly as asking a philosopher to teach music, or vice versa.

And it is totally unnecessary, particularly in the social sciences but also in the humanities. For if members of these disciplines are not *already* conducting studies on issues germane to social justice (and, of course, to other things as well) then they are simply derelict in their duty. If historians, sociologists, anthropologists, economists, and philosophers are ignoring poverty, unemployment, war, environmentalism, etc., no exhortations to the contrary are likely to improve matters.

Colleges and universities therefore ought to cease and desist forthwith from labeling themselves in this manner, and from promoting all extant programs to this end. It is unseemly to foist upon its faculty and students any one point of view on these highly contentious issues. It would be *just* as improper to do so from a free enterprise, limited government private property rights perspective as it is from its present stance in the opposite direction. For additional material critical of these initiatives, see Michael Novak[1].

Of course, social justice may be defined in yet a third manner: as favoring justice in the "social" arena, as opposed to other venues. Here, all intellectual combatants would favor the promotion of this value; the only difference is that leftists, for example, mean by this some version of egalitarianism, while for libertarians justice consists of the upholding of private property rights. For a college to uphold social justice in this sense would be highly problematic, in that two very different things would be connoted by this phrase.

---

[1] http://www.firstthings.com/ftissues/ft0012/opinion/novak.html

13 Discrimination: An Interdisciplinary Analysis

Discrimination has been treated by large parts of the academic community as though it were not amenable to logical analysis, be it economic, ethical or political; as though the very consideration of alternative viewpoints were somehow unsavory. The philosophy of "feminism," "human rights," "multiculturalism," and "political correctness" have so permeated intellectual discussion that criticisms of the mainstream view take on an aura of illegitimacy at the outset, even before arguments are heard in their behalf. This is highly unfortunate. If nothing else, John Stuart Mill's *On Liberty* should give us pause before closing our minds to alternative perspectives.

At one time in our recent history, the term "discriminating" had a positive value. It was a compliment. To say that a person was discriminating was to say that he was able to make fine distinctions. Today, of course, to say that someone is discriminating is to charge him with prejudice. This modern view is embodied in the so-called human rights codes of society, wherein it is illegal to discriminate against people on the basis of race, religion, sex, national origin, handicap, sexual preference, age, etc. Discrimination now carries a legal penalty—a fine, and even a jail sentence to back up the prohibition.

Reprinted with kind permission of Springer Science and Business Media from *Journal of Business Ethics* 11, no. 4 (1992): 241–54.

Classical Liberalism

Let us then consider an alternative philosophical treatment of discrimination, sometimes known as classical liberalism. It asks one and only one question: "When is the use of (state) force justified?" and gives one and only one answer: "Only in response to a prior rights violation." As such, this view must be sharply distinguished from theories of ethics. This is crucial, because there is all the difference in the world between claiming that a person should not be imprisoned or legally penalized for engaging in act X, and claiming that act X is moral. It is no contradiction to oppose the criminalization of discrimination on the basis of race, sex, national origin, etc., while at the same time declaring that such behavior is immoral and unethical. And that, indeed, is that stance maintained in the present paper. Discrimination is defended, here, in the very limited sense that perpetrators should not be incarcerated, fined, or otherwise interfered with by governmental authorities. The present writer, however, finds such behavior odious, and morally repugnant in the extreme.

Classical liberalism is predicated on the premise that we each own our own persons; we are sovereign over ourselves. We have property rights over our own bodies, and in the things we purchase, or receive through any other legitimate mode, such as gifts, inheritance, gambling, etc. (Nozick 1974, pp. 149–82). Intrinsic to this way of looking at things is that there are boundaries. My fist ends here, your chin begins there. If the former touches the latter, without being invited to do so, I have invaded you. The essence of this philosophy is that any barrier invasions such as rape, murder, theft, trespass or fraud are strictly prohibited.

Conversely, within one's own sphere the individual is free to do anything he wishes, provided only that he does not violate the rights or borders of others. Conceivably, people might be hurt deeply by friendship or patronage withheld, but it is the individual's right to withhold benefits of this sort, since such acts of omission cannot rationally be interpreted as a boundary crossing. As long as an individual's person or property is not invaded, no indictable offence has occurred and, accordingly, no penalty—no fine or jail sentence—should ensue.

From this philosophy is derived "the law of association," namely, that all interaction between free, sovereign, independent individuals should be voluntary and on the basis of mutual consent. On issues of pornography, prostitution, free speech and drugs, the well-known phrase "anything between consenting adults should be allowed" demonstrates this philosophy. The classical liberal variant of this expression, in Robert Nozick's (1974) felicitous phraseology, is that "all capitalist acts between consenting adults" should likewise be allowed.

All acts, whether personal or commercial, should take place on the basis of mutuality. From this we derive that discrimination too is a right and, therefore, it should not be a criminal act to indulge—on whatever basis one chooses. But here it is important to emphasize that what is meant by "discriminate" is something very particular. It is to ignore, avoid, evade, have nothing to do with, another person. It most certainly does not imply the "right" to lynch or beat up or enslave or commit assault and battery upon someone from a despised group. If I don't like bald people with beards who wear glasses, for example, I don't have to have anything to do with them. I shouldn't be fined or jailed for refraining from dealing with them, according to this philosophy. On the other hand, I can't approach such people and punch them in the nose. I should be incarcerated if I indulge any acts of this sort. In other words, I can do anything I wish to people against whom I hold prejudices—provided only that I do not engage in border crossings, or violation of their space (persons and property rights). I can "cut them dead" (socially and commercially), but I cannot commit even the slightest violence against them.

Is it "nice" to discriminate against people? Is it "reasonable" to prejudge an entire group or persons, based on negative experiences with a small sample? Certainly not.[1] In the popular belief, discriminators are

---

[1] A very eloquent statement in behalf of this view was made by Booker T. Washington, on May 31, 1897 during the unveiling of sculptor Augustus Saint-Gaudens's monument to the 54th Regiment of Massachusetts Volunteer Infantry, the first black fighting unit to take part in the Civil War. It was made to commemorate its participation in the battle to capture Fort Wagner, during which campaign the regiment sustained heavy losses:

> The black man who cannot let love and sympathy go out to the white man is but half free. The white man who would close the shop or factory against a black man seeking an opportunity to earn an honest living is but half free. The white man

hateful and wicked for not wanting to have anything to do with certain groups of people. As well, they are deemed illogical in that they over-generalize from a small sample to an entire population.[2] However, the issue presently facing us is not the moral or scientific status of discriminators. We are primarily concerned whether the individual has a right to act in this way, and with the economic implications of this philosophy, not with whether or not it is nice or reasonable for him to do so.

Human rights

Let us examine the "human rights" viewpoint in light of classical liberalism. Current "human rights" legislation only applies to commerce and sometimes to clubs, but not to personal interactions. This is puzzling because the advocates of such laws usually regard interpersonal relations as more important than commerce. Contemplate the fact that all heterosexuals discriminate against half the population in the choice of sexual partners. As do homosexuals. It is only bisexuals who are not guilty of this practice. (But most bisexuals presumably discriminate on other criteria: beauty, health, youth, wealth, honesty, sense of humor, common interests, personality, etc.) Therefore, if we consistently carry through on the anti-discrimination philosophy, we ought to punish everyone except bisexuals. Or consider marriage patterns. There is very

---

who retards his own development by opposing a black man is but half free. The full measure of the fruit of Fort Wagner and all that this monument stands for will not be realized until every man covered by a black skin shall, by patience and natural effort, grow to the height in industry, property, intelligence and moral responsibility, where no man in our land will be tempted to degrade himself by withholding from his black brother any opportunity he himself would possess. (*Toronto Globe and Mail*, Dec. 15 1989, p. A 16)

[2] If one considers the word "prejudice" etymologically, it means to pre-judge. That is, to make up one's mind about an issue before all the facts are in. But suppose you open up a door, go into a room, and close the door behind you, and then lo and behold, you are confronted by a tiger sitting on a couch. Do you act empirically, in a nonprejudicial manner, and go up to the tiger to engage in a close examination, to see if this particular member of the species will act like most of its fellows, and begin to maul you? Or do you take one look, and then head quickly for the nearest exit, based on your general experience and knowledge of the breed, before you know the facts about this particular animal? Most people would act in a prejudiced manner in this regard, and would not apologize for it. (I owe this example to Walter Williams.)

little intermarriage, relative to the totals, across racial, ethnic and religious categories. From this one can deduce that racism in general, or discrimination in particular, plays a significant role in marriage choices. To be consistent with the underlying philosophy of "human rights" advocates, when people apply for marriage licenses they should be asked: "Have you dated people from other backgrounds; did you give them a fair chance?" If not, no marriage should be permitted. Certainly, friendship patterns are based on all sorts of discriminatory patterns. Is this wrong? Perhaps; it might well be. Should this be punished by law? Hardly.

Some people maintain that we should enforce anti-discrimination legislation in commerce but not in personal relations[3] because a store, office, factory or workplace is "open to the public," while no such stricture applies to friendship and other personal relationships. Such a claim is hard to defend, however. A store could conceivably be open only to the blond blue-eyed public—all others are advised go elsewhere—or to the left-handed redheaded public—or base its clientele on whatever criterion it wishes to employ. There is no logical reason why an offer to commercially interact with some people should be interpreted as an offer to do business with all.

Second, "human rights" legislation is applied in a biased way. For example, with regard to considerations of national origin, many countries discriminate against foreign investment and treat the domestic variety more favorably. Tariffs discriminate against foreigners, so do immigration policies. University students from other nations commonly have to pay more for their education than citizens of the host country. These are all forms of discrimination based on national origin. And yet the

---

[3] There is a tradition amongst some civil libertarians (the British Columbia Civil Liberties Association is a strong case in point) that commercial liberties are very much inferior to personal ones. This sentiment finds expression, for example, in the denigration of commercial free speech rights (e.g., tobacco advertising) in contrast to the right to engage in free speech in the political or scientific arenas. One implication of this perspective, however, would be that the legal protections afforded the public policy statements "A subsidy for the XYZ cigarette company is in the public interest" or "Cigarette smoking is good for you" would be far stronger than those granted in behalf of the advertising statement "Buy XYZ cigarettes." In the classical liberal philosophy, in sharp contrast, no such distinction is maintained. On the contrary, liberty is conceived of as a "seamless garment," and no aspect of it is denigrated in behalf of any other.

response to these rights violations on the part of the human rights advocates, and civil libertarians, is curiously muted. This is difficult to reconcile with their position, since in other contexts they single out discrimination in business for particular opprobrium.

Let us consider some other examples. Women's consciousness-raising groups are not open to men, while legal sanctions have been applied against men's-only private clubs. Black Muslims do not allow white people to join them in prayer.[4] Similarly, Sikhs and Orthodox Jews, among many other religious groups, confine their prayer meetings to like-minded people. Boycotts of lettuce, grapes and other such union-inspired activities certainly discriminate against people who are despised, at least within parts of the counterculture. The Brownies, the Girl Guides, Boy Scouts, the YMCA, the YWCA, the Young Men's Hebrew Association or the Young Women's Hebrew Association, all discriminate on the basis of gender.

While some of these examples may seem frivolous, there is an important point to be made. Nondiscrimination is put forth as a basic human right. How, then, can there be exceptions? Surely, it is a basic human right not to be raped. Do we have exceptions incorporated into the law? No; the very idea is ludicrous. It is likewise a basic human right not to be murdered. Again, there are no exceptions. If it is a basic human right, we infer, exceptions are intolerable. The fact that exceptions to the laws prohibiting discrimination are not only intolerable but are instead widely espoused, even by defenders of the philosophy, indicates that it is not at all a basic human right not to be "victimized" by discrimination.

As well, many of these distinctions have been made with a certain amount of hypocrisy. Women's consciousness-raising groups are widely considered to be properly closed to men, but male-only private clubs have been subjected to intensive governmental pressure to change their membership practices. In many cities, women are allowed to join the Young Men's Christian Association, but men are not allowed to enroll

---

[4] In his most anti-white racist days Malcolm X was once asked if any white man—living or dead—would have been allowed to join the Black Muslims. He replied that John Brown would have been acceptable. See Breitman (1965, pp. 224–25).

in the Young Women's Christian Association. On many university campuses, there is provision for blacks-only dormitories and cafeterias; providing the same amenities for whites would be widely seen as anathema. At one major Pacific coast university, the administration had organized a homosexual appreciation week; when students organized a heterosexual appreciation week, they were punished by university authorities. In the U.S. House of Representatives, there is a widely recognized black caucus; no such white counterpart can even be contemplated, given the likely outraged response. "Black is beautiful" is a respected rallying cry for a significant minority of the population; anyone attempting to promote the counterpart "white is beautiful" would be summarily dismissed as a racist.

A possible defense of this state of affairs is that it is justified for the downtrodden and denigrated minority to discriminate against the majority, but not for the latter to undertake such actions with regard to the former. There is one obvious difficulty with such a response: it cannot be made compatible with the view that nondiscrimination is a basic human right. If it were so, then no one would have the right to discriminate against anyone at any time, for any reason.[5]

Another important point to consider is the backlash that special government treatment for minority groups has engendered. States Thomas Sowell (1990, p. 28): "One of the clearly undesired and uncontrolled consequences of preferential policies has been a backlash by nonpreferred groups. This backlash has ranged from campus racial incidents in the United States to a bloody civil war in Sri Lanka." In Canada, Marc Lepine entered the engineering school of the University of Montreal, and at gunpoint forcibly separated the male and the female students. Whereupon this person, who had previously complained about affirmative action benefits of women, cold-bloodedly murdered over a dozen co-eds. Feminists in Canada and elsewhere have unsuccessfully attempted to deny any connection whatsoever between this brutal and dastardly

---

[5] If we were to carry through fully and consistently on the logic of this premise, then blacks would have the right to rape and kill whites; Indians could legally steal from non-Indians; Jews could have "open season" on Germans.

act, on the one hand, and resentment against governmentally imposed preferential treatment for women on the other.

Why only include race, religion, sex, national origin, handicap, sexual preference, and age among the categories upon which it is illegitimate to discriminate? Why not also consider under this rubric people who are fat, drunk, stupid, smelly, ugly, short, bald, color blind, tone deaf, or humorless? One response to this *reductio ad absurdum* might be that the presently legally protected categories are justified in terms of one's ability to change. If a person cannot alter his condition, it becomes impermissible to discriminate against him; if he can, it becomes permissible.

But there are difficulties with this rejoinder. First, why is it morally relevant? Even if an inveterate rapist for some reason could not change his desire to indulge in such activity, it would still be just to visit physically violent sanctions against him to make him cease and desist. Second, this argument cannot possibly explain the present distinction between categories which are and which are not legally protected from discrimination. For example, changes in religion are relatively easy to incorporate, at least in comparison to an alteration in height. And yet discrimination on the basis of religious belief is commonly proscribed, but not that based on bodily size.

Another response might be that such categorization is made on the basis of the level of suffering undergone by the minority group. But those who are fat, drunk, stupid, smelly, ugly, short, or bald are also denigrated. Surely these people suffer just as much if not more from discrimination as do some of those who are not legally recognized as "minorities."

Many so-called human rights advocates would happily add these additional categories to the list of people against whom it would be illegal to discriminate. While a short fat bald man with splotchy skin, glasses and a squeaky voice can make an important contribution to society, he does not look the part, and is usually reimbursed and befriended accordingly. Maybe we should incorporate into the law a prohibition against discriminating against such persons. However, if we keep adding to the list, no one in our society will be able to interact with *anyone* on a truly voluntary basis.

Harm from discrimination?

Why do the "human rights" advocates champion these ideas? One possibility may be that they identify with and want to protect the underdog against suffering. But there is a strong objection to this view: the underdog does not greatly suffer—at least in the economic sense—from private discrimination. To be sure, there is some harm which does befall a minority group which is the target of discriminatory behavior. Certainly, such groups of people are better off if the majority is favorable to them, or at least views them with indifference. But the injury is minimal. It could not be otherwise, given that Jews and Chinese have long been amongst the groups most highly discriminated against in our society, and yet have incomes far in excess of the average (Sowell 1981a; 1981b; 1983).

In order to see why this is so, it is incumbent upon us to briefly review the economics of boycotts, of which discrimination is only a particular case. The reason boycotts are almost always relatively unsuccessful (even when engaged in on the part of millions of people, over many years, such as in the case of South Africa) is because of the failsafe mechanism which necessarily accompanies them (Abedian and Standish 1985; Hutt 1964). To the extent that a boycott is successful, it worsens the economic condition of the "victimized" group—at least initially. For example, if the boycott is through employment—the majority will not hire the minority—the wages of the minority decrease, and/or their unemployment rate increases. If the majority will not sell food to them, the price they become willing to pay for these items rises. As this process continues, their plight worsens. But, as their condition declines, it becomes more and more financially tempting on the part of both boycotters and nonboycotters to deal with these targets of the discriminatory behavior, in spite of the initial prejudice which lead to the boycott in the first place. For example, if racial prejudice leads to whites refusing to hire blacks, thus lowering their wage levels, "this would mean an opportunity for some employers to reap unusually high profits by concentrating on hiring members of such low-wage groups. Even if employers of all other groups were too blinded by prejudice to seize this opportunity, it would leave a great opportunity for extra high profits by employers belonging to the same ethnic group" (Sowell 1975,

p. 165). A successful boycott, in other words, carries within it the very seeds of its ultimate failure.[6]

But what of the plight of the minority during this process? Are they not grievously harmed in the interim? Not at all. So well does this "fail safe" mechanism operate that it is all but impossible to find evidence of the incidence of such boycotts. That is, it cannot be shown that there are greater profits to be earned in hiring such minority members, as there would be were they being victimized by discriminatory boycotts.

> The experience of employers hiring members of an ethnic group that has lower earning and/or higher unemployment rates does not show remarkable success, and in many cases elaborate and costly programs have produced very meager results, even when subsidized by large government grants. (Sowell 1975, p. 165)

Silberman Abella (1984) claims to have shown harmful effects on the well-being of minority groups as a result of discrimination, but her methodology is questionable on several grounds (Block and Walker 1985). For example, she allocates the entire difference between black and white earnings (that cannot be statistically explained by quantifiable variables) to discrimination, thus ignoring other possible sociological and cultural differences which cannot be so easily quantified; to wit, she regards years of schooling as a homogeneous good, even though there are great disparities in the quality of schooling received across racial categories, even though the subject specializations are widely

---

[6] This accounts for the fact that the South African economy is doing quite well, despite a deep-seated, well-entrenched, long-standing boycott against it. When most civilized nations refuse to buy South African products, their prices fall, which makes it almost impossible for those interested in wealth maximization to continue to resist making purchases from that country. Similarly, when most civilized nations refuse to sell to South Africa, the prices obtainable rise, making it more and more costly to continue the boycott. The better organized the boycott, and the more people who take part in it, the more quickly its internal contradictions become apparent.

A similar economic analysis may be applied to the problems facing the authorities now engaged in the "war against drugs." The more opium producers killed, the more heroin captured, the more marijuana burned, the more poppy fields sprayed with poison, the higher will be the prices of these illegal drugs, due to falling supply. But the higher the prices, the more the incentive which remains to create still other sources of supply.

disparate—and correlated with income. That is to say, blacks are often concentrated in fields with lower average earnings.

Perhaps the best refutation of the methodology has been penned by Sowell (1990, p. 25), who states:

> When two groups differ in some way—in income, for example—and 20% of that difference is eliminated by holding constant some factor x (years of education, for instance) then in a purely definitional sense statisticians say that factor x "explains" 20% of the difference between the groups . . .
>
> The potential for misleading explanations can be illustrated with a simple example. Shoe size undoubtedly correlates with test scores on advanced mathematics examinations, in the sense that people with size three shoes probably cannot, on average, answer as many question as correctly as people with size twelve shoes—the former being much more likely to be young children and the latter more likely to be older children or adults. Thus shoe size "explains" part of the math-score difference—in the special sense in which statisticians use the word. But nobody can expect to do better on a math test by wearing larger shoes on the day it is taken. In the real sense of the word, shoe size *explains* nothing.
>
> When a statistician testifies in court that his data can "explain" only 40% of income disparities between groups by "controlling" for age education, urbanization, and whatever other variable may be cited, the judge and jury may not realize how little the words "explain" and "control" mean in this context. Judge and jury may conclude the other 60% must represent discrimination. But virtually no statistical study can control for all the relevant variables simultaneously, because the in-depth data, especially along qualitative dimensions, are often simply not available. By controlling for the available variables and implicitly assuming the unaccounted-for variables do not differ significantly between groups, one can generate considerable residual "unexplained" statistical disparity. It is arbitrary to call that residual "discrimination."

Looked at another way, groups with visible, quantifiable disadvantages often have other, not-so-visible, not-so-quantifiable disadvantages as well. If statistics manage to capture the effect of the first kinds of disadvantages, the effects of the second kind become part of an unexplained residual. It is equating that residual with discrimination that is the fatal leap in logic.

The economics of the "pay gap"

There is an objection often put forth against our claim that the people subjected to private discriminatory behavior are not harmed by it. Are not the wages, salaries and incomes of women reduced because of economic discrimination against them? The so-called wage gap is offered as contrary evidence to our thesis. The fact is that at present the female/male income ratio is about 0.63. This ratio has been rising very slightly for the last few years, but over the past few decades has shown a great stability (Block and Williams 1981; Block and Walker 1985; Paul 1989; Levin 1984, 1987). For every dollar the male earns, the female earns sixty-five cents. Isn't this evidence of actual harm not based on law or government or violence or coercion or boundary trespasses but rather on private discrimination? Paradoxically, the answer is *no*.

There are two reasons for taking this stance. First of all, there is the statistical explanation. Yes, the average wage of all females divided by the average wage of all males is 0.65—there is no dispute about that. But this gross statistic hides more than it reveals. As it turns out, the explanation for this state of affairs is not at all discrimination against women, but rather the asymmetrical effects of the institution of marriage on male and female incomes. Matrimony is strongly associated with increased male incomes and decreased female incomes. The so-called "pay gap" of 35 percent associated with the wage ratio of 0.65 is almost entirely due to the asymmetrical effects of marriage. The plain fact of the matter is that the division of housework, child-care, shopping, cooking and other such activities is very unequal within most marriages. As well, married women's attachment to the labor force is vastly below that of men (Hoffmann and Reed 1982; Sowell 1984).

This can be shown in two ways. First, segregate the population by marital status, and derive a female/male income ratio for each subcategory. Block and Walker (1985) divided their sample into the ever and the never married. (The former classification consists of married, divorced, separated and widowed; the former, as its name implies, is comprised only of those people who have never been married.) When calculated in this manner, the ratio for the ever marrieds falls to below 0.40; that for the never marrieds rises to unity. In other words, the "pay gap" increases from 33 percent for all females to a truly horrendous 60 percent for the ever married females. By contrast, the pay gap for all females decreases from the 35 percent level to virtually zero for the never married females. Does this mean that the employer has a particular hatred for married women? This is the only interpretation consistent with the "feminist" mythology. However, contradictorily, in this view, the prejudiced male is supposed to favor married women, given, of course, that they are "barefoot, pregnant and in the kitchen." He is presumed to hate single women—those who do not marry, presumably because they have no respect for men and patriarchal institutions. But the statistical findings indicate the very opposite. When the data are broken down by marital status, it is not the single women, the never marrieds, who "suffer." Rather, it is the marrieds who do.

The ratio for full-time employed never marrieds in Canada ranges between 82.9 and 109.8, depending upon date (1971 or 1981), and educational background (Block and Walker 1985, p. 51). For never married persons aged thirty years old and above, Block and Walker (1982, p. 112) found a female-male income ratio of 0.992 for 1971; for comparable ever married, the ratio was 0.334. For U.S. data, Sowell (1984, p. 92) reports:

> Women who remain single earn 91% of the income of men who remain single, in the age bracket from twenty-five to sixty-four years old. Nor can the other 9% automatically be attributed to employer discrimination, since women are typically not educated as often in such highly paid fields as mathematics, science, and engineering, nor attracted to physically taxing and well paid fields

as construction work, lumberjacking, coal mining, and the like. Moreover, the rise of unwed motherhood means that even among women who never married, the economic constraints of motherhood have not been entirely eliminated.

As it happens, the wage ratio of nonmarried males to married males is about the same as between all females and all males. Namely, there is a "gap" of some 35 percent. Interestingly, there have been no analysts who have come forth with the claim that this is due to discrimination. Does this finding indicate that employers discriminate against bachelors? No. It is due to accounting practices which are not designed for economic analysis. The married male has an "assistant", in effect, helping him to earn that income. It is true that only his name appears on the check, but she is earning it too. She might have helped put him through college. She engages in all sorts of ancillary activities which contribute to his success. However, in the statistical accounts, she is not credited with helping to earn this money. She spends this money in many cases, but governmental statistical agencies typically do not take cognizance of the fact that she has helped to earn it.

It is thus erroneous to deduce from these statistics that discrimination can account for the male-female wage disparity. The reason women on average only earn 65 percent as much as males, is because their productivity is only 65 percent of theirs. This is not necessarily due to any inherent economic weaknesses on their part, however. As we have seen, the explanation is marital status. According to the best statistical estimations, never married women and never married men have equal productivity, and thus equal salaries. Married women are only 65 percent as productive as men in the market on average because they specialize in raising children and taking care of the household. Even those women who have advanced degrees or training do not typically keep up with the least developments in their professions; at least, they do not do so as assiduously as their married male counterparts.

Now let us consider the second reason in favor of the marriage asymmetry explanation of the wage "gap," *vis-à-vis* the discrimination or exploitation hypothesis. Notice the logical implications of the discrimination model. Assume that the productivity of males and females is exactly equal to each other. Assume the productivity of both to be at the level of $10 per hour.[7] Suppose further that the wage for males is $10 and for females it's $6.50 an hour, in order to maintain our ratio of 65 percent. Under these conditions, it would be as if the woman has a little sign on her lapel stating, "Hire me, and if you do I'll bring you an extra $3.50 an hour in pure profit." If the employer hires a woman, he can keep this $3.50, with no extra effort on his part. It goes without saying that all profit-maximizing employers would be vitally interested in discriminating in favor of additional returns. Without question, they would hire the women. But suppose that the employer is a sexist, who hires the man. If so, he will tend to go broke. His competitors, the employers who hire females, will be able to undersell and drive him to the wall.

It is ludicrous, economically speaking, to suppose that anything like this could long endure: that employers could discriminate against equally productive women, and yet remain in business for any appreciable amount of time. Yet, this is precisely the scenario implied by the discrimination hypothesis. Similarly, it is also an implication of this discrimination theory that profits would be positively correlated with the proportion of female employees, both across firms and industries. That is to say, if employers can really exploit women by paying them less—due to rampant discrimination—then they would earn more profits, the more women they have on their payrolls. But this, too, bespeaks economic illiteracy. Profits tend to equalize, *ceteris paribus*. If 50 percent profits can be earned in industry A, and 1 percent in B, then investment will tend to leave the latter for the former. But as capital leaves B, this raises the profit level to be derived there; similarly, as money comes flooding in to the greener pastures of A, it lowers returns. What will be the effect of a law that compels employer to pay "equal pay for work of equal value?" Suppose the law requires employers to pay women $10 an hour when their productivity is really

---

[7] We focus on productivity—or more strictly marginal revenue product—because that is why employers pay wages—to obtain productivity from their employees. It is a well-known axiom in economics that wages tend to reflect the level of productivity of the workers. See Samuelson (1970, chap. 20).

only worth $6.50, on average. An employer would be very reluctant to hire such people. If he does, he will lose money on each employee he takes on; eventually he will be forced into bankruptcy. As a result, the unemployment rate for women will be higher than it would otherwise have been, in the absence of such pernicious legislation. This is precisely the same effect as that of the minimum wage law. It functions so as to price women out of the labor market.

Consider the case of the ugly secretary and the beautiful secretary. In the real world, beautiful secretaries have an advantage over ugly ones. It may not be appropriate to discuss this economic phenomenon in certain circles; beauty may be strictly irrelevant to the job at hand; this phenomenon may be hurtful to nonattractive women, but that is the way the actual economy, and general society, functions. One might ask, how is it that ugly secretaries ever get a job if just about everyone is prejudiced in favor of beauty? The answer is a phenomenon expressed in economic jargon as "compensating differentials." The market works in such a way that the salaries that less fortunate women can attract decreases, making them a better bargain in the labor market. Comeliness is preferred, other things equal, but if other things are not equal, namely wages, then even those who discriminate in its favor may not choose to indulge their tastes in this way.

If the law mandates that all women be paid the same salaries, however, the underdog (the unattractive secretary) would be hurt the most. For under this condition it would be more difficult for those women to obtain jobs in the first place. Under the present system of free and flexible market wages, at least they can find employment. The same analysis applies to any despised group, whether discriminated against on the basis of gender, race, national origin, beauty or age.

If a law is passed saying a young person cannot be paid less than an older one, that deprives the young person of his saving grace in the market, namely, the ability to work for slightly less money. In nature, weak animals have a compensating differential. The porcupine is otherwise frail, but is has quills; the skunk is powerless but it uses odor as a defense; the deer is fragile, but it can run very fast. If these compensating differentials were somehow to be taken away, these animals would be well nigh doomed to extinction. In like manner, if the ability to work for less until they can gain experience is taken away from young people, their unemployment rate increases. This is precisely the scenario which obtains in the modern era, due to minimum wage legislation. Equal pay legislation would do for women what the minimum wage has done for teenagers. All true feminists—those who espouse public policies which have the effect of benefiting women, as opposed to mouthing pious platitudes about their intentions to this end—must therefore oppose such wage controls.

Rights and discrimination

If private discrimination is virtually powerless to harm its intended victims, government discrimination (Demsetz 1965; Higgs 1977; Lundahl and Wadensjo 1984; Stiglitz 1973) and state and private violence are entirely another matter (Louw and Kendall 1986; Williams 1989). The confusion between these two superficially similar phenomena[8] may account for the popularity of "human rights" legislation on the part of people who favor the downtrodden. In the 1940s and 1950s blacks in the Southeastern United States certainly did suffer from private violence. The Ku Klux Klan and others engaged in lynchings, cross burnings, and other terroristic activities. This is certainly an uninvited border crossing—the chins of these downtrodden groups were infringed upon by the fists of the aggressors. However, this is not at all what is meant by private discrimination.

Before proceeding further, therefore, a sharp distinction must be made between public and private discrimination. In the classical liberal world-view, only private individuals have a right to discriminate. Government may not legitimately engage in such behavior. We all pay taxes in order to finance government services. If the state singles out one group, Catholics or Punjabis for instance, and either subsidizes or

---

[8] There is all the world of difference between the invasive use of force, on the one hand, and the peaceful but assertive refusal to interact, on the other. Indeed, in the entire realm of political philosophy, there is scarcely a distinction important to make, nor one easier to make. Nevertheless, for many people, the distinction between these two concepts is hard to discern. This is all the more reason to make it clearly and repetitively.

penalizes them, this is unfair and improper. Affirmative action is an instance of government discrimination. For devastating critiques of this program, see Levin (1987), Roberts (1979, 1982), Sowell (1982, 1990), Williams (1982a).

There is a very important implication of this premise for public universities. To be admitted to state institutions of higher learning, entrance exams—usually based on intelligence and/or knowledge—have to be passed. In the terminology we are now using (Hagen 1977), the university discriminates on behalf of those who are thereby accepted as students. But other people were rejected; that is, they were discriminated against on the basis of their lack of knowledge or intelligence. This is improper and should not exist, in the philosophy under discussion. True, if public universities were to adopt a strict policy of nondiscrimination on the basis of mental acuity, they would cease to exist as centers of higher learning; if they wished to continue to discriminate on this ground, and to do so legitimately, they would have to be privatized.

Another very important distinction to be drawn in this regard is that between discrimination and the initiation of violence. The former is (relatively) benign, the latter malignant. Only the former is compatible with a regime which respects individual rights as adumbrated above; the latter certainly does not. However, it is also crucial to differentiate between private and public discrimination. It is vitally important to do so, because there is often a superficial resemblance between the two phenomena. Yet, as the latter but not the former also incorporates the initiation of violence, it and it alone is intractable from the point of view of the victims.

Consider in this regard that spate of infamous legislation known as Jim Crow (Williams 1982b).[9] Here, rights were violated on a massive scale, and great harm was perpetrated. Blacks had to sit at the back of the bus because of legal requirements. If they tried to take a seat anywhere else, they would be jailed. Similarly, they were legally restricted

---

[9] An economically similar system of law is the case of apartheid in South Africa (Williams 1989; Louw and Kendall 1986; Hutt 1964).

in terms of the washroom and drinking fountain facilities (Wharton 1947; Welch 1967).

Contrast this with a very different scenario. Instead of this back-of-the-bus practice being mandated by law, suppose that it were the result of merely private discrimination. We assume, then, that in the ex-Confederate states of Dixie that a view existed to the effect that the appropriate place for blacks was in the back of the bus, and that this is a widely upheld belief on the part of the majority white population, although not—and this crucial—buttressed by supportive state intervention. In such a case, the typical entrepreneur would say to himself, "How can I maximize profits, given this situation?" On the assumption that blacks wanted to ride on the front of the bus, but were prevented from doing so by the owners of the extant bus firms, this entrepreneur would start another bus line, one on which blacks can ride anywhere they want—front or back—as long as they pay for this privilege.

The problem in the Jim Crow South was that this would have been illegal. Entrepreneurs were required to obtain a permit or franchise in order to start up a competing bus line. But the same statist powers that forbade blacks the front of the bus also prohibited entrepreneurs from coming to the rescue of the minority group in this commercially competitive way. Operation permits to alternative bus firms were simply not granted (Wiprud 1945; Moore 1961; Eckert and Hilton 1972). In this instance the underdog could not be helped by the market—not through any fault of private discrimination, but because of the far more deleterious public variety.[10]

In the event, to continue our historical exegesis, blacks had to wait decades until the political realities became such that a majority of the electorate finally repealed Jim Crow. Had the market been allowed to operate freely at the outset, the effects of this pernicious legislation could have been rendered ineffective in the short time that it would have taken

---

[10] If the majority refuses to sell food to the minority, other people will leap into the void, in order to "exploit" the relatively hungry minority. They will be lured by the prospect of being able to earn greater profits, but in so doing, they will drive down the food prices the minority will have to pay. It is only if the majority utilizes force or violence to keep such profit maximizing good samaritans away from the minority that this process will not work.

an entrepreneur—black or white, it makes no difference—to set up a competing bus line. The market, in other words, is potentially the best friend of the downtrodden black minority group. Free enterprise is not the enemy. When it is obviated by state power, however, as occurred, unfortunately, in the case we are considering, this help remains only that—a potential.

"Human rights" advocates are so enthused about the so-called rights of people not to be discriminated against, that they neglect the real rights of people to engage in discrimination. Consider people forced to send their children to school where the teacher is gay. Parents resent this strongly, but are often unable to resist. Why not look at these people as underdogs and defend their rights? Surely, homosexuals have a right to practice the lifestyle of their choice. But inflicting themselves upon unwilling recipients is hardly consonant with the law of free association.

There is also the case of Nova Scotia school board which ruled that a teacher who carried the AIDS antibody and thus might likely develop this dread disease was to be returned back into his sixth grade classroom. Imagine the agony of parents forced to send a child to a place where they think there might be a chance of his contracting a fatal disease.[11] A case could easily be made that these parents are the underdogs. Our failure to defend people in such a position stems from moral myopia—the rights of some people are more important than the rights of others.

Expressing it that way implies, however, that rights can conflict with one another.[12] Properly understood, however, this cannot occur. If

---

[11] To be sure, scientific evidence indicates that AIDS cannot be disseminated by casual contact of the sort likely to be engaged in by schoolchildren in the classroom. But this is hardly relevant to the point at issue, namely the right of free association. People may wish to avoid contact with others for the most frivolous or scientifically erroneous of reasons. The question is, do they have a right to do so? And the answer is clear, at least for those who take individual liberty seriously.

[12] Suppose a white (black) female prostitute refuses to conduct her business with a black (white) male would-be customer. It might be argued, at least in jurisdictions where prostitution is not prohibited, that since she is engaged in a clearly commercial venture, and thus can be construed as being "open to the public," that she be legally forced to entertain all customers who can meet her price (and also that she not price discriminate on the basis of race). But if she is forced to do so, this is a violation of women's rights; if not, it constitutes racial discrimination, and thus a violation of the rights of minority group members.

there is a seeming contradiction between rights, one of them is not really a right. People do not have a right against other people that they have to interact with whether they want to or not, as the so-called human rights philosophy would have it.[13] Rather, in the classical liberal philosophy, people should be free to do whatever they please as long as they don't violate the space of other people by invasion.

What are the free speech implications of our analysis? Statements specifically discriminating against particular groups of people have a long pedigree in the civil liberties debate. They have been characterized as "hate literature." They are displeasing, even malevolent. But banning them is a clear violation of free speech rights.[14] Surely, any philosophy which takes seriously our rights of free expression would be exceedingly uncomfortable with a juridical proscription of "racist" statements.

This contradiction, of course, does not arise under classical liberalism, which countenances only negative rights; e.g., the right not to be murdered, raped, stolen from (Block 1986). Here, there can be no conflict in rights, for the woman is seen as the sole owner of her own body, with the right to dispose of it exactly as she wishes. And this includes the right to engage in sexual relations with anyone she chooses, for any reason acceptable to her.

[13] A similar analysis arises with regard to exceptions that are commonly made to the anti-discriminatory laws. For example, it is seen as illicit to discriminate between males and females, but there are separate (but equal?) washroom facilities assigned to men and to women. If this really were a matter of rights, such exceptions would not, could not, be tolerated. Similarly, discrimination between the sexes blatantly occurs in the field of sports, and is accepted by otherwise consistent adherents of the "human rights" philosophy: namely, there are separate divisions for males and females in university, Olympic and professional sports. For example, male and female basketball, tennis and volleyball players do not compete against each other; nor do track and field athletes. (Such an occurrence would hardly be allowed, in the case of race; could we countenance separate sports leagues for whites and blacks? For Jews and Gentiles? The very idea would be preposterous in the "human rights" world-view, and yet the very same principles apply to gender distinctions.) There is little doubt that were there only one athletic event, open to members of both sexes, that there would be virtually no female representatives who could successfully compete. Florence Griffith-Joiner, for instance, might hold the female world record for the 100-meter dash, but if she had to compete directly with males, she would not have even qualified to enter the Olympics.

[14] In classical liberalism, free speech rights are interpreted as but an aspect of the more basic rights to private property. For example, if someone breaks into my house at 3:00 a.m., and starts reading in a loud voice the sonnets of Shakespeare, he may not properly object if I toss him bodily out onto the street that I have violated his right of free speech. He has no right of free speech—on my property. He has such a right only on his own property, or on that (a hall, auditorium, newspaper advertisement, etc.) which he has rented from someone else.

The sociobiology of sexism

Now that we have established that private sexism, like racism, is impotent to greatly harm the economic well-being of the "victimized" group (in sharp contradistinction to sexist and racist policies pursued by government bodies, or the violence employed by states or individuals), we venture into an exploration of the question of why it is that sex discrimination exists in the first place. (What is meant by sexism in this account is first making distinctions between men and women, and then treating members of the two genders differently.) The most common explanation for this is that people are nasty, perverse and misanthropic. The problem with this hypothesis, apart from being circular, is that it in no way comes to grips with why the nastiness and perversity which is undoubtedly part of the human condition is channeled into "anti-female" directions.

The sociobiological account of sexism does not fail on these grounds. Consider the following case: a ferryboat capsizes and there is only one lifeboat available. The common sexist order of preference is women (and children) first and only then men, a long way second. Why is it that we have this deeply embedded sexist idea that women are to be placed on a pedestal in this way? Why not let women take their chances along with men, in the mad dash for the lifeboat? In the widely popular "feminist" analysis, this is because men regard women as little better than children in terms of intelligence, physical strength and maturity, and if children should be saved first because of their relative weakness, then so should women.

The sociobiological explanation of this event provides a sharp contrast (Wilson 1974). In this view, the women-and-children-first rule came about because it ensured the survival of our species. Women are biologically far more precious than men, and any species that does not base its actions on this rule is thus far less likely to survive than one that does. This is why the chivalristic notions are so deeply embedded in our psyches: the human race has been acting on these principles for aeons of time. Those parts of the race which did not have along ago died out.

Consider Germany, Poland and the Soviet Union after World War II; practically an entire generation of men in these countries were killed; the lives of the women were, by and large, spared, at least relatively speaking. A gigantic proportion of men in each military age cohort were wiped out: women of childbearing age tended to survive. Is this even noticed by the Germans, Poles and Soviets very much in the modern day, in terms of demographic implications? No. The next generation is just as large and just as well educated. It was almost as if this tragic loss had simply not occurred. Compare that scenario to the following hypothetical case. Suppose three-quarters of the women of the Soviet Union of childbearing age were killed, but hardly any of the men, the exact reverse of what actually occurred. What would be the demographic results in such a case? They would be no less than catastrophic. Not only would there be great danger for the next generation in these countries: the real question would be whether there would *be* any next generation or not!

Suppose that there were two races of apes, otherwise equally fit to survive, which had different customs regarding warfare. One group of apes (call them the human apes) did not allow their females to fight: instead, they tried to protect them as much as possible. When fighting took place it was with the expendable males in the front lines. The other group of apes (call them extinct) either pushed the women forward to the front lines of battle or were egalitarian—no "spurious" distinctions were made between the males and the females, they all went out and fought on an equal basis. Which group would survive? Obviously, the first group, the "human" apes, because like it or not women are more precious when it comes to survival of the species. This is so because one male and 25 females can leave as much progeny as 25 males and 25 females are capable of producing. That is, 24 of the males are all but extraneous to the process. It may be nice to have them around—at the very least they can furnish added protection—but biologically speaking their roles are as necessary for the survival of the human species as are drones for the survival of bees. That is why farmers commonly keep one bull for 25 cows—and not the other way around. However incompatible with the "feminist" view of the world, this biological fact simply cannot be denied.

This is a very powerful explanation of why women are dealt with as if they are much more precious than men. Because they *are*. Some people don't care about the survival of the human race, but this is irrelevant. We are now trying to understand why discrimination between men and women is so deeply embedded in the human psyche, and in the sociobiological analysis we have found a logical explanation. This is a positive enterprise, to which truth and falsity apply, not a normative one, which pertains to the categories of good and bad, like and dislike. In other words, this perspective may be incompatible with the worldview of the "feminists," but the evidence in its behalf is overwhelming, nonetheless.

Conclusion

Our interdisciplinary account of discrimination—utilizing insights from economics, politics, philosophy, sociology, biology, statistics and history—lends credence to our public policy recommendation: that this behavior, although immoral in many cases, should not be prohibited by law. Many of the goals of people of goodwill—for peace, prosperity and tolerance—will, paradoxically, be more likely of attainment under a legal regime which allows for the free association of individuals on a strictly voluntary basis, rather than under one which compels such interaction. The latter can often backfire, as racial violence on university campuses, following affirmative action and mandatory "politically correct" thought eloquently attest. So far has our present society lost sight of its classical liberal historical roots that the case for liberty in human relationships may seem to some to be vaguely racist, sexist, or otherwise morally objectionable.

14 A Libertarian Case for Free Immigration

"None are too many."—Reply of an anonymous senior official in the government of Canadian Prime Minister McKenzie King to the question, "How many Jews fleeing Nazi Germany should be allowed into this country?"[1]

All merchants shall have safe and secure exit from England and entry to England, with the right to tarry there and to move about as well by land as by water, for buying and selling by the ancient and right customs, quite from all evil tolls, except (in time of war) such merchants as are of the land at war with us. And if such are found in our land at the beginning of the war, they shall be detained, without injury to their bodies or goods, until information be received by us, or by our chief justiciar, how the merchants of our land found in the land at war with us are treated; and if our men are safe there, the others shall be safe in our land.[2]

Reprinted with kind permission of the Ludwig von Mises Institute from *Journal of Libertarian Studies* 13, no. 2 (1998): 167–86.

[1] Abella and Troper (1982, p. ix). I owe this citation to Phil Bryden and Jenny Forbes.
[2] From chapter 41 of the Magna Carta, cited in Thorne *et al.* (1965, p. 133). I wish to thank Ralph Raico for bringing this quotation to my attention.

Libertarianism

Libertarianism is a political philosophy; as such, it is a theory of the just use of violence. Here, the legitimate utilization of force is only defensive: one may employ arms only to repel an invasion, i.e., to protect one's person and his property from external physical threat, and for no other reason. According to Murray N. Rothbard:

> The libertarian creed rests upon one central axiom: that no man or group of men may aggress against the person or property of anyone else. This may be called the "nonaggression axiom." "Aggression" is defined as the initiation of the use or threat of physical violence against the person or property of anyone else. Aggression is therefore synonymous with invasion.
>
> If no man may aggress against another, if, in short, everyone has the absolute right to be "free" from aggression, then this at once implies that the libertarian stands foursquare for what are generally known as "civil liberties:" the freedom to speak, publish, assemble, and to engage in . . . "victimless crimes."[3]

I shall contend that emigration, migration, and immigration all fall under the rubric of "victimless crime." That is, not a one of these three *per se* violates the nonaggression axiom.[4] Therefore, at least for the libertarian, no restrictions or prohibitions whatsoever should be placed in the path of these essentially peaceful activities. Before considering the specifics, let us clear the decks of one possible misconception: that the libertarian can be a "moderate" on this question, advocating fully opening the borders at some times, completely closing them on other occasions, and leaving them slightly ajar if it seems warranted. Typically, such a policy is advocated based on considerations of assimilation, as in the following statement of "plain-spoken reasoning" by William F. Buckley:

---

[3] Rothbard (1978, p. 23). For another definitive vision of libertarianism, see Hoppe (1993a).
[4] For a listing of dozens of other archetypes, none of which necessarily violate the libertarian nonaggression axiom, and all of which are reviled by many, see Block (1976).

At various points in history we have opened, and then gently closed, our borders, pending economic and social assimilation. If there is dogged unemployment, there is no manifest need for more labor. If pockets of immigrants are resisting the assimilation that over generations has been the solvent of American citizenship, then energies should go to accosting multiculturalism, rather than encouraging its increase.[5]

Such a position, whatever its merits on other grounds, is simply not available to the libertarian, who requires consistency with Rothbard's nonaggression axiom. Pragmatic matters such as assimilation can form no part of the libertarian world-view. The only issue is: do emigration, migration, and immigration constitute, *per se*, a physical trespass against person and property or a threat thereof? If so, then libertarians must oppose them totally; if not, they must oppose any and all limits to them. There does not appear to be any middle ground or compromise position consistent with libertarianism.[6] That is, if the transfer of peoples does indeed constitute a violation of the libertarian axiom, as does murder, rape, theft, etc., then it must be completely prohibited. There can be no countenance for *partially* restricted immigration,[7] any more than for *partially* restricted murder. Buckley-type pragmatism applied to murder would mean that in some decades there should be no law at all opposing this heinous act, in other epochs we should very strictly prohibit it, and that in still other time periods we should adopt a more moderate position, perhaps allowing only a certain number of murders. Perhaps our choice should be dictated by life expectancy, or numbers of elderly people in the population.[8] Say what you will about the pragmatic benefits of this idea, it clearly falls outside the purview of libertarians.

---

[5] Buckley (1997, p. 20).

[6] For the view that at least on some issues the libertarian position occupies a middle ground, or compromise, see Block (1997, pp. 211–38).

[7] We are here implicitly assuming that the migrant will find a private property owner who is willing to take him in. Below, we subject this assumption to intensive examination.

[8] This would constitute a "modest proposal" for solving the Ponzi scheme elements of social security bankruptcy. We could hold "open season" on retirees, while protecting the lives of those still in the labor force.

Rothbard makes much the same point in another context:

"Economic power," then, is simply the right under freedom to refuse to make an exchange. Every man has this power. Every man has the same right to refuse to make a preferred exchange.

Now, it should become evident that the "middle-of-the-road" statist, who concedes the evil of violence but adds that the violence of government is sometimes necessary to counteract the "private coercion of economic power," is caught in an impossible contradiction. A refuses to make an exchange with B. What are we to say, or what is the government to do, if B brandishes a gun and orders A to make the exchange? This is the crucial question. There are only two positions we may take on the matter: *either* that B is committing violence and should be stopped at once, *or* that B is perfectly justified in taking this step because he is simply "counteracting the subtle coercion" of economic power wielded by A. Either the defense agency must rush to the defense of A, or it deliberately refuses to do so, perhaps aiding B (or doing B's work for him). *There is no middle ground!*[9]

The identical situation exists with regard to migration. Here, A, the migrant, is peacefully coming to visit his friend or relative in another land.[10] Whereupon B pounces on him, and forces him at the point of a gun to return to his place of origin. What should the libertarian defense agency do? Again, *there is no middle ground!* It must either support A or B. It cannot possibly do both.

The legality of migration is an all-or-none matter: either migration is *per se* legitimate, in which case it would be improper to interfere with it in any way, or it is *per se* invasive, in which case it should be prohibited, totally and comprehensively, just as in the case of murder and rape.

---

9 Rothbard (1970, p. 229), emphasis in original.
10 For how long? Who knows? Whose business is it anyway?

Emigration

Ponder the barriers to emigration which long existed behind the Iron Curtain, and still do for countries such as North Korea and Cuba. Civilized people of all ideological dispositions regard these as barbarous relics from the past—harking back to a time of serfdom, or actual slavery. A country which will not allow its citizens to leave is nothing better than a vast jail, no matter how many Olympic medals the prisoners may have won, no matter how many Sputniks the inmates may have launched.

Such a stark statement can be made on the basis of the libertarian philosophy. For here, people own themselves absolutely. It is a moral outrage for them to be enslaved by the state. Restrictions are sometimes justified on the grounds that would-be emigrants have benefited from public education, provided free of charge by the government. They are compelled to pay exit fees, or are prohibited from leaving outright, on the ground that they will take with them information given to them by the state, which continues to be "its" property. Since there is no way to leave without taking this education with them, the emigrants are prohibited from departing. We in the West, for the most part, see this merely as an excuse for a quasi-slave system—as an attempt to cover unlawful imprisonment with a thin veneer of legitimacy and property rights. But no state provides education to the populace "for free." On the contrary, schooling is financed from funds taken from the people in the first place, through taxes.

Even if, somehow, the government gave education to the citizens for free, it would still not follow that governments are entitled to enslave them on this ground. No, the only slavery even arguably compatible with libertarianism would be that agreed to in advance by freely contracting parties—a sort of "indentured servitude" for life. But no such contracts have ever been signed. Thus, there is no warrant to assume that the hapless people suffering from communism or Nazism were treated appropriately,[11] even under our heroic assumption of "free" education.

---

[11] For another analysis of the view that state actions can be justified on the basis of a "contract" which was never signed, see Spooner (1966).

As a matter of fact, one may interpret the curious historical institution of slavery[12] along these lines. That is, chattel slavery is but a special instance of the lack of freedom to emigrate. What makes it slavery is that the slave cannot quit, or emigrate from the situation, any time he feels like picking up and leaving. If he could, it would not be slavery but merely a peculiar voluntary employment contract. In other words, the right of emigration is so important that its absence implies outright slavery.

There is a further connection between emigration and immigration. Suppose the world contained one totalitarian country, while the rest of them were "free." If all other nations enact immigration prohibitions, this is tantamount to the imposition of emigration restrictions by the government of the one country from which people wish to flee. While it is a basic implication of the libertarian nonaggression axiom that people have a right to emigrate, at least one other nation must allow them to immigrate, or the exercise of this right will become impossible as a practical matter.

Migration

If there is to be a third category, migration, distinct from immigration and emigration, then it must be confined to that aspect of travel during which a person is neither under the control of the host country (emigration) nor the receiving one (immigration). It would apply to the ocean, after the migrant has vacated the country of origin, e.g., Cuba, or traveled to that small no-man's land or demilitarized zone between such places as North and South Korea.

There is no real difficulty for the libertarian in such a case. Shooting down a fleeing family in cold blood, no matter which nation is doing the killing, is murder. Should this have to be said, that murder is contrary to the libertarian axiom of nonaggression? Within limits, it matters not one whit why the persons involved are escaping—whether

---

[12] See Hummel (1996), for a thorough-going analysis of slavery.

for economic reasons, or to have a freer life, or because they are tired of totalitarianism.[13]

Immigration

A moment's reflection will convince any disinterested party that immigration is not necessarily invasive. Immigration consists of no more than moving to a foreign country. For the purist libertarian, national boundaries are only lines on a map, demarcating one "country" from another; there is no such thing as a legitimate nation-state. According to Rothbard:

> There can be no such thing as an "international trade" problem. For nations might then possibly continue as cultural expressions, but not as economically meaningful units. Since there would be neither trade nor other barriers between nations nor currency differences, "international trade" would become a mere appendage to a general study of interspatial trade. It would not matter whether the trade was within or outside a nation.[14]

Therefore, immigration across national boundaries should be analyzed in an identical manner to that migration which takes place within a country. If it is noninvasive for Jones to change his locale from one place in Misesania to another in that country, then it cannot be invasive for him to move from Rothbardania to Misesania. Alternatively, if migration across international borders is somehow illegitimate, this should apply to the domestic variety as well.

As long as the immigrant moves to a piece of private property whose owner is willing to take him in (maybe for a fee), there can be nothing untoward about such a transaction. This, along with all other capitalist acts between consenting adults, must be considered valid in the libertarian world. Note that there is no freedom of movement of the person *per*

---

[13] Of course, if they are themselves murderers, and are escaping to another country in order to avoid paying the just penalties for their foul deeds, or are escaping with private property stolen from its rightful owners, this is an entirely different matter. No longer do we have here innocent people merely attempting to better their own lives. Now, the "migrants" are themselves the criminals.

[14] Rothbard (1962, p. 550). See also Rothbard (1978), and Mises (1983).

se. This is always subject to the willingness of property owners in the host nation to accept the immigrant onto their land. Rothbard explains:

> The private ownership of all streets would resolve the problem of the "human right" to freedom of immigration. There is no question about the fact the current immigration barriers restrict, not so much a "human right" to immigrate, but the right of property owners to rent or sell property to immigrants. There can be no human right to immigrate, for on *whose* property does someone else have the right to trample? In short, if "Primus" wishes to migrate now from some other country to the United States, we cannot say that he has the absolute right to immigrate to this land area; for what of those property owners who don't *want* him on their property? On the other hand, there may be, and undoubtedly are, other property owners who would jump at the chance to rent or sell property to Primus, and the current laws now invade their property rights by preventing them from doing so.[15]

It is almost a certainty that there will in fact always be "other property owners who would jump at the chance to rent or sell property to" immigrants. If this is not obvious based on common sense experience, the economics of discrimination suggests no other possible conclusion.[16] If there are many owners who refuse to rent or sell to immigrants, the price the latter will have to pay will be high. But this will tend to induce those landowners on the margin to agree to accept immigrants. It must be the rare case indeed where in a country of millions of property owners there is not a single one willing to accept newcomers, even at the very highest prices they are willing to pay. In such a rare case, all those who adhere to libertarianism must indeed unite in opposing immigration,[17] for, with Rothbard, there is no one "on whose property. . . someone else ha[s] the right to trample."

---

[15] Rothbard (1982, pp. 119–20).

[16] On this topic, see Becker (1957), and Sowell (1975, 1983).

[17] That is, opposing it totally, as private property rights violations. However, even in this case there would be no need for a law prohibiting immigration, only one banning trespass in general.

But this is a theoretical curiosity, not something relevant to reality, or to public policy analysis. In real-world countries, certainly including the U.S., there can be found thousands, if not millions, of landowners willing to sell or rent space to people from all parts of the globe, no matter how obscure. For example, restaurateurs specializing in the foods common to foreign lands may wish to hire authentic foreign-born cooks. As a practical matter, it is inconceivable that some citizen property owners, whose families themselves immigrated in the past, would not be interested in taking in their countrymen, particularly at the very high remuneration available if most landlords do not wish to deal with the immigrants.

The case is equally clear for allowing immigrants to settle on unowned land. When there is virgin territory, there is no legitimate reason for immigrants (or domestic citizens) to be prevented from bringing it into fruitful production. States Rothbard: "*Everyone* should have the right to appropriate as his property previously unowned land or other resources."[18] "Everyone," presumably, includes immigrants as well as citizens or residents of the home country.

Mises, from a utilitarian rather than a natural-rights libertarian position, considered immigration an important element of freedom and progress:

> The principles of freedom, which have gradually been gaining ground everywhere since the eighteenth century, gave people freedom of movement. The growing security of law facilitates capital movements, improvement of transportation facilities, and the location of production away from the points of consumption. That coincides—not by chance—with a great revolution in the entire technique of production and with drawing the entire Earth's surface into world trade. The world is gradually approaching a condition of free movement of persons and capital goods.[19]

---

[18] Rothbard (1982, p. 240), emphasis added. See also Hoppe (1993a).
[19] Mises (1983, p. 58).

One last point under this topic. If immigration were *per se* invasive, then, perhaps with the exception of Indians,[20] as Americans are all either immigrants or descended from them, our occupancy of this country would be legally questionable. Since no advocate of immigration restrictions has ever expressed any such reservations, there is a problem of logical consistency here.

Objections

Let us now deal with several possible objections to the foregoing.

Allowing unrestricted immigration is equivalent to allowing the invasion of a foreign army.

States Mises:

> Under present conditions, the adoption of a policy of outright *laissez faire* and *laissez passer* on the part of the civilized nations of the West would be equivalent to an unconditional surrender to the totalitarian nations. Take, for instance, the case of migration barriers. Unrestrictedly opening the doors of the Americas, of Australia, and of Western Europe to immigrants would today be equivalent to opening the doors to the vanguards of the armies of Germany, Italy, and Japan.[21]

It must be remembered that these words were first published in 1944, and written some time before that; hence, perhaps, the fear of military invasion. But this appears to be an idiosyncratic use of language. No advocate of *laissez faire* capitalism ever conceived of this position as anything akin to total pacifism. Unrestricted immigration, in this perspective, does not at all include allowing invading armies *carte blanche* access to the home country.[22] On the contrary, it refers to peaceful settlement

---

[20] But the ancestors of native peoples, too, had to come from somewhere. If so, then they, too, are at least indirectly "guilty" of the crime of immigration.

[21] Mises (1969b, p. 10).

[22] This would apply, also, to carriers of communicable diseases. They are, in effect, if not by intention, an "invading army" in that if they are allowed in the recipient country, they will spread their germs to innocent people.

therein. It is perfectly consistent with the libertarian philosophy to oppose with the utmost determination an invading army, while throwing completely open the doors to peaceful settlers.

Unrestricted immigration will create or exacerbate unemployment.

This objection illustrates nothing so much as economic illiteracy. It assumes that there is only so much work in a nation to be done, and that if immigrants do more of it, there will be just that much left for present occupants. If it were true, any and every technological advance would prove a dire threat to our economy.[23] For example, the pick and shovel, to say nothing of the truck, can do the work of thousands of people, compared to teaspoons, or, better yet, bare fingernails. Are we to rid ourselves of these technological advances in order to improve our economy, and combat unemployment? Hardly.

Unrestricted immigration will reduce the real wages of the workers already in residence.

This contention, more perhaps than any other, explains the vicious opposition to immigration traditionally displayed by union leaders such as Cesar Chavez.[24] This charge, however, cannot be denied; it is true that under some circumstances, workers in the receiving country (and capital and land in the country of origin), will lose out.[25] Conversely, capitalists and landowners in the receiving country gain from the cooperation of a larger supply of labor, and workers remaining in the country of origin gain from the increased local scarcity of their services.

The owner of any resource, labor or any other, tends to be subject to a loss in wealth, at least relatively, when confronted by increasing supplies of a substitute factor of production. It is possible that these losses as a producer will be more than offset by gains as a consumer (due to the lower prices of final goods), but this need not at all be the case. It is also possible for an individual domestic worker's loss in wages to be more

---

[23] See Hazlitt (1979), Mises (1969b, p. 105), and Simon (1989).
[24] See Mehlman (1997, p. 30).
[25] See Mises (1966, pp. 377, 627).

than offset by gains in his invested wealth (e.g., he may have pension funds invested in stock ownership), but again, this need not be the case.

But as Hoppe has shown, people have the right only to the physical aspects of their property, not to its value.[26] For the latter is determined on the market by the human actions of thousands of people, exercising their demand for and providing supplies of commodities. To say that X has a right to the value of his property is thus to say that he has a right to make economic decisions for these thousands of other people whose choices determine the value of his property, a manifest absurdity.

Unrestricted immigration will increase crime.

There is no doubt that were the U.S. to open its doors to all and sundry, some number of criminals would take advantage of this opportunity. There are good "pickings" to be had here, after all.

But this is really an indictment of our criminal justice system,[27] not of open immigration. Nowadays, liberals wax eloquent about the cost of crime. The bill for incarcerating a criminal exceeds that of tuition at our most prestigious universities. When one imagines hordes of immigrants coming to this country, committing crimes, and then putting additional strain on our very limited supply of jails, it is easy to contemplate the closing of the borders.

In actuality, a libertarian society serious about crime would not experience so much of it in the first place. For one thing, it would legalize drugs. It is the prohibition, not the use of drugs, that leads to criminal behavior. The very high prices of illegal drugs which are due to prohibition, and are not intrinsic to addictive substances themselves, serve as a magnet for the underworld. When alcohol was prohibited, it was associated with criminal gang activity; when it was legalized, this connection was cut asunder.[28]

A libertarian society, moreover, would get tougher on genuine criminals. There would be no more cozy jails with color TVs, air

---

[26] Hoppe (1993a).

[27] See Rothbard (1970; 1978, pp. 215–41).

[28] For more on this point, see Block (1993, pp. 107–18; 1996, pp. 433–36), Boaz (1990), Friedman (1989), Hamowy (1987), Szasz (1985), and Thornton (1991).

conditioning, or recreation rooms. If indentured servitude for convicts were brought back, prisons could be run by private enterprise. Instead of draining taxpayers of vast amounts of money to house inmates, they could turn a profit.

Under such a system, apart from the undoubted harm they would perpetrate on their victims, immigrants who become criminals would not cost "society" a dime. On the contrary, through their sweat and tears they could be forced to make a positive contribution.

Unrestricted immigration will promote welfarism.

The argument here is that immigrants come to our shores not to breathe the heady wine of economic freedom, but to avail themselves of our stupendously generous welfare system. This is not so much a quarrel with immigration as it is with welfare. Says Hoppe in this context:

> It would also be wrongheaded to attack the case for free immigration by pointing out that because of the existence of a welfare state, immigration has become, to a significant extent, the immigration of welfare bums, who, even if the United States is below the optimal population point, do not increase but rather decrease average living standards. For this is not an argument against immigration but rather against the welfare state. To be sure, the welfare state should be destroyed, root and branch. However, the problems of immigration and welfare are analytically distinct, and they must be treated accordingly.[29]

Let it be said loudly and clearly: end welfare for all people, but at the very least for immigrants and their descendants, and by definition immigrants will no longer be attracted to our shores in order to receive such funds.

But there is another problem with this line of argument: it proves far too much. For if immigrants are to be prohibited from entry into this country on the ground that they *might in the future* go on the welfare rolls, and thus, in effect, steal from the longsuffering taxpayer, Pandora's

---

[29] Hoppe (1995, p. 25).

box will be flung wide open. If we can physically invade people for what they *might* do in the future,[30] the sky is the limit. Surely we can engage in preventive detention of all teenaged males—the guilty along with the innocent—on the ground that this cohort commits more than its proportionate share of crimes. But surely this would be a great injustice.

And what about childbearing for the present occupants of this great country of ours? It cannot be denied that any children born today might, some years into the future, avail themselves of our welfare program. But if we can preclude the entry of immigrants on this ground, this goes as well for having babies. Becoming pregnant ought to be a crime, on these grounds. At least the Chinese communists limited people to one child per couple. If opponents of totally open immigration on the ground that they might become welfare recipients are logically consistent, they would have to oppose any childbearing, whatever.[31]

Legally unrestricted immigration is indeed the libertarian position, the only possible libertarian position, but it should not be implemented until every other plank in this program is first put into effect.

This is a very powerful objection to the argument being presented here. For suppose unlimited immigration is made the order of the day while minimum wages, unions, welfare, and a law code soft on criminals are still in place in the host country. Then, it might well be maintained, the host nation would be subjected to increased crime, welfarism, and unemployment. An open-door policy would imply not economic free-

---

[30] Make no mistake about it: an immigration barrier is a physical invasion of innocent people. Here comes Mr. X, say, from Turkey, peaceably going about his business of settling on the land of his cousin in Arkansas, for example. Yet, before he can get there, the minions of the government interfere with his peaceful right of passage, and either jail him or forcibly return him to his country of origin.

[31] One might argue that the rich could escape this implication, by, say, posting a bond so that their children never need become welfare recipients. This might or might not work, depending upon such matters as future inflation, productivity, and precisely how these bonds are financed. In any case, however, it would also be possible to eliminate this argument by merely requiring that all *immigrants* sign an agreement never to go on welfare, and/or by posting a bond so that *their* children never need become welfare recipients.

dom, but forced integration with all the dregs of the world with enough money to reach our shores.

However strong this objection may be, Rothbard, albeit arguing in another context, provides us with the definitive rebuttal.[32] Rothbard noted that Alan Greenspan, in his youth, was a strong advocate of a gold standard,[33] but as head of the Fed, never from him a word of this has been heard.[34] Has Greenspan changed his mind? Or is he a total hypocrite? In Rothbard's view, neither is true. On the contrary, Greenspan *does* favor *laissez faire* capitalism and gold, but only on a high philosophical level where he doesn't have to *do* anything about it. In contrast, he does not champion it as a practical matter, for then he would be called upon to show some evidence of his beliefs. Says Rothbard:

> There is one thing, however, that makes Greenspan unique, and that sets him off from (the) Establishment. . . . And that is that he is a follower of Ayn Rand, and therefore "philosophically" believes in *laissez faire* and even the gold standard. But as *The New York Times* and other important media hastened to assure us, Alan only believes in *laissez faire* "on the high philosophical level." In *practice* in the policies he advocates, he is a centrist like everyone else because he is a "pragmatist." . . .[35]
>
> Thus, Greenspan is only in favor of the gold standard if all conditions are right: if the budget is balanced, trade is free, inflation is licked, everyone has the right philosophy, etc. In the same way, he might say he only favors free trade if all conditions are right: if the budget is balanced, unions are weak, we have a gold standard, the right philosophy, etc. In short, *never* are one's "high philosophical principles" applied to one's actions. It becomes almost piquant for the Establishment to have this man in its camp.

---

[32] Rothbard (1987).

[33] Greenspan (1966).

[34] Although see Bradford (1997, p. 40).

[35] Rothbard (1987, p. 3).

This, it must be acknowledged, is a devastating critique of the Greenspan position. And, if this be so, we cannot avoid the conclusion that the same argument constitutes a knock-out blow against the defense of immigration restrictions on the ground that every other aspect of full free enterprise must be reached.

There is a certain pattern underlying the position of these "postponement libertarians," the paleo-libertarians who favor full, free, open, and unrestricted immigration—but only after the entire libertarian vision has been attained. The underlying coherence of this perspective is that we should, whenever possible, attempt to achieve the same results now, under statism, as would ensue were we to be living in the fully free society.

Take the case of the bum in the library. What, if anything, should be done about him? If this is a private library, then the plumb-line or pure libertarian would agree fully with his paleo cousin: throw the bum out! More specifically, the law should *allow* the owner of the library to forcibly evict such a person, if need be, at his own discretion. Cognizance would be taken of the fact that if the proprietor allowed this smelly person to occupy his premises, he would soon be forced into bankruptcy, as normal paying customers would avoid his establishment like the plague.

But what if it is a public library? Here, the paleos and their libertarian colleagues part company. The latter would argue that the public libraries are *per se* illegitimate. As such, they are akin to an unowned good. Any occupant has as much right to them as any other. If we are in a revolutionary state of war, then the first homesteader may seize control. But if not, as at present, then, given "just war" considerations, any reasonable interference with public property would be legitimate.[36]

The paleos or postponement libertarians take a sharply divergent view: one should treat these libraries in as close an approximation as possible to how they would be used in the fully free society. Since, on that happy day, the overwhelmingly likely scenario is that they will be

---

[36] One could "stink up" the library with unwashed body odor, or leave litter around in it, or "liberate" some books, but one could not plant land mines on the premises to blow up innocent library users.

owned by a profit maximizer who will have a "no bums" policy,[37] this is exactly how the public library should be treated right now. Namely, what we should do to the bum in the public library today is exactly what would be done to him by the private owner: kick him out.

There are difficulties with this stance. First, as we have already seen, it is extremely likely that in the fully free society, virtually all immigrants would be taken in by a landowner in the host country. Therefore, if the paleos are to remain consistent with their own position, they should eschew all legislated immigration barriers.

Second, and even apart from this consideration, the postponement libertarian perspective is vulnerable to rebuttal by *reductio ad absurdum*. If we should not allow unrestricted immigration until we have achieved the free society, but instead should curtail immigration in an effort to approximate what would take place under a fully libertarian society, let us apply this insight to other realms of controversy.

Public schooling is a disaster. Certainly, in the present journal, there is no need to document such a claim.[38] That being the case, the libertarian position is clear: get rid of public education, forthwith, even if we have not attained complete liberty in other sectors of society.

But those who would be true to the paleo-libertarian position on immigration cannot avail themselves of this conclusion. Instead, they would have to ask: what would education be like in the free society? They would then have to endeavor to treat public schools as much like that as possible.[39] But if there is one thing that is clear, it is that in the free society the educational industry, like all others, would allow competition. How, then, to apply this principle? Simple. Embrace educational vouchers. Get in harness with those such as Milton

---

[37] Consider the Body Shop, or Ben and Jerry's Ice Cream, or any other "ethically oriented" company. Even they operate in this manner. That is, they may donate a part of their profits to unsavory enterprises (from a libertarian point of view), but they presumably do not employ "bum" types of people in the manufacture of their products.

[38] But for a curious and very limited defense of public education, see Levin (1977).

[39] The postponement libertarians could not advocate privatizing all public schools since the remainder of the economy is not yet fully free. They are limited to treating public property in manner as similar as possible to how it would be used in the free society.

Friedman who have long advocated this form of competition for the public schools.[40]

Here is a second example. The U.S. welfare policy is a disaster. The libertarian position is once again crystal clear: abolish welfare forthwith, no matter what the status of the remainder of the economy.[41] But the paleo or postponement libertarians are once again precluded from embracing so clear, just, and simple a solution. If they are to remain true to their immigration position, they will have to reason as follows: the problem with welfare as presently constituted is that it has a built-in marginal tax rate of 100 percent. If the dole is now $500 per week and the recipient earns a salary of $100, this payment will be reduced to $400, leaving the welfare "client" no better off financially. But thanks to Milton Friedman's negative income tax plan,[42] this problem can be overcome.[43]

Unrestricted immigration will assault the institutions which make a free society possible in the first place.

This, too, is a very powerful objection, for it cannot be denied that many of the people who might enter the U.S. under an open-door policy come from parts of the world where freedom is nonexistent, unheard of, or denigrated.

---

[40] Friedman (1962).

[41] True, it is harsh on the poor to totally eliminate welfare while the minimum wage, anti-peddler laws, etc., are still in effect. But two wrongs do not make a right. Just because the state victimizes the poor by making it illegal, and thus difficult, to earn money, does not make it right for government to injure a second group of people, taxpayers, and demand money from them at the point of a gun so as to transfer some of their funds to the first set of victims. In any case, were welfare to be totally eliminated right now, this would set up irresistible forces to end such employment barriers. This is analogous to the case for eliminating immigration restrictions on behalf of breaking up welfare. If hordes of poor foreigners poured onto our shores in order to take advantage of generous welfare provisions, that would immeasurably hasten the day that they were eliminated.

[42] Friedman (1962).

[43] Let it be remembered that each of these examples is a *reductio* of the paleo position on immigration. I certainly do not favor school vouchers or the negative income tax. My claim is only that if the postponement libertarians remain true to their views on immigration, logic will force them to embrace these latter positions as well.

Nevertheless, the case for free immigration is not without a response. First of all, the U.S. is no longer the freest country in the world, if it ever was; there are several others which beat us out for this honorific. Thus, not all immigrants are likely to be less conducive to freedom than are we.[44] Second, there have been immigrants in our history who have improved our freedom immeasurably. The names Ludwig von Mises, Friedrich A. Hayek, Israel Kirzner, William Hutt, Ludwig Lachmann, Hans Hoppe, Yuri Maltsev, Kurt Leube, James Ahiakpor, George Ayittey, Nathaniel Branden, Barbara Branden, Sam Konkin, Harry Watson, David Henderson, and Ayn Rand leap immediately to mind in this context. A closed-door policy in the past might well have made it impossible for these people to contribute to our society. And this is to say nothing of all the children and grandchildren of immigrants who have made significant contributions. How could it be otherwise, given that virtually all of us are "the children and grandchildren of immigrants?"

Third, just how, precisely, is it contemplated that the new immigrants will bring in to disrepute the mores, habits, and institutions which undergird our liberties? The most likely method is through voting. That is, hordes of people from other continents will come to our shores, settle down, and then vote for Nazism, communism, welfare statism, or some such. It cannot be rationally denied that this is a plausible scenario. The only problem with it is that it, again, assumes a real world situation (one with a welfare state, a pro-criminal penal system, etc.) instead of the ideal libertarian one. It is crucial that this not be done, however. For if it is, we conflate these other issues with that of immigration; we are seemingly arguing against an open-door policy, when actually, our real problem is with welfarism, criminal

---

[44] The restrictionist might reply: let us limit immigration to those countries which are actually freer than our own. But people who come to the U.S. from totalitarian countries are likely to do so because they *dislike* such regimes. Many of the strongest supporters of freedom in the U.S. are first- and second-generation Polish-Americans, Lithuanian-Americans, Cuban-Americans, etc. In any case, this is a mere empirical issue, unworthy, perhaps, of even noting. Underlying it, at least for the libertarian, is that immigration is a victimless crime, and should no more be legally banned than should prostitution or drug use.

coddling, etc. If we are to generate a *libertarian* theory of immigration, we must argue in a *ceteris paribus* manner.[45]

It is the same in this case.[46] The real difficulty here concerns promiscuous voting, not immigrants who might vote "incorrectly." The problem, even apart from new entrants to our country, is that those who are already citizens now have the "right" to vote on, not whether or not, but how much of other people's property they can legally steal through the ballot box. *This* is the real threat to liberty. In a free society, all the wrong-thinking immigrants in the world would be powerless to overturn (what is left of) our free institutions, for there would be no possibility of voting to seize other people's property.

But suppose these foreign hordes enter our pure libertarian society where no such decisions are even allowed to be politically contemplated, let alone enacted, and then proceed to do just that. After all, at one time in our history we were far more free than we are now. It was people—many of them, it must be conceded, immigrants—who undermined our free institutions.

One answer is that we never had a fully libertarian society. Had we, the courts would have ruled against any property-grabbing initiative or referendum. The police would have dealt firmly with any property-destroying or denigrating riots engaged in by communist or Nazi or welfarist immigrants. On the assumption that these foreigners were civilians, not an actual invading army, there seems little reason to believe they would have succeeded in their nefarious "foreign" schemes.

But suppose they did, somehow, overturn us, in a fully peaceful manner (perhaps through the sheer eloquence of their oratory), so that no physical sanctions against them would be compatible with libertarianism. Then what? Then we have a division between the libertarian axiom of nonaggression and what might considered, from the pragmatic or utilitarian point of view, to be the good society.

---

[45] Rothbard (1978, pp. 238–39) argues in this way when he refutes the objection of the Russian menace to a stateless U.S. society.

[46] This objection is but a variation of the first one considered, above. Only now instead of bearing rifles, the invading "army" will be issued votes, as soon as they have been naturalized.

But this should occasion no surprise or any embarrassment for the libertarian position. If you pack enough into your assumptions, you can overturn any principle, even an entirely appropriate and valid one such as the libertarian nonaggression axiom. For example, suppose that the all-powerful "Martians" threaten that unless we kill innocent person A, they will blow up the world. Surely, then, we would be presented with a stark choice indeed: violate the libertarian basic premise, or bring forth the end to all human life. One response might be "Justice though the heavens fall!" Another might be to say that the libertarian axiom is pro-life in all but such contrived situations. Or, to treat more realistic scenarios where utilitarianism and libertarianism might diverge, there is the fact that if we outlawed homosexuality, or engaged in preventive detention of male teenagers, we would undoubtedly reduce the incidence of AIDS and crime, respectively. Happily, we shrink back from such perversions of justice, because of elemental decency, e.g., adherence to the libertarian nonaggression axiom. Should we do any less in the case of immigration? Certainly not.

Conclusion

If one is against immigration, there are ways to reduce it which are fully compatible with libertarianism. For one thing, unilaterally declare full free trade with all nations. Trade in goods, services, and capital is an economic substitute for immigration. That is, there are two ways to right any imbalance between capital and labor: bring labor to the areas where population is below its optimum size (immigration), and bring capital and goods to the areas where they are below their optimum sizes (free trade in capital and goods). As the former are typically far cheaper than the latter, a regime of full free trade would eliminate much of the economic incentive toward migration.

Are libertarians moderates or extremists on the issues of emigration, migration, and immigration? The libertarian position on migration does *not* constitute a compromise in that it is indubitably an all-or-none proposition: either migration is totally legitimate, in which case there should be no interferences with it whatsoever, or it is a violation of the nonaggression axiom, in which case it should be banned, fully. I have argued in this paper that the former position is the only correct one.

But libertarianism constitutes a compromise position on this issue in two other senses. First, immigration is allowed if and only if there are property owners willing to sponsor (presumably for a fee, but not necessarily so) the new entrants, and not otherwise. Second, there are people on both right and left who oppose borders totally open to peaceful settlement (Chavez, Buckley), and libertarians find themselves safely on the other side of this unholy alliance.

For example, states Buckley: "The idea of totally open borders—anybody who wants to can come on in—is the stuff of libertarian fancy, nice for tone poems by such as Ayn Rand, but not very good national policy."[47]

It is not often that viewpoints are so starkly contrasted. We have, at least in this case, achieved real disagreement. It is clear that whatever the merits of this conservative perspective, it is not a libertarian one. Buckley is absolutely correct in labeling this Ayn Rand viewpoint as libertarian—and no one who dissents from it can to that extent call himself a libertarian.

---

[47] Buckely (1997, p. 20).

15 Secession

The law of free association is a crucially important implication of the rights of private property (in physical material, and in our own bodies). For if we cannot freely associate with others on a mutually-voluntary basis, our property rights are to that extent abrogated.

The most serious denigration of property rights in persons and thus in free association is, of course, murder. No one favors such behavior (killing in self-defense is entirely another matter) so this is not at all controversial. Another grave violation of the libertarian code of nonaggression against nonaggressors and their property is slavery (or kidnapping, which is short-term slavery). This, too, is nondebatable.

There are, however, many institutions, actually favored by "respectable" commentators on political economy, which partake of slavery to a greater or lesser extent. All laws against "discrimination" are violations of free association, because they force two parties, one of which who wishes to have nothing to do with the other, to interact despite these desires. When a store owner is forced to sell to customers against his will, and is not free to snub any of them on whatever racial, sexual, religious etc., basis he chooses, he is to that extent a slave. The difference between such laws and outright slavery is only one of degree: in *each*

Printed with kind permission of Mr. Llewellyn H. Rockwell, Jr. This article was initially posted on http://www.lewrockwell.com website.

case, the essence of the matter is that people are forced to associate with others against their will. Another instance is forced unionism. Our labor legislation forces employers to "bargain fairly" with those they would prefer to avoid entirely.

Perhaps the most important violation of the law of free association, at least on pragmatic grounds, occurs in the political realm. This is crucial, because other infringements, such as affirmative action, union legislation, etc., stem from political sources. If freedom of association in the realm of affirmative action is the right to discriminate, and in the field of labor the right to hire a "scab," then when it comes to the political realm, it is the right to secession.

Those who are not free to secede are, in effect, partial slaves to a king, or to a tyrannous majority under democracy. Nor is secession to be confused with the mere right to emigrate, even when one is allowed to take one's property out of the country. Secession means the right to stay put, on one's own property, and either to shift alliance to another political entity, or to set up shop as a sovereign on one's own account.

Why should the man who wishes to secede from a government have to vacate his land? For surely, even under the philosophy of statists, it was the people who came first. Government, in the minarchist libertarian view, was only instituted by them in order to achieve certain ends, later, after they had come to own their property. That is to say, the state is a creation of the people, not the people a creation of the state. But if a government was once invited in, to provide certain services, then it can also be uninvited, or invited to leave, or expelled. To deny this is to assert that the government was there first, before there were even any people. But how can this be? Government is not a disembodied entity, composed of creatures other than human (although, perhaps, there may be legitimate doubts about this on the part of some); rather, it is comprised of flesh and blood, albeit for the most part evil, people.

Given, then, that secession is a human right, part and parcel of the right to free association, how can we characterize those who oppose this? Who would use force and violence, of all things, in order to compel unwilling participants to join in, or to remain part of, a political entity they wish to have nothing to do with? Why, as would-be slave holders, of a sort. Certainly not as libertarians.

Thus, it is nothing short of amazing to find that there are commentators who actually call themselves libertarians and yet oppose the rights of secession. Were these people to remain consistent with this view, they would be logically forced, also, to give their imprimatur to union and anti-discrimination legislation, surely a *reductio ad absurdum*.

One of the grounds upon which so-called libertarians oppose secession, the right to be left alone politically speaking, is that those who wish to secede might be less than fully perfect in various ways. For example, the Confederate states practiced slavery, and this is certainly incompatible with libertarian law.

Let us assume away the awkward historical fact that this "curious institution" was operational in the North, too. After all, we are making a philosophical point, not a historical one. Let us posit, arguendo, that the North came to its confrontation with the South with totally clean hands as far as slaveholding, or, indeed, any other deviation from libertarian law is concerned (e.g., tariffs, high taxes, etc.). That is, the North is a totally libertarian entity, the South a morally evil one. (I know, I know; I'm only talking here for argument's sake.)

Would that premise be a valid rationale for the North to, in effect, enslave the South, and thus violate its rights of free association? It would not.

If it was proper for the North to hold the South captive against its will, the implication is that India was not warranted in seceding from England in 1948 since the former practiced suttee; that African countries were not justified in departing from their European colonial masters since they practiced clitorectomy; that it would not have been permissible for the Jews in 1930s Germany to have left the jurisdiction of the Nazis since they, too, were doubtless imperfect in some way or other.

Let us move from the realm of the macro to that of the micro. If groups of imperfect people are not justified in seceding from groups of perfect people, what about individuals? If we rigorously apply the principle on the basis of which Confederate secession was opposed to the individual level, again we run into all sorts of counterintuitive results.

For example, divorce. Under this "logic" no spouse could leave another if the departing one were less than perfect.

In the words of Clyde Wilson: "If the right of secession of one part of a political community is subject to the moral approval of another, then there really is no right of secession." Either you have the right of free association and secession, or you do not.

If secession is always and everywhere justified, what, then, is the proper libertarian response to the existence of suttee, slavery, clitorectomy, etc., in other countries (e.g., in seceding territories)?

Under libertarian free market anarchism, it would be permissible for a private defense agency to invade private property if a crime is occurring there (if a mistake is made in this regard, libertarian punishment theory, the topic for another day, kicks into gear; in this type of society, even the police are not above the law). If A is about to murder B in A's house, A may not properly object when the police kick in his door to forestall this dastardly act. Thus, free market competing defense agencies could have gone into the South to free the slaves, but once this was done, given that there were no other crimes occurring, and that due punishment was meted out to the evil-doers, that would be the end of the matter. There would be no further interaction. The South (or India in the case of suttee) would then be allowed to go its own way.

Under limited government libertarianism, the government of the North would take no steps to rid the sovereign Confederacy of its slavery (or India of its suttee). The purpose of the state in this philosophy is to protect its own citizens. Period. And, on the (historically accurate) assumption that the Confederacy showed no indication of invading the North, but merely wanted to be left alone to its own devices, that would be the end of the matter as far as the Northern government was concerned.

However, even under these assumptions individual abolitionists would be perfectly free, and, indeed, justified, in going in to the Confederacy, guns in hand, with the intention of ridding the South of this evil institution of slavery. But if things went poorly for them, they could not then scurry back to the North, tails between their legs, hiding behind their mama's skirts, because that would necessarily bring in the

Northern government into the fray. It would violate the noninvasion (except in self-defense) provision of limited government libertarianism, or minarchism.

There would be no "reconstruction." There would be no "indivisible" U.S.A. Rather, there would now be two totally separate countries. The U.S.A. and the Confederacy. Again, once slavery was ended, given that there were no other crimes occurring, and that due punishment was meted out to the evil-doers, that would be the end of the matter.

16 Legalize Drugs Now! An Analysis of the Benefits of Legalized Drugs

(with Meaghan Cussen)

Basic Constitutional Rights

Many argue that drug prohibition protects addicts from themselves by exerting parental control over their behavior. This government-enforced control, the anti-drug laws, strictly monitors addicts treatment of their own bodies. For example, the government decides that it wants to protect Fred Brown from destroying his body. The government, therefore, outlaws narcotics and, in effect, takes control of Fred's body. Under the United States Constitution and the anti-slavery laws, this hegemony should not happen. The guiding principles of the United States, iterated both in the Declaration of Independence and the Constitution, protect Fred's basic civil liberties to "pursue his own happiness" as long as he doesn't infringe on others' rights to life and property. With prohibition, Fred no longer has this constitutional right. He no longer controls his own body. Regulation has stripped him of his civil liberty. Fred's role of "owner of his own body" is taken away from him. This has, in effect, made him a slave.

Reprinted with kind permission of Blackwell Publishing from *American Journal of Economics and Sociology* 59, no. 3 (2000): 525–36. Meaghan Cussen graduated from the College of the Holy Cross, Worcester, Mass., U.S.A. in 1998 and wrote this paper with Dr. Walter Block while under his instruction as an economics student.

Are we being hysterical in categorizing present drug law as a form of servitude? No, our drug laws amount to partial slavery. We must all question the practices of roadblocks, strip-searches, urine tests, locker searches, and money-laundering laws. Philosophically speaking, drug prohibition severely threatens our civil liberties and is inconsistent with the anti-slavery philosophy and the founding documents of the United States. The legalization of drugs would give a basic civil liberty back to U.S. citizens, by granting them control over their own bodies.

Free Trade

Free trade benefits all parties. It can be assumed that if drugs were legalized, and thus were a part of the market, both the buyer and the seller would gain. Each time a trade occurs, the welfare of both parties is improved; if Joe sold you his shirt for $10, he would benefit because he obviously values the $10 more than the shirt. If he didn't, he would not have traded it. You would also gain from the trade because you obviously value the shirt more than you do the $10. If you didn't, then you would not have agreed to the deal. Free trade in the drug market works the same way. If Joe sells you marijuana for $10, he gains because he values the money more, and you gain because you value the drugs more. Whether or not another person thinks you should value the drugs more is not the question. That third party is not involved in the trade. The amount of pleasure the drug brings you is your motivation for buying it. Trade is a positive-sum game. Both parties gain, at least in the *ex ante* sense.

It cannot be denied that certain third parties will be offended by the drug transaction, on moral or ethical grounds. However, try to find any transaction that does not offend at least one person. Many people object to the sale of alcohol, cigarettes, birth control or animal products, but their feelings or beliefs do not stop these items from being sold. Marxists object to *any* market transactions because they see commercial activity as necessarily exploitative. There is obviously no pleasing everyone when it comes to market transactions. In our free-enterprise economy, however, anyone who participates in the market will benefit from it. "For all third parties who say they will be aggrieved by a legalized drug trade, there will be many more benefiting from the reduction in crime"

(Block 1993). "A third party can verbally oppose any given trade. But that opposition cannot be revealed through market choices in the same way that trade between the two parties indicates a positive evaluation of the transaction" (Block 1996, p. 434). Free trade of all goods contributes to the number of those who gain. In a free-market economy, everybody has opportunity to participate in the market, and therefore, equal opportunity to gain in a positive-sum transaction.

Not only would the legalization of drugs protect basic freedoms and lead to individual benefit through free trade, but it would also bring enormous benefits to society as a whole. The first and most important societal benefit is a reduction in crime.

Reductions in Crime

When addictive drugs are made legal, crime will decrease substantially, for four main reasons. First, the lowered price of narcotics will eliminate the theft and murder associated with their high prices. When drugs are legalized, law-abiding businesspeople will no longer be deterred by the illegality of drug commerce and will become willing to enter the market. With this increase of supply, assuming a less than proportional increase in demand, the price of narcotics will fall. Addicts who were formerly forced to steal, murder, and engage in illegal employment to earn enough money for their habits will be able to afford the lower prices. Therefore, these types of drug-related crimes will decrease.

Second, substance-related disputes such as gang wars and street violence will be reduced. Dealers will be able to use the courts to settle their disputes instead of taking the law into their own hands. Violations of rights within the drug business will be resolved through the judicial system, thereby decreasing gang violence, and saving the many innocent lives that often get caught in the crossfire.

Third, the drug business creates great profits for cartels. Cartels are often international organizations, many of which support terrorism and add to violent crime in America. If the narcotics market were open, drug revenues would be equally distributed by free-market forces, and would have less of a chance of supporting terrorist organizations, crime rings, and cartel activity and profit.

Finally, and most obviously, with transport, sale, and possession legalized, formerly illegal activities will now become society-approved business transactions. Crime, an act that breaks the law, which in its very insurrectional essence leads to societal instability, will be greatly reduced through the legalization of the inevitable activity of drug transactions.

The prohibition of alcohol in the 1920s provides us with a perfect case in point. The high crime rates during this decade were due to the existence of the black market, spawned from the government-enforced illegalization of alcohol. The black market led to the formation of major crime rings. The underground market for alcohol grew and led many profit-hungry entrepreneurs into a risky lifestyle of crime. Many were jailed due to transport, sale, and possession.

When Prohibition ended, alcohol-related crime ceased. The profit balloon driven by the limited supply of the illegal substance was deflated. The black market disappeared, along with all of the illegal activity associated with it. Crime rings were forced to disband and seek other means of income. How many crime rings exist today for the selling of alcohol? The answer is none. The reason is legalization.

In contrast, drug-related crime is skyrocketing. As Ostrowski (1993, p. 209) notes, "The President's Commission on Organized Crime estimates a total of seventy drug-market murders yearly in Miami alone. Based on that figure and FBI data, a reasonable nationwide estimate would be at least 750 murders a year. Recent estimates from New York and Washington are even higher." Anyone who questions whether prohibition is responsible for violence should note the relative peace that prevails in the alcohol and legal drug markets.

The Potency Effect

The end of Prohibition also brought the end of the dangerous potency effect. During Prohibition, it was in the best interests of the sellers to carry more potent forms of alcohol. Hence, an alcohol dealer would be more likely to carry vodka and other hard liquor instead of beer and wine because of hard liquor's greater value (per unit of volume). Therefore, people began drinking vodka and other hard liquor, which because of their high potency are more dangerous than beer and wine.

Alcohol-related deaths increased. This horrific result is known as the potency effect.

Fifty years after the repeal of Prohibition, the potency effect has been reversed. The average per capita consumption of alcohol has fallen to its lowest level ever (Hamid 1993, p. 184). In fact, people have begun switching to weaker alcohol alternatives, such as wine coolers and non-alcoholic beer. The legalization of alcohol reversed the potency effect. The legalization of drugs will do the same.

For example, the risks involved in transporting marijuana, a low-potency drug, for the purpose of sale are extremely high. It is in the best interests of the dealer to carry more potent, thus more expensive, drugs, which is why he or she will be more likely to carry cocaine because of its greater value (per unit of volume). Because cocaine is more potent, it is also more dangerous. Addicts face increased health risks when using cocaine as opposed to using marijuana. These health risks grow as potency increases. Stronger and more dangerous drugs such as crack, "ice," and PCP are substituted for the weaker, relatively safer drugs. The results are often deadly.

Health Benefits

The legalization of drugs would eliminate serious health risks by assuring market-driven high quality substances and the availability of clean needles. Prohibition in the 1920s created a market for cheap versions of alcoholic products, such as bathtub gin. Alcohol was diluted or adulterated in often dangerous ways. Needless deaths occurred because of the poor quality of the product. So is drug prohibition worth the health risks? Fly-by-night goods cannot always be trusted. If narcotics were legalized, purity could be all but guaranteed. Drugstores, held accountable by customers, would deliver safe products. Brand names would bring competition into the market and assure safer, better products. Doctors would now be able to monitor the drug use of seriously addicted patients. Poor quality would be a thing of the past.

In addition, clean needles would be readily available. Drug vendors and health care organizations would be able to provide clean needles for their customers and patients respectively. Today, needles are shared because they are difficult to obtain. About 25 percent of AIDS cases are contracted through the sharing of intravenous needles (Boaz 1990, p. 3). Legalizing drugs would eliminate this problem. "In Hong Kong, where needles are available in drugstores, as of 1987 there were no cases of AIDS among drug users" (*ibid.*).

When was the last time you heard of a diabetic contracting AIDS from contaminated needles? If insulin were prohibited, this situation would surely change for the worse.

Societal Benefits

Illegal drug sale creates a destructive atmosphere. When a criminal culture emerges, a community is torn apart. A booming black market fosters a large criminal presence. Casual recreational users are forced to come in contact with criminals to make their purchases, as prohibition makes it impossible to make a legal transaction. Additionally, basically good citizens often deal with and, unfortunately, become influenced by, the criminals of the area (Boaz 1990, p. 2).

Inner-city youths, surrounded by the booming black market, are influenced by the sheer amount of money dealers make and often fall into a life of crime (Boaz 1990, p. 2). These youths often see themselves as having the choice of remaining in poverty, earning "chump change," or pursuing a life of crime and making thousands of dollars a week. Which do you think all too many young people will choose?

The black market presence often leads to the corruption of police officers and public officials. Police, on average, make $35,000 a year. When they arrest the denizens of the drug world who make ten times that amount, it is often difficult not to be tempted into a life of crime.

> Drug corruption charges have been leveled against FBI agents, police officers, prison guards, U.S. customs inspectors, even prosecutors. In 1986, in New York City's 77th Precinct, twelve police officers were arrested for stealing and selling drugs. Miami's problem is worse. In June 1986, seven officers there were indicted for using their jobs to run a drug operation that used murders, threats, and bribery. Add to that two dozen other cases of

corruption in the last three years in Miami alone. (Ostrowski 1993, pp. 296–307)

We must question a policy that so frequently turns police officers into the very outlaws they are authorized to bring to justice. We must question a policy that leads to the enormous success of those willing to break the laws of our society. We must question a policy that leaves a criminal profession in a position of great influence over our youth and other honest citizens. Milton Friedman put it best when he wrote, "Drugs are a tragedy for addicts. But criminalizing their use converts the tragedy into a disaster for society, for users and nonusers alike" (Friedman 1989).

Prohibit the Crime, Not the Drug

The laws of the United States prohibit violent acts against other citizens. This is consistent with the founding principles of our nation, which allow each free individual to pursue life, liberty, and happiness. The laws of the United States should not prohibit the intake of narcotics that only have an immediate effect on the individual consumer. If I ingest a drug, I am doing possible harm only to myself, and no other. If I subsequently act violently on account of my altered state of mind, only then am I doing harm to others. It is the subsequent action that is harmful, not the drug-taking itself. Since I am responsible for my actions, I should be arrested and punished only when I am violent. Alcohol is legal even though people commit rapes, murders, beatings, and other violent crimes when they are drunk. Yet if a person commits these crimes when intoxicated, he or she is held responsible for them. A mere substance should not and does not serve as an excuse for the violent acts. The ingestion of alcohol is not illegal *per se*. The same standard should be applied to the use of presently illegal drugs.

It should also be noted that every narcotic does not turn the user into a crazed, enraged lunatic capable of all sorts of violent crimes. In fact, it is just the opposite. Most drugs induce lethargy. Remember that opium, now illegal, was used quite often in England, China, and the United States, and tended to induce stupor. The use of traditional opiates did not render users violent. In fact, no drug is "as strongly associated with violent behavior as is alcohol. According to justice Department statistics, 54 percent of all jail inmates convicted of violent crimes in 1983 reported having just used alcohol prior to committing their offense" (Nadelmann 1989, p. 22). This statistic renders the prohibition of drugs rather than alcohol a legal inconsistency.

Save the U.S. Taxpayer Money

According to the U.S. Department of Justice, federal, state, and local governments currently spend over $20 billion per year on drug enforcement. In 1992, there were more than one million arrests for drug law violations. In 1993, 60 percent of the seventy-seven thousand federal prisoners were incarcerated for drug-related crimes (Miron and Zwiebel 1995, p. 176). Jails are crowded and large amounts of tax dollars are being spent on enforcement efforts that only aggravate the problem. We can add to this sum the amount of money spent on research and medical care for those infected with AIDS and other diseases caused by needle sharing.

With legalization, the tax dollars spent on enforcement would be saved. The availability of clean needles would reduce the rate of AIDS infections, and would consequently reduce the amount of money spent on medical care, to say nothing of the reduction in human misery.

Don't Help Inflate Criminals' Profit Balloons

If we continue with the same anti-drug policies, we are only helping drug lords get richer. Each time a bust occurs and a shipment is captured and destroyed, the criminals benefit. The seizure reduces supply and takes out one or more black market participants. According to the laws of supply and demand, with a decrease in drug supply, black market prices will rise, creating a larger profit for suppliers. So, every time we think we are winning a battle in the war, we are really strengthening the enemy rather than weakening it. The way to win is not by fighting the alligators, but by draining their swamp (Block 1993, p. 696). It is better to ruin drug lords' businesses by deflating the profit balloon than by acting in a way (i.e., prohibition) that only benefits them. "By taking the profits out of [drugs], we could at one full swoop do more to reduce their power than decades of fighting them directly" (Holloway and Block 1998, p. 6).

At present, governmental control of the drug lords, while minuscule, is as effective as it will ever be in any sector of society (Thornton 1991). Just think, even in jails, where the lives of residents are completely controlled by the government, drugs still have not been eliminated. If the government cannot even control the drug trade within its own house, how can it expect to control it within the entire nation? Are we to imprison the whole citizenry in an attempt? Legalization will take the profits out of the narcotics industry.

Elasticity of Demand for Drugs

Many believe the elasticity of demand for narcotics is very high. If drugs are legalized and their prices fall, the amount purchased will increase by a large amount. This is not the case. In fact, the elasticity of demand for drugs in general is very low for three main reasons. First, narcotics are seen as necessities for drug users, not luxuries. "While one might severely reduce demand for [luxuries] in the face of an increased price, or even give it up entirety in the extreme, this does not apply to [necessities]" (Block 1993, p. 696). This behavioral pattern indicates that drugs are indeed low-elasticity goods. In fact, there is really no good reason to assume that many Americans would suddenly start to ingest or inject narcotics even if given the legal opportunity.

Second, most people recognize the danger of drugs and will avoid them no matter what the price. Third, if drugs are made legal, they will no longer have to be pushed. If they are sold over the counter to adults, criminals will no longer have to pawn these goods off on innocent youths. Competition will be high and dealers will have no reason to resort to this extreme measure. Certainly, market competition will occur which may result in advertisements targeting particular age groups. However, this would have a negligible effect compared to drug pushers' current youth-targeted tactics.

Finally, we should realize that legalization would cause potency to fall. With normalized supply, people will begin purchasing weaker, safer drugs. This normalized supply, along with the low elasticity of demand for narcotics, will lead to only a small increase in consumption.

Government Regulations

A main driver of anti-drug legislation is the concern that government would be sanctioning an immoral and destructive activity, viewed as sinful in the eyes of many in the population. However, the legalization of drugs does not mean that government and society would sanction their use. Alcohol and cigarettes are legal but we have pretty successful campaigns against these substances. Gossiping and burping are also legal, but you never see a government-sponsored advertisement advocating catty behavior or belching in public. Are we as a society to prohibit automobile racing, extreme skiing, the ingestion of ice cream and fried foods because they may have a detrimental effect on human health? No. Dangers associated with these activities cannot be measured. "Such inherently unquantifiable variables cannot be measured, much less weighed against each other. Interpersonal comparison of utility is incompatible with valid economic analysis" (Block 1996, p. 435). We cannot allow such legal inconsistencies to take place.

Legalizing drugs would eliminate these inconsistencies, guarantee freedoms, and increase the efficiency and effectiveness of the government's anti-drug beliefs. If drugs were legalized, taxes could be cut with the elimination of government expenditures on enforcement. All of the money saved could be used to promote anti-drug campaigns. Private organizations could take over the tasks of inspecting and regulating. A minimum age of twenty-one would be mandated for the consumption of drugs. Transactions would take place in a drugstore, with upstanding suppliers. Drugs could safely be administered, with clean needles, in hospitals where medical professionals could monitor and rehabilitate the addicted. MADD (Mothers Against Drunk Driving) is a good example of a successful anti-substance-abuse campaign. Private, nonprofit groups like this one could help in the fight against drug abuse.

Currently, we are not by any means winning the war on drugs. Our futile attempts at enforcement only exacerbate the problem. We need to de-escalate the war rather than continue fighting the over twenty-three million adult Americans who are obviously determined to enjoy themselves as they see fit (Boaz 1990, p. 5). We must also remember that those that need to be deterred the most, the hard-core drug users, are the least likely to be stopped (Ostrowski 1993, p. 205). Our law enforcement is not working to contain and control the very people the anti-drug laws are designed to control. The war on drugs has done little to reduce narcotics use in the United States and has thus proved counterproductive (Holloway and Block 1998, p. 6). Philosophically and practically speaking, drugs should be legalized. This act would prevent our civil liberties from being threatened, reduce crime rates, reverse the potency effect, improve the quality of life in inner cities, prevent the spread of disease, save the taxpayer money, and generally benefit both individuals and society as a whole.

17 Libertarianism and Libertinism

There is perhaps no greater confusion in all of political economy than that between libertarianism and libertinism. That they are commonly taken for one another is an understatement of the highest order. For several reasons, it is difficult to compare and contrast libertarianism and libertinism. First and most important, on some issues the two views do closely resemble one another, at least superficially. Second—perhaps purely by accident, perhaps due to etymological considerations—the two words not only sound alike, but are spelled almost identically. It is all the more important, then, to distinguish between the very different concepts these words represent.

Libertarianism

Libertarianism is a political philosophy. It is concerned solely with the proper use of force. Its core premise is that it should be illegal to threaten or initiate violence against a person or his property without his permission; force is justified only in defense or retaliation. That is it, in a nutshell. The rest is mere explanation, elaboration, and qualification—and answering misconceived objections.[1]

Reprinted with kind permission of the Ludwig von Mises Institute from *Journal of Libertarian Studies* 11, no. 1 (1994): 117–28. This article was initially published as an introduction to the Portuguese translation of *Defending the Undefendable* (Porto Alegre, Brazil: Instituto de Estudos Empresariais 1993).

Libertarianism is a theory about what should be illegal, not what is currently proscribed by law. In some jurisdictions, for example, charging in excess of stipulated rent levels is prohibited. These enactments do not refute the libertarian code since they are concerned with what the law is, not with what it should be. Nor does this freedom philosophy technically forbid anything; even, strictly speaking, aggression against person or property. It merely states that it is just to use force to punish those who have transgressed its strictures by engaging in such acts. Suppose that all-powerful but evil Martians threatened to pulverize the entire Earth and kill everyone on it unless someone murdered the innocent Joe Bloggs. The person who did this might be considered to have acted properly, in that he saved the whole world from perishing. But according to the doctrine of libertarianism he should still be guilty of a crime, and thus justly punishable for it. Look at it from the point of view of the bodyguard hired by Bloggs. Surely, he would have been justified in stopping the murder of his client.[2]

Note that the libertarian legal code speaks in terms of the initiation of violence. It does not mention hurting or injuring or damaging. This is because there are so many ways of harming others that should be legal. For example, opening up a tailor shop across the street from one already in business, and competing away its customers, surely offends the former firm; but this does not violate its rights. Similarly, if John wanted to marry Jane, but she agreed instead to marry George, then once again a person, John, is harmed; but he should have no remedy at law against the perpetrator, George. Another way to put this is that only rights violations should be illegal. Since in this view people only have a right to be free of invasions, or interferences with their persons or property, the law should do no more than enforce contracts, and safeguard personal and private property rights.

Then there is the phrase, "against a person or his property." This, too, must be explicated, for if libertarianism is predicated on punishing uninvited border crossings or invasions, then it is crucial to know where

---

[1] For further explication, see Rothbard (1970, 1978, 1982), Hoppe (1989, 1990b, 1993a), and Nozick (1974).

[2] For this example, as for so much else, I am indebted to Murray N. Rothbard.

your fist ends and where my chin begins. Suppose we see A reach his hand into B's pocket, pull a wallet out of it, and run off. Is the pickpocket guilty of a crime? Only if the previous possessor of the wallet were the legitimate owner. If not, if A were the rightful owner merely repossessing his own property, then a crime has not been committed. Rather, it occurred yesterday, when B grabbed A's wallet, which he is now repossessing.

In the case of the human body, the analysis is usually straightforward. It is the enslaver, the kidnapper, the rapist, the assaulter, or the murderer who is guilty of criminal behavior, because the victim is the rightful owner of the body being brutalized or confined.[3] Physical objects, of course, present more of a problem; things don't come in nature labeled "mine" and "thine." Here the advocate of *laissez faire* capitalism relies on Lockean homesteading theory to determine border lines. He who "mixes his labor" with previously unowned parts of nature becomes their legitimate owner. Justice in property is traced back to such claims, plus all other noninvasive methods of title transfer (trade, gifts, and so on).

"Uninvited," and "without permission" are also important phrases in this philosophy. To the outside observer, aided voluntary euthanasia may be indistinguishable from murder; voluntary sexual intercourse may physically resemble rape; a boxing match may be kinesiologically identical to a street mugging. Nevertheless there are crucial differences between each of these acts: The first in each pair is, or at least can be, mutually consensual and therefore legitimate; the latter cannot.

Having laid the groundwork, let us now relate libertarianism to the issues of prostitution, pimping, and drugging. As a political philosophy, libertarianism says nothing about culture, mores, morality, or ethics. To repeat: It asks only one question, and gives only one answer. It asks,

---

[3] In the religious perspective, none of us "owns" his own body. Rather, we are the stewards of them, and God is the ultimate "owner" of each of us. But this concerns only the relation between man and deity. As far as the relationship between man and man, however, the secular statement that we own our own bodies has an entirely different meaning. It refers to the claim that we each have free will; that no one person may take it upon himself to enslave another, even for the former's "own good."

"Does the act necessarily involve initiatory invasive violence?" If so, it is justified to use (legal) force to stop it or punish the act; if not, this is improper. Since none of the aforementioned activities involves "border crossings," they may not be legally proscribed. And, as a practical matter, as I maintain in *Defending the Undefendable*, these prohibitions have all sorts of deleterious effects.

What is the view of libertarianism toward these activities, which I shall label "perverse?" Apart from advocating their legalization, the libertarian, *qua* libertarian, has absolutely no view of them at all. To the extent that he takes a position on them, he does so as a nonlibertarian.

In order to make this point perfectly clear, let us consider an analogy. The germ theory of disease maintains that it is not "demons," or "spirits," or the disfavor of the gods that causes sickness, but rather germs. What, then, is the view of this theory of disease on the propriety of quarantining an infected individual? On the electron theory of chemistry, or of astronomy? How does it weigh in on the abortion issue? What position do germ theoreticians take on the Balkan War? On deviant sexual practices? None whatsoever, of course. It is not that those who believe germs cause disease are inclined, however slightly, toward one side or the other in these disputes. Nor is the germ theorist necessarily indifferent to these disputes. On the contrary, the germists, *qua* germists, take no position at all on these important issues of the day. The point is, the germ theory is completely and totally irrelevant to these other issues, no matter how important they may be.

In like manner, the libertarian view takes absolutely no moral or valuative position on the perverse actions under discussion. The only concern is whether the actions constitute uninvited initiatory aggression. If they do, the libertarian position advocates the use of force to stop them; not because of their depravity, but because they have violated the one and only libertarian axiom: nonaggression against nonaggressors. If they do not involve coercive force, the libertarian philosophy denies the claim that violence may properly be used to oppose them, no matter how weird, exotic, or despicable they may be.

Cultural Conservatism

So much for the libertarian analysis of perversity. Let us now look at these acts from a completely different point of view: the moral, cultural, aesthetic, ethical, or pragmatic. Here, there is, of course, no question of legally prohibiting these actions, as we are evaluating them according to a very different standard.

But still, it is of great interest how we view them. Just because a libertarian may refuse to incarcerate perverts, it does not mean he must remain morally neutral about such behavior. So, do we favor or oppose? Support or resist? Root for or against? In this dimension, I am a cultural conservative. This means that I abhor homosexuality, bestiality, and sadomasochism, as well as pimping, prostituting, drugging, and other such degenerate behavior. As I stated in Part I of my three-part interview in *Laissez Faire Books* (November 1991):

> The basic theme . . . of libertarianism (is that) all nonaggressive behavior should be legal; people and their legitimately-held private property should be sacrosanct. This does not mean that nonaggressive acts such as drug selling, prostitution, etc., are good, nice or moral activities. In my view, they are not. It means only that the forces of law and order should not incarcerate people from indulging in them.

And again, as I stated in Part III of the same interview (February 1992):

> I don't see libertarianism as an attack on custom and morality. I think the paleolibertarians have made an important point: just because we don't want to put the pornographer in jail doesn't mean that we have to like what he does. On the contrary, it is perfectly coherent to defend his right to engage in that profession and still detest him and his actions.

In order to better pinpoint this concept, let us inquire as to the relationship between a libertarian and a libertine. We have already defined the former term. For our purposes here, the former may be defined as a person who loves, exults in, participates in, and/or advocates the morality of all sorts of perverse acts, but who at the same time eschews all acts of invasive violence. The libertine, then, will champion prostitution, drug addiction, sado-masochism, and the like, and maybe even indulge in these practices, but will not force anyone else to participate.

Are libertarians libertines? Some clearly are. If a libertarian were a member of the North American Man-Boy Love Association, he would qualify.[4] Are all libertarians libertines? Certainly not. Most libertarians recoil in horror from such goings-on. What then is the precise relationship between the libertarian, *qua* libertarian, and the libertine? It is simply this. The libertarian is someone who thinks that the libertine should not be incarcerated. He may bitterly oppose libertinism, he can speak out against it, he can organize boycotts to reduce the incidence of such acts. There is only one thing he cannot do, and still remain a libertarian: He cannot advocate, or participate in, the use of force against these people. Why? Because whatever one thinks of their actions, they do not initiate physical force. Since none of these actions necessarily does so,[5] the libertarian must, in some cases reluctantly, refrain from demanding the use of physical force against those who engage in perversions among consenting adults.[6]

The libertarian may hate and despise the libertine, or he may not. He is not committed one way or the other by his libertarianism, any more than is the holder of the germ theory of disease required to hold any view on libertinism. As a libertarian, he is only obligated not to demand a jail sentence for the libertine. That is, he must not demand incarceration for the nonaggressing, non-child molesting libertine, the

---

[4] The issue of children is a daunting and perplexing one for all political philosophies, not just libertarianism. But this particular case is rather straightforward: Any adult homosexual caught in bed with an underage male (who by definition cannot give consent) should be guilty of statutory rape; any parent who permits such a "relationship" should be deemed guilty of child abuse. This applies not only to homosexual congress with children, but also in the case of heterosexuals. There may be an issue with regard to whether the best way to demarcate children from adults is with an arbitrary age cutoff point, but given such a law, statutory rape should certainly be illegal. And this goes as well, for child abuse, even though there are continuum problems here as well.

[5] Of course, as a matter of fact, many if not all pimps, for example, do initiate unjustified violence. But they *need not do so,* and therefore pimping *per se* is not a violation of rights.

[6] I owe this latter point to Menlo Smith.

one who limits himself to consensual adult behavior. But the libertarian is totally free as a person, as a citizen, as a moralist, as a commentator on current events, as a cultural conservative, to think of libertinism as perverted, and to do what he can to stop it—short of using force. It is into this latter category that I place myself.

Why, then, as a cultural conservative, do I oppose libertinism? First and foremost, because it is immoral: Nothing could be more clear than that these perversions are inimicable to the interest and betterment of mankind. Since that is my criterion for morality, it follows that I would find these activities immoral. Furthermore, however, libertines flaunt the "virtue" of their practices and are self-congratulatory about them. If a "low rung in hell" is reserved for those who are too weak to resist engaging in immoral activities, a lower one still must be held for those who not only practice them but brag about them, and actively encourage others to follow suit.

Other reasons could be given as well. Consider tradition. At one time I would have scoffed at the idea of doing something merely because it was traditional, and refraining because it was not. My every instinct would have been to do precisely the opposite of the dictates of tradition.

But that was before I fully appreciated the thought of F. A. Hayek. From reading his many works (for example, Hayek 1973), I came to realize that traditions which are disruptive and harmful tend to disappear, whether through voluntary change, or more tragically, by the disappearance of societies that act in accordance with them. Presumably, then, if a tradition has survived, it has some positive value, even if we cannot see it. It is a "fatal conceit" (Hayek 1989) to call into question everything for which good and sufficient reason cannot be immediately given. How else can we justify the "blindly obedient" practice of wearing ties and collars, for example?

Tradition, however, is just a presumption, not a god to be worshipped. It is still reasonable to alter and abolish those traditions which do not work. But this is best done with an attitude of respect, not hostility, for that which has worked for many years.

Religious belief furnishes another reason to oppose libertinism: Few sectors of society have been as strong in their condemnation of perversity.

For me in the early 1970s, however, religion was the embodiment of war, killing, and injustice. It was an "unholy alliance" of the Crusades, the Inquisition, religious wars, virgin sacrifice, and the burning at the stake of "witches," astronomers, nonbelievers, free thinkers, and other inconvenient people. At present, I view this matter very differently. Yes, these things occurred, and self-styled religious people were indeed responsible. But surely there is some sort of historical statute of limitations, at least given that present religious practitioners can in no way properly be held responsible for the acts of their forebears. Religion now seems to me one of the last best hopes for society, as it is one of the main institutions still competing valiantly with an excessive and overblown government.[7]

To analyze in brief our present plight: We suffer from far too much state interference. One remedy is to apply moral measurement to government. Another is to place greater reliance on "mediating" institutions, such as the firm, the market, the family, and the social club, particularly organized religion. These organizations—predicated upon a moral vision and spiritual values—can far better provide for mankind's needs than political regimes.

Another reason why I oppose libertinism is more personal. I have come to believe that each of us has a soul, or inner nature, or animating spirit, or personhood, or purity, or self-respect, or decency, call it what you will. It is my opinion that some acts—the very ones under discussion, as it happens—deprecate this inner entity. They are a way of committing mental and spiritual destruction. And the practical result of these acts, for those able to feel such things, is emptiness and anomie. They may ultimately lead to physical suicide. And this destruction of individual character has grave repercussions for all of society.

---

[7] It cannot be denied that the economic statements representing many religions are hardly ringing endorsements of economic freedom and free enterprise (see Block 1986 and 1988). This would include pastoral letters from the U.S. Catholic Bishops, the Canadian Conference of Catholic Bishops, the Papal Encyclicals and the numerous statements on such matters from the Reformed Jewish and many Protestant denominations. Nonetheless religious organizations, along with the institution of the family, are still the main bulwark against ever-encroaching state power. They play this role, in some cases, if only by constituting a social arrangement alternative to that provided by government.

Examples: Prostitution and Drugs

As an example of this destruction of the individual, consider prostitution. The sinfulness of this act—for both buyer and seller—is that it is an attack upon the soul. In this it resembles certain other forms of conduct: engaging in sex without love or even respect, fornication, adultery, and promiscuity. Prostitution is singled out not because it is unique in this regard, but because it is the most extreme behavior of this type. True, prohibition drives this "profession" underground, with even more deleterious results. True, if the prostitute is a self-owner (that is, she is not enslaved), she has a right to use her body in any noninvasive manner she sees fit.[8] These may be good and sufficient reasons for legalization. However, just because I oppose prohibition does not mean I must value the thing itself. It would be a far, far better world if no one engaged in prostitution, not because there were legal sanctions imposed against it, but because people did not wish to so debase themselves.

At the opposite end of the scale, in a moral sense, is marriage, certainly an institution under siege. The traditional nuclear family is now seen by the liberal cultural elite as a patriarchal, exploitative evil. Yet it is no accident that the children raised on this model don't go out on murderous rages. Of course, I am not saying that sex outside of the bounds of matrimony should be outlawed. As a libertarian, I cannot, since this is a victimless "crime." As a cultural conservative, however, I most certainly can note that the institution of marriage is under attack as never before, and that its resulting weakness has boded ill for society. I can vociferously maintain that imperfect as real-world marriages are, they are usually vastly superior to the other possible alternatives for taking care of children: the tender mercies of the state, single parents, orphanages, and so on.[9]

For another example, consider drug-taking. In my view, addictive drugs are no less a moral abomination than prostitution. They are soul destroyers. They are a slow, and sometimes a not-so-slow, form of suicide. Even while alive, the addict is not really living; he has traded in a

---

[8] A legal right, but not a moral right.
[9] For an analysis of the government's attack on marriage and the family, see Carlson (1988), and Murray (1984a).

moment's "ecstasy" for focused awareness and competence. These drugs are an attack on the body, mind, and spirit. The user becomes enslaved to the drug, and is no longer master of his own life. In some regards, this is actually worse than outright slavery. At least during the heyday of this "curious institution" during the nineteenth century and before, its victims could still plan for escape. They could certainly imagine themselves free. When enslaved by addictive drugs, though, all too often the very intention of freedom becomes atrophied.

I am not discussing the plight of the addict under the present prohibition. His situation now is indeed pitiful, but this is in large part because of drug criminalization. The user cannot avail himself of medical advice; the drug itself is often impure, and very expensive, which encourages crime, which completes the vicious cycle, and so on. I am addressing instead the circumstances of the user under ideal (legalized) conditions, where the substance is cheap, pure, and readily available, where there is no need of shared needles, and medical advice on "proper" usage and "safe" dosage is readily forthcoming.

There are certain exceptions, of course, to this rather harsh characterization. Marijuana may have some ameliorative effects for glaucoma sufferers. Morphine is medically indicated as a pain reliever in operations. Psychiatric drugs may properly be used to combat depression. But apart from such cases, the moral, mental, and physical harm of heroin, cocaine, LSD, and their ilk are overwhelming and disastrous.

Why is it moral treason to engage in such activities, or, for that matter, to pollute one's brain with overindulgence in alcohol? It is because this is a subtle form of suicide, and life is so immeasurably valuable that any retreat from it is an ethical and moral crime? Life, to be precious, must be experienced. Drugs, alcoholism, and the like are ways to drop out of life. What if using these controlled substances is seen as a way of getting "high," a state of being that is exhilarating? My response is that life itself should be a high, at least ideally, and the only way to make it so is to at least try. But it is the rare person who can do anything virtuous at all, while "under the influence."

Once again I reiterate that I am not calling for the legal abolition of drugs. Prohibition is not only a practical nightmare (it increases crime, it breeds disrespect for legitimate law, and so on) but is also ethically impermissible. Adults should have a legal (not a moral) right to pollute their bodies as they wish (Block 1993; Thornton 1991). To the objection that this is only a slow form of suicide, I reply that suicide itself should be legal. (However, having said this as a libertarian, I now state as a cultural conservative that suicide is a deplorable act, one not worthy of moral human beings.[10])

We are thus left with the somewhat surprising conclusion that even though addictive drugs are morally problematic, they should not be banned. Similarly with immoral sexual practices. Although upon first reading this may be rather unexpected, it should occasion no great surprise. After all, there are numerous types of behavior which are legal and yet immoral or improper. Apart from the ones we have been discussing, we could include gossip, teasing the mentally handicapped to their faces and making great sport of their responses, not giving up one's seat to a pregnant woman, cheating at games which are "for fun" only, lack of etiquette, and gratuitous viciousness. These acts range widely in the seriousness with which they offend, but they are all quite despicable, each in its own way. And yet it is improper to legally proscribe them. Why not? The explanation that makes the most sense in this quarter is the libertarian one: None of them amounts to invasive violence.

Mea Culpa

Previously, when I argued for the legalization of avant-garde sexual and drug practices (in the first edition of *Defending the Undefendable*), I wrote about them far more positively than I now do. In my own defense, I did conclude the introduction to the first edition with these words:

---

[10] That is, apart from extenuating circumstances such as continuous excruciating pain, intractable psychological problems, and the like. We have said that the essence of morality is the promotion of the welfare of mankind. In instances such as these, it is conceivable that suicide may be the best way to accomplish this. In any case, the response to these unfortunate people should be to support them, not to punish them. Certainly, the imposition of the death penalty for attempted (failed) suicides—practiced in a bygone era—would be the very opposite of what is required.

The defense of such as the prostitute, pornographer, etc., is thus a very limited one. It consists solely of the claim that they do not initiate physical violence against nonaggressors. Hence, according to libertarian principles, none should be visited upon them. This means only that these activities should not be punished by jail sentences or other forms of violence. It decidedly does not mean that these activities are moral, proper, or good.

However, when it came to the actual chapters, I was altogether too enthusiastic about the virtues of these callings. I waxed eloquent about the "value of the services" performed. I totally dismissed the moral concerns of third parties. I showed no appreciation of the cultural conservative philosophy. Nowadays, when I reread these passages, I regret them. It seems to me that the only fitting punishment is not to delete these chapters, but to leave them in, for all the world to see.

Marriage, children, the passage of two decades, and not a little reflection have dramatically changed my views on some of the troublesome issues addressed in this book. My present view with regard to "social and sexual perversions" is that while none should be prohibited by law, I counsel strongly against engaging in any of them.

One reason I defended several of them some twenty years ago is that I was so concerned with the evils of initiatory violence that I failed to fully realize the implications of defending these other activities. I was fooled by the fact that while many of these depraved acts are indeed associated with violence, none of them are intrinsically so, in the sense that it is possible to imagine them limited to consenting adults. Attempting in the strongest possible way to make the point that initiatory violence was an evil—and indeed it is—I unfortunately lost sight of the fact that it is not the only evil. Even though I, of course, knew the distinction between the legal and the moral, I believed that the only immoralities were acts of aggression. For years now, however, I have been fully convinced that there are other immoralities in addition to these.

The mistake I made in my earlier writing, it is now apparent to me, is that I am not only a libertarian but also a cultural conservative. Not only am I concerned with what the law should be, I also live in the moral, cultural, and ethical realm. I was then so astounded by the brilliance of the libertarian vision (I still am) that I overlooked the fact that I am more than only a libertarian. As both a libertarian and a cultural conservative, I see no incompatibility between beliefs which are part of these two very different universes of discourse.

Part Three:
LANGUAGE

18 Watch Your Language

Language is crucial to clear communication. It makes distinctions. We can hardly express ourselves without it. Our very thoughts can either be brought forth, or not, depending upon whether we have sufficient verbiage with which to attain this end. If the pen is mightier than the sword because it can determine the direction in which this weapon is aimed, then words are even mightier than the pen, for without the former the latter is useless.

Which words have we lost? Which have been thrust down our throats by the forces of socialism, statist feminism, and political correctness? What changes are imperative, if we are to even have a chance to turn things around in a more freedom-oriented direction?

Ms.

Mrs. and Miss have been all but taken from us, and we have been given the execrable Ms. in their place. This is a crucial loss, for the modern language in this regard papers over, nay, obliterates, the distinction between the married and unmarried state for women, while the "archaic" words positively exult in this distinction. This alteration has become so

Printed with kind permission of the Ludwig von Mises Institute. This article was initially posted as "Daily Article" on http://www.mises.org website.

well entrenched by the "inclusive" language movement that even some ostensibly conservative writers and periodicals have adopted it.

Why is this a tragedy? Because it is a disguised attack on the family. Whether the feminists accept this or not, virtually all heterosexual bondings are initiated by the male of the species. (There are good and sufficient sociobiological reasons why this should be the case.) Anything that promotes this healthy and life-affirming trend must be counted as a good; anything that impedes it as a bad. If it is easy to distinguish between married and unmarried females, male initiative is to that extent supported; if not, then the opposite.

If unmarried males are given incentive to approach unmarried females, this supports the institution of marriage and heterosexuality. To the extent they approach married women, this not only undermines marriage, one of the main bulwarks of society, but directly attacks civilization by exacerbating jealousy and intra-male hostility.

Why have the feminists urged Ms. upon us? Ostensibly, because it is "unfair" to distinguish between women on the basis of marital status, but not men. If so, then far better to urge the analogous distinction Mister and Master for married and unmarried men, than to lose that for women. We live in a complex age; surely any institution which simplifies it, by costlessly giving us more information, not less, is to be applauded.

But the softening of this distinction between Mrs. and Miss has implications far removed from any questions of "fairness." This can be seen by asking *"Quo bono"* from Ms? Those who benefit from making single women less available to heterosexual men are homosexual women, plus all those concerned with the so-called overpopulation problem. In economics, when there are large numbers of people or anything else involved, it is commonly assumed that at least some are on the margin.

In this case, there are males on the margin between approaching a female or not, and females on the margin between hetero- and homo-sexuality. Ms. moves society in the diametric opposite direction from the desirable in both these dimensions.

One argument against refusing to adopt to this modern consensus is that people should have the right to choose their own names. If someone wants to change from Cassius Clay to Muhammad Ali, or from

Don McCloskey to Dierdre McCloskey, that is their business. Polite people will refer to them by their chosen, not their given, names.

But this does not at all apply to titles. If I call myself King Block, or Emperor Block, no one need follow suit on this out of considerations of etiquette. Ms. is a title, not the name of any person. When in doubt, always use Miss, not Mrs. The former is or at least should be an honorific, not lightly to be bestowed in ignorance.

And the same analysis applies to using "he" to stand for "he" or "she," or "him" for "him" or "her." Our writing has become convoluted, and singular and plural no longer match, in an attempt to defer to the sensibilities of self-styled feminists. There is nothing more pathetic than a conservative magazine, attempting to score points against a feminist idea, and yet feeling constrained to use such "inclusive" language.

Could we have as successfully criticized Marxism, had we felt constrained to couch our attacks in Marxist language?

Developing Countries

It is errant leftism to call the underdeveloped countries of the world "developing." This is a triumph of will and good intentions over reality; many of these countries are retrogressing, not at all developing. Why not call a spade a spade and insist upon truth in political economy? Let us reserve the honorific "developing" for those countries which have, however imperfectly, embraced capitalism and are hence growing, and use "underdeveloped" or "retrogressing" for those, such as North Korea or Cuba, which still cling to central planning and government ownership, and as a result are in the process of moving back to the economics of the Stone Age.

Rent-seeking

In the literature of the Public Choice school of economic thought, the phrase "rent-seeking" is used to described what, even for them, is a rather despicable act: using the power of the state to capture wealth which would not be forthcoming through ordinary market transactions. Examples include minimum wages, farm subsidies, tariffs, etc.

But why use the rather innocuous word "rent" to indicate what is really (indirect) theft? Why not, instead, characterize such acts as loot-seeking, booty-seeking, pillage-seeking, plunder-seeking, swag-seeking, ransack-seeking, theft-seeking or plain old robbery (via the intermediation of the government).

This Public Choice practice actually denigrates either one or two things that go by the same name. One is the ancient and honorable institution of collecting rent for land, or houses, or other property, instead of selling them outright. Is there supposed to be something wrong with being a landlord? The other is the concept of economic rent which depicts something that has no foregone alternative.

For example, when the price of Rembrandts increases, this does not call forth an additional supply of these paintings; their fortunate owners gain an economic rent. But why should this be denigrated? As a matter of justice, these particular people made these investments; why should they not profit from them? And as far as economic efficiency is concerned, these higher prices still play an allocative role.

To conflate either of these activities with running to government for special grants of privilege to undermine one's competitors is thus an unwarranted attack on rational language. With friends like these, the freedom philosophy hardly needs enemies.

Social Justice

For any rational person, "social justice" would indicate a subset of justice focused more narrowly than the entire concept of just, presumably on "social" issues, whatever they are. But in the real word, this phrase applies not to a subcategory of justice, but rather to one particular perspective on justice, namely, that articulated by our friends on the left.

This places opponents of socialism, multiculturalism, etc., in the position of having to say that they oppose social justice. Wonderful, just wonderful. Far better to stick to our guns, to attempt to use language in a way we prefer, rather than have it dictated to us by our intellectual enemies.

In my view, we, too, should embrace "social justice." However, of course, instead of taking an egalitarian position on the concept, we utilize our tried-and-true insights involving personal and private property rights, negative liberties, homesteading, etc.

Tax Subsidies

The government does not tax the churches. The government does not (yet) tax (and control) the Internet. Is this fair? Not at all, maintain some. These are tax subsidies. The government is subsidizing churches and e-mail, forcing the rest of us to pay more as a result. That is one way to look at the matter.

Another, a far more appropriate way, is that these are not subsidies at all. When some of us are allowed to keep our own hard-earned money in our pockets, to spend as we please and not as our masters in Washington D.C. wish, this is hardly a subsidy. Rather, this is part and parcel of private property rights. To take the opposite position is to implicitly acquiesce in the notion that the state really owns the entire wealth of the populace, and anything they leave us is an act of generosity, or subsidy.

This is nonsense on stilts. We are the legitimate owners of all we produce, and government doesn't have a penny they didn't first mulct from us.

* * * *

Tom Bethell on Property Rights

Tom Bethell is fast becoming a "point man" on the subject of private property rights. This reputation was initially garnered with the publication of his book *The Noblest Triumph: Property and Prosperity through the Ages*.

This was followed up with his *Wall Street Journal* column of December 27, 1999 entitled "Property Rights, Prosperity and 1,000 Years of Lessons." Evidently, Bethell didn't read, or at least not carefully enough, my critique of his book published in the Fall 1999 issue of the *Quarterly Journal of Austrian Economics*, because he is up to his old tricks again: pretending to be an advocate of the private property philosophy while actually undermining it.

A quote from his latest missive:

The great legal innovation of this millennium was equality before the law, which first evolved in England. In the courts of common law, all men were seen to be created equal. This had momentous economic consequences. The new equality of status encouraged the freedom of contract and the rise of an exchange economy. The transmission of property became increasingly "horizontal"— from seller to buyer—and decreasingly vertical—from father to son. Wealth was democratized. It was acquired by those who, by virtue of their labor and ingenuity, merited it rather than inherited it. Contract superseded status.

Now this is more than passingly curious. Why does Bethell think fathers work so hard, save their money, innovate, etc., if not to help their sons in particular and their families in general?

The vertical vs. horizontal distinction is a good one. And, yes, Bethell is also correct in identifying the vertical relationship as the evil one, contrary to economic freedom and private property rights, and the horizontal one as the good one, consistent with these desiderata. But to claim that inheritance is contrary to merit, exchange and economic liberty is almost purposefully perverse. Very much to the contrary, inheritance, and, for that matter, gifts given during one's life, are integral aspects of horizontal or voluntary institutions.

If Bethell is in such great opposition to inheritance, and if he wishes to act in a manner consistent with this perspective, then he must also oppose fathers giving their children birthday gifts, wedding presents, putting them through school, giving them foreign-language lessons, etc. But more. Some parents read their young children stories at bedtime, keep them properly fed, hug and kiss them all the time, adorn their homes with music, art, books, love, etc. Others, while stopping short of child abuse (and sometimes not), give their children a very different kind of monetary and nonmonetary "inheritance." Is this "fair?" Of course not.

All children should choose their parents more carefully. But for the Bethell's of the world, this, presumably, is something to be changed by the force of law. We've got to "democratize" things, don't we?

A far better candidate for the role of oppressor in the vertical direction is the government, curiously not mentioned by our private-property-rights advocate. This is what philosopher Henry Maine was referring to when he famously recommended "contract" not "status." In the bad old days, members of the government ruling class acquired wealth from commoners not on the basis of voluntary trade, but through various forms of statist compulsions. This is what Bethell should be opposing in the name of private property rights, not, forsooth, voluntary gift-giving.

* * * *

The Cuban Boy Controversy

What to do with six-year-old Elian Gonzalez? The position of Clinton and Reno is clear. Do not make this into a political football. Allow the courts or the INS or indeed, pretty much anyone else, to decide, as long as they make a determination in favor of Castro. We can reject the views of these Waco killers out of hand; they have already far too clearly established a record with regard to the rights of children.

The liberal's views are also distressingly clear. One would have thought that they would favor keeping the Cuban boy in this country. After all, they are hardly well known as advocates of parental (that is, father's) rights over children. But this episode is a major embarrassment for Castro and evidently the soft spot of liberals for communist dictators is stronger than their aversion to family values.

Nor have feminists acquitted themselves with distinction. This must be the first time in the history of the universe that they gave anything but short shrift to the wishes of the father, and completely ignored those of the mother.

And what of the Cuban-Americans? They have vociferously campaigned for the right of this young immigrant to stay in the U.S. But if they really felt this strongly, they would have spirited him away a long time ago.

The only group to be unsure about this whole episode are the libertarians. And with good reason, I shall argue. This is a case where the various libertarian principles apply only tangentially, and in seeming conflict.

Why?

Let us begin by considering the case for keeping Elian in the U.S. First of all, there is no clear evidence that the boy's father really wants his son brought back to Cuba. He has, of course, testified to this effect, but anything said by anyone in that island nation has to be taken with a grain of salt; in a totalitarian dictatorship, all such statements are made under duress. The only way to determine the veracity of the father's wishes would be if he repeated them in a relatively free country such as the U.S.

But even that would not be enough. He would have to do so, here, in the company of his entire family and indeed anyone else likely to be harmed by Fidel in revenge. But even that would not be enough to justify shipping Elian back to Cuba.

It is a basic axiom of penology that no one should be imprisoned unless he has committed a crime. Cuba is nothing more than a large jail. For proof of this, one need look no further than the very people with whom Elian escaped. And thousands more Cubans who have voted with their feet in a similar manner. A prison is a place from which people try to leave, but are forcibly prevented from doing so by their jailor. If Cuba does not fit this bill, it is difficult to see why not.

Elian, of course, has committed no crime. Therefore, to consign him to prison, even one as large as Cuba, would be a travesty of justice. If his father truly wishes for this result, and is willing to act to attain this end, then he is guilty of child abuse and should himself be incarcerated.

This point would be crystal clear even to liberals if, instead of a Cuban boy fleeing from that country, it was a Jewish boy attempting to escape from Nazi Germany. No one, perhaps excluding the U.S. Nazi party, would advocate us turning our backs on a child in such a case. Why the difference? This is because our *intelligencia* see the communists as much more benign than the Nazis. However, in terms of the number of citizens murdered, Mao (sixty million) and Stalin (twenty million) have it all over Hitler (ten million). In terms of percentage of total population killed, moreover, the communist Pol Pot is the "champion."

Now let us consider the case for returning Elian home to his father. It is a basic postulate of libertarianism that the parents have the right to bring up the child. With the unfortunate death of Elian's mother, this right passes on to the father. There is, of course, one caveat: if there is any child abuse, all bets are off; these rights, and much more, are ended.

The problem is, where precisely is the cut-off point between responsible child rearing and abuse? When parents stub out their cigarettes on the stomachs of their children, this point is clearly passed. When a parent spanks his child for not doing his homework or brushing his teeth, clearly it is not.

What, then, of the present case? Is it *per se* child abuse to bring up progeny in Cuba? This would mean that all parents now living in that troubled island nation are guilty of this crime. When and if this communist country is liberated, all heads of families (who have not at least tried to escape at the risk of their lives) should be punished. This seems rather far-fetched, because, say what you will about Castro, in terms of mass murder he is no Mao, Stalin, Hitler or Pol Pot.

And yes, were a black slave in Georgia in 1830 to insist that his son, now free in the North be brought back to live with him, or were a Jew in Nazi Germany in 1943 to make the same demand regarding his son living safely in, say, Canada, each would reasonably be considered guilty of child abuse. But the same cannot be said for Cuba *vis-à-vis* the U.S.

For those who doubt this, consider the following. America is not the freest country in the world. Contrary to fans at basketball games, we are not number one. According to the rankings put forth in the book *Economic Freedom of the World* 1975–1995[1], Hong Kong, Singapore and New Zealand are all freer.

Suppose that a distant cousin or an uncle from say, New Zealand, kidnapped an American child and kept him there on the ground that his country was freer than the U.S., and it would therefore be child abuse to return him (I owe this example to Jeff Tucker).

---

[1] Gwartney, Lawson, and Block (1996).

Would we give such a claim any credence? Hardly. We would give it the back of our hand. In like manner, just because the U.S. is undoubtedly a more free country than Cuba does not logically imply it is child abuse to raise a child there. And if not, then, at least for the libertarian, the father's wishes are paramount.

What, then, is the solution? We must ensure that the return of the child is really the wish of Elian's sole surviving parent. This can be accomplished by allowing Juan Miguel Gonzalez, along with his family and friends, to come to Florida to pick him up. (I assume that Elian is too young to make this decision for himself.) Then, he and only he should be allowed to decide.

19 Taking Back the Language

In my last column,[1] I claimed that language was important in the ideological battle for the free society. If we allow our "friends" on the statist left to seize the linguistic high ground, we make the battle more difficult for ourselves. We must use words which help us make the case for *laissez faire* capitalism, not those insisted upon by the other side. Let us now continue this process of "deconstructing" language to these ends with some more examples.

Filthy Rich

This phrase is uttered with an attitude of disgust. The implication is that wealth is always attained illegitimately.

This, of course, is sometimes true, but certainly not always. That is, there are indeed illicit methods of attaining riches, such as through theft, or Murder Inc., or fraud, or in a myriad of other ways which violate the libertarian axiom of nonaggression against nonaggressors, and upon the rights to person and property upon which it is based.

But the usual targets of this loathsome epithet are not crooks or killers; nor are the overwhelming majority of wealthy people thieves.

Printed with kind permission of the Ludwig von Mises Institute. This article was initially posted as "Daily Article" on http://www.mises.org website.

[1] "Watch Your Language."

Rather, the targets are businessmen who have earned vast wealth by enriching the lives of their customers. The presumption, then, is that if a person is well-to-do, he came by his possessions honestly. Instead of denigrating the rich we ought to hold ticker-tape parades in their honor.

And we ought to consider using the counterpart phrase "filthy poor," not to depict those who through no fault of their own are impoverished, but rather those, the "undeserving poor" of an earlier era, who are able-bodied, but do little to help themselves, and everything they can to pull the rest of us down to their level.

Privileged

Properly used, this term applies to those who have been given special advantages denied to the ordinary person. In olden days, this word would be used, for example, to describe a guild member who could engage in commerce prohibited to those who were not so privileged.

Nowadays, "privileged" would well apply to the beneficiaries of government imposed affirmative action; these people are given contracts, jobs, admission to university, etc., denied to others with identical and even superior qualifications, but with the wrong skin color, gender or sexual proclivities.

But this is not at all the way the word is used in the modern benighted epoch by our leftish pundits, teachers, clergy, and editorialists. Instead, this word is employed to describe the children of the rich.

"This child comes from a wealthy family in Scarsdale," it is said. "He is privileged."

But this is nonsense on stilts. As long as the parents of the Scarsdale child earned their money honestly, their children were given no unfair advantage. Using "privileged" to refer only to the children of the affluent is just another way of asserting that wealth is *per se* exploitative.

This, however, is Marxist claptrap, and ought to be dismissed out of hand. We might as well denigrate as "privileged" all children of loving parents, because these kids have a benefit not enjoyed by the victims of child abuse.

Unearned Income

According to the arbiters of language down at the friendly revenue office, earned income stems from labor. In very sharp contrast, "unearned income" is generated from profits, investment, interest, etc.

This is, presumably, because work by the sweat of the brow is noble, uplifting and in the public good, while risking one's capital in order to earn a profit by benefiting consumers is the very opposite.

Since when have the Marxists taken over the IRS? If the U.S.S.R. could rid itself of its Marxists, can we not do the same for our very own made-in-the-good-old-U.S.-of-A. Infernal Revenue Service?

Freeman

Recently, the flagship publication of the Foundation for Economic Education changed its name from "Freeman" to "Ideas on Liberty." This was reportedly done to distinguish this magazine from a militia organization, which called itself "The Freemen" and ran afoul of federal law.[2]

But the FEE's Freeman had been publishing for decades. It had long been an honorable periodical, but in this decision it has illustrated exactly what should not be done in the battle of ideas. Surely a better course of action would have been to sue for name infringement.

We must protect our own banners, emblems and heritage, not give them up at the first sign of difficulty. Shall we one day, at this rate, eschew "liberty," "property," "free enterprise," "libertarianism?" We will, if this sort of abnegation becomes a precedent.

Ultra

There are ultra-conservatives, but, amazingly, there are no ultra-liberals. Where have all the ultra-liberals gone? (To be sung to the tune of the popular anti-war song.)

"Ultra" refers to a person with whose ideas the speaker disagrees. That is why Mother Teresa was not ultra-generous, but anyone to the

---

[2] For the full story on this group, see "Who Are the Freemen?" (http://www.lewrockwell.com/orig/tucker2.html).

right of George Bush becomes an ultra-conservative. It is time, it is long past time, to begin a search for ultra-liberals under each bed; or, better, to leave off this name calling of ultra, which applies only to one side of the aisle.

Eer

It is much the same with the suffix "eer." There are "profiteers," because profits are undoubtedly evil and obnoxious. Ask Fidel, he'll tell you. But there is no such thing as a "wageer," even though the salaries of some of our leading athletes and actors have catapulted upward of late. This is because workers are always downtrodden, never greedy, at least according to the fourth estate.

* * * *

A Defense of Book Burning

In a recent column "The Comstocks Try for a Comeback on Long Island,"[3] Gregory Bresiger took issue with a group of Irishmen who had planned to burn 700 copies of the book *Angela's Ashes* by Frank McCourt. This is a story of the author's childhood, which does not place Irish culture in a good light.

Bresiger has pulled out all the stops in his opposition. He quotes from Ray Bradbury's novel *Fahrenheit 451*, and even resorts to a quote from Malachy McCourt, McCourt's brother, concerning this practice in *Hitler's Germany*. He implies that book burning is but the first step on a path which leads to people burning, intolerance and the "crushing of ideas."

One argument against book burning is that of unintended consequences: those who engage in these acts sometimes only succeed in more heavily popularizing the object of their scorn and hatred. But this hardly justifies calling them "hyenas" or "blundering clowns."

Nor is there any justification for calling out the big guns of tolerance, Erasmus, Spinoza, John Stuart Mill and John Milton. For the key,

---

[3] http://www.lewrockwell.com/bresiger/bresiger8.html

here, ignored by Bresiger, is the distinction between public and private book burning.

With regard to the former, I am in total and enthusiastic support of Bresiger. The government simply has no business burning books, or doing much of anything, for that matter.

However, private book burning, of the sort engaged in by the Irish opponents of Frank McCourt's *Angela's Ashes* is entirely a different matter. Burning one's own books is part and parcel of private property rights. In opposing private book burning, leaping calumny on the heads of those who engage in this activity, Bresiger is treading on the edge of private property rights violations.

If I own a book, I have a right to burn it. Period. While Bresiger never comes out and states that book burning ought to be illegal, this is strongly suggested by his linkage of this practice to Hitler, hyenas, and people burning.

I wonder what is his view of flag burning? Here, as in book burning, the libertarian position ought to be clear: people have a right to burn or otherwise destroy any of their own private property. Any law prohibiting from doing just that is an illicit one.

20 Word Watch

Stakeholder

A new word has crept into our lexicon, courtesy of our friends on the left. It is "stakeholder" and it is the entering wedge of yet another attack on private property rights.

In the good old days, a firm had contractual obligations to its suppliers, to its employees, and to its customers. The only obligation it had to its neighbors was the one we all have to each other: to refrain from threatening or engaging in initiatory violence against them and their rightfully owned property.

But all of this is now out of date. Thanks to the new dispensation, all of these people, and a whole host of others as well, must now be invited into the boardroom, there to join with the nominal owners of the firm in setting policy. And, to add insult to injury, these "stakeholders" may even sometimes get to outvote the owners of shares of stock.

How does this work? Under the stakeholder theory, anyone with any connection at all to the business, no matter how tenuous, now has a quasi-ownership right over the firm's property.

Thus, it is no longer a matter of pleasing customers, or seeing them take their business to competitors and suffering as a result. Now, customers

---

Printed with kind permission of the Ludwig von Mises Institute. This article was initially posted as "Daily Article" on http://www.mises.org website.

have the right to actually set policy. Employees, in this philosophy, are not merely owed an honest paycheck for an honest day's work; in addition, they have the right to put their two cents in to the decision-making process. And ditto for neighbors, politicians, passersby and other busybodies.

One problem with this attempt to foist "economic democracy" on an unsuspecting public is to determine the number of votes owned by each of these constituencies. There seems to be no obvious answer to this question apart from "one man one vote." But if any Tom, Dick or Harry can get a vote without actually investing in a company, why would anyone in his right mind set up a corporation?

More basically, the problem with this scheme is that it amounts to theft. How else can you categorize a plan which forces the owner of property to share its control with others, no matter who they are, who did not share in the creation of the business? If "stakeholders" want to have a say in how a firm is run, let them invest in it. If they do, they are no longer stakeholders, but rather investors. Another difficulty is that "stakeholding" seems to be a one-way street.

All the nosey passersby seem to get a property right in the company, but the owners of the firm, for some strange reason known only to our friends on the left, do not obtain a similar right to their property (this is on the assumption that they have any). But logical consistency is only the "hobgobblin of little minds," so perhaps it is reasonable that stakeholding should not be a two-way street. Why ruin a perfect concept?

Getting something for nothing

According to a libertarian who ought to know better, "one of the basest human motives [is] the desire to get something for nothing."[1]

Now, there is, of course, a sense in which this is totally unobjectionable. Theft, for example, is a way to "get something for nothing," and is the paradigm case of an illegitimate act from the libertarian perspective.

---

[1] B. Bradford, *Liberty Magazine*, May (2000), p. 7.

However, there are other possible scenarios in which depictions of this phrase are not at all incompatible with the free-market philosophy. To condemn the attempt to get something for nothing is thus to over-generalize; it is to throw the baby out with the bath water.

Charity is one case in point. The recipient of voluntary welfare does nothing improper, whatsoever. A person may be down on his luck, or simply forgot his wallet, or was the victim of a mugging. He asks a passerby for a buck for carfare, or for a cup of coffee, or for some change with which to make a phone call, and receives it. He thereby got "something for nothing," but certainly offends no law which should remain on the books.

When I first met Murray Rothbard as a young man, he allowed me to bask in his presence. He would invite me to his home, he and his wife Joey would feed me, I was allowed to listen to and even partake in the conversation of this great man. Certainly, I gave him nothing, and he gave me plenty. I was far from the only aspiring young libertarian with half-baked ideas who Murray took under his wing.

In a very real sense, I and all these others "got something for nothing." True, it is possible to argue that the ordinary giver to charity, and Murray Rothbard, the Mother Teresa of libertarianism, didn't get nothing from the recipients of their donations. Rather, they got some sort of satisfaction from the doing of a good deed.

However, to resort to this line of argument is to acquiesce in the notion not that getting something for nothing is "a base human motive," but that it is impossible. In this view, even the victim of a crime gets "something:" e.g., the satisfaction that the robber took no more than he did, or refrained from murdering him.

Or take another case: I am holding a $100 bill in my hand, and the wind takes it off, to who knows where. Surely, I gain nothing from this occurrence; but if it floats into someone else's possession, he gains something for nothing. To deny this possibility is to engage in fallacious tautological reasoning. It is not only possible to get something for nothing, this need not be a base human motivation at all.

The critics of obtaining something for nothing also overlook the concept of consumer and producer surplus. The grocer has thousands of oranges on hand. If he does not sell them soon, they will rot, and then it would cost him money (in addition to the purchase price) to dispose of them. For him, these oranges are not only nothing (zero value) they are an actual burden (negative value).

I have just finished running a marathon race, and those oranges look like liquid gold to me. So the grocer sells a few of them to me. He gets something for nothing (actually, for minus values). Although I pay a few pennies for each, so great is my thirst I would have been willing to pay many dollars for these oranges had I been asked to do so. The difference to me between what I would have been willing to pay (the greater value) and what I actually did pay (the lesser value) is my consumer surplus. No one else can know this amount, but for me it is, in effect, found money.

Or, in other words, I just got something for nothing in terms of consumer surplus as did the grocer in terms of producer or seller surplus. This is part and parcel of the "magic of the marketplace," and should not be denigrated.

Free Rider

A concept seen by mainstream economists with fear, loathing and disgust is that of the "free rider." Anyone who gets a value for which he does not pay (another version of "getting something for nothing") is relegated to the depths in neoclassical economics. The free rider is evidence, for them, of economic inefficiency, a so-called "market failure" and charged with committing the sin of an "external economy."

The typical example of this horror is when a person benefits from the fact that his neighbor washes his car, or trims his lawn, or keeps his house in good repair. These actions tend to maintain or upgrade the real estate values of the first homeowner's property, and presumably increase his enjoyment of his holdings (e.g., the view improves).

Why is this so bad? For one of two reasons. We can become enraged at the free rider because, horrors, he is getting something for nothing. Alternatively, we can view him with disdain because the creator of the free ride, the good neighbor, is not doing enough to beautify his own premises, and is thus "cheating" the free rider out of even greater benefits.

Damned if you do, damned if you don't, seems to be the motto of the neoclassical economist. Whether blaming the recipient of the positive externality for being an ingrate, or the donor for not doing enough for the former, one thing is clear: government must step in, for without the tender loving care of the state, this neighborhood will surely go to the dogs.

What nonsense. As Murray Rothbard (1997, p. 178) has stated in one of the most insightful comments in all of economics,

> A and B often benefit, it is held, if they can force C into doing something . . . any argument proclaiming the right and goodness of, say, three neighbors, who yearn to form a string quartet, forcing a forth neighbor at bayonet point to learn and play the viola, is hardly deserving of sober comment.

If people are nice to one another, if they smile at each other, well and good. If we appreciate what Einstein and Mozart have given us, if we are "free riders" on them, again well and good. We are all the beneficiaries of those who came before us. This is part and parcel of civilized living, and is no cause for alarm.

21 Continuing to Watch Our Language

In past columns on Watching Your Language,[1] I made the point that it is important for us who espouse the freedom philosophy to be aware of the importance of language. If we get pushed into the linguistic corner our intellectual enemies have prepared for us, it is even more difficult to make the case in favor of *laissez faire* capitalism. In these previous attempts to wrestle with this challenge, I tried to set the record straight with regard to the following words and phrases: Ms., developing countries, rent-seeking, social justice, tax subsidies, property rights, filthy rich, privileged, unearned income, freeman, ultra, profiteer, book burning, stakeholder, getting something for nothing, free rider, swamps and prejudice.

It is now time to add a few new terms to this list. They are as follows: opportunism, red states-blue states, liberal and libertarian. Let us consider them in turn.

Opportunism

In ordinary language, "opportunism," or "opportunistic," are pretty neutral words. Even, possibly, slightly positive, in that they indicate that

Printed with kind permission of Mr. Llewellyn H. Rockwell, Jr. This article was initially posted on http://www.lewrockwell.com website.
[1] See "Watch Your Language," "Taking Back the Language," and "Word Watch."

someone is taking initiative, availing himself of opportunities, etc. (In medicine, the word applies to disease-carrying agents which take advantage of opportunities to spread. However, this is a bit outside our realm of interest; in any case, no one blames germs, so there is hardly a negative connotation to the word.[2])

In mainstream economics, for example, the *American Economic Review*, on the other hand, "opportunistic" is now being used as a synonym for cheating or shirking. Here, is an example, of this phenomenon:

> Economic models of incentives in employment relationships are based on a specific theory of motivation: employees are "rational cheaters," who anticipate the consequences of their actions and shirk when the marginal benefits exceed costs. We investigate the "rational cheater model" by observing how experimentally-induced variation in monitoring of telephone call center employees influences opportunism. A significant fraction of employees behave as the "rational cheater model" predicts. A substantial proportion of employees, however, do not respond to manipulations in the monitoring rate. This heterogeneity is related to variation in employee assessments of their general treatment by the employer.[3]

Things have even gotten to a pass where such language has seeped in to mainstream popular publications; for example, see *The Economist*, 4/2/05, p. 15.

What is wrong with this? What is wrong is that as in the case of "rent-seeking," a perfectly neutral, or even "good" word is used to carry "bad" baggage. Rent-seeking, as used by economists, the Public Choice School is the main culprit here, is an equivalent of downright theft, through the political process. By tying "rent" to "thievery," one tars the former with the brush of the latter. One undermines the ancient and honorable practice of collecting rent. True, it cannot be denied, economists who use language in this way do not have in mind landlords

---

[2] See on this http://www.aegis.com/topics/oi/
[3] http://ideas.repec.org/a/aea/aecrev/v92y2002i4p850-873.html

charging rent to tenants. Rather, they are thinking of economic rent, the difference, for example, between what a baseball player's salary as an athlete, and, say, his next best job as a mechanic or bus driver. But that is irrelevant. Why use a perfectly good word like "rent" to depict legal theft?

In like manner, taking advantage of opportunities is the hallmark of the entrepreneur. But if "opportunism" is widely conflated with cheating, then entrepreneurship, and indeed profit seeking, is thereby impugned. But we need all the help we can get for acts such as these. Thus, we should strive mightily not to equate opportunism with cheating or shirking. Why not use the words for this purpose "cheating" or "shirking?" Why pick on poor old opportunity seeking?

Red States-Blue States

As these words are commonly used, blue states refer to those, many of which are located along both coasts of the U.S. (on the East Coast, the ones toward the north), whose occupants voted mainly for the Democratic Party. Red states refer those in the center of the nation ("flyover country" in the words of those occupying both coasts) that voted preponderantly for the Republican Party.

But this is confusing. Every time I hear these phrases mentioned in this manner I have to do a bit of internal mental switching. This is because red is a color I associate most with Communism, and, I can't help it, I link the Democrats more closely than I do the Republicans with U.S.S.R.-style government ownership of property and control over the economy. Thus, I have to tell myself that even though red applies to the left side of the political spectrum (economically speaking) it still refers to people in states who preferred the Republican Party. Awkward. (Not that the war-monger, tariff and tax-raising George Bush can be considered a free enterpriser; it is just that, gulp, had Kerry won there would not even be the veneer of free enterprise to hide the Bush-style lurch to the left.)

Why have the powers that be decided upon switching colors and political linkages in this way? I don't know for sure. I can only speculate. My thought is that this is an attempt on their part to sever the connections between political philosophy and hue in the eyes of the public. And why, in turn, should they want to do this? Again, another conjecture; maybe they think that colors are shorthand for views in political economy, and they want to reduce the very limited additional clarity of thought such cues might afford.

In any case, the connection between color and political perspective is an interesting one, even if somewhat confusing. The Italian fascists wore black shirts. But Hitler, the person who perhaps most personifies fascism, was actually a greenie, left-wing environmentalist, anti-smoking nut (remember, the Nazis were the National Socialist Party). Speaking of the modern greens, the anti-market worshippers of Gaia, they are really watermelons: green on the outside, but red on the inside. These people have a strong but unrequited desire to control the lives of other people and their property. For a while, they "successfully" hitched their wagon to the communist, or red movement, but this all came unglued in 1989, at which point they switched their allegiance to the greens. Complicating matters is that the favorite color of the Levellers in seventeenth-century England, according to Murray Rothbard, the first libertarian political movement, was green. Who, then, are the true greens?

Returning to fascism, the Blueshirts were an Irish Fascist movement during the 1930s, led by General Eoin O'Duffy, and Jose Antonio's Falange were also Blueshirts. So fascism now can claim black and blue, which has a certain appropriateness. On the other hand, there is brown as in brownshirts (we'll not mention UPS in this regard), another fascist group. Further complicating matters is that the combination of red, white and blue has stood for fascism for quite a long time now.[4]

(I would like to acknowledge help from several friends of mine on linking colors and political movements. They are Tom DiLorenzo, Stephan Kinsella, David Gordon, Lew Rockwell, Jeff Tucker and Ralph Raico.)

---

[4] See on this Charlotte Twight, "America's Emerging Fascist Economy" (http://www.amazon.com/exec/obidos/tg/detail/-/0870003178/lewrockwell).

Given that communism is red, and that the coastal states are politically pink, at least closer to red than anything else, and that the states in the center of the country who voted for Bush are closer to fascism, and there is historical precedent for categorizing that belief system as blue, then the way these color names are actually bandied about is an inversion of the truth in such matters.

So, what, then, should we do about the 180-degree confusion of the colors red and blue as applied to the various states? Simple; the same thing as in all these other cases of verbal abuse: refuse to go along. I know, I know, it is confusing if everyone else calls Arkansas, for example, a red state and you call it a blue one. But the same holds true with any of these other words: opportunism, Ms., developing countries, rent-seeking, social justice, tax subsidies, property rights, filthy rich, privileged, unearned income, freeman, ultra, profiteer, book burning, stakeholder, getting something for nothing, free rider, swamps and prejudice. If we do not make a statement with words, they will soon enough be taken away from us.

Liberal and Libertarian

Precisely the same thing has long ago occurred with "liberal." In one epoch, long, long ago, a liberal was one who believed in peace, private property rights, limited government and free markets. That perfectly good word was seized by our friends on the left, and now we must resort to "classical liberal," or "liberal, European style," if we wish to distinguish ourselves from the likes of Ted Kennedy, John Kerry or Hillary Clinton. The same thing occurred with "gay," and I take my hat off to Joe Sobran for having attempted to rescue that particular word. We have got to fight, fight, fight to keep hold of verbiage important to us.

Something of the sort now even seems to be occurring with the word "libertarian." When the likes of Milton Friedman can publicly call himself a "small L libertarian,"[5] the end might not be near, but it is ominously approaching. This Nobel Prize-winning economist is not a libertarian, big or small L, it matters not. He favors school vouchers, the

---

[5]   Milton Friedman, Wikipedia. http://www.self-gov.org/mfriedman.html

continuation of the Fed, the negative income tax, the anti-trust law; he was the father of tax withholding (although to be fair to him, he later on apologized for this), road socialism (he opposes the privatization of streets and highways) and fiat currency (he is derisive toward advocates of the gold standard). It is true he is sound as a bell on things like free trade, rent control, minimum wages, etc., but this scarcely supports a claim to libertarianism.[6]

Of course, in the context of the major talking heads, Friedman is a libertarian. At least, he is probably the most libertarian of any person they have ever had contact with. When they say that *even* Milton Friedman takes thus and such a position, it pretty much defines one end point of the political spectrum. Anyone even more libertarian than he, forsooth, falls right off the end of the realm of respectability.

What are we to do in the face of such challenges? Well, try to hold on to as much verbal turf as we can. At least, let us be aware of these problems. This is a necessary, albeit hardly sufficient, condition for confronting them.

---

[6] http://www.lewrockwell.com/rothbard/rothbard43.html

22 Voluntary Taxes: Abusive Language and Politicians

(with William Barnett)

In his March 20, 2002 letter to the *Wall Street Journal* "'Tough-Guy' Proposals for Indiana's Budget," that state's Governor Frank O'Bannon calls "for increases in two minor, voluntary taxes—on cigarettes and riverboat admissions."

"Voluntary taxation?" "Voluntary taxation" is an oxymoron if ever there was one; it is similar to "jumbo shrimp," "an important trifle," or "a square circle." "Voluntary taxation" is a downright contradiction in terms, since if there is anything that taxation is not, it is voluntary. The proof is, if you do not pay, your property is forcibly confiscated and/or you go to jail. "Coercive taxation" is a redundancy, because once you comprehend the former word in this phrase, you know the meaning of the latter is a constituent part of that understanding.

This is but one—though a typical one—example of the way politicians abuse the language in attempting to deceive the people about the true nature of their actions.

Printed with kind permission of Mr. Llewellyn H. Rockwell, Jr. This article was initially posted on http://www.lewrockwell.com website. William Barnett II is Chase Distinguished Professor of International Business and Professor of Economics at Loyola University, New Orleans.

Does the good governor mean that purchasers of cigarettes/entrants onto riverboats don't have to pay the relevant tax if they don't want to? Or does he mean that they don't have to pay the tax if they don't buy cigarettes/enter riverboats? It is not likely that he intends the former. If the former, then, of course, all taxes are voluntary; e.g., one could avoid property taxes on residential property or sales taxes on food merely by going homeless or not buying food, respectively. In the latter case, perhaps one could survive by foraging in dumpsters. Similarly, he might mean that income taxes are really voluntary, in that you can choose not to earn an income, in which case you are not subject to the tax. That is, because voluntary choice determines whether or not a tax applies, the levy in question is not really compulsory.

But if this were true, then robbery would no longer be a crime. A robbery victim could simply choose not to own anything. That, surely, would foil any would-be thief. Or, an intended murder victim could be offered the choice of a slow, painful death by torture or administering to himself a dose of a quick, painless poison. This would no longer be murder. Instead, utilizing the "logic" of Governor O'Bannon, it would become a (voluntary) suicide.

C'mon, Governor, give us a break! Using the coercive power of government to relieve people of their hard-earned wealth is bad enough, but debasing the language (no doubt quality education is a top priority for this servant of the people) in the process only adds insult to injury.

23 Language, Once Again: Civil War, Inclusive Language, Economic Warfare, National Wealth

Civil War

What took place in 1861 in the U.S. was *not* a "civil war." There were *not* two contending armies, each one trying to rule the other. Rather, this was a war over secession.

For an example of a true civil war we might consider the Spanish Civil War of 1936. There, two groups fought each other, and each wished to rule over the entire country. On the one side were the fascists, under Franco; on the other side were the communists.

Why call what happened in the mid-nineteenth century in the U.S. a "Civil War?" A true civil war, as we all know, is between two contending parties, each of whom wants to rule the other, or, govern the entire society, composed of both elements.

In the war of 1861, this applies, full well, to the North. But the South did not want to rule the North, nor the entire country composed of both. It only wanted to separate from the North, or secede from the union. In my view, it takes "two to tango." You can't have a civil war if only *one* side wants to rule the other.

Printed with kind permission of Mr. Llewellyn H. Rockwell, Jr. This article was initially posted on http://www.lewrockwell.com website.

Here are some more accurate names for that tragic event:
A. Neutral
    1. War of 1861
    2. War between the North and the South
    3. War between the states

B. Slightly pejorative
    4. War of Southern Secession
    5. War for Southern Independence

C. Very pejorative
    6. War of Northern Aggression
    7. Lincoln's War
    8. War to Prevent Southern Independence
    9. Second American War for Independence
    10. The Third American War for Independence
    11. The Rape of the South by the North

D. Radical
    12. First War of Southern Secession

The first category, A. Neutral, includes three entries, all of which are nondebatable. That is, they are highly descriptive, and, presumably, will not offend anyone. They are: War of 1861, War between the North and the South, and War between the states. No one could rationally object to War of 1861, or, perhaps, War of 1861–1865. After all, those were the undisputed years of the fighting. Nor can the geographical descriptions, war between the North and the South or between the states, be rejected. They are, it cannot be denied, highly accurate, and not under contention.

The second category, B, is slightly pejorative in that it explicitly blames the North for the conflagration. Both War of Southern Secession and War for Southern Independence indicate that it was the North that attempted to force an unwilling South into something of which it no longer wanted to be part. Were the North and the South a married couple, we might say that the South wanted a divorce, and the North was unwilling to grant one to it. We have a phrase that describes such an event between a man and a woman: marital rape.

But what about slavery, it might be objected? If there is any true rape going on in this situation, it was not perpetrated by the North against the South. Rather, both literally and figuratively, it far better describes what the South was doing to the slaves.

Not so, not so. For there was slavery in the North as well! It gives the North way too much credit to put matters in this way. As both parts of the country were guilty of enslaving innocent people,[1] this horrific crime cannot be used to distinguish the parties. Slavery, as it were, gets cancelled out of the equation, and we are left with one group of people who no longer wanted to politically associate with another group of people, and yet were forced to do just that, against their will.

As well, there were several New England states that seriously discussed secession in the 1820s, as a protest against slavery, not in its support, and there were no hues and cries from "progressives" that this would have been illegitimate.[2]

In category C, we arrive at very pejorative appellations that quite properly indicate the guilt of the North and innocence of the South in no uncertain terms. The War of Northern Aggression, Lincoln's War,[3] the War to Prevent Southern Independence, the Second American War for Independence, and the Third American War for Independence[4] all lay the blame squarely on the guilty party. The rape of the South by the North does this in spades.

The South fought a valiant battle against the North.[5] Unfortunately, the latter vastly outnumbered them, both in terms of men and material.

With category D, we arrive at the most radical of all nomenclature: the First War of Southern Secession. The implication is that what

---

[1] For the argument in favor of legalizing *voluntary* slavery, an entirely different matter, see Block (1999, 2001, 2003, 2004, 2006).

[2] For a defense of secession, see Adams (2000); Gordon (1998); Kreptul (2003); McGee (1994); Rothbard (1967).

[3] DiLorenzo (2002) makes the case for this appellation.

[4] Since the War of 1812 was the second. I owe this point to Larry Sechrest.

[5] See the movie, "Gods and Generals" (http://www.godsandgenerals.com).

occurred in 1861 will once again take place, only this time the results will be very different. A group that would likely welcome this eventuality is the League of the South (http://www.dixienet.org/). More power to them.

Inclusive Language

When I was a young lad, the people who caught fish were always called "fishermen." Nowadays, those who perform this task are referred to as "fishers." Why the sudden, ok, not so sudden, change? This obviously stems from the genus political correctness, species, feminism. "Fisher" is inclusive of males and females, while "fisherman," seemingly, excludes the latter. A similar analysis applies to "actor" and "actress," to "firefighter" and "fireman." The former two of each of these pairs, "actress" and "fireman," although in use for eons, have now been banished down the memory hole. There used to be "chairmen"; now, there are only "chairs" in polite society. Why? This can only be to satisfy the perverse desires of feminists. In the pre-feminized language, the male nomenclature typically included both genders. That is, although women rarely were firemen or fishermen, they most certainly *could* be, insofar as the language was concerned.[6]

And why do feminists favor such language? Much like the natives of cargo cult fame,[7] they feel that if they can but change something superficial, then real results are sure to follow. That is, males and females will be treated equally, if inclusive language is but utilized by all. Just as cargo cult members do not realize there are good and sufficient reasons why airplane delivery of goods is strictly limited to legitimate airports, feminists do not appreciate there are compelling economic and biological reasons why females, on average, earn less money than do males.[8] A similar phenomenon seems to be operating with regard to blacks in

---

[6] True, there never was any such thing as a "farmerman." There were always, and ever, only "farmers." This would appear to be an exception that proves the rule.

[7] These pre-civilized people believe that if they build runways, out of straw or other handy material, in the middle of the jungle, airplanes will swoop down out of the sky and deliver cargo to them. (See on this http://en.wikipedia.org/wiki/Cargo_cult)

[8] See chapter 12 of the present book for an elaboration of this claim.

television shows and movies. They are typically portrayed as doctors, lawyers, professors, scientists, mathematicians, engineers, in numbers far in excess of their actual representation in these professions. This is yet another example of the triumph of hope over reality.[9]

Further, these innovations really bollix up the language.[10] Consider the following confusions between the singular and the plural:

"'If you love someone, set them free' (Sting); 'It's enough to drive anyone out of their senses' (George Bernard Shaw); 'I shouldn't like to punish anyone, even if they'd done me wrong' (George Eliot)."[11]

One way out of this infelicity is to use the plural instead of the singular. "For instance, instead of 'As he advances in his program, the medical student has increasing opportunities for clinical work,' try 'As they advance in their program, medical students have increasing opportunities for clinical work.'"[12] Or, "Each professor decides their own reading lists."[13] But, who wants to be confined to the straightjacket of use of the plural forever. What did the singular ever do to deserve such a fate?

Another objection is based on logic. Inclusive language replaces every use of "man" it can get its hands on, and replaces it with "human." For example, "man" becomes "human," "mankind" gets converted to "humankind," "straw man" morphs into "straw person," etc. Often "person" is substituted. For example, "He went to the store" becomes "A person went to the store."

The problem, here, is with the last part of "human" and "person," namely, "man" and "son." If the feminists were logically consistent, they would first insist on "huwoman," instead of human." But this too

---

[9] Another explanation for this phenomenon is to try to get the masses of people to become comfortable with, and accustomed to, females and blacks in nontraditional high prestige occupations, as a support for affirmative action policies that elevate their numbers there compared to what they would have been in the absence of such unjust programs. I anxiously await the fictional depiction of old fat Jews such as myself as sports heroes, sexual studs and rap singers.

[10] http://www.adoremus.org.

[11] http://www.english.upenn.edu/~cjacobso/gender.html

[12] *Ibid.*

[13] http://www.marquette.edu/wac/neutral/NeutralInclusiveLanguage.shtml

presents difficulties as "woman" ends in the dread "man." Maybe "hudaughter" should be used instead of "human" and "perdaughter" in place of person.

Economic Warfare

Pundits are accustomed to utilizing the language of war and strife to depict economic relationships. This is confusing, irrational and misleading. For the dismal science addresses mutual benefit, or positive sum games. All participants gain whenever a trade, a purchase, sale, rental agreement, job, etc., gets consummated; necessarily so in the *ex ante* sense, and in the overwhelming majority of cases *ex post*.

For example, if I purchase a newspaper for $1, it is an apodictic undeniable truth that at that moment, I ranked the periodical more highly than the money I had to pay for it. Why else, for goodness sakes, would I have been willing to engage in this commercial transaction was this not so? I *anticipated* that I would benefit from this trade. Even in the *ex post* sense, from the vantage points of afterward, in virtually all such cases I and everyone else in this position gains. Rare is the case where I, or anyone else for that matter, regrets the purchase of a paper on the ground that there was no good news in it after all, and that was what the buyer was seeking and expecting.

Consider in this regard, then, concepts such as "price war," or "hostile takeover." Here, it would appear, there is not mutual benefit occurring in the market, but rather an antagonistic relationship. Nothing could be further from the truth.

Take the latter first. This charge is fueled by the spectre of corporate raiders who swoop down on a helpless firm, engage in a "hostile takeover," sell off its assets, and fire all the employees. There are numerous fallacies here. First of all, unemployment is created by artificially boosting wages above workers' productivity. If the minimum wage law, or a union, insists that an employee be paid $10 per hour, but he is only worth $7 in terms of productivity, he will be unemployed, period. This has nothing to do with so-called hostile takeovers. Yes, people are fired, but unemployment is no higher in industries that witness such activities than in any other.

But do not corporate raiders sometimes dismember firms for their assets? Indeed, they do. However, they only earn a profit when these selfsame assets are actually worth more in other areas of endeavor than where they were first deployed. This means that if jobs are lost in one corporation, they will be created in others, to the places where the assets are now more productively employed, thus *raising* wages.

Another socially beneficial effect of the corporate raider concerns salaries of chief executive officers. Many commentators complain that CEO salaries have hit the stratosphere, and constitute an unconscionable exploitation of the workingman. Suppose that the capital value of a firm would have been $100 million if the CEO salary was "moderate," but, because of a stupendous compensation package, it is now worth only $10 million. Such a firm would be ripe for the pickings of a corporate raider. He would purchase this business for, say, $11 million, fire the parasitical CEO, watch the firm's value rise to its "proper" $100 million, and pocket a hefty $89 million in profit. The corporate raider is to outrageous CEO salaries what the canary is to coal mine safety; only he does the bird one better: not only does he warn of a problem, he solves it in one fell swoop. Yet, government, in jailing people like Michael Milken, has obliterated this beneficial market mechanism. And now they have the audacity to complain of out-of-control CEO pay.

As for "hostility" there is no such thing between the buyer and seller of stock. The only "hostile" person is the CEO who was ripping off the firm. But when we say that in the market there is only peaceful cooperation, we mean on the part of those who engage in any specific transaction; e.g., the newspaper buyer and seller. Third parties, of course, can always be hostile. A Marxist, for example, might have his nose put out of joint by *all* commerce. He is "hostile" to all of them. So what?

What of price war? This, too, is a linguistic contortion. When grocers, or filling stations, for example, lower their prices in an attempt to attract customers, they are very far from having a "war" with those who buy from them. Very much the *opposite* is the case. As far as the relation of these vendors with each other, the supposed participants in this "war," they are in the same position as the too-high-salaried CEO and the corporate "raider." They are third parties to all these transactions, and, as such, have no standing in any of them. They cannot reveal or demonstrate (Rothbard 1997) their hostility. That is, when customer A purchases groceries or gasoline from seller a, seller b might not like it, but he is not part of this transaction.

National Wealth

We have often been told that the richest X percent of the people own Y[14] percent of the national wealth. It is usually far more than their proportion of the population, as might be expected in the context of not exactly equal wealth on the part of all people. But this X percent of the population do not own *any* of the national wealth. They, of course, can claim *all* of their own wealth, but *none* of anyone else's.

Putting matters in terms of national wealth, and then noting that it is unequally distributed, is a recipe for complaints on the part of the poorest elements of the population, and their self-styled spokesmen.

Implicit in this notion is the idea that the best way to attain "equity," defined, typically, as almost absolute income equality, is to take income or wealth from the rich and simply give it to the poor. One could do so by instituting a highly progressive income or wealth tax.

There are many problems with any such course of action. First, it reduces the incentive of both rich and poor to earn income and be productive. The former will not work as hard, at the margin, if what they produce will be taken from them. But this applies to the latter as well, since they will not be *given* as much of the wealth of other people if they earn their own.[15] Second, "equity" is not at all the same thing as "equality." The first term denotes fairness, while the second merely indicates a certain mathematical relationship. But what is so fair about expropriating, at the point of a gun, money from those who have earned it, and giving it to those who have not? Third, a country that engages in such practices to a great degree may well approach "equality," but it will be only equality of the sort where everyone starves equally.

---

[14] Eugene Paczelt suggested this term to me as problematic.

[15] A popular bumper sticker reads: "Work harder. Millions of welfare recipients are counting on you."

Fair Trade

What could be fairer than "fair trade?" The superficial answer is that nothing could be. But a more careful analysis of language reveals that there is nothing at all fair about "fair trade," and that really fair trade is free trade.

Let us begin by defining our terms. "Fair trade," thanks to the perversion of language, is a system where people are prevented from trading as they wish. Instead, barriers to trade are enacted, in order to counteract environmental and labor standards prevailing in other countries.[16] In other words, if an exporting country in South America or Africa pays wages lower than those deemed appropriate by busybodies and do-gooders in the first world, tariffs and even quotas will be placed in the path of imports emanating from that source. Why it is "fair" to create unemployment in these third world countries by forcing wages above productivity levels is never explained.

Taken to its logical conclusion, and where else are we to take it, "fair" trade is really an attempt to remove any competitive advantage that these nations might have *vis a vis* those in Europe or North America. If we could impose the same stringent labor and environmental legislation on these countries as now prevails domestically, exports from these poorer areas would no longer be competitive with the product of locals. Ultimately, this would pretty much spell the death knell for *any* trade between rich and poor global communities.

This would harm all of those in wealthy countries, particularly the less well off there. But the biggest victims would be inhabitants of the poorer sectors of the world. It is no accident that those parts of Africa, in an earlier century, that came into contract with the more advanced West (that is, those on the coast) developed more quickly than those internal to that continent, where traders seldom ventured.[17] Most global trade takes place *within* the advanced areas, not between them and those suffering from dire poverty. To deprive these parts of the world of the relatively little trade they presently enjoy would be to treat the poor,

---

[16] http://en.wikipedia.org/wiki/Fair_trade
[17] Bauer (1981, 1984); Bauer and Yamey (1957).

then, in a particularly vicious way. Is it any accident that those most intent on promoting "fair trade" are the leftists who have infested the labor and left-wing environmental movements in the West? This is far from the only instance where those who pose as the friends of the poor are actually their greatest enemies.

In very sharp contrast, *free* trade[18] is the last best hope for the poor, of all nations, as well as for promoting worldwide specialization and division of labor, which benefits all trading partners, at least in the *ex ante* sense.

---

[18] http://en.wikipedia.org/wiki/Free_trade

Bibliography

Abedian, I., and B. Standish. 1985. "Poor Whites and the Role of the State: The Evidence," *South Africa Journal of Economics* 52, no. 2.

Abella, Irving, and Harold Troper. 1982. *None is Too Many: Canada and the Jews of Europe, 1933–1948,* Toronto: Lester and Orpen Dennys.

Adams, Charles. 2000. *When in the Course of Human Events: Arguing the Case for Southern Secession,* New York: Rowman & Littlefield.

Alchian, Armen A. 1977. *Economic Forces at Work,* Indianapolis, Ind.: Liberty Fund.

Anderson, Benjamin M. 1917. *The Value of Money,* New York: Macmillan.

Anderson, Martin. 1989. *The Christian Science Monitor,* January 4; reprinted in Block 1990a.

Anderson, William, Walter Block, Thomas J. DiLorenzo, Ilana Mercer, Leon Snyman, and Christopher Westley. 2001. "The Microsoft Corporation in Collision with Antitrust Law," *The Journal of Social, Political and Economic Studies* 26, no. 1.

Armentano, Dominick T. 1982. *Antitrust and Monopoly: Anatomy of a Policy Failure,* New York: Wiley.

———. 1972. *The Myths of Antitrust,* New York: Arlington House.

Bacon, Kenneth A. 1989. "College Seniors Fail to Make Grade," *Wall Street Journal,* October 9.

Barnett, Randy E., and Don B. Kates. 1996. "Under Fire: The New Consensus on the Second Amendment," *Emory Law Journal* 45.

Barnett, William II. 1989. "Subjective Cost Revisited," *Review of Austrian Economics* 3, no. 1.

Bauer, Peter T. 1987. "Population Scares," *Commentary* 84, no. 5.

———. 1984. *Reality and Rhetoric: Studies in the Economics of Development,* Cambridge Mass.: Harvard University Press.

———. 1981. *Equality, the Third World, and Economic Delusion,* Cambridge, Mass.: Harvard University Press.

Bauer, Peter T., and Basil S. Yamey. 1957. *The Economics of Under-developed Countries,* Chicago: University of Chicago Press.

Baumol, William J. 1963. "Urban Services: Interactions of Public and Private Decisions," in Howard G. Schaller, ed., *Public Expenditures Decisions in the Urban Community,* Baltimore: Johns Hopkins University Press.

Becker, Gary. 1964. *Human Capital,* New York: National Bureau of Economic Research.

———. 1957. *The Economics of Discrimination,* Chicago: University of Chicago Press.

Belton, Beth. 1996. "Bad Data: Flawed Economic Reports Rattle Markets, Rifle Pocketbooks," *USA Today,* December 3.

Benson, Bruce L. 2001. "Restitution as an Objective of the Criminal Justice System," *The Journal of the James Madison Institute* 15 (Winter).

———. 1989. "Enforcement of Private Property Rights in Primitive Societies: Law Without Government," *Journal of Libertarian Studies* 9, no. 1.

Bidinotto, Robert. 1994. "Crimes and Moral Retribution," in Robert Bidinotto, ed., *Criminal Justice? The Legal System vs. Individual Responsibility,* Irvington-on-Hudson, N.Y.: Foundation for Economic Education.

Bish, Robert L., and Robert Warren. 1972. "Scale and Monopoly Problems in Urban Government Services," *Urban Affairs Quarterly* 8, no. 1.

Block, Walter. 2006. "Epstein on Alienation: A Rejoinder," *International Journal of Social Economics* 33, no. 3/4.

———. 2004. "Are Alienability and the Apriori of Argument Logically Incompatible?," *Dialogue* 1, no. 1.

———. 2003. "Toward a Libertarian Theory of Inalienability: A Critique of Rothbard, Barnett, Gordon, Smith, Kinsella and Epstein," *Journal of Libertarian Studies* 17, no. 2.

———. 2001. "Alienability, Inalienability, Paternalism and the Law: Reply to Kronman," *American Journal of Criminal Law* 28, no. 3.

———. 1999. "Market Inalienability Once Again: Reply to Radin," *Thomas Jefferson Law Journal* 22, no. 1.

———. 1998. "Roads, Bridges, Sunlight and Private Property: Reply to Gordon Tullock," *Journal des Economistes et des Études Humaines* 8, no. 2/3.

———. 1997. "Compromising the Uncompromisable: The Austrian Golden Mean," *Cultural Dynamics* 9, no. 2.

———. 1996. "Drug Prohibition, Individual Virtue and Positive Economics," *Review of Political Economy* 8, no. 4.

———. 1994. "Libertarianism vs. Libertinism," *Journal of Libertarian Studies: An Interdisciplinary Review* 11, no. 1.

———. 1993. "Drug Prohibition: A Legal and Economic Analysis," *Journal of Business Ethics* 12.

———. 1992. "Discrimination: An Interdisciplinary Analysis," *Journal of Business Ethics* 11.

———, ed. 1990a. *Economics and the Environment: A Reconciliation,* Vancouver, B.C.: Fraser Institute.

——. 1990b. "Earning Happiness Through Homesteading Unowned Land: A Comment on "Buying Misery with Federal Land" by Richard Stroup," *Journal of Social Political and Economic Studies* 15, no. 2.

——. 1990c. "Private Property, Ethics and Wealth Creation," in Peter L. Berger, ed., *Toward an Ethic of Wealth Creation,* San Francisco: Institute for Contemporary Studies.

——. 1989a. "Population Growth: Is it a Problem?," in Peter S. Ross, Sheila Riordon and Susan MacArtney, eds., *Resolving Global Problems into the 21st Century: How Can Science Help?,* Proceedings of the Fourth National Conference of Canadian Pugwash, Ottawa: CSP Publications.

——. 1989b. "Ludwig von Mises and the 100% Gold Standard," in Llewellyn H. Rockwell, Jr., ed., *The Meaning of Ludwig von Mises,* Lexington, Mass.: Lexington Books.

——. 1988. "Economics of the Canadian Bishops," *Contemporary Policy Issues* 6, no. 1.

——. 1986. *The U.S. Bishops and Their Critics: An Economic and Ethical Perspective,* Vancouver, B.C.: Fraser Institute.

——. 1983. *On Economics and the Canadian Bishops,* Vancouver, B.C.: Fraser Institute.

——. 1982. "Economic Intervention, Discrimination, and Unforeseen Consequences," in Walter Block and Michael A. Walker, eds., *Discrimination, Affirmative Action, and Equal Opportunity,* Vancouver, B.C.: Fraser Institute.

——. 1980. "On Robert Nozick's 'On Austrian Methodology,'" *Inquiry* 23, no. 4.

——. 1979. "Free Market Transportation: Denationalizing the Roads," *Journal of Libertarian Studies* 3, no. 2.

——. 1978. "Abortion, Woman and Fetus: Rights in Conflict?," *Reason,* April.

——. 1977. "Coase and Demsetz on Private Property Rights," *Journal of Libertarian Studies* 1, no. 2.

——. 1976. *Defending the Undefendable,* New York: Fox and Wilkes.

——. 1975. "On Value Freedom in Economics," *The American Economist* 19 (Spring).

Block, Walter, and Daniel Coffey. 1999. "Postponing Armageddon: Why Population Growth isn't Out of Control," *Humanomics* 15, no. 4.

Block, Walter, and Matthew Block. 1996. "Roads, Bridges, Sunlight and Private Property Rights," *Journal des Eonomistes et des Etudes Humaines* 7, no. 2/3.

Block, Walter, and Michael A. Walker. 1985. *Focus on Employment Equity: A Critique of the Abella Royal Commission on Equality in Employment,* Vancouver, B.C.: Fraser Institute.

Block, Walter, and Robert W. McGee. 1989. "Information, Privilege, Opportunity and Insider Trading," *Northern Illinois Law Review* 10, no. 1.

Block, Walter, and Roy Whitehead. 2005. "Compromising the Uncompromisable: A Private Property Rights Approach to Resolving the Abortion Controversy," *Appalachian Law Review* 2, no. 4.

Block, Walter, and Walter E. Williams. 1981. "Male-Female Earnings Differentials: A Critical Reappraisal," *Journal of Labor Research* 2, no. 2.

Boaz, David. 1997. *Libertarianism: A Primer,* New York: Free Press.

———. 1991. "The Public School Monopoly: America's Berlin Wall," in *Liberating Schools: Education in the Inner City,* Washington, D.C.: Cato Institute.

———, ed. 1990. *The Crisis in Drug Prohibition,* Washington, D.C.: Cato Institute.

Bonavia, Michael. R. 1954. *The Economics of Transport,* London: Cambridge University Press.

Bookchin, Murray. 1970. "Toward an Ecological Solution," *Ramparts,* May.

———. 1989. "Death of a Small Planet," *The Progressive,* August.

Bradford, William R. 1997. "Greenspan: Deep-Cover Radical for Capitalism?," *Liberty* 11, no. 2.

Bramwell, Anna. 1989. *Ecology in the 20th Century,* New Haven, Conn.: Yale University Press.

Breitman, George, ed. 1965. *Malcolm X Speaks: Selected Speeches,* New York: Grove Press.

Brown, Byron. 1992. "Why Governments Run Schools," *Economics of Education Review* 11, no. 4.

Brownlee, O.H., and Walter W. Heller. 1956. "Highway Development and Financing," *American Economic Review* 46, no. 2.

Buchanan, James M. 1969. *Cost and Choice: An Inquiry into Economic Theory,* Chicago: Markham.

———. 1975a. "Public Finance and Public Choice," *National Tax Journal* 28, no. 4.

———. 1975b. *The Limits of Liberty,* Chicago: University of Chicago Press.

Buchanan, James M., and George F. Thirlby. 1981. *LSE: Essays on Cost,* New York: New York University Press.

Buchanan, James M., and Gordon Tullock. 1971. *The Calculus of Consent: Logical Foundations of Constitutional Democracy,* Ann Arbor: University of Michigan Press.

Buckley, William F., Jr. 1997. "Immigration Advocates Resist Reasoning," *Conservative Chronicle,* February 12.

Burchard, John. 1970. "Design and Urban Beauty in the Central City," in James Q. Wilson, ed., *The Metropolitan Enigma,* Garden City, N.Y.: Doubleday.

Carlson, Allan C. 1988. *Family Questions,* New Brunswick, N.J.: Transaction Publishers.

Coase, Ronald H. 1960. "The Problem of Social Cost," *Journal of Law and Economics* 3, no. 1.

Coleman, James, and Thomas Hoffer. 1987. *Public and Private High Schools: The Impact of Communities,* New York: Basic Books.

Commoner, Barry. 1990. *Making Peace with the Planet,* New York: Pantheon Books.

Conquest, Robert. 1990. *The Great Terror Edmonton,* Alberta: Edmonton University Press.

———. 1986. *The Harvest of Sorrow: Soviet Collectivization and the Terror-Famine,* New York: Oxford University Press.

Cooper, Norman L. 1971. *Urban Transportation: An Answer,* Bloomington: Indiana University Press.

Cuzán, Alfred G. 1979. "Do We Ever Really Get Out of Anarchy?," *Journal of Libertarian Studies* 3, no. 2.

Demsetz, Harold. 1965. "Minorities in the Market Place," *North Carolina Law Review* 43, no. 2.

DiLorenzo, Thomas. 2002. *The Real Lincoln: A New Look at Abraham Lincoln, His Agenda, and an Unnecessary War,* New York: Random House.

——. 1990. "Does Capitalism Cause Pollution?," *Contemporary Issues Series,* no. 38, St. Louis, Mo.: Center for the Study of American Business.

Eckert, Ross D., and George W. Hilton. 1972. "The Jitneys," *Journal of Law and Economics* 15, no. 2.

Ellis, Howard S. 1934. *German Monetary Theory 1905–1933,* Cambridge, Mass.: Cambridge University Press.

Encyclopedia Talmudit. 1976. Vol. 10, Jerusalem: Encyclopedia Talmudit Publishing.

Enke, Stephen. 1955. "More on the Misuse of Mathematics in Economics: A Rejoinder," *Review of Economics and Statistics* 37.

Epstein, Richard A. 1992. *Forbidden Grounds: The Case Against Employment Discrimination Laws,* Cambridge, Mass.: Harvard University Press.

Evers, Williamson M. 1996. *Victim's Rights, Restitution and Retribution,* Oakland, Calif.: Independent Institute.

——. 1978. "The Law of Omissions and Neglect of Children," *Journal of Libertarian Studies* 2, no. 1.

——. (n.d.). "Political Theory and the Legal Rights of Children," unpublished manuscript.

Foreman, David. 1990. "Only Man's Presence Can Save Nature," *Harpers Magazine,* April.

Friedman, David. 1978. *The Machinery of Freedom: A Guide to Radical Capitalism,* New Rochelle, N.Y.: Arlington House.

Friedman, Milton. 1989. "An Open Letter to Bill Bennett," *Wall Street Journal,* September 7.

——. 1985. "Capitalism and the Jews," in W. Block, ed., *The Morality of the Market: Religious and Economic Perspectives,* Vancouver, B.C.: Fraser Institute.

——. 1977. *Friedman on Galbraith and on Curing the British Disease,* Vancouver, B.C.: Fraser Institute.

——. 1962. *Capitalism and Freedom,* Chicago: University of Chicago Press.

——. 1960. *A Program for Monetary Stability,* New York: Fordham University Press.

Friedman, Milton, and Anna J. Schwartz. 1963. *A Monetary History of the U.S., 1867–1960,* New York: National Bureau of Economic Research.

Friedman, Milton, and Rose Friedman. 1979. *Free to Choose: A Personal Statement,* New York: Avon Books.

Gall, Peter A. 1984. "Regulation of Picketing under the B.C. Labour Code: Some Cracks in the Institutional Foundation," in J.M. Weiler and P.A. Gall, eds.,

The Labour Code of British Columbia in the 1980s, Vancouver, B.C.: Carswell Legal Publications.

Goodman, John C., Richard L. Stroup *et al.* 1991. *Progressive Environmentalism: A Pro-Human, Pro-Science, Pro-Free Enterprise Agenda for Change,* Dallas, Texas: National Center for Policy Analysis.

Gordon, David, ed. 1998. *Secession, State, and Liberty,* New Brunswick, N.J.: Transaction Publishers.

Graber, David M. 1989. "Mother Nature as a Hothouse Flower," *Los Angeles Times Book Review,* October 22.

Graham, Grace. 1963. *The Public School in the American Community,* New York: Harper & Row.

Greenspan, Alan. 1966. "Gold and Economic Freedom," in Ayn Rand, ed., *Capitalism: The Unknown Ideal,* New York: Signet; reprinted from *The Objectivist.*

Grubel, Herbert G., and Josef Bonnici. 1986. *Why is Canada's Unemployment Rate so High?,* Vancouver, B.C.: Fraser Institute.

Gwartney, James, Robert Lawson, and Walter Block. 1996. *Economic Freedom of the World 1975–1995,* Vancouver, B.C.: Fraser Institute.

Hagen, John. 1977. "Finding Discrimination: A Question of Meaning," *Ethnicity* 4.

Hahn, Robert W., and Robert N. Stavins. 1991. "Incentive-Based Environmental Regulation: A New Era from an Old Idea?," *Ecology Law Quarterly* 18, no. 1.

———. 1989. "Economic Prescriptions for Environmental Problems: How the Patient Followed the Doctor's Orders," *Journal of Economic Perspectives* 3, no. 2.

Hahn, Robert W., and Gordon L. Hester. 1989. "Where Did All The Markets Go? An Analysis of EPA's Emissions Trading Program," *Yale Journal on Regulation* 6, no. 1.

Halbrook, Stephen P. 1995. "Congress Interprets the Second Amendment: Declarations by a Co-Equal Branch on the Individual Right to Keep and Bear Arms," *Tennessee Law Review* 62, no. 3.

Hamid, Ansley. 1993. "To the Editor of the Commentary," in *Drugs in America: The Reference Shelf,* New York: H.W. Wilson.

Hamowy, Ronald, ed. 1987. *Dealing With Drugs: Consequences of Government Control,* San Francisco: Pacific Institute.

———. 1984. *Canadian Medicine: A Study in Restricted Entry,* Vancouver, B.C.: Fraser Institute.

Haritos, Z. 1974. "Theory of Road Pricing," *Transportation Journal* 13 (Spring).

Haveman, Robert H. 1970. *The Economics of the Public Sector,* New York: John Wiley and Sons.

Hayek, Friedrich A. 1990. *Denationalisation of Money,* London: Institute of Economic Affairs.

———. 1989. *The Fatal Conceit: The Errors of Socialism,* Chicago: University of Chicago Press.

———. 1976. *Choice in Currency: A Way to Stop Inflation,* London: Institute of Economic Affairs.

——. 1973. *Law, Legislation and Liberty,* Chicago: University of Chicago Press.

——. 1960. *The Constitution of Liberty,* Chicago: University of Chicago Press.

——. 1948. "A Commodity Reserve Currency," in *Individualism and Economic Order,* Chicago: University of Chicago Press.

Hazlitt, Henry. 1979. *Economics in One Lesson,* New Rochelle, N.Y.: Arlington House.

——. *The Failure of the New Economics: An Analysis of the Keynesian Fallacies,* New York: Van Nostrand.

Heinlein, Robert. 1959. *Starship Troopers,* New York: Berkley Medallion.

Henderson, David R. 2001. *The Joy of Freedom: An Economist's Odyssey,* New York: Financial Times/Prentice Hall.

Higgs, Robert. 1977. *Competition and Coercion: Blacks in the American Economy, 1865–1914,* Cambridge: Cambridge University Press.

Hoffmann, Carl, and John Reed. 1982. "When is Imbalance not Discrimination?," in Walter Block and Michael A. Walker, eds., *Discrimination, Affirmative Action, and Equal Opportunity,* Vancouver, B.C.: Fraser Institute.

Holcombe, Randall G. 1997. "A Theory of the Theory of Public Goods," *Review of Austrian Economics* 10, no. 1.

Holloway, Jason, and Walter Block. 1998. "Should Drugs Be Legalized?," *West Coast Libertarian* 18, no. 2.

Hoppe, Hans-Hermann. 2001. *Democracy, the God that Failed: The Economics and Politics of Monarchy, Democracy, and Natural Order,* New Brunswick, N.J.: Transaction Publishers.

——. 1995. "Free Immigration or Forced Integration," *Chronicles* 19, no. 7.

——. 1993a. *"Review of The Economics and Ethics of Private Property", Studies in Political Economy and Philosophy,* Boston: Kluwer.

——. 1993b. "Banking, Nation States, and International Politics: A Sociological Reconstruction of the Present Economic Order," in *The Economics and Ethics of Private Property,* Boston: Kluwer.

——. 1990a. "Man, Economy, and Liberty," *Review of Austrian Economics* 4, no. 1.

——. 1990b. "Review of *The Justice of Economic Efficiency,*" in S. Littlechild, ed., *The Austrian School of Economics,* London: Edward Elgar.

——. 1989. *A Theory of Socialism and Capitalism,* Boston: Kluwer.

Hoppe, Hans-Hermann, Jörg Guido Hülsmann, and Walter Block. 1998. "Against Fiduciary Media," *Quarterly Journal of Austrian Economics* 1, no. 1.

Horowitz, David. 1991. *Deconstructing the Left,* Lanham, Maryland: Second Thoughts Books.

Horwitz, Morton J. 1977. *The Transformation of American Law: 1780–1860,* Cambridge, Mass.: Harvard University Press.

Hummel, Jeffrey R. 1996. *Emancipating Slaves, Enslaving Free Men: A History of the American Civil War,* Chicago: Open Court.

——. 1990. "National Goods Versus Public Goods: Defense, Disarmament, and Free Riders," *Review of Austrian Economics* 4, no. 1.

Hutt, William H. 1989. "Trade Unions: The Private Use of Coercive Power," *Review of Austrian Economics* 3, no. 1.

Hutt, William H. 1973. *The Strike Threat System: The Economic Consequences of Collective Bargaining*, New Rochelle, N.Y.: Arlington House.

Hutt, William H. 1964. *The Economics of the Colour Bar*, London: Andre Deutsch.

Jackman, William T. 1916. *The Development of Transportation in Modern England* 1, Cambridge: Cambridge University Press.

Jasay, Anthony de. 1997. *Against Politics: On Government, Anarchy, and Order*, London: Routledge.

Jasay, Anthony de. 1985. *The State*, Oxford: Basil Blackwell.

Jencks, Cristopher. 1985. "Is the Public School Obsolete?," *The Public Interest* 80.

Kates, Don B., Jr., Henry E. Schaffer, John K. Lattimer, George B. Murray, and Edwin H. Cassem. 1995. "Guns and Public Health: Epidemic of Violence or Pandemic of Propaganda?," *Tennessee Law Review* 62, no. 3.

Kates, Don B., Jr. 1992. "Bigotry, Symbolism, and Ideology in the Battle over Gun Control," *Public Interest Law Review* 31.

——. 1991. "The Value of Civilian Arms Possession as Deterrent to Crime or Defense Against Crime," *American Journal of Criminal Law* 18.

——. 1990. *Guns, Murder, and the Constitution: A Realistic Assessment of Gun Control*, San Francisco: Pacific Research Institute.

——. 1986. "The Battle over Gun Control," *Public Interest Law Review* 84.

——, ed. 1984. *Firearms and Violence*, San Francisco: Pacific Research Foundation.

Kaufman, Wallace. 1994. *No Turning Back: Dismantling the Phantasies of Environmental Thinking*, New York: Basic Books.

Kinsella, Stephan N. 1998/1999. "Inalienability and Punishment: A Reply to George Smith," *Journal of Libertarian Studies* 14, no. 1.

——. 1996a. "New Rationalist Directions in Libertarian Rights Theory," *Journal of Libertarian Studies* 12, no. 2.

——. 1996b. "Punishment and Proportionality: The Estoppel Approach," *Journal of Libertarian Studies* 12, no. 1.

Kirzner, Israel. 1973. *Competition and Entrepreneurship*, Chicago: University of Chicago Press.

Kleck, Gary. 1991. *Point Blank: Guns and Violence in America*, New York: Aldine de Gruyter.

Kleck, Gary, and Britt Patterson. 1993. "The Impact of Gun Control and Gun Ownership Levels on City Violence Rates," *Journal of Quantitative Criminology* 9.

Klitgaard, Robert, and Ruth Katz. 1983. "Overcoming Ethnic Inequalities: Lessons from Malaysia," *Journal of Policy Analysis and Management* 2, no. 3.

Kreptul, Andrei. 2003. "The Constitutional Right of Secession in Political Theory and History," *Journal of Libertarian Studies* 17, no. 4.

Kropotkin, Petr A. 1970. *Selected Writings on Anarchism and Revolution*, Cambridge, Mass.: M.I.T. Press.

Krueger, Anne. 1974. "The Political Economy of the Rent-Seeking Society," *American Economic Review* 64, no. 3.

Krutilla, John V. 1963. "Welfare Aspects of Benefit-Cost Analysis," in H. Schaller, ed., *Public Expenditure Decisions in the Urban Community,* Washington, D.C.: Johns Hopkins Press.

Landes, Elisabeth M., and Richard A. Posner. 1978. "The Economics of the Baby Shortage," *Journal of Legal Studies* 7.

Lange, Oscar, and Fred M. Taylor. 1938. *On the Economics Theory of Socialism,* Minneapolis: University of Minnesota Press.

Leoni, Bruno. 1961. *Freedom and the Law,* New York: Van Nostrand.

Leoni, Bruno, and Eugenio Frola. 1977. "On Mathematical Thinking in Economics," *Journal of Libertarian Studies* 1, no. 2.

Levin, Michael. 1987. *Feminism and Freedom,* New Brunswick, N.J.: Transaction Books.

———. 1984. "Comparable Worth: The Feminist Road to Socialism," *Commentary* 74, no. 3.

———. 1977. *Why Race Matters,* Westport, Conn.: Praeger.

Lieberman, Myron. 1989. *Privatization and Educational Choice,* New York: St. Martin's Press.

Lincoln Highway Association. 1935. *The Lincoln Highway,* New York: Dodd, Meade.

Locke, John. 1955. *Second Treatise of Civil Government,* Chicago: Henry Regnery.

———. 1960. "An Essay Concerning the True Origin, Extent and End of Civil Government," in P. Laslett, ed., *Two Treatises of Government,* Vols. 27–28, Cambridge: Cambridge University Press.

Lott, John R., Jr. 1998. *More Guns, Less Crime: Understanding Crime and Gun Control Laws,* Chicago: University of Chicago Press.

Lott, John R., Jr., and David B. Mustard. 1997. "Crime, Deterrence and Right to Carry Concealed Handguns," *Journal of Legal Studies* 26, no. 1.

Louw, Leon, and Frances Kendall. 1986. *South Africa: The Solution,* Bisho Ciskei: Amagi Publications.

Lundahl, Mats, and Eskil Wadensjo. 1984. *Unequal Treatment: A Study in the Neoclassical Theory of Discrimination,* New York: New York University Press.

Machan, Tibor. 1990. *Capitalism and Individualism,* New York: St. Martin's Press.

———, ed. 1982. *The Libertarian Reader,* Totowa, N.J.: Rowman and Littlefield.

Manne, Henry A. 1966a. *Insider Trading and the Stock Market,* New York: Free Press.

———. 1966b. "In Defense of Insider Trading," *Harvard Business Review* 44, no. 6.

Margolis, Julius. 1955. "A Comment on the Pure Theory of Public Expenditure," *Review of Economics and Statistics* 37.

Mauser, Gary. 1992. "Gun Control in the United States," *Criminal Law Reform* 3.

Mauser, Gary, and Richard A. Holmes. 1992. "An Evaluation of the 1977 Canadian Firearms Legislation: An Econometric Approach," *Evaluation Research* 16.

McGee, Robert. 1994. "Secession Reconsidered," *Journal of Libertarian Studies* 11, no. 1.

——. 1991. "A Theory of Secession for Emerging Democracies," *Asian Economic Review* 33, no. 2.

——. 1988. "The Case for Privatizing Money," *The Asian Economic Review* 30, no. 2.

——. 1987. "The Place of Ludwig von Mises in the History of Monetary Thought," *The Asian Economic Review* 29.

McGee, Robert, and Walter Block. 1994. "Pollution Trading Permits as a Form of Market Socialism, and the Search for a Real Market Solution to Environmental Pollution," *Fordham University Law and Environmental Journal* 6, no. 1.

Mehlman, Ira. 1997. "Funding Fraud," *National Review,* March 24.

Menger, Carl. 1950. *Principles of Economics,* Glencoe: Free Press.

Mill, John S. 1956. *On Liberty,* New York: Bobbs-Merrill.

Mills, Stephanie. 1989. *Whatever Happened to Ecology?,* San Francisco: Sierra Club Books.

Miron, Jeffrey A., and Jeffrey Zwiebel. 1995. "The Economic Case Against Drug Prohibition," *Journal of Economic Perspectives* 9, no. 4.

Mises, Ludwig von. 1983. *Nation, State, and Economy,* New York: New York University Press.

——. 1981. *The Theory of Money and Credit,* Irvington-on-Hudson, N.Y.: The Foundation for Economic Education.

——. 1969a. *Socialism,* Indianapolis, Ind.: Liberty Fund.

——. 1969b. *Omnipotent Government: The Rise of the Total State and Total War,* New Rochelle, N.Y.: Arlington House.

——. 1966. *Human Action,* Chicago: Regnery Publishing.

——. 1957. *Theory and History: An Interpretation of Social and Economic Evolution,* New Haven, Conn.: Yale University Press.

——. 1952. *Planning for Freedom,* South Holland, Penn.: Libertarian Press.

Mohring, Herbert. 1965. "Urban Highway Investments," in Robert Dorfman, ed., *Measuring Benefits of Government Investments,* Washington, D.C.: The Brookings Institution.

Mohring, Herbert, and Mitchell Harwitz. 1962. *Highway Benefits,* Evanston, Ill.: Northwestern University Press.

Monroe, Paul. 1940. *Founding of the American Public School System,* New York: Macmillan.

Moore, Thomas G. 1961. "The Purpose of Licensing," *The Journal of Law and Economics* 4.

Morriss, Andrew P. 1998. "Miners, Vigilantes, and Cattlemen: Overcoming Free Rider Problems in the Private Provision of Law," *Land and Water Law Review* 33, no. 2.

Mundell, Robert. 1961. "Optimal Currency Areas," *American Economic Review* 51, no. 4.

Murray, Charles. 1997. *What it Means to Be a Libertarian,* New York: Broadway Books.

———. 1984a. *Losing Ground: American Social Policy from 1950 to 1980,* New York: Basic Books.

———. 1984b. "Affirmative Racism: How Preferential Treatment Works against Blacks," *The New Republic,* December 31.

Nadelmann, Ethan. 1989. "The Case For Legalization," *Washington Post,* October 8.

Narveson, Jan. 1987. "Have We A Right to Non-discrimination?," in Deborah C. Poff and Wilfred J. Waluchow, eds., *Business Ethics in Canada,* Scarborough: Prentice-Hall Canada.

National Safety Council. 1977. *Accident Facts,* Chicago: National Safety Council Research Department.

Netzer, Richard. 1952. "Toll Roads and the Crisis in Highway Finance," *National Tax Journal* 5, no. 2.

Noble, Charles M. 1971. "Highway Design and Construction Related to Traffic Operations and Safety," *Traffic Quarterly,* November.

Novak, Michael. 1986. *Will it Liberate? Questions about Liberation Theology,* New York: Paulist Press.

Novak, Michael *et al.* 1984. *Toward the Future: Catholic Social Thought and the U.S. Economy—A Lay Letter,* New York: Lay Commission on Catholic Social Teaching and the U.S. Economy.

Nozick, Robert. 1974. *Anarchy, State, and Utopia,* New York: Basic Books.

Ohashi, T.M., and T.P. Roth, eds. 1980. *Privatization: Theory and Practice,* Vancouver, B.C.: Fraser Institute.

Olson, Mancur, Jr. 1965. *The Logic of Collective Action,* New York: Schocken Books.

Oppenheimer, Franz. 1975. *The State,* Montreal: Black Rose Books.

Ostrowski, James. 1993. "Has the Time Come to Legalize Drugs?," *USA Today Magazine* 119, reprinted in *Drugs in America: The Reference Shelf,* New York: H.W. Wilson.

Owen, Wilfred. 1956. *Metropolitan Transportation Problem,* Washington, D.C.: Brookings Institution.

Parks, Lawrence M. 1998. "Creating Money Out of Nothing," *FAME Fed Watch Report,* no. 1., New York: Foundation for the Advancement of Money.

Patinkin, Don. 1965. *Money, Interest and Prices: An Integration of Monetary and Value Theory,* New York: Harper & Row.

Paul, Ellen F. 1989. *Equity and Gender: the Comparable Worth Debate,* New Brunswick, N.J.: Transaction Publishers.

Paul, Ron, and Lewis Lehrman. 1982. *The Case for Gold,* Washington, D.C.: Cato Institute.

Peterson, Shorey. 1950. "The Highway from the Point of View of the Economist," in Jean Labatut and Wheaton J. Lane, eds., *Highways in Our National Life: A Symposium,* Princeton, N.J.: Princeton University Press.

Peterson, Willis L. 1991. *Principles of Economics: Micro,* Boston: Richard D. Irwin.

Petro, Sylvester. 1957. *The Labor Policy of the Free Society,* New York: Ronald Press.

Pierce, Truman M. 1964. *Federal, State, and Local Government in Education,* Washington, D.C.: The Center for Applied Research in Education.

Pigou, Arthur. 1912. *Wealth and Welfare,* London: Macmillan.

Polsby, Daniel, and Don B. Kates. 1998. "American Homicide Exceptionalism," *University of Colorado Law Review* 69, no. 4.

Porrit, Jonathan, and David Winner. 1988. *The Coming of the Greens,* London: Fontana.

Posner, Richard. 1975. "The Social Cost of Monopoly and Regulation," *Journal of Political Economy* 83.

Radford, R.A. 1945. "The Economic Organization of a POW Camp," *Economica* 12.

Raimondo, Justin. 2000. *An Enemy of the State: The Life of Murray N. Rothbard,* Amherst, Mass.: Prometheus Books.

Rathje, William L. 1989. "Rubbish!," *Atlantic Monthly,* December.

Rawls, John. 1971. *A Theory of Justice,* Cambridge, Mass.: Harvard University Press.

Regulation and Automobile Safety. 1975. Washington, D.C.: American Enterprise Institute for Public Policy Research.

Renshaw, Edward F. 1962. "The Economics of Highway Congestion," *Southern Economic Journal,* April.

Report Newsmagazine. 2001. February 19.

Reynolds, Morgan O. 1984. *Power and Privilege: Labor Unions in America,* New York: Manhattan Institute for Policy Research.

Rifkin, Jeremy. 1987. "Time Wars: A New Dimension Shaping Our Future," *Utne Reader,* Sept./Oct.

Rifkin, Jeremy. 1980. *Entropy: A New World View,* New York: Bantam.

Robbins, Lionel. 1932. *An Essay on the Nature and Significance of Economic Science,* London: Macmillan.

Roberts, Lance W. 1982. "Understanding Affirmative Action," in Walter Block and Michael A. Walker, eds., *Discrimination, Affirmative Action, and Equal Opportunity,* Vancouver, B.C.: Fraser Institute.

——. 1979. "Some Unanticipated Consequences of Affirmative Action Policies," *Canadian Public Policy* 5, no. 1.

Ross, William D. 1956. "Comment," *American Economic Review* 46, May.

Roth, Gabriel. 1967. *Paying for Roads—The Economics of Traffic Congestion,* Baltimore, Maryland: Penguin Books.

Rothbard, Murray N. 1997. *Logic of Action II,* Cheltenham, U.K.: Edward Elgar.

——. 1991. *The Case for a 100 PerCent Gold Dollar,* Auburn, Ala.: Mises Institute.

——. 1990. "Law, Property Rights, and Air Pollution," in Walter Block, ed., *Economics and the Environment: A Reconciliation,* Vancouver, B.C.: Fraser Institute, reprinted from *Cato Journal* 2, no. 1.

——. 1989. "The Hermeneutical Invasion of Philosophy and Economics," *Review of Austrian Economics* 3, no. 1.

——. 1987. "Alan Greenspan: A Minority Report on the New Fed Chairman," *The Free Market* 5, no. 8.

——. 1983. *The Mystery of Banking,* New York: Richardson and Snyder.

——. 1982. *The Ethics of Liberty,* Atlantic Highlands, N.J.: Humanities Press.

——. 1981/1982. "Hayek's Denationalized Money," *The Libertarian Forum* 15, no. 5/6.

——. 1978. *For a New Liberty,* New York: Macmillan.

——. 1977. "Toward a Reconstruction of Utility and Welfare Economics," *Occasional Paper,* no. 3, San Francisco: Center for Libertarian Studies.

——. 1975. *America's Great Depression,* Kansas City, Kans.: Sheed and Ward.

——. 1973. "Value Implications of Economic Theory," *American Economist* 17.

——. 1970. *Power and Market: Government and the Economy,* Menlo Park, Calif.: Institute for Humane Studies.

——. 1967. "The Principle of Secession Defended," *Colorado Springs Gazette Telegraph,* Pine Tree Column, October 3.

——. 1962. *Man, Economy and State,* Los Angeles: Nash Publishing.

Rothstein, Richard. 1996. "The Real Cost of Education: What the Numbers Tell Us," *Dissent* (Spring).

Rubin, Charles T. 1994. *The Green Crusade: Rethinking the Roots of Environmentalism,* New York: Free Press.

Sale, Kirkpatrick. 1989. "Presidential Matters," *Resurgence,* no. 132, January– February.

Samuelson, Paul A. 1970. *Economics,* New York: McGraw Hill.

——. 1956. "Social Indifference Curves," *Quarterly Journal of Economics* 70, no. 1.

——. 1955. "Diagrammatic Exposition of a Theory of Public Expenditure," *Review of Economics and Statistics* 37, no. 4.

——. 1954. "The Pure Theory of Public Expenditure," *Review of Economics and Statistics* 36, no. 4.

Savas, E.S. 1974. "Municipal Monopolies versus Competition in Delivering Urban Services," in Willis D. Hawley and David Rogers, eds., *Improving the Quality of Urban Management* 8, *Urban Affairs Annual Reviews,* Beverly Hills, Calif.: Sage Publications.

Schmidt, Emerson P. 1973. *Union Power and the Public Interest,* Los Angeles: Nash Publishing.

Scholefield, Joshua, and Archibald W. Cockburn, eds. 1932. *Pratt and MacKenzie's Law of Highways,* London: Butterworth.

Schumacher, Ernst F. 1973. *Small is Beautiful,* New York: Harper & Row.

Sechrest, Larry J. 1999. "Rand, Anarchy, and Taxes," *The Journal of Ayn Rand Studies* 1, no. 1.

Siegan, Bernard. 1972. *Land Use without Zoning,* Lexington, Mass.: Lexington Books.

Silberman, Rosalie Abella. 1984. *Equality in Employment: A Royal Commission Report,* Ottawa: Ministry of Supply and Service.

Simon, Julian. 1990. "The Unreported Revolution in Population Economics," *The Public Interest* 101.

——. 1989. *The Economic Consequences of Immigration,* Oxford: Basil Blakwell.

——. 1981. *The Ultimate Resource,* Princeton, N.J.: Princeton University Press.

Simons, Henry C. 1948. *Economic Policy for a Free Society,* Chicago: University of Chicago Press.

——. 1936. "Rules vs. Authority in Monetary Policy," *Journal of Political Economy* 34, reprinted in *Economic Policy for a Free Society 1948,* Chicago: University of Chicago Press.

Skoble, Aeon J. 1995. "The Anarchism Controversy," in Tibor R. Machan and Douglas B. Rasmussen, eds., *Liberty for the 21st Century: Essays in Contemporary Libertarian Thought,* Lanham, Maryland: Rowman and Littlefield.

Smerk, George M. 1965a. *Urban Transportation: The Federal Role,* Bloomington: Indiana University Press.

——. 1965b. "Subsidies for Urban Mass Transportation," *Land Economics,* February.

Smith, Adam. 1965. *An Inquiry into the Nature and Causes of the Wealth of Nations,* New York: Modern Library.

Sowell, Thomas. 1990. *Preferential Policies: An International Perspective,* New York: Morrow.

——. "Preferential Policies," in A. Anderson, and L. Bark, eds., *Thinking About America: The United States in the 1990s,* San Francisco: Hoover Institution Press.

——. *Civil Rights: Rhetoric or Reality,* New York: Morrow.

——. 1983. *The Economics and Politics of Race: An International Perspective,* New York: Morrow.

——. 1982. "Weber and Bakke, and the presuppositions of 'Affirmative Action,'" in Walter Block and Michael A. Walker, eds., *Discrimination, Affirmative Action, and Equal Opportunity,* Vancouver, B.C.: Fraser Institute.

——. 1981. *Ethnic America,* New York: Basic Books.

——. 1976. *Patterns of Black Excellence,* Washington, D.C.: Ethics and Public Policy Center.

——. 1975. *Race and Economics,* New York: Longman.

Spooner, Lysander. 1966. *No Treason,* Colorado Springs, Colo.: Ralph Myles Publisher.

Stiglitz, Joseph E. 1973. "Approaches to the Economics of Discrimination," *American Economic Review* 63, no. 2.

Stonier, Alfred W., and Douglas C. Hague. 1964. *A Textbook of Economic Theory,* New York: John Wiley and Sons.

Strabo. 1949. *The Geography of Strabo,* London: Heinemann.

Stringham, Edward. 1998. "Justice without Government," *Journal of Libertarian Studies* 14, no. 1.

Stroup, Richard L. 1988. "Buying Misery with Federal Land," *Public Choice* 57.

Szasz, Thomas. 1985. *Ceremonial Chemistry: The Ritual Persecution of Drugs, Addicts, and Pushers,* Holmes Beach, Fla.: Learning Publications.

Tannehill, Morris, and Linda Tannehill. 1970. *The Market for Liberty,* Lansing, Mich.: self-published.

Thorne, Samuel E. *et al.* 1965. *The Great Charter: Four Essays on Magna Carta and the History of Our Liberty,* New York: Pantheon.

Thornton, Mark. 1991. *The Economics of Prohibition,* Salt Lake City: University of Utah Press.

Tideman, Nicholaus T., and Gordon Tullock. 1976. "A New and Superior Process for Making Social Choices," *Journal of Political Economy* 84, no. 6.

Tiebout, Charles M. 1956. "A Pure Theory of Local Expenditures," *Journal of Political Economy* 64, no. 5.

Tinsley, Patrick. 1998. "With Liberty and Justice for All: A Case for Private Police," *Journal of Libertarian Studies* 14, no. 1.

Tripp, Alker. 1950. "The History of the Modern Highway in England," in Jean Labatut and Wheaton J. Lane, eds., *Highways in Our National Life: A Symposium,* Princeton, N.J.: Princeton University Press.

Tucker, William. 1990. *The Excluded Americans: Homelessness and Housing Policy,* Chicago: Regnery-Gateway.

Tullock, Gordon. 1980. "Efficient Rent Seeking," in J.M. Buchanan, R.D. Tollison, and G. Tullock, eds., *Towards a Theory of the Rent Seeking Society,* College Station: Texas A&M University Press.

——. "The Welfare Cost of Tariffs, Monopolies and Theft," *Western Economic Journal* (now *Economic Inquiry*) 5.

U.S. Bishops' Pastoral Letter on Catholic Social Teaching and the U.S. Economy. 1984. Origins: NC Documentary Service, November 15, no. 22/23.

U.S. Bureau of the Census. 1976. *Statistical Abstract of the United States,* Washington, D.C.: U.S. Government Printing Office.

Vickrey, William. 1974. "Breaking the Bottleneck by Sophisticated Pricing of Roadway Use," *General Motors Quarterly* (Spring).

——. 1963. "Pricing and Resource Allocation in Transportation and Public Utilities," *American Economic Review* 53, no. 1.

Vonnegut, Kurt. 1982. "Harrison Bergeron," in Walter Block and Michael A. Walker, eds., *Discrimination, Affirmative Action, and Equal Opportunity,* Vancouver, B.C.: Fraser Institute.

Walker, Michael A. 1988. *Privatization: Tactics and Techniques,* Vancouver, B.C.: Fraser Institute.

——, ed. 1976. *The Illusion of Wage and Price Control,* Vancouver, B.C.: Fraser Institute.

Walters, Alan A. 1968. *The Economics of Road User Charges,* International Bank for Reconstruction and Development, Staff Occasional Paper No. 5, Baltimore: Johns Hopkins University Press.

Webb, Sydney, and Beatrice Webb. 1922. *English Local Government,* New York: Longmans, Green.

Weiler, Paul. 1980. *Reconcilable Differences,* Toronto: Carswell.

Welch, Finis R. 1967. "Labor-Market Discrimination: An Interpretation of Income Differences in the Rural South," *Journal of Political Economy* 75, no. 3.

West, E.G. 1983. "Are American Schools Working? Disturbing Cost and Quantity Trend," *Cato Institute Policy Analysis* 26.

Wharton, Vernon L. 1947. *The Negro in Mississippi,* Chapel Hill: University of North Carolina Press.

Williams, Walter E. 1989. *South Africa's War Against Capitalism,* New York: Praeger.

———. 1982a. "On Discrimination, Prejudice, Racial Income Differentials, and Affirmative Action," in Walter Block and Michael A. Walker, eds., *Discrimination, Affirmative Action, and Equal Opportunity,* Vancouver, B.C.: Fraser Institute.

———. 1982b. *The State Against Blacks,* New York: McGraw-Hill.

———. 1978. "Tuition Tax Credits: Other Benefits," *Policy Review* (Spring).

Wilson, Edward O. 1974. *Sociobiology: The New Synthesis,* Cambridge, Mass.: Harvard University Press.

Winch, David M. 1963. *The Economics of Highway Planning,* Toronto: University of Toronto Press.

Wiprud, Arne C. 1945. *Justice in Transportation: An Expose of Monopoly Control,* New York: Ziff-Davis.

Wollstein, Jaret B. 1974. *Public Services Under Laissez Faire,* New York: Arno Press.

Wooldridge, William C. 1970. *Uncle Sam, the Monopoly Man,* New Rochelle, N.Y.: Arlington House.

Index of Names

Index of Subjects

www.ingramcontent.com/pod-product-compliance
Lightning Source LLC
Chambersburg PA
CBHW082128290526
45794CB00008B/2970